MARIA LYDIG DALY

DIARY OF
A UNION LADY
1861-1865

EDITED BY

HAROLD EARL HAMMOND

Introduction to the Bison Books Edition
By Jean V. Berlin

UNIVERSITY OF NEBRASKA PRESS • LINCOLN

© 1962 by Funk and Wagnalls Company, Inc.
Reprinted by arrangement with HarperCollins Publishers, Inc.
Introduction to the Bison Books Edition © 2000 by the University of
Nebraska Press
Manufactured in the United States of America

♾

First Bison Books printing: 2000
Most recent printing indicated by the last digit below:
10   9   8   7   6   5   4   3   2   1

Library of Congress Cataloging-in-Publication Data
Daly, Maria Lydig, 1824–1894.
Diary of a Union lady, 1861–1865 / Maria Lydig Daly; edited by Harold
Earl Hammond; introduction to the Bison Books edition by Jean V.
Berlin.
  p. cm.
Originally published: New York: Funk & Wagnalls, 1962.
Includes index.
ISBN 0-8032-6623-5 (pa: alk. paper)
1. Daly, Maria Lydig, 1824–1894—Diaries. 2. United States—His-
tory—Civil War, 1861–1865—Personal narratives. 3. New York
(N.Y.)—History—Civil War, 1861–1865—Personal narratives. 4. New
York (N.Y.)—Social life and customs. 5. New York (N.Y.)—Biography.
I. Hammond, Harold Earl, 1922–   . II. Title.
E601.D155   2000
974.7′103′092—dc21
[B]
99-089818

INTRODUCTION TO THE BISON BOOKS EDITION

Jean V. Berlin

At the turn of the twenty-first century, we have accepted certain notions about the Civil War as self-evident truths. We think of Lincoln as a great and beloved leader; that Northern support for the war effort was nearly universal; and that the North itself was a united, even monolithic unit—despite historians' efforts to show us otherwise. The truth about life in nineteenth-century America is very different from what we sometimes think it is. Maria Lydig Daly's Civil War diary brings to life a portrait of a sorely divided society and a president as much hated as loved. The reader may not like Daly (and there is much about the woman to dislike), but there is no denying that she describes vividly the upper-class society of New York City during the war and reminds us that as many factors divided Northerners as united them. Her malicious and entertaining comments on New Yorkers high and low as well as national figures provide fodder for many points of view and keeps the reader wondering what she will say next.

But for all this, *Diary of a Union Lady, 1861–1865* remains surprisingly unknown. Published in the flurry of works issued to mark the centennial of the Civil War, it was quickly overshadowed, and the emphasis on the history of Southern women that came later has only pushed it further into the historiographical background. Though Daly did not polish and rewrite her narrative as did Southern diarist Mary Chesnut, her catty remarks, witty sallies, and astute insights combine to make an enjoyable as well as important book, and one that has its own lessons to teach us about history.

The Dalys were very active in New York society. Maria Daly's family connections as well as Judge Charles P. Daly's political eminence admitted them to the highest circles in the city. They were friendly with George Strong (another diarist and prominent citizen), knew all the politicians of the day, and dabbled in the arts and good works.[1] Daly's frequent references to Albert Bierstadt, Frederick Church, and other well-known painters of the Hudson

River School underlined the couple's participation in the artistic scene of the day. Their attendance at various charitable fairs, theater productions, operas, dinner parties, and receptions was typical for the upper class in New York. Perhaps most interesting was the judge's close friendship with Edwin Booth, John Wilkes Booth's brother, which continued after Lincoln's assassination. The Dalys also knew George Bancroft and many other contemporary men of letters.

New York City during the Civil War was an exciting place, where many men made fortunes in war-related speculation, but far more suffered the ravages of rampant inflation and stagnant wages. While the nouveau riche indulged themselves at Tiffany's, the lower classes could not put food on the table. Any attempts by laborers to organize and bargain for better wages were met with employers' hiring free blacks, which heightened racial tension. The Emancipation Proclamation worsened working-class fears by raising the specter of a large unemployed black population drifting north to find work. The Conscription Act of 1863 proved unpopular when workers realized that the wealthy could buy their way out of the military by paying a three-hundred-dollar bounty to hire a substitute, while the poor could not evade service and faced the prospect of returning from war either unable to work or unable to find work because all the jobs had been taken by African Americans. The lottery to enact the federal draft was scheduled for July 1863, in the midst of this volatile atmosphere. The riots, which followed within days of the draft, raged for seventy-two hours, left more than one hundred dead, and ruined hundreds of businesses and properties. The well-to-do, Republicans, and African Americans were the targets of the wrath of a crowd many believed to be Irish in leadership and composition. Daly was torn: on the one hand, she deplored the reckless violence; on the other, she sympathized with the Irish and laborers.[2] These sympathies go a long way toward explaining her dislike of African Americans. Later in 1863 Judge Daly would aid the women who formed the Workingwomen's Protective Union, and he and his wife remained active in the women's labor movement until their deaths.[3]

Maria Daly's feelings about African Americans were quite typical for her time. For many, the Civil War was about the Union, not slavery, and they could not see how the two were inextricably entwined. Daly herself had no decided views on slavery and positively disliked abolitionists. Her sympathy for the Irish laborers made her receptive to their claims that free blacks were pricing them out of jobs, and she was clearly uneasy with the idea that blacks could also claim all the rights and prerogatives of whites. But the events that swirled around her did still affect Daly to some degree. She was markedly uncomfortable at the manner in which blacks were singled out during the Draft Riots, and her comments upon viewing a black regiment are somewhat poignant:

> It was a very interesting and a very touching sight to see the first colored regiment from this city march down the street for the front. They were a fine body of men and had a look of satisfaction in their faces, as though they felt they had gained a right to be more respected. Many old, respectable darkies stood at the street corners, men and women with tears in their eyes as if they saw the redemption of their race afar off but still the beginning of a better state of affairs for them. Though I am very little Negrophilish and would always prefer the commonest white that lives to a Negro, still I could not but feel moved (278).

Change, however glacial, was taking place inside Maria Daly.

More perceptive were her views of the fanaticism driving some abolitionists and Southern women. "It is a pity that the abolition female saints and the Charleston female patriots could not meet in fair fight and mutually annihilate each other," she wrote, undoubtedly echoing the prayer of many a northern politician and general (143). She early observed that reports of Southern atrocities on the battlefield would bring about the very retribution Confederates sought to avoid and blamed "these demoniac Southern women, whose pride and arrogance have had so much to do with this fearful state of things" (139–40, 158). The women of New Orleans, she wryly observed, "would rather be buried beneath the ruins of their homes than be left to the mercy of the barbarous Yankees—these barbarous creatures who have done nothing but feed their hungry and clothe their naked since they took their pestilent city" (155). She also worried that the North was weakened by its young folk, a generation she saw as starting the decline of a once-great nation, a refrain heard from the seventeenth century to this day. She fretted that "in America, the *young* rule; all is subservient to them" but could offer no real evidence to support her contentions (95).

What is perhaps most startling in *Diary of a Union Lady* to modern readers is Daly's attitude toward Lincoln. Today, when Lincoln is a secular saint, it is hard to remember what strong feelings of revulsion he inspired during his own lifetime. In 1860 when he emerged as the Republican candidate for president, he was a backwoods lawyer who had served briefly in Congress more than a decade earlier. He had achieved some renown during his 1858 debates with Stephen Douglas, but he was still relatively unknown and won the presidency only because of sectional divisions. For someone of Daly's patrician background and Democratic loyalties, Lincoln was anathema, and his wife, the controversial Mary Todd Lincoln, little better. Daly's initial remarks were quite condescending: "He cannot gather himself up easily for an effort, but all agree [he] is a conscientious, honest fellow, most unfit for his high position, not realizing the peril of the country, content to be President and have Mrs. Lincoln dress herself up and hold levees" (86). It was with the release of the Emancipation Proclamation that her rhetoric gathered invective: "There is no law but the despotic will of poor Abe Lincoln" (179). By 1864 she could hold her spleen no longer, going so far as to collect all the vicious rumors she had heard about the presidential couple, hoping to publish them (304-5). When Lincoln was assassinated, she fretted that he would become a martyr and never be forgotten, as he deserved to be. Her attitude shows that great men often inspire as much loathing as they do love. Military men get off much more lightly in her narrative. McClellan remained a hero until the end. Sherman, she declared, was a good Democrat—news which would have greatly astonished that gentleman. She very much liked and approved of General Grant and his wife Julia, commenting in November 1865 that "the General looks as if much given to persistent deep thoughts" (371–72). One wonders if events between 1866 and 1876 did anything to shake her good opinion of this commander.

Daly also berated her family members, particularly her father and her sister, Maggie, whose daughter would become the guardian of her journal. The rifts in her family created by her marriage are never far from her thoughts, and she had not completely reconciled herself to the idea that she had had to choose between her family and her husband. She found the financial consequences of her decision galling and was insecure about both her person and her position. Born into a wealthy family that traced its roots back to the start of white settlement in New York, Daly personified American aristocracy. The fact that she was still unmarried at thirty-one, when she first met her husband-to-be, argued that she was a plain and/or headstrong woman who did not receive many offers of marriage. Though the judge appeared to be her ideal mate, his origin as the son of Irish immigrants and rise as a self-made man (from cabin boy to jurist) made her quite defensive about his abilities and natural virtues. To many in her social cohort, he was a jumped-up Irishman who should have stayed in his place. Equally offensive to those in her class would have been his Catholicism, and Daly ends by over-compensating and sounding more Catholic than the judge himself, although she remained an Episcopalian until her death. On the whole, she was well aware of her good fortune in what she referred to as "the dreadful lottery of matrimony" (191). She consistently portrayed her husband as a paragon and bragged about his intellect, influence, and good nature. Though a bit sad that she had no children, she was nonetheless content in her marital state, or if not, confided no such doubts to her diary.

Maria Lydig Daly was undoubtedly a difficult woman, and her stream of critical remarks can become tiresome. Particularly troubling is the amount of space she fills in her diary cutting down other women, such as Arabella Griffith Barlow, wife of Gen. Francis C. Barlow. That her friend had married an attractive man ten years her junior who was achieving national military renown seems to have chafed Daly. For those familiar with Arabella Barlow's wartime record, Daly's comments seem cruel. Barlow died in July 1864 of a fever contracted while working at the battlefront hospitals of the Army of the Potomac. She had followed her husband throughout the war, helping with the wounded in any way that she could and joining the United States Sanitary Commission. She excelled at finding sources of food and other necessities in the wartorn countryside and often focused on duties other than actual nursing. When Daly's great and good friend Harriet Whetten reported in September 1862 that "Arabella . . . has been living, it seems, very comfortably at government expense at the hospital at Harrison's Landing near her husband's regiment" and concluded that she had been doing nothing but lounge around as "the men told her that there had not been a lady near them to sit beside them a moment for ten days," both Whetten and Daly were ignorant of Barlow's real efforts (172–73). Whetten, alone of Daly's female friends, remained uncriticized, perhaps because she passed along gossip and perhaps because she remained single. As a spinster, she posed no social threat to Daly. George Templeton Strong's wife came in for harsh words about her appearance; "painted like a wanton," sniffed Daly, although one man protested that she was "very pretty and very young looking," while saying he could not see the cosmetics (321 and 332). " 'Put on your glasses and thank Providence you are near-sighted, then,' " snapped Daly (332). Daly also gave short shrift to Strong's war work, observing "they say very kindly and charitably that Mrs. George Strong went down with rouge pot, crinoline, and maid to attend to the wounded and came home having washed the faces of seven men" (134).

This entertaining but malicious by-play has led some readers to compare Daly's diary to that of Mary Chesnut. While the women shared some superficial characteristics, their differences are deeper. Chesnut considered herself a writer, and the fact that she reworked, rewrote, and edited her journals over the years is well-known.[4] With one eye on immortality, Chesnut took into account later historical judgments to modify and amplify her text, giving her work an occasionally eerie prescience. Daly did no such thing. *Diary of a Union Lady* is clearly composed of her off-the-cuff impressions, kept as an aide-mémoire of an exciting and important time. That she left them to a family member rather than destroy them does suggest she had an idea of their historical value and wished to share them with her relations. It may also have been a bid for the sort of immortality denied her by her childlessness. In the end, however, it is clear that Daly had neither the subtlety nor the vision of Chesnut, although her style has a flavor all its own.

Perhaps the most important lesson we can draw from Daly is that contemporary impressions are often wrong. Many of her judgments are impossible for most Americans to accept today. From her work we should comprehend how hard it is for anyone, regardless of education, wealth, and background, to see and understand what is going on with any degree of accuracy or clarity. We all have prejudices, which cloud our minds, and it behooves us to question the motives behind our own beliefs. Above all, Daly's diary should enjoin us to take a good hard look at ourselves.

NOTES

1. Allan Nevins and Milton Halsey Thomas, eds., *The Diary of George Templeton Strong*, 4 vols. (New York: The Macmillan Company, 1952).

2. For the most recent account of New York City during the Civil War, see Edwin G. Burrows and Mike Wallace, *Gotham: A History of New York City to 1898* (New York: Oxford University Press, 1999), 852–905.

3. Mary Elizabeth Massey, *Women in the Civil War* (1966; rpt., Lincoln: University of Nebraska Press, 1994), 145.

4. C. Vann Woodward, ed., *Mary Chesnut's Civil War* (New Haven: Yale University Press, 1981), xv–xxix.

CONTENTS

Foreword • *xv*

Preface • *xvii*

Personalities in the Diary • *xxi*

Introduction • *xxxvii*

1861 • *1*

1862 • *93*

1863 • *211*

1864 • *273*

1865 • *327*

Index • *385*

FOREWORD

Readers of this volume will quickly perceive that it offers them a special treat. As Count Gurowski was the inimitable purveyor of masculine gossip in Washington during the Civil War, Mrs. Maria Lydig Daly was an inimitable purveyor of the feminine gossip of New York. Like the Count, she knew a great many important people, and heard much at first hand of historic occurrences. Her record, if read tolerantly and with a proper sense of humor, is endlessly entertaining. That she was a very silly woman at times quickly becomes evident, but it is equally clear that she was goodhearted, and her inanities and follies can be overlooked for the value of her clear-eyed observation of the social scene, her numerous good stories, and her occasional flashes of shrewd insight.

The wife of an honest, witty, and eloquent judge, the friend of many copperhead leaders of New York, and an ornament of the better Irish-American circles of the city, Mrs. Daly had peculiar opportunities for recording valuable bits of history. She could set down what Catholic circles thought of the war, could give a special view of recruiting and the draft riots, and could offer a Democratic account of such political events as the election of Horatio Seymour to the governorship. Her own fervent Unionism, like her husband's, was unquestioned. But she has some very catty things to report about the President, and probably gave her own color to an almost incredible statement quoted from a daughter of General James Wadsworth: "Lincoln is a miserable creature whose inordinate conceit and vanity make his stupidity and vulgarity unendurable." She notes with relish that Fitz-John Porter remained a hero to Democrats after his dismissal from the army: "the people seem disposed to make a lion of anyone reprimanded or disgraced by the Administration." And she expresses a hearty wish that the six New England States with their twelve Senators could be cut down to size by consolidation into one.

For all her flightiness, this vivacious woman often showed her ability to make an accurate estimate of character. Her little portrait of Jessie Benton Frémont, a woman so brilliant, positive, and truthful, but also so imperious in manner, is perfect. Her slightly malicious sketches of the personages at the memorable Century Club dinner in honor of Bryant's seventieth birthday are nearly as good. She pronounces Fernando Wood a "scamp," dismisses Archbishop John Hughes with faint praise, and seizes at once upon an apt characterization of Francis Meagher of the Irish Brigade—a man born to die as rebel on the gallows with a resounding speech in his mouth. Throughout her record she scatters bits of social and economic history. She notes that even in the dark days following Fredericksburg places of amusement were crowded, and fashionable painters like Bierstadt were getting higher prices than ever, while people were buying diamonds at Tiffany's without asking their price; inflation and war profits had changed New York by the end of 1862. It is also clear, however, that many of the best New Yorkers were making heavy sacrifices in time, money, and effort for the Union cause, and that a great deal of enthusiasm was put into the reception of the Russian fleet, the Sanitary Fair, and the lionizing of such returned heroes as Farragut. Professor Hammond, who has written the biography of Judge Daly, deserves our thanks for adding to it this entertaining and useful document.

San Marino, California   ALLAN NEVINS

PREFACE

The diarist's niece, Mrs. Emy Otto Hoyt, allowed me the use of documents and papers originally belonging to Judge and Mrs. Daly when I was doing research for Judge Daly's biography, *A COMMONER'S JUDGE, The Life and Times of Charles P. Daly* (Boston: Christopher Publishing House, 1954). Among this material, which previously had been inspected only by a few members of the family, was the voluminous personal diary of Judge Daly's wife, Maria Lydig Daly. Mrs. Hoyt, now deceased, is the only person I know to have read the diary in its original form. She informed me that Mrs. Daly wished the diary to remain secret until persons discussed in it were no longer living. Mrs. Hoyt was one of these persons.

"Translation" is a more appropriate term than "transcription" for the task of getting the diary into the form of a typed manuscript, for Mrs. Daly's handwriting was indescribably bad and such incidentals as punctuation, sentence structure, and spelling were ignored in her haste to set the multitudinous thoughts of an active mind down on paper. Such errors have been corrected in the editing process, and the frequent negative references to Mrs. Daly's sister (Emy Otto Hoyt's mother, Margaret Lydig Otto) which were heavily crossed out by Mrs. Hoyt have been restored. This task occupied several years of arduous labor on the part of my wife and myself, one reading aloud while the other typed, and both stopping frequently to study a word or a name. The diarist's two large handwritten volumes came to nearly eight hundred typewritten manuscript pages. Only the first volume is presented here.

Then came the chore of identifying the hundreds of persons Mrs. Daly mentions—sometimes with a first or last name only, and occasionally with a nickname or a literary reference (i.e., "King Log" for Abraham Lincoln, a reference to Aesop's fable, *Frogs Asking for a King*). Delightful though this game of "hide and seek" is to the historian, it becomes frustrating when an obscure "Mr. Brown" or a "Miss Smith" cannot be identified or distinguished from a hundred others. All identifiable personages mentioned in the diary have been given footnotes in the text; persons frequently mentioned are listed in a separate "cast of personalities." The most important events referred to have been briefly described either in footnotes or in longer italicized passages.

Grateful appreciation in bringing the *Diary of a Union Lady* to light is extended to my wife, Helen Stegmann Hammond, without whose encouragement and assistance this volume might never have been organized; to Emy Otto Hoyt, who permitted me the use of the original manuscript; to Mr. and Mrs. Henry L. Corbett (Mrs. Corbett is Emy Otto Hoyt's eldest daughter) for their aid and encouragement in the publishing of both Judge Daly's biography and Mrs. Daly's diary; to Mrs. William A. W. Stewart (Mrs. Corbett's sister) and Mrs. Alfred O. Hoyt (wife of Emy Otto Hoyt's son) for bringing the Daly materials to the attention of Professor Allan Nevins of Columbia University, who then referred them to me; to Mr. David Lydig Frothingham, who made the legal arrangements necessary for releasing the diary for publication; to Allan Nevins, one of America's greatest living historians, for urging me to complete this project, for preparing me academically for such work, and for providing the present Foreword; to Carter Davidson, President of Union College in Schenectady and my superior when I began to work on the diary, and to George

Stoddard, Chancellor of New York University, for encouraging research and scholarship on the part of their faculties; to John W. Knedler, Jr., Dean of University College, for his forbearance in allowing the diary to take precedence over many other important chores; and to Bayrd Still, Chairman of the History Department at New York University, for reading the Introduction and making a number of constructive suggestions concerning it.

Thanks also goes to Robert Zuckerman, a student of mine at the University, for assisting me at the library during the final weeks of preparation, and to Rigmor Jones, Sandra Brozman, and Libby Glasgow for typing various portions of the final manuscript.

HAROLD E. HAMMOND
Professor of History
New York University

PERSONALITIES IN THE DIARY

ADAM BADEAU, brigadier general of the Union Army toward the latter part of the Civil War, is referred to variously by Mrs. Daly as "our friend," "very observant and thoughtful," "genuine, appreciative and very kindly," and as "extremely ugly and insignificant looking." Badeau was a faithful reporter of the latest war news, and in his capacity as military secretary to General Grant from March 1864 to the end of the war, he kept Mrs. Daly posted regularly on developments along the battlefronts. Unquestionably, Badeau's high regard for the Dalys contributed to the frequency with which the Grants visited in the Daly home after the war.

GEORGE BANCROFT, whose reputation as a historian, cabinet officer, and diplomat was established before 1861, represented aristocracy of the best sort to Mrs. Daly. In this volume of the diary, the Bancrofts are mentioned as being present at banquets, public ceremonies and other events to which the Dalys were also invited, but in later years the relationship became much more intimate. After the war Mrs. Daly cultivated the Bancrofts and even stayed with them at their Newport summer home. Although she took every opportunity to get close to the Bancrofts, Mrs. Daly rather disliked George Bancroft, and occasionally tried to prove to herself in the diary that Judge Daly was undoubtedly the superior man and intellect.

ARABELLA GRIFFITH BARLOW, who married General Francis C. Barlow in April 1861 (he went directly to war the moment the ceremony was concluded), was an intimate of Mrs. Daly, but as was so common in Mrs. Daly's relationships with her own sex, she rarely had a good word to say about Mrs. Barlow. Mrs. Daly referred to General Barlow as "Arabella's boy-

husband" because she was some ten years older than her husband: "The woman who opened the door told us there was a
young soldier and his mother in the parlor." The friendship
was valuable in that Mrs. Daly received reports from the
battlefield through the General's letters to his wife. Mrs. Barlow died early in 1865, and Mrs. Daly mourned the loss of
"poor Belle."

FRANCIS C. BARLOW, referred to in the diary as "Frank," rose
from the rank of lieutenant in 1861 to brigadier general the
next year for meritorious service. He saw active service at
Fortress Monroe, and in the battles of Chancellorsville and
Gettysburg. He was first wounded in the battle of Fair Oaks,
and seriously wounded at Spotsylvania. With Grant's army,
Barlow was credited with the capture of Johnston's division
and participated in the final pursuit of Lee's army. "Arabella
declares that he loves fighting for the sake of fighting and is
really bloodthirsty." Although Mrs. Daly hinted that Barlow's
promotion to brigadier general was due to the Judge's influence, she credited his valor in his promotion to major general.

HENRY WARD BEECHER, the clergyman-orator abolitionist leader,
was an object of Mrs. Daly's ridicule as one of "the firebrands
which have set fire to the smouldering discontent of the South."
The diarist's scorn for the man whose sermons often drew as
many as 2,500 people did not abate, and toward the end of
this volume Mrs. Daly referred to Beecher's "muscular Christianity" and described him as a man "thoroughly wise in his
own conceit and confident of his own ability to direct the universe."

ALBERT BIERSTADT, popular landscape painter during the mid-
nineteenth century, was a particular favorite of Mrs. Daly. She
attended most of Bierstadt's showings, and he was frequently
a guest in the Daly home. Typical paintings were "The Rocky
Mountains" and "Pike's Peak."

EDWIN THOMAS BOOTH, brother of John Wilkes Booth and the
leading stage actor of his day, became an intimate friend of
Mrs. Daly during the Civil War, and afterward she served

almost as his private confessor. It's probable that Judge Daly was responsible for cultivating Booth's friendship at the outset, for it was appropriate that the widely regarded Shakespearean scholar Daly should cultivate the greatest living Shakespearean actor. Mrs. Daly describes Booth as "so silent and dark and Gawain-looking," but she cannot resist a prankish little sarcasm: "He would lose half his popularity if [his female admirers] had heard what I heard this evening of his new love." When Booth's brother shot Lincoln, Mrs. Daly grieved, "Poor Edwin Booth is ruined by his brother's act. His engagement of marriage is broken, his future as an actor blasted. . . . The melancholy Dane; he will look and act more naturally than ever."

JAMES TOPHAM BRADY, justice of the Supreme Court in New York City during the period covered in the present volume, was a personal crony of Judge Daly. Long before he married Mrs. Daly's sister Catherine, the Judge and Mrs. Daly, Brady and Kate Lydig were a "foursome." When James T. Brady died in 1869, his younger brother John R. Brady ascended to the Supreme Court and served in that capacity until his death in 1891. Mrs. Daly was not entirely guiltless of playing matchmaker in getting James T. Brady together with her sister: "After [the guests] left, Judge Brady came in and we had a little talk about Kate. If they should like each other, it would be very pleasant for us, but I dare not take any part in bringing it about. It is too great a responsibility." Mrs. Daly describes Brady as possessing "a very clear mind, great imitative powers, and [as] very capable in conversation, witty and clever at repartee."

MICHAEL CORCORAN, an Irish immigrant, enlisted in the Irish 69th New York Regiment as a private, was elected colonel of the Regiment in 1859, and by 1861 he was commissioned a brigadier general. When the 69th Regiment left New York at the outset of the war, Mrs. Daly reports that the Judge marched with them down Broadway. So ardent was Daly's patriotism that, armed with a revolver, he followed Corcoran's regiment to Camp Seward on Arlington Heights and helped to guard the ramparts when there was a threat of attack. But Corcoran was taken prisoner at the Battle of Bull Run, and Thomas Francis Meagher took his place—much to Mrs. Daly's annoyance. Judge Daly was untiring in his efforts to get Corcoran exchanged, and when he finally returned to New York, he was given all the welcome a returning hero could expect. Corcoran saw a good deal of action during the next year, but on December 27, 1863, he died of natural causes. Mrs. Daly attributed his death to the rigors of imprisonment and military life.

CHARLES PATRICK DALY, Mrs. Daly's husband, is the real hero of the diary. One would expect Mrs. Daly to have recorded more of her husband's witticisms, but she doubtless omitted them in the interest of preserving his dignity. The Judge is the only person close to Mrs. Daly who escaped her caustic wit. Her love was so heavily laced with hero worship that it becomes difficult to separate the image from the man. According to his wife, the Judge deserved a much higher position than his own ambitions allowed, and Mrs. Daly was unceasing in her efforts to promote him through her many highly placed friends and acquaintances. Her particular ambition was that the Judge serve on the U.S. Supreme Court.

SIR DOMINICK DALY, Provincial Secretary of Canada from 1840 to 1846, lieutenant governor of Prince Edward Island from 1854 to 1859, and governor of South Australia from 1861 until his death in 1868, was Mrs. Daly's claim to the Judge's noble heritage. She was delighted when Sir Dominick sent the Judge a seal ring with his coat of arms. In the diary, Mrs. Daly attempts to establish the myth that the Judge was a blood relative of Sir Dominick. Although Sir Dominick was not in the United States during the war, he was a faithful correspondent to the Dalys, and the diary reports some interesting opinions from a foreign observer about the rebellion.

GEORGE THOMAS DAVIS, "our friend from Greenfield, Massachusetts," is frequently mentioned in the diary as a close personal friend of the Dalys. After a political career in Massachusetts, he represented that state in Congress, beginning with 1851.

Always mentioned by Mrs. Daly in most respectful tones, Davis is described by the diarist as "a delightful companion. He knows all the literary celebrities of Massachusetts and was Webster's intimate friend." Davis' position permitted some interesting observations, such as—"Mr. Davis likewise told us that he heard Mrs. Lincoln abusing Cameron, the Secretary of War, in plain English. . . . I have to write to Mrs. Lincoln and tell her that she is right in her opinion and to do her best to induce the President to remove him."

JEFFERSON DAVIS was treated with considerable respect by the diarist until the end of the war. She considered him "probably the best of all" of the Southern leaders, and stated that "as far as I am concerned, I would as willingly be ruled by Jeff Davis as by poor Lincoln, and I suppose many feel the same." Her admiration was for strong leadership and discipline, which she bemoaned was so lacking in the North: "Jefferson Davis is the head; Lee's and Jackson's orders are obeyed." But the idol fell from his pedestal in the hour of defeat: "If we execute him, we should make him a martyr. Let him go and he is only a miserable failure whom no one will care for, from whom we shall have nothing to fear." In the end, when Davis was finally captured, Mrs. Daly commented, "Poor wretch! I have no sympathy with his cause nor his ambition, but I cannot but feel sorry for him. What torture of mind he will suffer until his end comes!"

JOHN ADAMS DIX, veteran politician and staunch New York City Democrat, was naturally well known to the Dalys, since the Judge was another of the city's leading Democrats. This makes Mrs. Daly's inaccuracy concerning Dix's political career somewhat difficult to understand. She introduces him in the diary as a former Senator, Minister to France and Secretary of War. Actually, he was a U.S. Senator from 1845 to 1849, postmaster of New York City, and Buchanan's Secretary of the Treasury for a few months in the beginning of 1861. He was named commander of the Department of the East in July, 1863, but he never served as Secretary of War. For four years *after* the War, he was U.S. Minister to France, which would lead one to

believe that Mrs. Daly added information to the earlier passages
later on in her life. He abandoned the Democrats after the war
and became Republican Governor of New York for one term.
Mrs. Daly was proud of the fact that her husband administered
the oath to Dix when the latter became a major general in the
Union Army.

JOHN CHARLES FRÉMONT, explorer, political adventurer, and
soldier of fortune, irritated Mrs. Daly sorely, as did his wife
Jessica, daughter of Senator Thomas H. Benton of Missouri. If
the diarist quoted Judge Daly correctly, the Judge was not
alone in his opinion that Frémont was "an incapable, obstinate,
selfish, conceited, and unscrupulous man." And to this Mrs.
Daly adds, "His wife Jessie is very ambitious, and between
them they might be looking to the main chance rather than
the good of their country. They would be nothing loath to
be the heads of a Western republic." It was through Baron
von Gerolt, Mrs. Daly tells us, that the Dalys got to know the
Frémonts personally. But when Mrs. Frémont continued to
play up to Mrs. Daly, the diarist experienced a temporary
change of heart and admitted to liking Mrs. Frémont, even
though she could never be popular in New York: "Nobody
likes so much fresh breeze and so much sunlight; it disturbs
the lazy and frightens the hypocritical."

BARON FRIEDRICH VON GEROLT, Prussian minister to the United
States during the Civil War, was an intimate of the Dalys
even before the diary was begun. The Baron and members of
his family stayed at the Daly home for weeks at a time, and
the favor was reciprocated when the Dalys went to Washington. The Gerolt children provided Mrs. Daly with an
opportunity to offer her views on child-rearing and young people's manners and behavior. Of the baron, Mrs. Daly comments, "Baron Gerolt is truly philosophical. He says that it is
quite impossible to judge anything in this country by a European standard; that no one can tell how this war may end or
what may be the consequences." And of Mrs. Gerolt, "She
has, it would seem, a truly aristocratic and German contempt
and want of consideration for those beneath her. . . . Baron

Gerolt himself is considerate, however, in the extreme, and is one of the most lovable men I have ever met. He is the *noble* side of the family too. Madam is not; she belonged to the literary circle."

ULYSSES SIMPSON GRANT, commander of the Union forces, does not appear in the diary until 1863, because he was relatively unknown before that time. The battle of Vicksburg thrust him before the public eye, and Mrs. Daly immediately became one of his ardent admirers. After reciting the famous remark Lincoln made about Grant's brand of whisky, Mrs. Daly moralized, "It is lamentable that drunkenness is so common among our officers." After the war was won, Judge Daly became active in organizing a hero's welcome for the General in New York, and it was on this occasion that the Dalys became intimate with the Grants. The Dalys attended the opera with the Grants, entertained one another, and on numerous occasions during the years immediately following the war, Grant and his wife were dinner guests in the Daly home. Mrs. Daly describes Grant as "exactly like his portrait—most positive, honest-looking . . . firm in keeping his personal base"; Mrs. Grant as "simple, natural, not handsome, but pleasant looking; a slight cast in the eye, but fine teeth and a pleasant, honest smile."

TOWNSEND HARRIS, U.S. Consul-General and then Minister to Japan from 1859 to 1862, became a close friend of the Dalys during the war years and remained so until his death in 1878. The 1858 treaty Harris negotiated with Japan called for the visit of some seventy Japanese delegates to the United States, and undoubtedly as a result of Daly's close association with Harris, the Judge served as host to a group of Japanese jurists with the delegation. Mrs. Daly was fascinated with Harris' descriptions of Japan. So interested was Mrs. Daly in what Harris had to narrate during long evenings spent in the Daly home that she never did get around to evaluating Harris the personality: "Mr. Harris has always something interesting to tell us. Last evening he described scenes he had witnessed in Siam. He must have great powers of adaptation."

ROBERT EDWARD LEE, General of the Confederate Armies, is treated respectfully by the diarist and is generally employed as a model to which the Union officers fail to correspond: McClellan "stands idly on this side of the Potomac, whilst Lee is recruiting and furnishing himself in Virginia." Then again, bemoaning another of Lee's victories, the diarist writes, "Truly God has a controversy with this people; He raises for us no deliverer." Upon the occasion of Lee's surrender to Grant, Mrs. Daly comments charitably, "I hope the animosity that has so long reigned will now pass away. May God comfort and change the hearts of our so long vindictive foes!" Later, Mrs. Daly tells of the refusal of Judge Daly to meet Lee personally because he deserted the United States flag after having said that nothing would induce him to do so. This is followed by the remark, "He is in Richmond subsisting upon U.S. rations. What a future for a descendant of Washington!"

MARY TODD LINCOLN, wife of the President, was a favorite target of Mrs. Daly. "Mrs. Lincoln behaves in the most undignified manner possible, associating with Wyckoff and Sickles, with whom no lady would deign to speak; but she seems to be easily flattered." In a most uncharitable description of Mrs. Lincoln, Mrs. Daly wrote that "she looks like a vulgar, shoddy, contractor's wife who does not know what to do with her money," and that "It is humiliating to all American women who have to economize and struggle and part with their husbands, sons, and brothers in these sad times, to see this creature sitting in the highest place as a specimen of American womanhood." She commented on the occasion of the 1864 election, "Lincoln, a rail-splitter, and his wife, two ignorant and vulgar boors, are king and queen for now, and candidates for election." And following the assassination, Mrs. Daly could only commiserate briefly, "Poor Mrs. Lincoln!"

CATHERINE LYDIG BRADY, referred to as "Kate" or "Katie" in the diary, was Mrs. Daly's sister. In order of birth, the children of Philip and Catherine Mesier Lydig were Maria, Margaret (Maggie), Catherine (Kate), Philip (Phil), David, Rosalie, and Florence (Fuggie). Catherine married James T. Brady. At the time of this marriage, the diarist felt chagrined that a younger sister should receive all the attention and approval she considered herself to have been denied at the time of her own courtship and marriage. But the wound healed, and Kate continued to appear everywhere with her older sister.

CATHERINE MESIER LYDIG was Mrs. Daly's mother. Mrs. Lydig's father, John Suydam, was the son of Hendrick Rycker (Suydam being an adopted name), a prominent New York merchant, and her mother was Jane Mesier of Poughkeepsie. The diarist was quite harsh with her mother and never forgave the difficulties she experienced at the time of her marriage. "Spent the morning in Laight Street and had all my old grievances renewed by the sight of the preparations for Kate's marriage. I tried hard to keep them down but could not. Poor Mother, nature has given her little brains; she has not one ounce of spirit."

DAVID LYDIG, Mrs. Daly's younger brother, does not emerge as a real personality in the first volume of the diary because he was still very much of a boy. "David has returned from his European travels, I fear with little profit. The dear boy is a fine specimen of the country gentleman, with little appreciation, however, as yet, of art, science or literature." And later, "David has just returned home from Milford, and as the government has had recourse to drafting, I fear for him. He is so strong. The weak and miserable and mean will get off." During the war, David attended an agricultural college, and Mrs. Daly expressed the hope that he would occupy the "country gentleman's" status of her grandfather Lydig, after whom young David had been named.

DAVID LYDIG, Mrs. Daly's paternal grandfather, was in her opinion her "real" father. The author of most of the Lydig fortune, he retired about 1832 and divided his time between his town house at 34 Laight Street and his West Farms estate. Mrs. Daly frequently refers to him as "Dear grandpapa Lydig." She often reminisces about "my dear grandfather Lydig, whom I loved so very dearly, better than anyone in the world.

I cannot think of him now, even after more than twenty years of separation, without feeling the tears come. The love between us was so pure, so disinterested on my part, so reverential, so perfect in its trust." Bemoaning the fact that her grandfather never knew Judge Daly, the diarist comments, "How much he would have appreciated Charles! How much they are alike. They have the same aristocratic tastes and habits."

MARGARET LYDIG OTTO married a Karl Otto of Germany and lived in Switzerland for the remainder of her life, with the exception of a few visits home. She was the mother of Emy Otto Hoyt, to whom Mrs. Daly entrusted the care of her diary and who made this publication possible. On the one hand, the diarist wished that her sister had married differently and lived close to her, and on the other hand she writes, "I am glad to be released from further correspondence with her." Bitterness continued throughout life between the sisters, dating from the Lydig family's initial rejection of Mrs. Daly's choice of a husband: "Had a letter from Mag. She thinks most favorably and says that I must have quite realized my ideal in my husband. She is right for once. I am happy enough to be able to afford to forgive those who caused me so much trouble and pain and so insulted him."

MARIA MESIER LYDIG, paternal grandmother of Mrs. Daly and wife of the elder David Lydig, was the daughter of Peter and Catherine Slecht Mesier, descendants of original Dutch settlers of New Amsterdam. Mrs. Daly was the namesake of her grandmother Lydig. "Grandmother, with her passionate temper but wholesome rule," is described by the diarist at one point as "my true mother."

PHILIP LYDIG is mentioned more often in the diary than any other blood relation. The diarist felt very close to brother "Phil," through whom she experienced the terrors of war vicariously. Phil is described by the diarist as the "most intellectual" member of her living family. Her fears began when "Phil has succeeded, I fear, in getting a commission as lieutenant in the regular army and a staff appointment. He'll make a splendid figure, but it makes my heart ache to think of it," and reached a climax when "Phil has just come in to say that he has received a telegraph from General Parke to say that if he has his commission, he [Parke] would like him to join him at once at Annapolis to go on to Burnside's expedition, which is destined for Yorktown and sails in a few days. May God protect him. I feel that he does his duty in going, but it is dreadful to have this anxiety." Phil saw action at Roanoke Island, became a captain, participated in the battle of Fredericksburg, the battle for Richmond, and the capture of Petersburg at the end of the war when he was attached to the 9th Army Corps.

PHILIP LYDIG, Mrs. Daly's father, worked with his father, retired, lived in his father's town house and country estate, and contributed little beyond the rearing of his family. Mrs. Daly did not regard him highly. "If father could but realize how much he made us lose, some thousands at least, by his sad mistake and unreasonableness, he would make it up; but he does not. That he deeply regrets the part he had in the matter [of her marriage], he takes every opportunity, unlike my mother's near family connections, to show us." When Mrs. Daly asked her father for an old house and four acres at West Farms, or even the privilege of buying it, Philip Lydig refused. She commented, "It is all for the best, doubtless, and I will try to remember Who has permitted it, and look upon the rest as agents only. Thus I may keep my heart from hardening, but the selfishness of this family is terrible."

GEORGE BRINTON MCCLELLAN, Commander of the Army of the Potomac from the disaster of the first Battle of Bull Run until November 1862, was well known to the Dalys before the war. Though maligned for his caution and apparent unwillingness to engage in battle, McClellan gave much-needed training and organization to the Union forces while he was top commander. Mrs. Daly joined in the chorus of ridicule, at last, which led to the reinstatement of Halleck to the top position: "McClellan, they now say, is incapable, and is striving after the Presidency, instigated by his wife." A year later, the diarist experienced a change of heart and wrote, "How virulent the Republicans are against McClellan." When, early in September 1864, the Democrats nominated McClellan in Chicago, Mrs. Daly was jubilant and pledged to win converts to his side. In the election debate which followed, she argued, "Who can be worse? If McClellan would be the experiment, what was Lincoln?" Later, she wrote, "The Republicans may deny it . . . but the soldiers were not allowed to vote for McClellan."

THOMAS FRANCIS MEAGHER, stormy petrel and former Irish revolutionary, fled to the United States just in time to escape banishment to Van Diemen's Land, and settled in New York. The Dalys first came to know Meagher when he volunteered for service in Colonel Corcoran's 69th Regiment, and in the beginning they were favorably impressed. Then came Bull Run, and Corcoran was taken prisoner. Early reports of this occurrence in the diary praise Meagher's conduct, but soon after Meagher replaced Corcoran as Colonel of the Regiment, his role at Bull Run became that of master intriguer. From the moment Meagher was elevated to the rank of brigadier general, he became the principal villain of the diary. He is described as having a "very domineering, arrogant disposition," as being "very despotic, ambitious" and "double-faced," and of being drunk during the battle of Bull Run.

BERNARD O'REILLY, chaplain of the 69th Regiment, became an intimate friend of the Dalys and appears frequently in the diary. Born in County Mayo, Ireland, in 1820, O'Reilly emigrated to Canada in 1836, attended Laval University, and was ordained a priest in 1843. Later he entered the Society of Jesus and was assigned to St. John's College, Fordham, N.Y. Father O'Reilly's influence over Mrs. Daly was so great that she considered becoming a Catholic. In 1861, she described him as "unostentatious, refined, intellectual," and ended her narration of his heroic conduct on the battlefield at Bull Run with the accolade, "Behold, indeed, an Apostle of Christ, a follower of his self-denying Master!" He inspired her to say, at a later date, "There is something great in that sanctified character which cannot be reached by any other. It approaches the nearest to the imitation of Christ." After the war, O'Reilly withdrew from the Jesuits and devoted himself to literature. His publications were many, most of them devoted to Catholic history, and he received special recognition from Pope Leo XIII for his scholarship.

BARON CARL ROBERT ROMANOVICH VON DER OSTEN-SACKEN is first mentioned in October 1862, and thereafter appears as a frequent visitor in the Daly home. First Secretary to the Russian Legation to the United States during the Civil War, Osten-Sacken was an enthusiastic supporter of "the American experiment." "He wants a book to be written upon America, showing how the remarkable growth is produced, how towns are formed from settlements, etc.; in fact, the whole organism! He asked Dr. Lieber, but he [Lieber] said that the difficulty would be that no European could be made to believe that an American was born with all this organism in him and developed it as naturally as he breathed." When the Russian fleet made its historic "goodwill tour" to New York during the war, the Baron promised to take the Dalys aboard the flagship to attend Greek Orthodox services.

EDWARD PELTZ, land speculator and close friend of the Dalys, is often referred to as "Father Peltz" because of his great age at the time the diarist wrote about him. Daly and Peltz had been engaged in land speculation in Minnesota and Wisconsin, but Judge Daly discontinued that form of investment soon after his marriage. More the visionary and idealist than the hard-headed business man, Peltz soon had Mrs. Daly involved in his endless schemes to encourage emigration to the Midwest. Although she claimed that such transactions were making her "quite business-like, quite scheming," she is soon subsidizing the old man's trips to Washington, D.C., to induce Secretary Seward to become involved with their essentially humanitarian proposals. At one point in the diary (see pages 203–204), Mrs. Daly writes a short biography of this "splendid old fellow—so disinterested, so generous, so free from pettiness."

EDWARDS PIERREPONT, judge, cabinet officer, and diplomat, was a personal friend of Judge Daly and was associated with him in a number of organizations. Pierrepont served on the bench of New York City's Superior Court from 1857 to 1860, and retired to private law practice just before the war began. A staunch supporter of Lincoln and Grant, he served as attorney-general in 1875 and was United States ambassador to Britain from 1876 to 1877. Mrs. Daly sought Pierrepont's aid in obtaining a commission for her brother Phil, and she tells us that Pierrepont delivered it to her personally. Since he was conversant with Lincoln and most of the high government officials in Washington, his conversations with the Dalys make interesting reading. All was not smooth between the diarist and Pierrepont, however. When Dix and Pierrepont supported Lincoln in the 1864 campaign, she felt that they had disgraced themselves.

VALDEMAR RUDOLF RAASLOFF, Danish minister to the United States during the Civil War, was one of the diplomats whom the Dalys entertained at their home. He was frequently a dinner guest of the Dalys. The diarist found him a challenging companion, and he prodded her into expressing some of her strong opinions in her notebook—"Colonel Raasloff is a very disputatious, very intelligent, agreeable man. He rallied me very much upon my American spirit." Possessed of strong views on almost any subject, according to Mrs. Daly, Raasloff is quoted on everything from the Catholic Church ("one of the only stable influences in America") to politics ("Raasloff says that we are ripe here for a despotism") to the costs of war ("Raasloff thinks peace on any terms would be better for us than this ever-increasing frightful debt.")

WINFIELD SCOTT, U.S. Army Chief of Staff from 1841 to 1861, was a hero of the Indian and Mexican Wars, and was a good friend of the Dalys. Before the first Battle of Bull Run—which was fought against his wishes—Scott told the Judge "that with 2,000 men he could defend [Washington] even without any intrenchments against 20,000 for twenty-four hours." A Southerner by birth, Scott was loyal to the Union and opposed to secession. He, unlike others in Washington, foresaw a long war, based on the Union's lack of preparedness. He retired on

November 1, 1861, and was honored with a formal call by Lincoln and his entire cabinet. "Dear old warrior! Gallant old chief! They say that he is the greatest general now living," wrote Mrs. Daly.

WILLIAM HENRY SEWARD, Lincoln's ambitious Secretary of State, was not one of the diarist's favorites, though she did appeal to him for favors from time to time. "Charles seems to think that Seward is not the man for the occasion; he is too wrapped up in self. So long as you will listen whilst he preaches, well, but he cannot believe in anyone else nor see the wisdom in those who differ from him," and later, "Seward, I suppose, could not believe that anyone could be wiser than himself." Mrs. Daly was far from alone in her opinion of the man who proposed to Lincoln that he sit back and relax and allow an expert to run the government for him. In December of 1862, Mrs. Daly somehow got the impression that Seward had resigned from the cabinet, but in this she was mistaken, and she never bothered to correct her error in subsequent references to the man.

MARY SHEAFF, "Cousin Mary," is the target in the diary for some of Mrs. Daly's most caustic remarks: "I told Cousin Mary Sheaff today that if her branch of the family did not wake up soon that we should get ahead of them. . . . I like to tease her a little."

JAMES SHIELDS, judge, soldier, and politician, emigrated to the United States from Ireland at an early age, studied law, served in the Illinois Legislature in 1836, and became a judge of the Illinois Supreme Court in 1843. He distinguished himself in the Mexican War and emerged a major general. Governor of the Oregon Territory from 1848 to 1849, he served in the U.S. Senate from 1849 to 1855 and from 1858 to 1859. He was made a brigadier general of Union volunteers on August 19, 1861, prior to which he was engaged in mining operations in Mexico. He fought at Winchester and in the Shenandoah Valley, was defeated at Port Republic in June 1862, and resigned his commission in 1863. From this point on, he lived in California, where he pursued a rather undistinguished political career. In the beginning of the diary, Mrs. Daly looked upon Shields almost as her protégé, and she did what she could to foster his career. Two things upset her very much, however—the rumor that Shields was running with a "Miss Cahil" and the General's inability to see that Meagher was making a fool of him. These two factors caused her to say, quite correctly, "The General is not a well-balanced character."

Miss Harriet Douglas Whetten, Mrs. Daly's only intimate woman friend, is one of the few ladies whom Mrs. Daly treated with consistent kindness in her diary. Mrs. Daly evidently went in for a little matchmaking which failed, for she comments at one point, "I'm glad that Harriet is not his [Shields'] wife. She might have lost her illusions." When Miss Whetten determined upon joining the nursing corps of Miss Dorothea Dix, Mrs. Daly became very upset and protested, "If I were [one of] the *boys*, I should not want a lady about my sickbed," but despite the failure of her plea that Miss Whetten abandon her war career, the diarist wrote, "I love her dearly, for she has very noble qualities. She is generous, affectionate, intelligent and high minded." Katherine Prescott Wormeley, in *The Other Side of War*, describes Miss Whetten as a tall, symmetrical woman who played an active and heroic part in the nursing work of 1862.

INTRODUCTION

Candor would be lacking if a diarist knew who, or how many, would read things into his interpretations of events at some later date. The reader's fascination lies perhaps in the diarist's not knowing—and not caring. One of the charms of Mrs. Daly's diary is that she revealed her feelings without inhibition and expressed her many prejudices with great poignancy. Her lack of reserve in reacting to situations in which she was either an observer or a participant provides the *Diary of a Union Lady* with an abundance of spice and interest.

An understanding of Mrs. Daly's past, family connections, marriage, social milieu, and economic status are all-important to a full appreciation of what she thought and felt and wrote. Equal in importance, perhaps, to all of these factors is an understanding of Judge Daly's stature in the New York City Mrs. Daly wrote about, for his opinions and associations were paramount in the viewpoints and personalities discussed in the diary.

Before a description of the diarist and a review of the career of her husband, however, must come something about the scope and content of the diary itself. This volume includes only the years 1861 through 1865—the war years and some of their aftermath. The second and larger volume, as yet unpublished, covers the postwar period, with the last entry being made on July 29, 1893—one year before the lady's death. Our present concern is with the war years and with the nature of the diarist's coverage of what these years were like in New York.

Scope and Content

The diary was begun during a trip the Judge and Mrs. Daly made to Washington, D.C., at the end of January, 1861. Talk

of war was on everyone's lips, and doubtless Mrs. Daly's mo-
tivation in taking up her pen at this point was to preserve, for
rereading in the future, the immediate impressions of a coming
national emergency.

Except for this single Washington entry and a few written
while Mrs. Daly vacationed in the country, the diary concerns
itself with the city of New York, its people, and the impact
of the war on the city. She records New York's immediate response to Lincoln's call for volunteers and money; the regiments preparing for and marching off to war; the role the ladies
of New York played in assisting the war effort; the work of
the Sanitary Commission and the celebrated Sanitary Commission Fair to raise money for the Union cause; the Draft Riots
of 1863; the visit of the Russian fleet to New York; and the
sacrifices some New Yorkers imposed upon themselves while
the wives of war-profiteers spent lavishly on extravagances.

Mrs. Daly's coverage of the war itself is somewhat vague and
frequently inaccurate. A good deal of effort has been expended
by the editor to distinguish the diarist's emotional reactions
from the facts and to clarify and enlarge upon her sometimes
casual references to battles of great significance, for the lady
left much to be desired in her narration of the progress of the
war. This need not have been, for a number of newspapers
were brought into the Daly home every day; the Judge discussed the war with the important politicians and diplomats who
frequented his home; and Mrs. Daly was kept posted from the
front by such personal friends as Adam Badeau, General
Grant's secretary.

Politics assumes sufficient importance in the diary for a separate section of this introduction to be devoted to it, but most
of the diarist's political commentary reflects the attitude of a
traditionally Democratic city to Republican national leadership
during wartime. On local politics, Mrs. Daly's remarks are
especially valuable, for the Judge was a local politician and a
Union Democrat who numbered among his personal friends im-

portant Copperheads (the "Peace Democrats," who opposed Lincoln's war policy) in the city.

In addition to recording military and political history, the diary reveals how the wealthy and prominent of the city lived during the war, as well as the effect of the war upon the poor. People from all walks of life enjoyed the hospitality of the Dalys, and the diarist often complains about the Judge's habit of bringing people "of little consequence" into their home and being "put upon" by them. Innumerable supper parties are described by Mrs. Daly, parties given in her own home or in the homes of other prominent New Yorkers, and the record she has made of conversations, dress, food, and almost everything else offers the reader a wealth of social history.

Equally valuable is the diarist's description of the cultural life of New Yorkers during the war. Not only did the Dalys regularly attend lectures, concerts, and the opera, but a number of celebrities visited their home during these years. Poets and writers and explorers and diplomats fraternized in the Daly home with actors, artists, and educators. The art exhibits at the Tenth Street Studio building and the Shakespeare tricentennial celebration, in which the Judge took a leading part, are well described.

As for the economic picture, Mrs. Daly describes the effect of war economy on New Yorkers, complains bitterly about inflation and a depreciated currency, high taxes, and the increasing cost of living. Although she had had a considerable dowry fixed upon her by her father, and although the Judge's salary was reasonably high in that day, she constantly reiterates her claim of a shortage of money. Things did not become so bad, however, that she had to discharge either of her two servants or to concern herself over the almost certain loss of a hundred-dollar loan to the aged Edward Peltz.

Something has still to be said about Judge Daly, Mrs. Daly's family background and connections, the circumstances which caused Mrs. Daly to speak so bitterly about members of her family, the diarist's "frame of reference," and, finally, about New York City during the period in which Mrs. Daly wrote about it. Each of these topics contributes to a fuller understanding of the diarist herself and of her attitudes, opinions, and prejudices.

Charles Patrick Daly

The diarist's husband, Judge Daly, spent almost his entire life in New York City, and since he lived from 1816 until September, 1899, that life nearly spanned the century.

Born of Irish immigrant parents who arrived in America only two years before their only son was born, Charles Daly rose to eminence in the social, political, and intellectual circles of his day. A leader in many fields, he earned a reputation as patron of the arts, philanthropist, Shakespearean scholar, and sage. The Judge was careful in his scholarship, and his writings include the common law, juridical history, diplomatic treatises, and the history of drama. Columbia University conferred the degree of Doctor of Laws upon him in 1860 and engaged him—a man of almost no formal education—to lecture in the School of Law.

Judge Daly's active service on the bench is one of the longest in American jurisprudence. A justice of the Court of Common Pleas of the City of New York from his twenty-eighth to his seventieth year, he was Chief Justice for the last twenty-seven of his nearly forty-two years on the bench. The Common Pleas was considered the highest court in New York City during the nineteenth century, and it existed by that name from 1821 to 1896, when it was dissolved and its jurisdiction divided between the Supreme Court, the Superior Court, and the General Sessions Court. Judge Daly served on it during the most significant period of its life, from 1844 to 1885.

Two of the most celebrated of Judge Daly's cases were the Astor Place Riots Case in 1849 and the impeachment trial of Mayor A. Oakey Hall (1872) during the Tweed Ring scandals. Daly was known as "the incorruptible judge," and he fought Tweed and his cohorts with a vigor that nearly cost him his judicial position.

Daly held a governing role in the American Geographical Society, formed in 1852, almost from its infancy, and was president from 1864 to 1899. In this capacity he knew well such great men as Stanley, Humboldt, Hall, Hayes, Du Chaillu, and Peary. Indicative of the regard explorers had for him is the fact that there is a Lake Daly in the Arctic and a Cape Daly in Northern Greenland.

A Tammany man in his early career, Daly became a Union Democrat during the Civil War and belonged to the reform element of the Democratic party after the war. He assisted his personal friends George McClellan, Samuel J. Tilden, and Winfield Scott Hancock in their unsuccessful bids for the Presidency of the United States in the 1864, 1876, and 1880 elections. In his role as behind-the-scenes politician, Daly vigorously supported Grover Cleveland in his three bids for the Presidency. Though a onetime member of the New York legislature, Daly resisted the many offers of political advancement made to him, preferring "peace to power" for himself.

As a wit and orator of first rank, Daly acted as unofficial host for the city of New York, welcoming dignitaries, dedicating monuments, presiding over public meetings, and leading movements for improvement and reform.

Two minority groups were indebted to Judge Daly for his efforts—the Irish and the Jews. As champion of the rights of both groups, Daly's concern for their interests was tangible. President of the Friendly Sons of St. Patrick for a number of years, the Judge pursued his lifelong guardianship over distressed Irish immigrants in America, headed charities for Irish relief, and from the United States aided the movement for Irish independence. Daly was also close to the Jewish population of New York, and he was a guest of honor at all their important functions in the city. Author of *The History of the*

Jews in North America, the Judge contributed generously to Jewish charities and was instrumental in founding the Jewish Orphans' Home in the city.

The Lydig Family

Maria Lydig Daly was a descendant of two old and distinguished New York families—the Lydigs and the Suydams. Her parents, Philip Mesier Lydig and Catherine Mesier Suydam, were cousins, married in 1821. Maria was born on September 12, 1824, the first of ten children born to this union, only seven of whom survived infancy: Maria, Margaret, David (d. infant), Elizabeth (d. infant), David Suydam (d. infant), Catherine, Philip, David, Rosalie, and Florence.

Founder of the New York family of Lydigs was Philip Lydig. He was born at Schwab-Hall, Germany, in 1723, migrated to America in 1750, and established himself as a grain merchant in Philadelphia. In 1760, Philip Lydig moved to New York City and engaged in the business of supplying vessels with sea biscuit. At the time of the Revolution, his was the chief bakery in a city of eight thousand residents, and he is reputed to have engaged in espionage for General Washington. Active in soliciting funds for the construction of a German Lutheran Church at the corner of Frankfort and William Streets in New York, he was buried beneath that edifice in 1784.

Philip Lydig's marriage to the daughter of Peter Grim—Mrs. Margaret Ebert, widow of Philip Ebert—in 1763 added another old and distinguished American family to Mrs. Daly's background. One of the two children born of this union was David Lydig, Mrs. Daly's grandfather, and he inherited Philip Lydig's thriving business and considerable fortune gained from Revolutionary profiteering. One of his commercial acquisitions was the water power at Buttermilk Falls in the town of Cornwall, Orange County, New York. There he erected large mills for the manufacture of flour which supplied his wholesale outlet at South and Davis Streets in New York City. David Lydig's prosperity allowed him to purchase still another site. This property, supplied with water power and a mill, was the DeLancey estate, and it consisted of many acres adjoining the village of West Farms. A portion of this estate is today occupied by the Bronx Park Zoological and Botanical Gardens.

Born in New York City in 1764, David Lydig married Maria Mesier, daughter of Peter and Catherine Slecht Mesier, in 1790. The only child born of this marriage was Philip Mesier Lydig, Mrs. Daly's father. Head of the Mesier family was Peter Mesier, a wealthy New York merchant and property owner who came close to bankruptcy as a result of the fire of 1776 in the city. Another of Peter Mesier's daughters, Jane, married John Suydam, also a prominent New York merchant, and one of the children of this marriage was Mrs. Daly's mother. With the marriage of Mrs. Daly's parents, therefore, the Lydig, Mesier, and Suydam families were linked.

Philip Mesier Lydig was born in New York City in 1799, entered his father's business early, and married at the age of twenty-two. When his father, David Lydig, realized that the completion of Governor Clinton's Erie Canal meant that the flour producers of New York would have to gear their trade to a "wheat-belt" market, he shrewdly resolved to sell out his interests before his competitors became aware of the implications of a cheap transportation route for Midwestern grain producers and flour merchants. He therefore sold the "father-and-son" business, mills and all, and both David and Philip Lydig retired for the rest of their natural lives in the early 1830's. David died on June 16, 1840, and Philip Mesier Lydig inherited his entire fortune of more than half a million dollars (many millions in today's currency, and before inheritance taxes).

David Lydig had resided at 35 Beekman Street for over thirty-five years before he moved to 225 Broadway in 1819, into a block which claimed such well-known residents as John C. Coster and John Jacob Astor. At the same time that he sold his business he sold his town house to John J. Astor at a good profit, and a hotel was built on the site. A new residence was constructed at 34 Laight Street, and this became the town house of Mrs. Daly's family when David Lydig died. The diarist was born and reared at this address, and the family divided their time between the Laight Street home and their country estate at West Farms. Philip Lydig devoted the remainder of his life, after his early retirement, to rearing his large family, investing his money, and looking after his town house and his country estate.

Courtship and Marriage

Considering the origins of both the Judge and Mrs. Daly, the diarist's dichotomy on the matter of "class" becomes more understandable. The Judge was the son of poor Irish immigrants; he reared himself, educated himself, and rose to eminence from cabin boy to a leading figure in the city. Mrs. Daly, by contrast, belonged to the monied and "blood" aristocracy of New York, for the Dutch and German "old family" merchants were as highly regarded in the city during the nineteenth century as the Irish were despised. Further, the Lydigs, Suydams, and Mesiers belonged to the eminently respectable Lutheran and Dutch Reformed Churches, and Mrs. Daly's father went one step beyond this in respectability by joining the Episcopal Church. The "blue bloods" of nineteenth-century New York were Episcopalians, and the Roman Catholic faith, into which Judge Daly was born, claimed the city's lowliest.

Little wonder, then, that Philip Lydig, a member of the best clubs and societies of New York, objected to the courtship between his first-born and a man named Charles Patrick Daly. It must also have been difficult for Philip Lydig to believe that the Judge, who, though made respectable by his position, had been able to accumulate very little money on his own by his thirty-ninth year, was not interested in his daughter because of her money. Add to this the fact that Maria Lydig was in her thirty-second year and still unmarried in a day when girls usually married in their teens, and Philip Lydig's suspicions bear the weight of logic. And so began a conflict between father and daughter which she could never forget.

In November and December of 1855, just after Judge Daly had turned thirty-nine, an innocuous series of letters arrived at his rooming house. The first invited him "very socially to meet a few friends at eight o'clock, 34 Laight Street," and it was signed "Mr. Lydig." Shortly after his visit to the Lydig home, the Judge received a note which read, "*The Art Student*, with Miss Lydig's compliments. She thinks she may recommend it and begs that Judge Daly will read it at his leisure. . . . Should he have no pleasanter engagement this evening, will he not join us at twenty-five Waverly Place at six o'clock and go with us to see *Rip Van Winkle*." Years later, when asked where he had met his wife, Judge Daly replied that he had met her at a party, and that upon first sight he had decided that she was the one and only woman whom he wished to marry. The feeling was mutual, subsequent correspondence showing the lady the more determined of the two as obstacles began to multiply.

Maria Lydig could hardly be regarded as a headstrong child at the age of thirty-two, despite the fact that she had been overprotected by a father who was almost always at home and was reluctant to see his patriarchy broken up. She was a woman who saw in the Judge her last opportunity to break away from her family and to enjoy the pleasures and benefits of marriage, and though she toyed with the idea of an elopement which would cut off her dowry and family money, the Judge was apparently cool to that idea. In a long letter to Daly early in 1856, Miss Lydig wrote, "Father, I fear, is a little insane. I do not think he will ever consent, but what is this to us? I am of age; so are you. What God has joined, let not man put asunder. Let neither our tempers or pride disjoin us."

Miss Lydig wrote a great many letters to Daly during 1856,

the year of their courtship and marriage, but it was a one-sided correspondence and we must follow the mounting crisis through Maria's reactions rather than those of the Judge. "Let not Father nor anyone else induce you to enter into any engagement to let me alone and dissuade me from loving you. Let not your own pride do so. As I said before, I am no one's chattel and my marriage is only of my own contracting." And again, "It may be next Autumn, it may be next Spring, but we shall be happy *despite unnatural and irrational parents*. Do aid me; don't be more virtuous than I. I shan't love you for it. Do nothing for the present but love. Yours affectionately, cast down but not in despair, afflicted, not shaken, having nothing and yet possessing all things, Maria."

Finally, Maria prodded her middle-aged bachelor into action, for a terse note appears in the Judge's papers from Philip Lydig which reads, "Returned this day from the country, and your note was placed in my hands. I have immediately called upon you, but finding you not at home, I will call again tomorrow evening at seven o'clock to discuss this painful affair." The result of the interview was evidently favorable, for Maria subsequently wrote to Daly, "I had a conversation with father this evening. He says he will always be happy to see you. He esteems and likes you and has not the slightest objection, dearest, to your coming to see me. He would, and willingly, that we should marry, were it not for this one impediment [religion], which I fear the poor soul has made a principle of thinking such."

The courtship continued throughout the summer of 1856, and so did the conflict between Maria and her father, until finally the impatient lady wrote in the late summer, "Can we not be privately married and each return to our respective homes until we see fit to live together? I feel that I am asking a great sacrifice of you to consent to this. You will gain with me, as an Irishman would say, only a certain loss—you an independent rich bachelor, but I do not think there would be any wretchedness in it [and] I might gain a little peace of mind." Such an arrangement was unsatisfactory to the "rich bachelor" before and now, and nothing was done until Maria's mother stepped into the situation and settled the matter.

My dear Judge:

Maria will not write this, although her father bade her; therefore, I do so. On mature consideration, Mr. Lydig and I think there is no one more likely, from your stability of character and high principle, to make our daughter happy, and we believe that, being both persons of moderate desires, with what she will have—which perhaps I should tell you, namely, $20,000 settled on herself—you will be able to live, if not luxuriously, at least comfortably. It is no great sum, but her father thinks it better to have something in reserve for a rainy day in the future.

As I am fully convinced that you seek her only for herself, if you can come down this evening early, do so. You were always a favorite with me, and I hope that all things may be so fortunate and happy that you and my daughter, with God's blessing, may live as happily together as her father and I, who, though not a person to make professions, I trust you may find an affectionate father.

Yours most sincerely,
C. M. Lydig

Soon the details of the arrangement were settled. In addition to the $20,000 dowry settled upon Maria (a fortune in that day), Philip Lydig agreed to buy for the newlyweds the only town house they ever occupied, 84 Clinton Place. Father and daughter located the proper house in the proper neighborhood, and Philip Lydig bought it outright for $12,000 cash. In addition to this, Maria had sums of money settled upon her in the estate of her grandmother, more due from the estate of her grandfather, and, of course, one seventh of Philip Lydig's considerable fortune when he died. Yet, in her diary, Mrs. Daly regarded this as insufficient, and brooded over the way her father had cheated her of her proper inheritance—this from a woman who was prepared to throw it all away several times.

They were married on September 27, 1856, after less than a year of courtship. Few details are available regarding the ceremony, and even the announcement of the event is limited to a letter from Daly's friend, N. P. Willis: "This is your wedding day, and a more beautiful one never made life and love's blessings wherewith to enjoy it." It is strange that the marriage of two such socially prominent persons should not have received wide attention by the social columnists, but evidently pains were taken to avoid publicity. The wedding was also apparently conducted outside of New York City, and part of Mrs. Daly's subsequent bitterness over the affair was over the absence of members of her family.

"Frame of Reference"

Many factors contribute to a person's "frame of reference," a term used to explain the diarist's attitudes, opinions, and prejudices. Included among these are heritage, marriage, economic and social status, religion, education—a multitude of factors.

The national political scene received as much attention from Mrs. Daly in the first volume of her diary as any other topic, partly because the country was at war and the future of every American depended heavily upon the leadership that could only originate in Washington, and partly because Mrs. Daly was married to a politician who belonged to the opposition party. There is little doubt that Mrs. Daly acquired most of the political attitudes she expresses in her diary by association with the Judge and his friends, for we find her trying to persuade her father that his political convictions are wrong and those of the Judge are right. Enough clues are offered in the diary, even if we ignore Philip Lydig's background and situation in life, to indicate that the diarist was not reared a Democrat.

Shocking to many readers today is the number and virulence

of the Lincoln-haters during the period in which he was making history, but it was only long after his death that Lincoln gained his full stature in the popular mind. Mrs. Daly's reference to "Uncle Ape," "King Log," and "the clod," as applied to Lincoln would be considered seditious, if not sacrilegious, today, but when one realizes that these epithets are being used by a convert to the oldest existing political party in America against the incumbent of a four-year-old minority party, they do not seem so extraordinary.

The reference to "King Log" is an interesting one, for in Aesop's fable, Jupiter sent the frogs a log for a king and they complained bitterly when it did nothing but float harmlessly on the top of the water. This is how many people in the North felt about Lincoln's conduct of the war during the first few years of his administration. Had she pursued the analogy further, however, she would have gotten to Aesop's moral, which was, "Better no rule than cruel rule." When the frogs also found the eel an unsatisfactory ruler, Jupiter sent a heron to rule them, who preyed upon them until there were none left. Mrs. Daly did say that she would prefer the rule of Jefferson Davis to Abraham Lincoln, though Davis was considered an arbitrary ruler by many Southerners.

When the 1864 election approached, Mrs. Daly forgot all about her earlier impatience with the vacillation and delays of McClellan when he commanded the Army of the Potomac, and she put all her energies behind the effort to drive "Lincoln and his host of locusts" out of Washington: "Today I have been writing out all the bad things I have heard of Lincoln and his wife, hoping to get them into the papers." These were the expressions of a political partisan who believed in 1864 that Lincoln had bungled the war hopelessly and had proved himself a weak and impotent ruler. But when her predictions of a McClellan landslide proved so far wrong (an easy miscalculation to make in a city in which Union Democrats and Copperheads were the two majority groups in 1864), the diarist comments in the good-natured manner with which most Americans receive defeat at the polls: "*Vox Populi, vox Dei!* So it must be for the best! All now left to us is to put the shoulder to the wheel and do our best to draw the governmental machine out of the slough."

Mrs. Daly takes a very dim view of New Englanders, most of whom she believes to be abolitionists. From the thunder which the Garrisons, the Beechers, the Stowes, and other literary and intellectual lights of New England made over the slavery issue, it was not odd that most of the country (on both sides of the Mason and Dixon line) thought that all New Englanders were warmongering abolitionists. And New England's historic, if not intellectual, connection with Great Britain helped Mrs. Daly to ball two strong prejudices into one and come up with an intrigue between the New England abolitionists and British Southern sympathizers to start the war and help the South to win. If all this seems fantastic today, it was quite plausible to New Yorkers in the 1860's, and such views were shared by a large number of people who moved in Mrs. Daly's circle.

The diarist's almost belligerent defense of the Irish and her sympathy with Irish causes needs almost no explanation in view of her marriage to the Judge. Although Mrs. Daly had evidently been reared in an atmosphere hostile to the Irish immigrants who fled from famine in the 1840's and flooded the New York labor market with unskilled laborers, all this changed when her courtship with the Judge began. After their marriage, Judge Daly attracted to his home many of the prominent Irish who entered or lived in New York.

It is also difficult today to conceive of the disdain accorded Irish immigrants during most of the nineteenth century. As "the most recent group to come over," they were relegated to the bottom of the social and economic scale, hated and exploited. Assigned to the worst slum housing and the most menial tasks, they were paid miserable wages and labored under brutal conditions. Little wonder, then, that they became unruly and malcontent. The culmination of their resentment was reached with the Draft Riots of 1863, during which they made helpless Negroes targets of their wrath. A good account of this is offered by the diarist.

The Judge was second-generation Irish, and identified himself only with the most "respectable" Irish element. When the Draft Riots began, he helped to organize a group of propertied citizens who armed themselves and went out to do battle with the Irish mobs that roamed the streets of the city. Not only his position, but his marriage to a woman from old New York families of wealth and reputation placed him beyond the abuse Irish New Yorkers normally received. Finally, the Judge's affluence after his marriage added to his respectability in the eyes of many.

Religion is another topic which Mrs. Daly dwelt upon considerably in her diary. Here again, she combated so well the objections her parents raised to marrying out of her faith that she very nearly became a convert to Roman Catholicism. If she shared the convictions of her Episcopalian family, she was doubtless somewhat anti-Catholic up to the thirty-second year of her life. Suddenly she was proposing to the Judge that he whisk her off to the Catholic bishop at Baltimore for a quick ceremony. In the present volume of the diary, her criticism of the Protestant Church, and particularly of the Episcopal clergy, is biting—often vicious. Her praise for the structure, organization, and clergy of the Roman Catholic Church, by contrast, is extravagant and almost worshipful. If these represented her true sentiments, it is amazing that she lived and died an Episcopalian.

Liberal though her marriage to the Judge made her, Mrs. Daly was never able to free herself from many of the prejudices which her family's social and economic status imposed upon her. She ridiculed people of great wealth on the one hand but identified with them on the other, and chafed when she could not compete with them on an equal footing. She paid lip service to the poor and humble, but regarded them with contempt. And on the matter of slavery, she abused slaveholders with as much vigor as an ardent abolitionist, and in the next breath expressed her revulsion toward being physically close to "niggers." She believed in a society stratified into distinct socio-economic classes, and when an Abraham Lincoln or a Thomas Francis Meagher or the wife of a former laborer who had made enough to allow certain luxuries stepped beyond his designated limit, she protested vigorously.

She was malicious toward most members of her own sex—especially the very attractive ones—but she was very human and very much a woman. It was quite natural for her to resent women who were able to make themselves more attractive than she, and it is not surprising that her only intimate woman friend during her adult life met spinster Dorothea Dix's specifications for the ideal nurse during the Civil War.

Mrs. Daly's New York—the 1820's and the 1860's

By contemporary standards, the New York into which Mrs. Daly was born in 1824 would be considered a small to medium-sized city, but its population of approximately 125,000 made it the largest city in the United States and one of the world's great metropolises. The degree to which the city fathers were "keeping up with the times" and with the increases in the city's population was a matter of conflicting report then, as it is today, for progress in any given area only sharpened the contrast with backwardness in other areas.

On the side of progressiveness, the celebrated Interment Law was passed in 1823, forbidding burials south of Canal Street; Maiden Lane was opened up, and improvements were made near Pearl Street; the Sharon Canal Company was incorporated for the purpose of supplying the city with water, with a capitalization of $560,000; a new burying ground was laid out between 40th and 42nd Streets and between Fourth and Fifth

Avenues, ten acres in all, at a cost of $8,449 to the city; the old
Potter's Field was leveled, and a beautiful park to be known as
Washington Square was formed on its site; Fulton Bank was
incorporated, and a new law taxing bank stock in the city
passed the state legislature in Albany; the Hudson River steam-
boat monopoly was dissolved by a decision of the United States
Supreme Court; and the New York Gas Company was granted
the exclusive privilege, for thirty years, of laying cast-iron
pipes in the streets south of Grand Street for the purpose of
lighting the streets of New York by gas, on the same terms
and at the same cost as oil.

On the negative side, historian Bayrd Still offers this un-
savory view of the city:

> Physically, in this generation, New York City suggested the
> carelessness of growing youth. Travelers of the 1820's—both
> native and foreign—complained of its unkempt and cluttered
> streets, its squalid, smelly slips, and its ever-present pigs. Bales
> and boxes of merchants' wares, or sawyers preparing wood for
> the market, often blocked the pedestrian's way. "The streets
> of New York are not to be perambulated with impunity by
> either the lame, or the blind, or the exquisitely sensitive in their
> olfactory nerves," warned a Glasgow printer upon his return
> to Scotland in 1823. "To use an American phrase, a person
> must be wide-awake not to dislocate his ankles by the in-
> equalities and gaps in the side pavements, or break his legs by
> running foul of the numberless movable and immovable in-
> cumbrances with which they are occupied."

In 1822 and 1823, New York was "again smitten by a great
calamity"—yellow fever, a plague which had claimed seven
hundred New Yorkers in 1803 and three hundred more in 1805.
As the panic swept over the city, a mass exodus began, and banks
and public offices were removed to the village of Greenwich.
The name "Bank Street" serves as a reminder of this migration
to escape the disease which this time claimed over 1,200 lives.

Still, the city's population increased from 123,706 in 1820 to 166,085 in 1826.

By the time Mrs. Daly began her diary early in 1861, New York's population had grown to nearly 800,000. The Erie Canal was only one of the factors which contributed to the city's growth. As wave after wave of immigrants descended upon the city, many dug in where they landed instead of moving westward. New York, which was fast becoming a social and intellectual center, attracted visitors of high caliber from all over the world, many of whom settled there. New York City became not only a national but an international marketplace, and this in a rapidly developing industrial age! And as her population grew, and as wharves and piers occupied more and more of the Manhattan shores, far-sighted realtors recognized the potential of the wildernesses of a generation before, and forward-looking city fathers set to work on a grand scheme for a city park which would stretch from 59th Street to 110th Street and from Fifth to Eighth Avenues, an area occupied by about five thousand squatters "living in the most abject manner" and including "eighty-five or ninety farm houses and about two hundred shanties, barns, stables, piggeries and bone factories." Cultivated New Yorkers now gathered at Cooper Union, the Academy of Music on 14th Street, and the Astor Library, all opened in 1854, to listen to great lectures, to enjoy the opera, or to read books they could not own. New and splendid hotels were rising all over the city to accommodate the ever-increasing flow of visitors, and some featured such novelties as steam heat in every room and steam-operated elevators. Even the trustees of Columbia University recognized the trend, and moved the campus beyond the hum of the city to 49th Street.

In 1861, the County Court House, popularly known as the "Tweed Court House," was begun in City Hall Park. It was completed ten years later, and its erection represented an estimated $8,000,000 in graft to the "Tweed Ring." In 1861,

George Opdyke was elected mayor of the city, to replace Fernando Wood, a Copperhead. In 1861, more than 100,000 citizens of New York gathered in Union Square to give rousing support to President Lincoln's call to arms—the largest mass demonstration ever staged in the city!

This was the New York of 1861, the year in which Mrs. Daly took up her pen to chronicle the life of the city during the most explosive event in American history.

DIARY OF A UNION LADY

Those who read the history of these times one hundred years hence will be able to appreciate its great historical importance. We are too near at present.

Maria Lydig Daly
Diary, page 128

1861

As the year 1861 opened, Washington, D.C., was a fitful city, seething with sedition, expectant of momentary invasion, and kept on edge by almost daily explosions from Capitol Hill. Congress was in a state of rebellion over the outcome of the previous November's four-way election, and all governmental business halted as men re-evaluated their positions and contemplated drastic changes.

No leadership could be expected from the Executive, for "Lame Duck" James Buchanan had grown tired and politically impotent from the war of words which he found wherever he turned. His Vice President, John C. Breckinridge, the choice of the South in the 1860 election, and three of his cabinet members were prominent Southerners, as were so many other government officials and employees who surrounded him. Buchanan, though a Pennsylvanian, was "a house divided" within himself, and he was unable to lift a finger to save the Union or preside over its dissolution. At last deserted even by his Southern friends, there was talk of kidnaping him so that Breckinridge could take over the government.

Washington, D.C., where geese and pigs still roamed the streets, and where slops and refuse were still emptied into the gutters, was vulnerable to any kind of attack. Its public buildings, half-completed imitations of Greek temples, were spread far and wide, and the city itself was innocent of natural barriers to aid in its defense. Besides, the city was still half-filled with

Southerners representing every social class, and the best military unit stationed there, the 3rd Militia National Rifles, largely went over to the South when the war began.

To rescue the nation's capital from panic and probable conquest, Lieutenant General Winfield Scott transferred his military headquarters from New York City to Washington, D.C., in December of 1860. Bent and weary, the 75-year-old hero of the War of 1812 and the Mexican War appealed to a petrified President and a secession-minded Secretary of War, John B. Floyd of Virginia, for means whereby Washington could be defended and Federal property in the South protected.

At this time, the total force of the United States Army consisted of some 16,000 regulars, commanded mostly by Southerners and spread thinly over the Pacific Coast and the American Southwest. During his twenty years of command over the Army, Virginia-born Scott had preferred Southern gentlemen as officers, and as a result West Pointers from the North like McClellan, Burnside, Sherman, Halleck, Hooker, and Rosecrans had retired to civilian life.

The Dalys couldn't have chosen a more hazardous time to visit Washington than January and February of 1861. South Carolina had left the Union on December 20, 1860; Mississippi followed on January 9th; Florida on the 10th; Alabama on the 11th; Georgia on the 19th; Louisiana on the 26th; and Texas on February 1. Secession talk was loud and menacing in both Virginia and Maryland, and if both of these states left the Union, Washington, D.C., would go with them. Violence was threatened on every side, and no one knew when and from what direction it would come.

January 31, 1861[1]

The Judge[2] and myself left New York to pay a long-

---

[1] Evidently Mrs. Daly did not date her entries at the outset of the diary. Events recorded under "January 31, 1861" occurred between early January and the date of the next entry, May 26, 1861.

[2] Charles P. Daly. See *Personalities in the Diary*, page xvi.

promised visit to Baron von Gerolt,[3] the Prussian Minister at Washington. We left New York on Saturday at 7 o'clock and encountered a terrific snowstorm. On reaching Philadelphia, we were obliged to take sleighs in order to reach the Baltimore depot. We arrived at Baltimore at about 3 o'clock in the morning and, being very tired, determined to spend the Sunday there at the Utah House and proceed on Monday morning to Washington. We found Baltimore not very interesting. We visited the Cathedral, walked around Monument Square, and in the evening went to deliver a letter of introduction which Mr. N. P. Willis[4] had almost obliged us to take with us to Mr. Kennedy, the Senator,[5] whom we found a very agreeable man and holding Union sentiments. Mrs. Kennedy is a lively, clever woman. At this house we met Chip Grey,[6] whose acquaintance we had made at the White Sulphur Springs two summers before, and a Mr. Thompson,[7] the editor of a literary paper at Richmond (who was called the modern Récamier)—both friends of Mr. Stanard of that city.

As the state of the country was, of course, the chief subject of discussion, they seemed to think that Maryland was sound for the Union, although there were many in favor of secession because they feared that in case Virginia joined the Cotton States, their soil would be the battleground. We passed an agreeable evening, and on Monday morning left for Washington, where we were warmly greeted by Baron von Gerolt and family.

---

[3] See *Personalities in the Diary*, page xviii.

[4] Nathaniel Parker Willis (1806–1867) was a poet and journalist, a well-known and highly successful figure in New York in the 1850's and a Washington correspondent during the war.

[5] Anthony Kennedy, U.S. Senator from Maryland (Unionist), 1857–63.

[6] Probably John Chipman Gray (1839–1915), a lawyer and educator who became aide-de-camp to General Gordon and major and judge advocate-general of United States volunteers on the staffs of Generals Foster and Gillmore. Later Story professor of law at Harvard Law School.

[7] John Reuben Thompson, editor of *The Southern Literary Messenger*.

Fearing that some attack might be made upon the capital, General Scott[8] had taken up his quarters in the city and was endeavoring to organize some plan for defending it. Although through the indecision and weakness, if not wickedness, of President Buchanan, he [Scott] was very much hindered and his propositions disregarded, for on the first consultation which he had with the President he had counseled a decisive stand and advised that immediate reinforcements should be sent to all the forts threatened—particularly to Fort Sumter. But the traitors about the President had prevailed and our octogenarian General is now doing all that he could to protect the capital from foes within and without. He told the Judge that with 2,000 men he could defend it even without any intrenchments against 20,000 for 24 hours, the city being built very advantageously, the streets being very wide and all radiating from a center.

Whilst in Washington, we passed our time principally in the Senate, where we always found a seat in the diplomatic loges. We heard Seward,[9] Douglas,[10] Thomson,[11] and Hale[12] speak, and heard one of Douglas' most able debates. Nothing ever interested me so much, although I was astonished to see the apathy with which the Senators generally listened and wrote or read their papers whilst such vital subjects were discussed and the government and integrity of the United States (so great a nation) hung upon their vote and upon their right appreciation of what was proposed, accepted, or rejected. Senator Mason of Virginia[13] struck me as violent-tempered,

---

[8] See *Personalities in the Diary*, page xxvi.

[9] William Henry Seward, Whig and Republican Senator from New York, 1849–61. See *Personalities in the Diary*, page xxvii.

[10] Stephen Arnold Douglas, U.S. Senator from Illinois, 1847–61; one of Lincoln's opponents for the Presidency in 1860.

[11] John Renshaw Thomson, U.S. Senator from New Jersey, 1853–62.

[12] John Parker Hale, U.S. Senator from New Hampshire, 1855–65.

[13] James Murray Mason, U.S. Senator from Virginia, 1847–61, was expelled from the Senate and became the Commissioner of the Confederacy to Great Britain and France in 1861.

selfish, and double dealing. Seward seemed to think that everything must go right, now that Lincoln, a Republican, was
elected President. The Senators from the Eastern states seemed
to have no other idea than that they were the victors and that
slavery and the South should suffer. Senator Crittenden of
Kentucky[14] seemed the only patriot except Thomson and
Douglas in the house. We met him afterwards at dinner at
Baron Gerolt's, as well as the Mayor of Washington[15]—who
was said to be a secessionist. We likewise met Major Dahlgren,[16]
the inventor of the gun which bears his name, a most unpretending, agreeable gentleman.

The Judge had several interviews with Seward and endeavored to shake his confidence on one occasion. After a long
argument, Seward said, "Oh Judge, you are so old a Democrat
that it is impossible for you to see anything from a Republican
point of view. There is no danger of civil war. It will all be over
in six weeks."

The Judge said that unless the Crittenden Compromise[17] was
adopted, namely, that the question of slavery in the territories
was abandoned, we would have civil war. "Suppose they attack
Fort Sumter," said the Judge, "what will you do then?"

"Oh," replied Seward, "don't say anything about it. They

---

[14] John Jordan Crittenden, Governor of Kentucky from 1848 to 1850, was
elected to the U.S. Senate five times between 1817 and 1861. As successor
to Henry Clay's Senate seat in 1842, he appropriately initiated the celebrated,
but never adopted, Crittenden Compromise of 1860–61.

[15] Mayor James E. Berret, a Breckinridge Democrat.

[16] John Adolphus Bernard Dahlgren was at this time in the ordnance
department at the Washington Navy Yard. On April 22, 1861, he became
commandant of the yard; in 1863 he was promoted to rear admiral and
from that year until June of 1865 commanded the South Atlantic Blockading Squadron.

[17] Senator Crittenden proposed that slavery be prohibited north of the old
Missouri Compromise line of 36°30′, and protected by law south of that
line; that new states could enter the Union with or without slavery, as they
chose; and that the fugitive slave laws be enforced. Since the Republicans
had just won the election on the issue of prohibiting slavery in the territories, Lincoln and his supporters had to reject the plan.

won't do it, and if they do, it will be time enough to think about it."

"Don't you think," said Charles, "that that had better be thought of before, so that you may be prepared?"

"Oh Judge," answered Seward, "your mind is diseased on the subject. We will never have civil war."[18]

We were in the Senate on the day that Louisiana seceded from the Union and saw her Senators Benjamin[19] and Slidell[20] take their leave—which they did with very eloquent, but very specious and abusive, speeches. It was a very sad sight to see the stars fading away out of our banner one by one. On leaving the Senate, the Judge met Benjamin and walked up Pennsylvania Avenue with him. In the course of conversation, Benjamin remarked, "We shall all be back here in two months, and you will join us. New York and several other states will come in. We don't care for most of the Eastern ones; they may stay out if they please; New York will certainly come."

The Judge said, "It would be very unwise for you to act on any such suppositon. Believe me," he said, "you will be entirely mistaken. No Northern states will ever enter your confederacy if you take these forcible measures to separate yourselves, except upon the point of the bayonet. You will unite us as one man in defense of this government."

Benjamin replied, "Oh, Judge, you are not a practical politician as we are. We know how people feel at the North."

Said the Judge, "I have lived all my life in New York and was born there. I think I ought to know something about the

---

[18] In 1850, Seward had prophesied that slavery would disappear either gradually and voluntarily, with compensation, or by force and violence. Eight years later he declared that "an irrepressible conflict" existed between pro- and antislavery forces.

[19] Judah Philip Benjamin, U.S. Senator from Louisiana, 1853–61, served as Secretary of State for the Confederacy from February 1862 until the war's end.

[20] John Slidell, U.S. Senator from Louisiana, 1853–61, became the Confederate Commissioner to France.

people, and, depend upon it, you will find the result to be as I tell you."

Mrs. Slidell, on a farewell visit to Madam von Gerolt, said that they would be back in Washington in March or April at the furthest and that she should not remove her furniture or all of her wardrobe—it would not be worthwhile (so confident were she and her husband of the success of the Confederates).

We spent our time agreeably at the Von Gerolts'. Sometimes in the evening several of the Corps Diplomatique would come in, and in my American ears it sounded strangely and unpleasantly to hear them discuss where they might be in 1862— whether in Montgomery or Chicago or some little Western country town. Every hour there was a change in sentiment. Today some conspiracy against the government was discovered, or troops were ordered to relieve Fort Sumter, or countermanded. Then the Compromise, it was thought, might be accepted; then great hopes were raised by the Peace Conference.[21] The political barometer rose and fell with the latest comer.

We went to one of the President's levees. I never saw so incapable a face as Buchanan's. Surely no woman would have been crazy enough, had he been in the profession of medicine, to entrust him with the health of her favorite poodle. And that was the poor, almost imbecilic looking man who was President of the United States and possessed more power than any constitutional monarch of Europe during his term of office. Indeed, when I looked over the two Houses [of Congress] I was struck with the want of statesmanlike looking men in both. There were clever, cunning looking men, but no broad-browed, wise, thoughtful heads, such as you expect in a lawgiver, among them.

---

[21] The State of Virginia summoned a Peace Convention which met on February 4, 1861, but the seceded states were not genuinely interested in it and it turned out to be something of a farce. Lincoln was convinced by the Convention that concessions which would satisfy the South could never be made by the North.

I heard Wigfall,[22] the Senator from Texas, pour forth an invective (no one could call it a speech); it was half crazy, a violent denunciation of what nobody had ever been guilty [of], full of foul language. Among other things he said was that he hoped to see this Union split into as many pieces as cannon could split glass. His manners whilst seated in his chair were such as would exile him from any drawing room and any other place except a barroom. He chewed and spat and sat with his heels on his desk and was so disgusting altogether that I should like to have hurled something at him myself. I hope that some-day he may meet with his deserts.

One evening we passed at Mr. Reverdy Johnson's,[23] the most able lawyer in Washington, where we were introduced by Judge Rockwell of Connecticut,[24] a delightful, amiable gentle-man whose death we heard of only a few days after our return home. On the morning of our departure, we had great hopes of the Union. Virginia had declared a majority for the Union, and the Border States, it was thought, would go with her. Charles dined with General Scott, who most politely declared that he should call and see me; but the Judge said that it was not worthwhile [for Scott] to use his valuable time in paying visits, that he [the Judge] would tell me his kind intentions since he [Scott] had already too much to do. Dear old warrior! Gallant old chief! They say that he is the greatest general now living, and notwithstanding that he is a Virginian, he is loyal to this government.

Indeed, most of the older men seem to be sound in Union principles. It is the younger whom the mischievous idea that state sovereignty is superior to that of the United States seems

22 Louis Trezevant Wigfall, U.S. Senator from Texas, 1859-61, became a brigadier general in the Confederate Army.

23 Reverdy Johnson (1796–1876), who was a member of the Peace Convention, was a Senator from Maryland, 1845-49 and 1863-68. He was to serve as counsel for the defense of Mrs. Mary E. Surratt in the trial of the eight conspirators in Lincoln's assassination.

24 John Arnold Rockwell, lawyer, jurist, and author, was a U.S. Representative from Connecticut, 1845-49.

to have misled. The doctrine is only since Calhoun,[25] who is said to have predicted that so soon as the Democratic Party (which has always favored the South) should lose its power, the Southern states would separate and form another confederacy, and all the last generation have been educated to this idea.

Although Mrs. Daly began to chronicle her trip to Washington on January 31, 1861, while she was in Washington, she evidently did not complete the account until some time after February 6. She tells us that she and the Judge returned from Washington the day that Virginia defeated a motion for secession—February 6, 1861. Enthusiasm in the North ran high when Virginia rendered such a vote by a 40,000 majority, but hope that such a critical state would remain within the Union dwindled rapidly over the next month. Mrs. Daly's almost despondent recitation of the February 6th action indicates that she made record of it long after the enthusiasm ran dry. Virginia did not actually secede (by a 3 to 1 vote) until May 23, 1861—more than a month after the fall of Sumter.

Unhappily, nothing is recorded in the diary about Lincoln's passage through New York, the inauguration, or the exciting developments which led to the fall of Fort Sumter. This latter event, however, shocked her into taking up her pen once more.

Major Robert Anderson, commander of the Federal forts in Charleston Harbor, South Carolina, considered his position at Fort Moultrie too vulnerable. Therefore, he dismantled the fort and moved his little garrison into Fort Sumter, which commanded the harbor. Although the size of Anderson's force constituted no threat to South Carolina, the move was interpreted as an act of aggression, and three envoys descended upon President Buchanan to demand the removal of all U.S. forces from Charleston Harbor.

Buchanan equivocated, and probably would have yielded to pressure from his Southern friends had changes not been made in his cabinet at this time which resulted in a more Unionist attitude. Kentucky-born Anderson was torn between

---

[25] John C. Calhoun, the great Senator from South Carolina, defended slavery and staunchly supported the doctrine of states' rights.

two loyalties, for he sympathized with the Southern cause and was bound by a strong sense of duty to the authority he represented.

Finally, Buchanan notified the Southern "ambassadors" that the U.S. garrison would not be withdrawn from Fort Sumter, and he authorized General Scott to send reinforcements. In consequence, the South Carolinians occupied Fort Moultrie and Castle Pinckney, drove off the Star of the West when it attempted to land reinforcements at Sumter, and joined other seceded states in confiscating government arsenals, customhouses, forts, and revenue cutters. Buchanan made no attempt to recover Federal property, and both he and Major Anderson were solicitous to avoid any incident which might precipitate war.

As the inauguration of a new Republican President approached, further developments at Fort Sumter were held in a state of suspension to see what the new President would do. Florida had allowed Fort Pickens in Pensacola harbor to be reinforced, but General Pierre G. T. Beauregard's troops hovered all about Sumter and prevented reinforcement or provisioning of the Fort. In the meantime, Anderson's supplies were running dangerously low, and pressure was immediately upon the new President to set about resolving the situation in one way or another.

General Scott advised abandonment of both Sumter and Pickens, the influential Seward favored conciliation, and of all Lincoln's advisors, only Montgomery Blair, Postmaster General, argued for taking a strong position on holding and supporting Sumter. Lincoln's reply to those willing to give in to secession was an order for the secret preparation of supplies and reinforcements for both Sumter and Pickens, and notification sent to the governor of South Carolina that an attempt would be made to supply Sumter peaceably.

Lincoln's intentions inflamed the South Carolinians, and General Beauregard demanded immediate surrender of Fort Sumter. Major Anderson refused, and on Friday, April 12, 1861, Fort Sumter was fired upon. Anderson capitulated before there was a single military casualty on either side.

*The Fort Sumter incident united the North more than any-
one would have believed possible in the preceding months.
On April 20, a quarter of a million people gathered in New
York's Union Square for a Union mass meeting, and rousing
speeches and the singing of the National Anthem resulted in
the formation of the Union Defense Committee to supply the
Federal government with money, troops, and whatever else
was required to wage war against the South. Over a million dollars was immediately subscribed, and by April 25, New York's
7th Regiment of militia arrived in Washington, D.C.*

*On April 19, the New York 7th Regiment, commanded by
Colonel Marshall Lefferts and consisting of 1,050 men, left
New York City. They were followed on April 21 by 550 men
in the 6th Regiment under Colonel Joseph C. Pinckney; 900
men of the 12th Regiment under Colonel Daniel Butterfield;
and 950 men of the 71st Regiment under Colonel A. S. Vosburgh. On the 23rd, 900 men under Colonel George Lyons
left as the 8th Regiment; on the 27th, 600 men of the 5th under
Colonel C. Schwarzwaelder departed for the front; on the
28th, 500 men of the 2nd went under the command of Colonel
George W. Tompkins; on the 29th, Colonel Michael Corcoran
led his 69th Regiment, consisting of 1,050 Irishmen, out of the
city; and on the 30th, the 9th Regiment under Colonel John
W. Stiles left with 800 men. In the same month that Sumter
was attacked, and within fifteen days of its fall, New York
City alone supplied the Federal government with 7,300 troops.*

Fort Sumter has been fired upon! Major Anderson[26] and his
160 men, after a brave defense, were obliged to evacuate it,
but with the honors of war, saluting his flag—that flag which
has never before been humbled since it first floated on the
breeze! There was great rejoicing over this inglorious victory

---

[26] Kentucky-born Robert Anderson, veteran of Indian wars and the
Mexican War, was rewarded, after the fall of Fort Sumter, with a brigadier-
generalship and the command of Union forces in his native state. Conflicting
loyalties resulted in a health failure, and he withdrew from active service in
the fall of 1861.

of 7,000 men over 160, who, without provisions and with their magazines surrounded by their burning officers' quarters, were at last obliged to leave it. The attack was unexpected at the last, so that Major Anderson with his small band had not sufficient time to remove the wood and other combustible matter within the Fort, into which, notwithstanding—the enemy saw it was on fire and knew how few were its defenders —they continued to pour in hot shells. The attack upon Fort Sumter has united all the North as one man against the South. Party is forgotten. All feel that our very nationality is at stake, and to save the country from anarchy (learning what South America and Mexico are) that every man must do his best to sustain the government, whoever or whatever the President may be. It is a sublime spectacle.

Sir Dominick Daly,[27] formerly Secretary General of Canada and Governor of Prince Edward Island, in calling to take leave of us said that now he had greater faith in our institutions than he had ever felt before, for although he had watched with the greatest interest the progress of America, he had always feared. But when he saw how every man rallied to the side of right, he began to believe in self-government. He begged the Judge to write him within a fortnight and tell him how things were, as he would like to have an unprejudiced account. He is a true gentleman—wise, unassuming, and with no English prejudices; but then, like the Judge, he is an Irishman and a Catholic. . . .

The 7th Regiment[28] have offered their services and left for Washington. Many of the sons of the richest men in the city are in its ranks, and mothers and wives are almost crazy at the thought of the dangers they are about to encounter. My two brothers can scarcely be kept at home, but father declares that he will not allow them to go as they know nothing of war and

---

[27] See *Personalities in the Diary*, page xvi.
[28] New York's 7th Infantry Regiment was mustered in on April 19, 1861, and left immediately for Newport News, Virginia. After two years of service in the Department of Virginia, it was mustered out in May 1863.

have never belonged to a regiment. Mr. Weston,[29] our clergyman, goes as a chaplain. It is a very brave act, for no one knows the dangers they may meet, nor in what force the secessionists may be at Annapolis since the 6th Massachusetts Regiment was fired upon in Baltimore.

There is much said about the readiness of Massachusetts and of her having been first in the field, but I think it is quite proper that she should be. It is preeminently her own quarrel. Her Wendell Phillips, Garrisons, Beechers,[30] and Stowes are the firebrands which have set fire to the smouldering discontent of the South.

Antislavery movements in America date back almost to the inception of the institution itself, but their first real victory did not occur until 1807, when Congress passed a law prohibiting further importation of slaves. Another major victory was won when the Missouri Compromise of 1820 prevented the spread of slavery to new Western territories destined to become states. Thus far, the control of slavery was mutually agreed upon by Northerners and Southerners alike, and some Southerners even experimented with such projects as compensation, deportation, and colonizing Negroes in Liberia.

Strong emotionalism was injected into the issue of abolition when William Lloyd Garrison published his first issue of the Liberator *in Boston on January 1, 1831. From this point forward, Garrison waged a war of words on Southern slaveholders and ridiculed them in the most vitriolic and insulting terms. So uncompromising was this man in his denunciations that he managed to offend almost as many people in the North as he did in the South. On October 21, 1835, Garrison was dragged through the streets by a Boston mob and nearly killed. He split the organized antislavery groups of the North, and*

---

[29] Sullivan Hardy Weston (1816–1887) was ordained a priest in 1852 and became assistant rector of New York's Trinity Episcopal Church, succeeding Bishop Wainwright. As chaplain of the 7th Regiment he was at the battlefront in 1861 and again in 1863.

[30] Henry Ward Beecher. See *Personalities in the Diary,* page xiv.

rapidly lost the support of the more respectable element asso-
ciated with abolitionism.

Whether due to, or despite, the influence of Garrison,
abolitionism increased in the North. Some 150,000 people had
joined the cause—including such respectables as Wendell Phil-
lips, John Greenleaf Whittier, and James Russell Lowell—by
1840, and in that year the Liberty Party ran James G. Birney
for President of the United States. Although Birney failed to
rally much support, the abolitionists did manage to seat Joshua
Giddings as the first abolitionist congressman.

Mrs. Daly's favorite targets among the abolitionists appear
to be Lyman Beecher, and his son and daughter, Henry Ward
Beecher and Harriet Beecher Stowe. Julia Ward Howe also
comes in for a few barbs. Mrs. Daly seems to share the feeling
of so many Irish-Americans of that period that the Negro is
the natural enemy of the Irish laborer, that slavery is wrong,
and that abolitionism is a menace imported from England.
There are many paradoxes here.

A few days since, I met the wife of Stoddard,[31] the poet, a
New England man and a great friend of Bayard Taylor[32] and
the *Tribune* circle—all rabid abolitionists. Of course she re-
peated what she heard, and said on my expressing myself as no
friend to free blacks, "But Mrs. Daly, if slavery is such a re-
proach to us, Europe will think much less of us. Even though
we are not so powerful, they must appreciate the moral principle."

It made me so angry that I could scarcely answer, so I said,
"My dear Mrs. Stoddard, I would much rather be feared than
respected by the European powers and do not believe that
they (especially England—who is always talking and inculcat-

---

[31] In addition to being a poet, Richard Henry Stoddard edited the literary
journal *Mail and Express.*

[32] Author, editor, and diplomat Bayard Taylor worked on the New York
Tribune in the 1850's, was U.S. Secretary of Legation in St. Petersburg,
Russia, in 1862–63, and served as minister to Germany in 1878.

ing this cheap philanthropy and sowing discontent between North and South) will respect the Yankees any more because they are no longer powerful. Let those who feel so concerned for the slaves at the South and who ask such sacrifices from slave-owners each buy one and then liberate them by degrees. Then I shall believe in the principle—the philanthropy which actuates the abolitionists."

In Texas they have obliged the U.S. troops to surrender, General Twiggs[33] having gone over to the secessionists. Some of his command refused to obey, and they were at last obliged to surrender and their U.S. flag, the stars and stripes, was trailed in the dust. This news has exasperated the whole North. We mean to test now in earnest who are the strongest, and if the European powers, whose respect my friend was so anxious about, will only let us alone, we will soon settle the question.

The 69th Irish Regiment[34] left after the 7th—which has been much lauded and magnified. I thought that the poorer men should be equally cheered and encouraged, and so I have presented the Regiment [69th] with a flag. Colonel Corcoran[35] sent me a most gallant message. I went with Mr. and Mrs. O'Gorman[36] to see the brave fellows off. Broadway was lined

[33] On February 23, 1861, while the issue of war or peace still hung in the balance, General David Emanuel Twiggs, commander of the Department of Texas, turned over his U.S. military property, including 19 army posts, to Texas. The fact that he still wore his U.S. Army uniform branded him a traitor in Northern eyes. General Scott evaded an inquiry of Twiggs' action until war made the issue academic.

[34] The 69th New York Regiment, known popularly as the "Irish Brigade," was the favorite of the Dalys. So intimate was the Judge's association with the 69th that a group known as the "Judge Daly Guards" was organized within the Regiment. A history of the 69th was written by Captain David P. Conyngham and published by William McSorley & Co. in 1867, entitled, *The Irish Brigade and Its Campaigns, with some accounts of the Corcoran Legion and Sketches of the Principal Officers.*

[35] Michael Corcoran. See *Personalities in the Diary,* page xv.

[36] Richard O'Gorman was a lawyer active in the Democratic party in New York as a "Peace Democrat," or Copperhead. This faction of the party opposed conscription, emancipation, and military arrests, and favored ending the war by negotiation.

the whole length of the march, the women pressing around to bid good-by to fathers, husbands, and brothers. To my surprise, I saw the Judge marching with them down Broadway. I know he wished he were going with them.

May 26, 1861

The 1st German Rifles[37] we likewise, through the instrumentality of Mrs. Manton and Mr. Bencard, raised a flag for, feeling that it was the foreigners who were going to fight our battles (and yet not more foreigners than were our fathers or grandfathers). My great-grandfather came from Germany just as these gentlemen, like Colonel Blenker or Stahel,[38] to seek a new country where he could live as he pleased without having to bow to a king or princes. Stahel is a nobleman of one of the first families in Hungary, and was desperately wounded, taken prisoner, and condemned to death. He took his mother's name in coming to this country.

Mr. William Rhinelander,[39] Dr. Gescheidt,[40] Mother[41] and

---

[37] Louis Blenker's "1st German Rifles" was attached to the 8th Infantry Regiment from New York City. It mustered in on April 23, 1861, left for Washington, D.C. on May 26, 1861, and served with the Army of Northeast Virginia until August 1861. Blenker, born in Germany, was active in his country's revolution of 1848 and was forced to flee. He came to New York, joined the army, and rose to brigadier general. He was mustered out of service on March 31, 1863, and died in October of that year of wounds received in Virginia.

[38] Julius Stahel was a Hungarian, known also as Count Sebastiani, who was in the Austrian army until 1848, when the Hungarian revolution broke out. He joined his countrymen and fought brilliantly, but had to flee the country when Austria put down the revolt. Stahel came to New York in 1859 and edited a German newspaper until 1861, when he joined the Federal army. He commanded the 8th New York Regiment at first Bull Run and saw much subsequent action, retiring in February 1865 as a major general of volunteers. After the war he served as U.S. consul at Yokohama, Japan.

[39] William Christopher Rhinelander was a New York real estate manager.

[40] German-born physician and author Louis Anthony Gescheidt made a fortune practicing medicine in New York City and retired in 1870. He is best known for a treatise on eye diseases.

[41] Catherine Mesier Lydig. See *Personalities in the Diary*, page xxi.

ourselves have united to give the Steuben Regiment[42] a flag. The Judge had likewise a little guide color made with the cross of fidelity (a German order given to Baron Steuben by the Margrave of Ansbach) painted upon it. Mr. Laing was kind enough to paint it for him. This is the only decoration Steuben ever wore, and he desired that it should be buried with him. We went down to the City Hall to see it presented, and it was a most impressive sight. The news of Ellsworth's[43] death had just arrived, and these men in their marching order went with blankets and knapsacks on their way to the steamer which was to take them to the seat of war—with their wives and sisters and mothers following them to say a last good-by. It was indeed a most affecting sight. Most of the officers are German noblemen. The Judge had the portrait of Steuben taken from the Governor's room, draped with the colors, and placed upon the balcony in view of the Regiment whilst he presented the colors, making a very appropriate speech which was received with great acclamation. Colonel Bendix[44] is one of the most soldierly men as I have as yet seen.

Mrs. Manton, Sophie, and Kate[45] have undertaken to present the 6th and 8th Regiments of Massachusetts with banners. The Judge and I thought that it would be much better to furnish

---

[42] "Steuben's Rangers" were attached to the 86th Infantry Regiment, organized at Elmira, New York, mustered in on November 20, 1861, and mustered out in June, 1865. Their leader was the son of Baron von Steuben (1730–94), who came to the United States in 1777 and became a major general in the Continental Army.

[43] Colonel Elmer Ephraim Ellsworth captured the imagination of the North by the colorful drills his Chicago and New York Zouaves performed. On the night of April 23, 1861, as Federal troops moved into Virginia, Ellsworth tore the Confederate flag down from the Marshall House, a hotel in Alexandria, Virginia. As he came down the stairs, the innkeeper shot and killed him, and in turn was killed by Ellsworth's aide. The funeral was held in the White House, and Lincoln rode in the procession. All the North mourned the young hero's death.

[44] John E. Bendix (1818–1877) was a colonel in the 7th New York Regiment of Volunteers from April 23, 1861, from which he resigned and became a colonel of the 10th New York Volunteers on September 21, 1861. He was mustered out of service on May 7, 1863, as a brigadier general.

[45] Catherine Lydig. See *Personalities in the Diary*, page xx.

those who were going out from amongst us and that particularly those of German descent should show their sympathy to the brave foreigners now lately arrived and settled among us from their old fatherland. Mrs. Manton's father was an intimate acquaintance of Steuben, and her brother was his godson. If dear grandpapa Lydig[46] were alive, he doubtless could have related many interesting anecdotes concerning him [Steuben].

May 30, 1861

I have been busily engaged in making havelocks out of white linen which the linen merchants mostly have kindly contributed for the 69th. I thought they should be as well cared for as the 7th, whom I fear, because they are gentlemen's sons, may receive more praise than they deserve. They are at last all finished and I have received a letter of thanks from Colonel Corcoran. The last I have sent on with the Judge on Friday last.

June 2, 1861

The Judge went to visit the Colonel at Camp Seward on Arlington Heights, leaving me home fearfully anxious all Sunday and Monday night. I was restless and alarmed as though I were on the battlefield myself. Today I received another letter from Colonel Corcoran in which he says that he had the honor of having the Chief Justice of the Common Pleas [Daly] for two occasions among the men in his command; that Judge Daly and Mr. O'Gorman volunteered when there was reason to believe in an attack upon the camp and stood upon the ramparts armed with revolvers. I knew that Charles must be in danger. I felt it here in my room. I had a dispatch from him yesterday, however, saying that he was now

---

[46] David Lydig. See *Personalities in the Diary*, page xxi.

at Baron Gerolt's and would not be home until the end of the
week—that he thought he might do some good by remaining.

June 5, 1861

 . . . I am very thankful that he [the Judge] has returned
safely, for I never feel that he is safe out of my sight during
this excitement. He is so impressionable. Mr. O'Gorman, who
is going to Europe in a fortnight himself, has now induced
him to drill, so I shall be left to myself, I suppose, more than
ever with a feeling that nobody can tell what may come of it.
Women must *trust*, and only by committing their loved ones
to that Divinity who shapes all ends can they ever be at peace.
Sometimes I am so anxious and distressed for the future, much
as I blame myself for it, that I almost wish I had never known
the blessedness of married life, but had lived as I once thought
to do—a single life without any care, anxiety, or interest in
the world—having nothing to lose at least.

June 7, 1861

 Yesterday, Judge Brady,[47] Kate, and myself took the
Sattler's boat to go and visit the different camps on the East
River. We touched at Riker's Island, where Hawkins' men[48]
are stationed, and then stopped at Fort Schuyler, where a
Colonel Baker's Regiment[49] now is. A storm coming on pre-
vented our going, as we had intended, to see McLeod Murphy's

---

[47] James Topham Brady. See *Personalities in the Diary*, page xv.

[48] Rush Christopher Hawkins raised the 9th New York Volunteers—
Hawkins' Zouaves—and served as their colonel. He commanded them until
their term expired in May 1863. He was brevetted a brigadier general in 1865.

[49] Edward Dickinson Baker, Lincoln's close friend in Washington, was
a Senator from Oregon when the war broke out. He came to New York
City and raised a "California Regiment," made up of New Yorkers and
Pennsylvanians. After a summer of training, Baker's men left for Washington. The President felt deep personal grief when Ned Baker was killed in
action at Ball's Bluff on October 22, 1861.

Regiment (which we shall have to do some other time) at Willett's Point.

As yet, Colonel Baker's Regiment is neither in uniform nor armed, but seems admirably drilled. It is chiefly recruited from Philadelphia, only one company being New Yorkers. One of the lieutenants told us that every man had paid $50 to recruit in New York, as they went on so slowly in Philadelphia. Judge Brady left Kate and myself in the cottages occupied by the keeper of the lighthouse whilst he went to see if he could find any conveyance to take us to the railroad, and was so long—nearly two hours—in returning that we missed the boat and could not think what had become of him. It seems that he had a pass to leave the Fort, but could not get back into it again, so we had to stay until six in the afternoon. I felt all the time that I wanted to be home to welcome the Judge, as he had tele-graphed that he would be here at five, but when we reached home at half-past eight, there was no Judge.

He arrived about half-past nine, full of news. He had re-mained at Baron Gerolt's earnest entreaty and had gone to Secretary Seward's reception, borrowing a dress coat from Mr. Schleiden, the Bremen minister.[50] It must have had a very amus-ing effect, as Mr. Schleiden is twice his size, being very tall and stout. Seward and he [the Judge] went to visit the 69th Regiment together. He says that Colonel Blenker met him and said, "Oh, Judge, why, you seem to know everyone here. Where are you staying? I shall call upon you." We thought that in New York he seemed to consider Mr. and Mrs. August Bel-mont[51] of paramount importance. He introduced Lieutenant Colonel Stahel to the Gerolts.

---

[50] Rudolph Matthias Schleiden (1815–1895), German politician and diplo-matist.

[51] Banker and diplomat August Belmont served as U.S. minister to the Netherlands from 1853 to 1857 and was chairman of the Democratic Na-tional Committee from 1860 to 1872. Agent of the Rothschilds, Belmont was regarded by Mrs. Daly as *crème de la crème* of New York society.

Among the captains in Colonel Blenker's Regiment is [Gustav] Struve, the German revolutionist. He is of noble birth. He told us that he had begun life as a diplomatist; then he was a judge; then an author and editor; then an advocate; then a revolutionist; and now a conservative soldier. When in prison, expecting every day to be shot, he had begun his history of the world, and in prison had completed two volumes. Now he said he had just finished it in good order, so he thought that he would change his sedentary life, which he thought was not good for his health. I laughed and said, "Well, Captain Struve, I never before heard of a man going to war for his health!"

In looking over these pages, I find that I have forgotten to chronicle a very pleasant day (I think the 28th of May) which we passed on Staten Island visiting the different camps there. We first went to Colonel Wilson's Zouaves, "Billy Wilson's Boys," as they are more commonly called, and found them, contrary to our expectations, a very orderly and quiet, disciplined body.[52] We made the acquaintance of one of the lieutenants, Gilloway, from Nashville, Tennessee. He said that he had joined them only a few days before and quite unexpectedly. On leaving home with some others, he had been stopped, sent back, his letters opened, and one [from] Russell of the *Times*[53] not returned to him, as well as $150 in his possession with which he had intended paying his travelling expenses. He thought, he said, he would get it back with interest before he was done with them, however. We saw and shook

---

[52] There was not general agreement on this point. In his well-known diary, edited by Allan Nevins and Milton Halsey Thomas, George Templeton Strong describes "Billy Wilson's crowd" as "a desperate-looking set" who carried revolvers and bowie knives in addition to conventional rifles, and boasted, "We can fix that Baltimore crowd! Let 'em bring along their pavin' stones; we boys is sociable with pavin' stones!"

[53] William Howard Russell, London *Times* correspondent to the United States during the Civil War, was a particular object of Mrs. Daly's ridicule. His attempt to report the war objectively was resented by Northern partisans like Mrs. Daly, and in her eyes he bore the further stigma of being the critical *Times* correspondent to Ireland in 1845. He was knighted in 1895 and died in 1907.

hands with Billy Wilson, a man very broad-shouldered, rather undersized, with a pair of black eyes which look as though they might blaze out like Drummond lights when excited. He wears only a private's uniform and exercises with his men and has great influence over them. We interested Miss Ives and Mrs. Rogers in them, meeting them in the road.

We then took a carriage and drove down to the fort building opposite Fort Hamilton, and whilst admiring the prospect, saw the steamer *Alabama* come in, towing a prize schooner with the Confederate flag flying, the Union Jack above it. We likewise went to Camp Scott, where Sickles' Brigade[54] is to be, a magnificent camping ground from whence 10,000 men, Colonel Wilkinson told us, could be sent in transports which could be at the wharves to any place desired in four hours without the public papers being aware of it. It must much annoy the government, I should think, to have everything published and give the enemy great advantage so that they can at once protect themselves. There seem to be plenty of spies in both camps, however. There is now every prospect of an engagement at Manassas Junction, where the enemy is in force. They say they have 147,000 men in Virginia, but General Scott is a host in himself.

June 10, 1861

Spent the evening at Mr. Golden's, where we were asked to meet Mr. Weston in honor of his return. Charles could not go with me as it was the first evening they had met to drill. I suppose it is right that every man should know how to use a bayonet, but it seems as if my heart strings tighten whenever

---

[54] The brigade organized at Camp Scott, Staten Island, by Colonel Daniel Edgar Sickles (later a major general) and mustered in the U.S. service for three years beginning June 20, 1861. Designated the 1st Regiment Excelsior Brigade, it was attached to the 70th Regiment of Infantry, U.S. Army. In the battle of Gettysburg, Sickles lost his right leg. In 1864, he was appointed U S. ambassador to Spain.

I hear him speak of the war. I know he would like the excitement of it. I thought him more of a philosopher. I would like to see him at the head of government. He has the mind to direct and that is more than the hands to execute. And there is such corruption and thieving and mismanagement, from the Governor, Morgan,[55] to the very newsboy who sells the catch-penny press of New York, that an honest man whom they might fear would be a great blessing to the country.

Lincoln, though a man of little practical ability, seems to be straightforward and honest, but Charles seems to think that Seward, the Secretary of State, is not the man for the occasion; he is too wrapped up in self. So long as you will listen whilst he preaches, well, but he cannot believe in anyone else nor see any wisdom in those who differ from him. Father Peltz[56] said that in some difficulty about immigrants which occurred whilst he [Seward] was governor of the state, he showed himself selfish and unprincipled.

We had a pleasant evening at Mrs. Golden's. When I came in alone, they all exclaimed, "What, no Judge? How sorry I am." When Charles came late in the evening for me, there was a general stir. I confess it pleased me and gratified me greatly. Mr. Weston came up to me and said, "The Judge is home again, Mrs. Daly, I see by your radiant look. What does he say they think in Washington?"

I answered, "Among other things, that the chaplain of the 7th has left golden opinions behind him, that he is held to be as good a soldier as any of the regiment."

[55] Edwin Denison Morgan's election as Governor of New York in 1858 represented a victory for political boss Thurlow Weed on both the state and national level. Morgan was a highly regarded New York City merchant before entering politics; served in the state legislature and as state and national Republican Party Chairman prior to becoming Governor; and was reelected Governor by more than 50,000 votes in 1860. In 1862, Morgan chose not to run for a third term, and despite the fact that the Democrats won that election, Weed persuaded the state legislature of 1863 to elect Morgan to the U.S. Senate.

[56] Edward Peltz. See *Personalities in the Diary*, page xxv.

"This is the very first compliment, Mrs. Daly," said Mr. Weston, "that you have ever paid me."

June 11, 1861

Spent the day at home and heard with distress of the engagement of our troops at Bethel and their loss, but I feel General Butler will soon recover it; he will not allow his prestige to be lost.[57] Charles has gone to a meeting of the Ethnological Society at Mr. Folsom's.[58]

June 12, 1861

Charles tells me that whilst away, he went to Alexandria and said it seemed as though it were Sunday. The stores were all closed, the wharves silent, no one but an occasional zouave to be seen. It was the first time he had ever been in a conquered city. He likewise visited the Navy Yard, where he saw Captain Dahlgren, who is in charge of the telegraph. He was about, he said, to explain to him and Baron Gerolt some plan of the campaign, but checked himself, saying, "Perhaps I had better be silent, although I know, gentlemen, you have no correspondence with the papers. They are so busy, however," said he, "and catch at everything in such a wonderful manner that we cannot be too careful, as it exposes our hand." The two gentlemen assured him that they thought he was quite right; they might perhaps in conversation inadvertently say more than might be prudent and they might not know to whom.

It is strange to find the press so unscrupulous, the abolitionist

---

[57] On June 10, 1861, an expedition was sent out from Fort Monroe, then under the command of Major General Benjamin Franklin Butler, to capture an entrenched camp of Confederates at Big Bethel on the road between Hampton and Yorktown. In the attack which followed, the Union forces bungled matters badly and were forced to retreat with some losses.

[58] Scholar and antiquarian George Folsom was president of the Ethnological Society and a leading light in the Historical Society of New York in his day.

press particularly, since it is their own quarrel. I hope that New England and her Mayflower pride may be a little taken down by the action of her English cousins on this matter. They evidently do not feel any very great sympathy with their American relatives—at least their Northern ones. Perhaps they at present feel more for their South Carolina ones, who would be glad, according to Mr. Russell of the *Times*, to have an English prince to reign over them; but that we cannot permit. The rule of the few over the many may be very agreeable for the few, but this continent is the home of the oppressed of the whole world and we want no English aristocrats here to foster, as in India, all native quarrels and then protect and then rule the weaker party until the whole continent owns her sway.

June 13, 1861

Had a delightful drive with Charles, Kate, and Judge Brady to Willetts Point last evening where we visited Colonel McLeod Murphy's regiment quarters there. It is to be a regiment of sappers and miners. The Colonel is a gentlemanly man, a native of Virginia, and originally an officer in the navy. He is a man of considerable literary ability. . . .

Today there are accounts that Beauregard is marching upon Washington, but I think they must be unfounded.

I saw the flag given to Wilson's men by Mr. Weston and Mr. Strong. Notwithstanding the reputation they had from the papers for disorderly conduct and bad character, they seem as well behaved as any other body of men I have seen. The Colonel signs himself, "Your comrad, William Wilson, Commanding Colonel," and goes through the exercises with his men just as though he were one of them. I could not hear Mr. Weston's address or Mr. Wilson's answer. All the officers went into Mr. Schmidt's and evidently were entertained there, some coming out moving their jaws still. Afterwards, a pipe and a package of tobacco were distributed to each soldier by the ladies of the parish, which gave great satisfaction. They were the first to direct their attention to Wilson's Regiment. Wilson came up the steps where we stood and thanked us, saying that he did not know what they should have done without the ladies of New York, the best ladies of the world. He thought that his enemy, Mayor Wood,[59] one of the greatest secessionists in the country, had been vilifying him and he would have put him [Wood] down and his brother-in-law, he continued, both of whom were secessionists. And if he had any authority, he would hang them as high as Haman.

Colonel Baker's Regiment, which we saw at Fort Schuyler, has likewise received marching orders.

The mistake at Bethel is still unexplained. Our friend Schaffner, the adjutant of the Steuben Regiment, says that there will be an investigation, that no one was told that the Townsend Regiment[60] were to have a white band upon the arm, etc. It looks as though General Butler were in fault. He sent too small a body of troops and too little artillery. A Mr. [Theodore] Winthrop[61] whom we knew is among those killed.

Lieutenant [Adam Jacoby] Slemmer of Fort Pickens is expected here. The Judge met and was introduced to him in

---

[59] When the Civil War broke out, Mayor Fernando Wood suggested that New York City secede from the Union along with the departing Southern states. The fact that an outspoken Copperhead could have been elected and reelected several times in the stormy years prior to the war indicates the Copperhead strength that existed. But Sumter changed the mood of the city, and few Copperheads dared to be as outspoken as Wood. In the 1861 contest, Wood lost the mayoralty to George Opdyke, but he staged a comeback the following year by being elected to Congress, where he served in the House sporadically until his death in 1881.

[60] Frederick Townsend organized the 3rd Regiment of New York State Volunteers, and was commissioned colonel in May of 1861. He commanded at Big Bethel, and at the close of the war was brevetted a brigadier general.

[61] Novelist and essayist (1828–1861), a native of New Haven, Connecticut. He marched to Virginia with New York's 7th Regiment on April 17, 1861, and remained as military secretary to General Benjamin F. Butler at Fortress Monroe, with the rank of major. He helped to plan the attack upon Little and Big Bethel, and lost his life bravely, but recklessly, on June 10. His widely admired works were published posthumously.

Washington. The Judge represents him as a gentle, feminine-looking man with a low voice. He had a more difficult post than Colonel Anderson himself.

I am sorry the Judge was so modest and did not call on General Scott. People of much less importance than himself call upon him and never think whether they are trespassing on his time; besides, Charles is a favorite with the old hero.

June 17, 1861

Since I last opened this, nothing has occurred with the exception of the evacuation of Harpers Ferry by the Rebels and the advance of the Federal forces to Leesburg. The circle seems to be closing around the Rebel army, and in the papers of today is a proclamation of Beauregard, one of the most infamous falsehoods that have ever been published, calling upon the Southern people to rise and defend their homes and the honor of their wives and daughters from the Northern mercenary hordes whose cry is beauty and booty. It only shows the weakness of his cause and proves, as Charles says, that any people who need such proclamations as this to rouse them must be already wavering.

General Dix called today to take his oath of office before the Judge. He is a major general. He has been senator, minister to France, Secretary of War,[62] and is now one of the most modest, unassuming gentlemen in the world. I found him in the parlor when I came, waiting for Charles. He came forward and said that he had been amusing himself by playing with my dog and reading my books. Opening one of them, he said, "Here is a passage which I have not read for a long time, and which stirs up very old memories," and he read [James] Thomson's description of morning, beginning,

---

[62] Mrs. Daly's information on Dix is inaccurate. See *Personalities in the Diary*, page xvii.

And soon observant of approaching day
The meek-eyed morn appears, mother of dews.
At first faint gleaming in the dappled East.

He read through the whole passage. "I entered the army,"
continued the General, "very early. At 15 I was a soldier and
at 19 an adjutant in a regiment stationed on the frontier. Of
course I often had sentry duty to perform We were obliged
to keep a little book and jot down the occurrences of the night.
I," said he half-bashfully, "used occasionally to insert some
poetical lines in mine, and the last time I remember seeing this
passage was when I wrote it on the frontier so many years ago."

General Dix thinks the war will not last longer than next
winter, that the leaders are heartily tired of it already. He said
that they assert that influential men in New York had promised
them 40,000 troops. He did not think they would risk a battle,
but would retreat to Richmond. I can scarcely believe it. He
spoke very dispassionately. It was he who, when Secretary of
War, gave the order—"Whoever attempts to take down the
flag of the United States, shoot him on the spot!"—and had a
principal share in inaugurating this Union movement in the
North.

The Judge has gone to drill. This afternoon he made my
heart leap by saying that he only wished he had joined one of
these regiments. I don't think he would have added anything to
his reputation. The Celtic blood, I suppose, asserts itself and
proves what is said of them is half-true—they can never be
philosophers. And yet, I think a judge should be quite pas-
sionless and incapable of being influenced and carried away by
the people with whom they associate. Of course, he is not so
when on the bench.

Last night, Mr. Young[63] passed the evening here. He

---

[63] William Young (1809–1888), a journalist, was born in England and
came to the United States in 1838. From 1848 until 1867 he edited the
Albion, a New York newspaper devoted to British news and interests.

thought, he said, that there was probably a good deal of truth in the reports we heard of the ill-treatment of Northerners at the South, and that they believed every Northern man an abolitionist and feared for their slaves.

Charles brought home *Vanity Fair*,[64] which contained a very clever caricature: a bale of cotton surmounted by a gigantic hand, wearing a chain, and many limbs crushing a manacled Negro (a small Negro) in its teeth; English of every rank, Prince Albert, the clergy, the army, the countryman with his hobnailed shoes on their knees before it, crying, "Great is God Cotton, and great are his people." It is called, "The Idol of England."

I wish that Charles was a senator or in the cabinet at this juncture; he has so clear a head that I feel sorry they have not the benefit of it. He has been as yet right in everything he predicted. He is much better fitted for the council chamber than the tented field, martial as his feelings are.

The first privateer was taken and brought into port yesterday. She was number one, and consequently the first who had taken letters of marque from Jeff Davis.[65] I hope it may be typical of the fate of all of them.

June 18, 1861

I passed the morning with Harriet Whetten[66] on Staten Island. She could not come up with me because she wished to see the supervisor who distributed the money given to the families of the soldiers in their absence on behalf of a sick protégé, a former Sunday school scholar of hers. . . .

---

[64] A weekly magazine devoted to political issues and given to satire. Edited by William Allan Stephens, this mildly Republican journal criticized many of Lincoln's war policies. It published only from December 1859 to July 1863. (In 1868 another magazine by this name began publication.)

[65] See *Personalities in the Diary*, page xvii.

[66] See *Personalities in the Diary*, page xxviii.

In the evening, Captain Cogswell of the regular army and Adjutant Schaffner and the major of the Steuben Regiment came in whilst we were rusticating in the garden—Charles on the top of a high ladder tying up vines, and I cutting flowers. Captain Cogswell wished the Judge to meet him tomorrow at twelve and supped him whilst he gave the Union Defense Committee[67] a good rating for their conduct in equipping the regiments under their care. They have spent, he says, $75,000 on one regiment alone, and what is more, they have grown rich in their vocation. How dreadful to steal the property of the brave fellows who are fighting our battles!

Adjutant Schaffner gave me an account of the fight at Great Bethel and the firing upon the *Albany*. Colonel Townsend's Regiment, he said, thought that they had done a very fine thing. One hundred and seventy of the 7th, the Steuben, having entirely routed the Regiment, did not find their mistake until, in hot pursuit of (as they supposed) a flying foe, they stumbled over a prostrate but unwounded soldier who undeceived them. It seems that General [Ebenezer W.] Peirce,[68] or rather "lawyer" Peirce, Colonel Townsend and staff were in advance and mounted and without scouts, so that the Steuben Regiment and Colonel Bendix took them for a company of the enemy's cavalry. General Peirce retired and retreated because, he told the

---

[67] The Union Defense Committee, formally organized on April 22, 1861, grew out of the Union Square mass meeting of April 20, 1861. Under the able leadership of John A. Dix, and then of Hamilton Fish when Dix went to war, the Committee raised over a million dollars immediately as a contribution to the war effort, organized and drilled volunteer troops, and put sixty-six New York regiments into the field by the end of the year in reply to Lincoln's call for seventeen regiments from the city. The financial management of the Committee's affairs by Simeon Draper & Co. created a good deal of scandal, and the Committee ceased to function in 1862—not, however, before it contributed a vast sum of money for the care of the widows and orphans of New York volunteers.

[68] Ebenezer W. Peirce, a brigadier general, was severely censured after Big and Little Bethel because his force of 2,500 retreated before the Confederate force of about 1,800. When his term expired, he reenlisted as a private soldier and soon rose again to the command of a regiment.

adjutant, he knew them to be friends. A strange way of treating friends, it seems to me, whilst at the same time he kept up a sharp fire upon them! The Steuben men behaved, it seems, admirably well under fire. It was well that they did not take to battery, as there was another masked battery in the rear and they would have lost a great number in the act.

Colonel Bendix wrote the Judge a very interesting letter; he wants the Judge to try and get him the equipment of another 1,000 men which General Butler will accept if armed and uniformed. Charles has gone to see General Dix about it.

June 21, 1861

Spent a most delightful day yesterday at Willett's Point in Camp Morgan, where McLeod Murphy's Regiment is encamped. According to agreement, he sent us an invitation to come and see the banners blessed and enjoy a clambake. So we left here at half-past nine in the morning, Judge Brady driving his delightful ponies; Charles, Kate, and myself forming the party. It was the perfection of a June day, and the time was delightful. . . .

June 26, 1861

Sunday evening last Mrs. [Wolcott] Gibbs[69] and Mr. and Mrs. D'Oremieulx[70] came to spend the evening with us. Mr. D'Oremieulx, who was originally a lieutenant at West Point but is now a teacher of French, gave us much information concerning the rebel commanders. Beauregard, he says, is a good officer certainly, but by no means an extraordinary one.

---

[69] Oliver Wolcott Gibbs (1822–1908) was a professor of physics and chemistry at the College of the City of New York from 1847 to 1863. He then moved to Harvard University as a professor of applied science.

[70] The wife of Theophile Marie D'Oremieulx was the former Miss Laura Wolcott Gibbs.

He has had no experience in the field and therefore no one can tell what he may be. Lee,[71] he says, is likewise a good scientific officer, but is only capable of carrying out the orders of others. He was the favorite aide of General Scott, and when he came forward to give in his resignation, saying that his allegiance to the state of Virginia obliged him, the old General exclaimed, "By God, Sir, it is *my* state."

"Yes, General, but I swore allegiance first to my state."

"You must have been devilish young, sir," said the General. "Leave the room, sir."

Jefferson Davis is probably the best of all, with the exception of Bragg,[72] but we have never heard much of any of them.

There is a rumor that the war will be over by August, but it seems too good to be true. I hope that the Administration will not get afraid and yield all that we have taken up arms for.

They [the South] wish, I was told, to throw the responsibility upon the Democratic party, being alarmed at what has been done. The South wants some rough treatment, and will never behave until she really feels that we are the stronger. It would be very natural, surely, to allow England to come South as well as North and we hemmed up between her two dependencies—which the South would then become. They refused this year to celebrate the 4th of July.

We have just had a visit from a sergeant in the 69th who told us of the long 17-mile march they had to Vienna to support the Ohio Regiment. We gave him some rum and water and a one-dollar bill.

Mary Linton sends me word that until I write in another spirit she will not answer my letters, lest there should be a breach made between us forever. How very absurd! I only

---

[71] See *Personalities in the Diary*, page xx.

[72] General Braxton Bragg was a hero of the Mexican War whose bravery at Buena Vista won him a lieutenant-colonelcy. He retired from the U.S. Army in 1856, and in February 1861 was commissioned a brigadier general in the Confederate Army. After the battle of Shiloh he became a full general.

wrote what I saw around me, precisely as she did, but no Southerner can bear contradiction, I suppose, from anyone. . . .

July 1, 1861

Nothing very important now seems to occur. There is a pause. Every day we expect to hear of something decisive from Virginia. General Dix has been called to Washington and given the command of Eastern Virginia.

Going down to the market this morning in the cars, two men next to me were talking over the times. One was the president of a bank in New Jersey and knew Mr. Archibald Gracie,[73] whom he pronounced a first-rate man. They seemed to think that everything was for the best.

"Now," says he, "what have they got at the South to compare with us? They always spend over their income. And what if their plantations do bring in over $75,000 a year? They spend it all aforehand. They talk about their having all the money now. What we've got to do is just do without. I get two suits of clothes a summer; this year I'll do without and wear the old ones. Why," said he, "just look at my shoes. These were an old pair I had huve away. I'll save $100 this summer that will pay the increase in taxes, and the women, instead of buying the silks and satins from France, will wear their old ones and dye old ribbons and wear their old bonnets instead of having one for summer, one for fall, one for winter, and one for spring. They'll make one do for the year round. My family, sir, spent $6,000 last year; this year they'll not spend more than $1,500, and the government nor me won't feel the difference."

This is the true spirit, and I thought I would try to do likewise!

---

[73] Archibald Gracie was a descendant of the Archibald Gracie who built Gracie Mansion in New York City. He was president of the Mobile, Alabama, branch of Baring Bros. before joining the Confederate Army, and was killed in action before Petersburg.

July 12, 1861

We spent the Fourth very agreeably at the West Farms[74] —Judge Brady, Mr. Weston, and ourselves—and had a very pleasant day. On the day afterward, Judge Brady drove me over to Mr. Bailey's, where we had promised to stay a few days at Fordham. It is a pretty place, but wants interest, and we felt that we wanted more freedom. It is a great mistake to be too polite and kind, but I think that it is rather ourselves than they who are at fault. We live so much to ourselves that every exertion is wearisome.

.   .   .   .   .   .

General McClellan[75] has at last won a victory and returned the enemy's position in Western Virginia. I hope it is the prelude to an entire overthrow and submission on the part of the rebels.

Charles today received a letter from Sir Dominick Daly in which he writes that the sympathies of the English people—the Liberals, who are three fourths of the population, are with us. His letter was a very gratifying one. After many expressions of regret, he mentions that one of the pleasantest events of his visit here was making the acquaintance, and he hopes the friendship, of his distinguished namesake. He begs Charles to accept a ring with his family arms, which he says, as he is entitled to, he hopes he [Charles] will wear despite his republican principles, as it will give them pleasure to have him own his connection with the family. It is a very pleasant incident, as it is so spontaneous on Sir Dominick's part. . . .

---

[74] West Farms was a tiny rural village in the Bronx distinguished by the presence of a railroad station during this period of the diary. The Bronx was "country," dominated by a few large estates which well-known New York families owned, like the Lydigs, the DeLanceys, the Astors, and the Morrises. The Lydig estate was later purchased by New York City as the site for the Bronx Park Zoo.

[75] See *Personalities in the Diary*, page xxiii.

July 15, 1861

We have had, Charles and I, a very pleasant few days all by ourselves at home. Today I went to see Mrs. Welford, who, after having been fourteen or fifteen years married, has just had a little girl—the first. I almost envied her her baby and wished it were mine; perhaps God will yet give us one. I do not care so much for myself, but I want Charles to have an heir to his name and reputation. We are very happy together as we are, and God knows I am thankful.

Today we had a letter from General Shields,[76] dated June 1st, who writes very dispiritedly about the country. He fears that we may have a military despotism and add another national suicide to the history of the world. I wish he were here to fight the battles of the Union. We want our generals. Mine was a strong, manly letter, full of sense.

Today too, we received news of the first real victory over 10,000 rebels under [Brigadier General Richard B.] Garnet in Western Virginia—which kills secession there!

General McClellan's dispatches are models, so modest and brief. General Scott will undoubtedly sustain his great reputation and, as he says, this will be his last and greatest campaign. A few days since, I read an anecdote worth recording of him concerning some one of the meddlesome busybodies who undertake to fight his battles for him and lay out his plans.

"General," said the man, "the country expects *action, action,* sir!"

"I know it," answered General [Scott], "but war is a science which is not learned in a day. I have studied it all my life. It requires three things:—*time,* money and patience, sir. And sir, the President has promised that I shall have all three!"

Charles cannot resist the cry of extras in the street and is taken in nearly every day by the newsboys, who to his question, "Are you sure now that it is news?" answer, "Yes, Cap-

---

[76] See *Personalities in the Diary,* page xxvii.

tain, indeed it is. Look here," pointing to three or four places in the paper at once.

This morning Mr. Peltz and I devoted to endeavoring to get money out of western property owners to encourage emigration to Minnesota.[77] I am growing quite business-like, quite scheming.

When war broke out on April 12, 1861, both sides responded with great enthusiasm and each predicted an early destruction of the enemy. Throughout the North, the reaction was a spontaneous giving of men, money, and everything else the government suggested. Having oversubscribed all of the Lincoln government's requests, the people of the North were impatient for results. Rumors of victory circulated almost daily for the first six weeks, and then grumbling set in against "the politicians in Washington" for doing nothing but making speeches.

Veteran General Scott knew the very probable result of sending raw recruits into battle, and he had no thirst for an early defeat which could mar his glorious career. And so bickering set in at the nation's capital, as politicians responded to the complaints of their constituents, unseasoned and elected company commanders chaffed at the bit for action, and the term of service for the three-month volunteers rapidly drew to a close. Under the enormous pressure brought to bear upon him, Scott finally capitulated and asked General Irvin McDowell, who was at this time stationed at the War Department in Washington, to submit a plan.

According to the plan, McDowell was to advance upon Beauregard, whose army was guarding the important railroad junction at Manassas which connected the train from Richmond with the train from the Shenandoah Valley. McDowell's force of 36,000 men should overwhelm Beauregard's 22,000, according to the plan, if General Robert Patterson's 14,350 men at Harper's Ferry could prevent Joseph E. Johnston's

---

[77] See Edward Peltz, *Personalities in the Diary*, page xxv: also Mrs. Daly's biographical sketch of him and description of his work on pages 203–204.

10,700 men from reinforcing Beauregard. The government en-
dorsed the plan, and on July 16 McDowell set out from Manassas for Centerville, just across the winding and sluggish
stream known as Bull Run.

Two days later, McDowell's men reached Centerville and
stopped. Their feet were sore, their food supply was low, and
they were tired. But even before they had left Washington,
Confederate spies in the nation's capital had supplied the South
with all the information they required to determine how they
would meet the onslaught. Patterson, resentful because Scott
would not give him his head, retreated from Johnston's force
instead of engaging it. His information was as bad as Johnston's was good, and as he retired before what he believed to
be an army of some 40,000 men, Johnston moved right by and
joined Beauregard on the 20th.

Sunday morning, July 21, came around before McDowell was
prepared to attack. This gave the spectators plenty of time in
which to make themselves comfortable for the big show, and
politicians, camp followers, and curiosity-seekers cluttered the
periphery of the proposed battleground. The fighting started
about 10:00 A.M., and by noon all was going well for the Union
forces. By 2:00 P.M., the critical point of the battle centered
about a hill topped by the Henry farmhouse. Fresh troops from
Johnston's army were ordered into the battle, and the Confederates took the hill. The Union troops began an orderly retreat.

What began as an orderly withdrawal turned into a rout, as
the brigade of E. Kirby-Smith followed up with a heavy discharge of musketry and a charge. As panic set in among the
Union troops and they began to flee, Beauregard ordered an
attack along the entire line of battle. The scene which followed
was sickening, as mounted officers competed with frantic foot-
soldiers to get away from the scene of the battle; it was every
man for himself. The spectators added to the confusion, as they
tried to avoid being trampled by men and horses.

All night long they stumbled into Washington—whipped,
demoralized, and pronouncing the imminent doom of the Capi-

*tol. But the pursuing enemy was only a phantom, for Beaure-
gard was too surprised by his victory to take advantage of the
situation.*

*The news of victory electrified the South, as it depressed
the North. Except for its morale value, however, the battle was
of no real military significance. Losses of life were negligible
—Union killed, 481; wounded, 1,011; missing, 1,216; Confederates killed, 387; wounded, 1,582—and although the North lost
the battle, it gained more from the defeat than it would have
from victory.*

*Bull Run proved the need for training, military discipline,
a good system of supply, and coordination of command. Defeat
spelled out for the North the need for many reforms, and they
set about instituting them at once. The battle also sobered the
people of the North and put an end to glib predictions of an
easy victory or an early and successful cessation of hostilities.*

July 22, 1861

This morning we felt flushed with victory, and I began
dictating terms to the rebels, lamenting only to Harriet Whetten, who is staying a day or two with me, that Jefferson Davis
would not be punished in a general amnesty.

This afternoon came distressing accounts of the sequel of the
capture of the batteries at Bull Run; namely, that a panic had
seized our troops, General Johnston had joined General Beauregard and had the Federal Army men in full retreat upon Washington with the loss of all of their artillery and 3,000 killed;
that it was a complete rout, General Blenker's brigade alone
making a stand and retreating in good order. God help us if
this is so. I trust we may receive better accounts tomorrow.
Charles has gone to the club to hear the last telegrams.

July 23, 1861

Only 300 or 500 killed, God be thanked. Two batteries
saved, but the army is signally defeated. What illumination and

rejoicing will there be in the Southern cities! Mary Linton will be in high spirits, and the steamer will take our disgraceful account to Europe.

Charles thinks that General McDowell was anxious to win renown before McClellan came up and began the attack too soon, and supposes that the order to retreat was given upon finding that they were about to be trapped in their advances in a place enclosed by masked batteries, which order—coming at the moment of apparent victory and the ammuniton wagons hurrying to the rear to bring fresh supplies of ammunition—created the panic.

Colonel Corcoran is said to be missing. Mr. Meagher[78] likewise, but I think he will be heard from. He is a mixture of apparent bravado and much prudence, if his face does not belie him. Never in my life did I feel as badly as when I saw this fearful, disgraceful news in the paper yesterday. It will prolong the war another year, if not three, and give European powers cause to consider the matter of recognizing the Confederacy as very probably their best policy.

July 24, 1861

As further intelligence comes in, hope and energy revives. Our loss is not as great as supposed, being perhaps not over 1,000, perhaps little over 500. The rebels, however, have taken a great many prisoners, among them Colonel Corcoran, it is supposed. The rebels have lost, it is estimated, from 3,000 to 4,000. Mr. Meagher, who showed great bravery, is safe in Washington. He had his horse killed under him whilst storming a battery.

Dear old General Scott says that it was the first time that he had shown himself a coward in yielding to the government and allowing an attack before he was ready. God protect Colonel

---

[78] See *Personalities in the Diary*, page xxiv.

McClellan's command! It has been, as General Scott [stated], no defeat, but only too great odds against us. Great acts of bravery have been done; the Fire Zouaves, the 69th and the 71st, and Blenker's 1st rifles having particularly distinguished themselves. Russell of the *Times* declares that he has never seen such fighting as the charges of the Fire Zouaves and the 69th. The dear, brave, warmhearted fellows! How glad I am that I showed my sympathy with them at first before they have made themselves forever celebrated. Their place in history will be beside the Green Mountain Boys in the War for Independence.

The interest which our foreign population have shown, the eagerness with which they have rushed to the rescue of their adopted country, is irrepressibly touching. It was all to save this country which they call the hope of the world.

Down with aristocrats! For cultivation and fine manners and luxurious living, we give up self-devotedness, disinterestedness, genuine emotion, love of our neighbors, and all the finer though more rugged elements of human nature. Down with aristocracy in our free country! Let our people be educated to respect free labor and independence and may God instruct their hearts and spread so among us the fear and love of Him that dishonesty and knavery may be banished from among us and we delivered from the rascally politicians and meddlesome editors and thieving public servants who dishonor this great republic!

July 28, 1861

The more we hear from those who were in the battle of Bull Run, the more exasperating does it seem. Had the officers behaved themselves well, had they been fitted to command, the victory would have been ours.

Meagher behaved very gallantly when the ensign who bore the green flag was killed. He seized it, and, calling to his men, "Remember Frontenez," charged and carried the battery, not perceiving that his horse was shot until he fell with him. Father

O'Reilly,[79] the chaplain, seeing the ensign fall, held the standard himself until Meagher came up and showed the greatest coolness and courage. He remained with Colonel Corcoran and was the last to leave the field. He was indefatigable in his attention to the wounded and dying. When parties of the enemy came up in search of prisoners, he lay down upon the ground and feigned death until they passed, and then continued his charitable work. Behold, indeed, an Apostle of Christ, a follower of his self-denying Master!

Brown, the clerk of the Common Pleas, has returned, and he too declared that had they been well-officered, they would have carried the day. Now the war must be a thing of time. Our prestige is gone and must be reconquered. It is a most lamentable and disgraceful thing to acknowledge, but our people have no moral feeling, no instinct of honor, no principle. Each man is out for himself; each one seeks how many dollars he can get out of his friends, his occupation, his place under the government. No one serves from purely patriotic feeling as in the old republics. Luxury has done all this, and we women are greatly to blame for our share therein, and the richer classes are more tainted with the mercenary miserable spirit than the poorer ones. This uprising of the people will, I trust, put the leaders of fashion, those dead respectables, in the obscurity which they deserve, and give a chance to the real aristocracy of nature to invade their ranks and make them recognize some other title to distinction than money and dancing masters' manners.

My flag, which I gave to the 69th, was lost. The ensign dropped it in his retreat, and as he escaped unhurt, has not dared to show his face. The Regiment declared that he shall be shot if he does. He is skulking somewhere about in Washington, and sent on to his wife for nine dollars to enable him to come home. But if he does, the Regiment vows vengeance for the disgrace. If anyone asks me about it, I shall say that one of

---

[79] See *Personalities in the Diary*, page xxiv.

the ensigns was killed and nothing more. The brave fellows shall not suffer for the fault of *one*. Besides, it was the first battle, and I would forgive the poor fellow and give him another chance.

Last Friday evening, the 26th, after having waited until half-past eight for Charles to come in, for he had gone down to meet the 69th Regiment who were expected on that day, he came in at last with two gentlemen, Mr. O'Conor[80] and Mr. John Savage[81] (from Washington, and a member of the 69th). He [Savage] had led the troops at Vienna and been in the fight. I found him one of the most attractive men I have ever met. He sang for us, after dinner, "The Temptation of St. Anthony," and then the war song of the 69th, "The Flag of Our Country Forever," which he composed himself and set to the tune of "Dixieland." It is an inspiring song; I must get it.

July 29, 1861

Yesterday afternoon, Mrs. [Wolcott] Gibbs came in and we talked over the state of the country. She gave us her experience in South Carolina. She vividly described her astonishment on her arrival at Charleston at finding so small a town, wooden houses, no paint, no libraries, no fine arts, no nothing. She describes Columbus as the best looking city she saw, but said the road was through pine barrens where she saw occasionally a poor looking farm house, as they appeared to her Northern eyes, and was told that those were the planters'. Her

---

[80] Charles O'Conor, distinguished New York lawyer, was active in politics and once ran on the Democratic ticket for lieutenant governor of New York. Identified with the Copperhead element during the war, O'Conor defended Jefferson Davis in his treason trial and won acquittal.

[81] Dublin-born John Savage fled to America in 1848 because of his revolutionary activities, and earned his living in the United States as a journalist and free-lance writer. With the outbreak of the Civil War, Savage joined the 69th Regiment. His best known works are *'98 and '48, the Modern Revolutionary History and Literature of Ireland* (1856); *Faith and Fancy* (1864); *Poems* (1867); and *Fenian Heroes and Martyrs* (1868).

idea of the Southern nabob was much lowered. At Columbus, she said, the most intelligent man she conversed with was their black coachman, John, who gave them all the information they gained. He drove them to the Hampton plantation, the largest in South Carolina. They saw some fifty or sixty slaves who had just been allowed to come home from Arkansas because they were homesick. John explained this by saying that if a nigger ever gets real homesick, he dies, and they knew the value of property if they knew nothing else. He said the North Carolinians were the real gentlemen. He had a wife and children up there, but he had been sold to that innkeeper who hadn't two ideas in his head. But he had always been accustomed to the society of gentlemen, poor fellow!

A few Sundays since, in going to church in the railcar, I heard two Negroes, as black as crows with white cravats, talking over the state of things. One, who spoke with very little Negro accent, said that he had been so long out of the country that he scarcely felt as though he belonged to it. He said that we have no aristocracy here, but that [there] was no such thing. He said the feeling was here, though there were no titles and that it would never succeed for, he said, a middle class had more respect for an aristocracy than the lower classes who did all the work and worked without hope.

"Now," said he, "you see in Spain, there never was such a state of things as there was in France. And then look out at the South," said he, "there is too much white blood enslaved to make them long comfortable."

That Black certainly understood himself, though he looked like a dressed-up baboon and little else to me. I have an antipathy to Negroes physically and don't like them near me.

Mrs. Gibbs described the conversation of their fellow passenger, a sick man from Jacksonville. He took, she said, a great fancy to her son-in-law, Mr. Tuckerman, and at last, despite his reserve, he used to listen to him. He told him that he had just been to New York for the first time, that it was an awful

big place, and "Oh," said he, "didn't the people live comfortable?" He didn't wonder how they brag so; he wished more
people from his part of the country would go there. He had
just been reading *Hamlet*, a play by Shakespeare. "It was a
clever play, wasn't it?" He had seen it acted in New York, so
he thought he would read it. Then he told Mr. Tuckerman that
he wished he would come and see him, that he had a snug place
and made eighty thousand a year.

"You must lay up a good deal then," said Mr. Tuckerman.
"No, I don't."

"Do you raise it by your corn or sugar or tobacco?"

"No," said he, "*natural* increase. I've a good lot of niggers,
and I buy every now and then and sell at a profit. I never raise
more corn or produce than enough to feed the stock. It don't
pay. Can't you come? Can't you tuck the old lady away somewhere, for maybe she might not like what she'd see at home. Is
she smart? Is she lively?"

"Now," said Mr. Tuckerman, "she knows as much as most
women of her age."

"Oh, it wouldn't do! She'd be shocked at the way I live,
maybe. You see, I'm a bachelor."

July 30, 1861

Yesterday Mr. George Davis[82] from Greenfield dined
with us. He is a delightful companion. He knows all the literary
celebrities of Massachusetts and was Webster's intimate friend.
He had just returned from Washington, arriving there on the
very day of the disaster at Bull Run. He said that his feelings
had been so harrowed by what he had seen and heard that he
wished himself under his own vine and fig tree once more. . . .

Mr. Davis likewise told us that he heard Mrs. Lincoln[83] abusing Cameron, the Secretary of War, in plain English. The dis-

---

[82] See *Personalities in the Diary*, page xvi.
[83] See *Personalities in the Diary*, page xx.

honest money-making thief, as bad almost as Floyd[84] in his
thieving from the government, but with a private purpose. I
have to write to Mrs. Lincoln and tell her that she is right in
her opinion and to do her best to induce the President to remove him.

Friday last, August 2nd, Father O'Reilly, the chaplain of
the 69th Regiment, dined with us in company with Mr. Dever
and Mr. Hardcross, whose name I rather think in no way belies
him. Father O'Reilly is an unostentatious, refined, intellectual
man about thirty-five years of age—a Jesuit. He says that the
two engagements at Bull's Run and Manassas were not a defeat,
that with the exception of two or three regiments who behaved
badly (who really ran away), all the rest behaved well and retreated in the presence of the enemy in good order. He thought
the rebels must have lost quite as many, if not more, than we,
for he heard the members of his own regiment saying, "Well,
if they shot Haggerty, I killed six of them for him; and besides,
our own batteries did fearful execution." He himself, he said,
had he a musket, could have done something. But as it was, he
ran away when he could do no good to go back when he might
be of service. Once, when sheltered behind a tree, the bullets
whizzed past so fast that he thinks they must have taken him
for an officer. One bullet, he said, struck his hat and turned it
round a little on his head. He brought home one of the fine
weapons belonging to the Black Horse cavalry. They were all
black, he said—black uniform and black plumes—and were the
élite of the South—all gentlemen of estate. As they passed like
a whirlwind, the 69th poured in a volley which literally mowed
them down.

Colonel Corcoran is at Richmond, a prisoner. It is said that
he would not give his parole, as that would prevent him from

---

[84] Buchanan's Secretary of War, John B. Floyd, was more than strongly
suspected of turning over Federal property to the South on the eve of the
war, and was believed to be guilty of personal corruption in the sale of
military sites.

serving again during the war. The Judge found out the under-ground railroad and sent him a message telling him, if he wanted money, to draw upon him. We shall have to save as much as possible this next year or two; I wish I knew what I could do to make something.

August 6, 1861

Went yesterday to see the 12th Regiment mustered out of service, and saw Frank Barlow, Arabella's boy-husband,[85] who is a lieutenant. He tells the same story about the inefficiency and ill-conduct of the officers and says that Colonel Butterfield[86] is a snob; that he did not know how to treat either his men or his officers; that none of them would ever serve under him again. We saw their dog, who has followed them all through Virginia.

Colonel [Milton] Cogswell of the Tammany Regiment[87] is in town and says that when the officers of his regiment are changed, he will not command them; that they are a set of pot-house politicians only and not equal to their men in any respect. This is what we have to contend with, for this rebellion seems to have been a conspiracy among the army officers. What will be the end of all this?

Went on Sunday to hear Father O'Reilly preach. His text was, "Judge not that ye be not judged," and it was an excellent sermon—perhaps a little too philosophical in the beginning. He has promised to write to me and to bring me some new flowers from Paris on his return. This was spontaneous on his part; I did not ask it of him, but I hope he will not forget it.

---

85 See *Personalities in the Diary*, pages xiii and xiv.

86 Dan Butterfield, Colonel of the 12th New York Militia, became General Hooker's chief of staff when the latter was commander of the Union forces. He achieved the rank of major general.

87 The "Tammany Regiment" was the 42nd Infantry Regiment from New York. Organized at Great Neck, N.Y., it was mustered in on June 22, 1861, was attached to Stone's Brigade, Division of the Potomac, and was mustered out in July 1864.

September 2, 1861, West Farms

We have been here about three weeks and I have not had leisure to sit down and write the events as they take place. Little has been done, and the papers only contain a great many extracts from Southern and European papers, which are very annoying to Northern readers and show what a dreadful mistake the battle of Bull Run was. We have lost our prestige. The Grand Army of the United States is not the imposing body it was imagined. In Missouri, we have lost General Lyon,[88] who has been the head and strength of the Union party in the state [New York], and although he lost his life in a bravely contested battle, wherein 5,000 Union troops held their ground against 25,000, still we can little afford to lose a good officer in this, our need.

The enlistment goes on slowly. When the enthusiasm of our people was at its height, the government, with narrow-sighted policy, refused to take but a certain number, and now it is difficult to fill up the regiments. Whilst the Confederates have, they say, 300,000 in Virginia alone!

At last we have had a success. The fleet from Fortress Monroe has taken Fort Hatteras in North Carolina and 300 prisoners, and stopped one of the most annoying battle ports which sheltered privateers.

Baron von Gerolt, the Prussian minister, and his family are at our house in Eighth Street and have now been here three weeks; they seem to find it very comfortable. He is now the oldest of the foreign diplomats in this country, and his judg-

---

[88] Brigadier General Nathaniel Lyon, a professional soldier and graduate of West Point, was stationed in "Bleeding Kansas" for several years prior to the outbreak of war. He was assigned to the St. Louis Arsenal early in 1861, and when the war began he seized Camp Jackson and armed volunteers. He captured Jefferson City, pushed into Missouri, and was killed in the Battle of Wilson's Creek on August 10, 1861. Many people attributed his death to General Frémont's blundering, since the latter was in command of the Department of the West at the time.

ment is so relied upon that the English government desired that his dispatches to his government should be sent to England [so] that they might be able to read what he said. He is a most lovable old man with all the politeness and affability of the old regime.

His wife is a real German, possessing strong sense, very practical, perfectly simple, natural, unassuming, economical. His daughters [are] all different from each other. Tomorrow we are to join them at Lake Mahopac, where they are going to stay a week or ten days. I love the girls, particularly the two younger ones. Although Carlotta is no doubt far the most estimable, useful, and etc., she does not interest me and I cannot tell why. I find that the five years I have passed away from our home has very much changed me. I see the faults of our home education more, and although powerless to help, cannot bear to see the girls growing up so selfish and so useless and so disrespectful of their elders. The three girls seem to take their own limited experiences and necessarily narrow views as the standard of their judgment by which, if not others, at least they will be governed. It is a great pity, because it prevents them from taking advantage of the experience and judgment of persons older and wiser and of more weight and importance in the world than themselves and gives them an impertinence of manner very offensive to others and injurious to themselves. It is this very spirit which has brought our country to this pass—the want of reverence for authority, of respect and consideration for parents, the self-will of the young and ignorant. Even the Indian tribes were wiser than we and never dared to question the will or the judgment of the sages of their tribe or family. Here every young woman has her private opinion to which everyone who wishes to please her must bow, and which is her standard of the wisdom and intellect of others.

Baron von Gerolt and family spent the day here with Baron [George W.] von Schaack, son of General von Schaack, who has come to offer his services to the United States. He is now a major in the Steuben Regiment and has left for Fort Monroe.

September 7, 1861

A victory at last! Fort Hatteras, which commands the entrance to Albemarle Sound, with 36 cannon, a thousand stand of arms, three vessels laden with cotton and tobacco, seven hundred prisoners, was taken by General Butler's late mysterious expedition from Fort Monroe. This changes the state of things materially. God grant a speedy success and a cessation of bloodshed!

> *On September 2, 1861, the spirits of Northerners were uplifted by the news that joint military and naval expeditions had taken Fort Hatteras and Port Royal in the Carolinas. This strategic area had been a source of irritation to the North, since from it raiders harassed Union merchantmen, and blockade-runners made port. General Ben Butler and Commodore Silas Stringham left Hampton Roads with fifteen ships on August 25, and arrived at Fort Hatteras the next day. Stringham's larger ships stood beyond the range of the Confederate cannon and blasted away at the fort with their potent Dahlgren guns. The Confederates surrendered as soon as they realized the hopelessness of their situation. Although McClellan now had a great opportunity to capitalize on the capture of the gateway to all Southeastern Virginia, he failed to make good on his advantage.*

The paper of this morning contains the news of the final emancipation of woman. Abdul-Aziz,[89] the new Sultan, declares that he renounces the Eden of Mohammed, that he approves of the Christian marriage and opens the doors of the seraglio to all

---

[89] Abdul-Aziz was Sultan of Turkey from 1861 to 1876. He showed some interest in Westernizing his country, but actually accomplished little in the way of reforms. Deposed on May 29, 1876, he died—murdered or a suicide—a few days later.

Turkish women, gives Christians equal privileges in his domin-
ions, and perfect religious liberty. Glory be to God!

September 9, 1861

A week ago, we left West Farms to spend a day or so
with Baron Gerolt at Lake Mahopac in Putnam County. We
stopped at White Plains to wait for the Dover Plains train, and
on the piazza of the hotel encountered no less a person than
Samuel E. Lyon, the lawyer, who, he told us, had moved to
New York. His daughter has married into the Army—Brigadier
General Smith, an intimate friend of McClellan, whom Mr.
Lyon called "Mac." He said that all the officers were unani-
mous in their desire to have McClellan nominated the major
general in case of accident to General Scott, which is a great
proof of his worthiness.

Attempts were made to arrest Johnston,[90] but I see by the
papers that he has reached Richmond.

We met Mr. Schleiden, the Bremen minister, and Colonel
Raasloff,[91] the Danish envoy, in the cars, going likewise to Lake
Mahopac, and in one of the most dreadful rains I was ever out
in, reached Croton Falls station and had to drive five miles to
the Lake. . . .

Colonel Raasloff is a very disputatious, very intelligent,
agreeable man. He rallied me very much upon my American
spirit!

"What," said he, "you do not pretend that you are invincible
after that great battle of Bull Run, Mrs. Daly? Now, we cannot
grant that! You must allow these people to be belligerents, since
you ask an exchange of prisoners—notwithstanding your anger

---

[90] Albert Sidney Johnston (1803–1862) was in command of the U.S.
Army's Department of the Pacific, but quickly resigned his commission
when the war broke out, and headed for Richmond. He received a warm
welcome and a commission as a full general in the Confederate Army, with
command of the Department of Kentucky.

[91] See *Personalities in the Diary*, page xxvi.

at European governments for so doing. You see, you have allowed it yourselves!"

I said no, we did not, that we did not pretend to keep to the
military etiquette any more than we did the courtly etiquette
of European countries, that he forgot we were semi-barbarians,
only half-skilled in the arts—civil, social and military—of Europe; that perhaps after two or three centuries of a standing
army and a strong government our army might be as perfect as
theirs, and we the people as accustomed to severe discipline,
but that we were now only beginning to learn. In the South,
he perceived that the cotton aristocracy had there very much
the advantage of us; their armies were better disciplined, being
pressed into service. They had a more European method of raising armies; namely, compulsion!

"Oh, yes," said he, "but you American ladies are very strong-
minded; you might almost raise an army amongst yourselves."

He is quite right. American women, I do not doubt, would
be quite as courageous as the men; they have an equal love of
adventure and excitement.

I find I can with great difficulty sit silent and hear the
Country attacked. Mr. [William] Young of the *Albion* has
been publishing such contemptuous editorials about the American squabble that I almost dislike him and hope that he may
keep his distance. We don't ask the assistance or advice of
Europeans. He gains his bread here, and if he thinks us all so
contemptible, pray why does he not return to glorious Old
England and his great naval memories, and his sister and brother,
sea princes and princesses of English Commodore blood? Russell too, I confess, I never wish to meet at an American's table.
We are too desirous of foreign approbation.

Baron Gerolt is truly philosophical. He says that it is quite
impossible to judge anything in this country by a European
standard; that no one can tell how this war may end or what
may be the consequences; that he thought for new levies our
troops behaved well; and that all proved the immense vitality

at the North. I believe the Judge talked the Dane [Raasloff] over to more Northern sentiments, as well as Mr. Schleiden.

This morning in the paper is a letter from the Emperor of Russia expressing his warmest sympathy with the Federal government, which will doubtless have the most beneficial effect upon other European governments. Alexander of Russia seems to be a really great and wise prince in his making peace with the English and French, his internal improvements, the emancipation of the serfs, his settlements, and in this, his kind and brotherly letter, he shows a large and liberal mind and a wise policy.

I have written today to General Shields to urge him to come on. I do not see why he should not take this prominent place for which nature has fitted him, now that there is an opportunity for him to distinguish himself.

September 13, 1861

Yesterday was my birthday. My dear mother had not forgotten it, although I had kept quite silent upon the subject. The years are almost too many, even though they are counted in kisses. Mother, it seems, had ordered an ice pitcher to be sent to me. Having no children keeps one young in feeling.

My life is a very pleasant one, my husband loving and affectionate, but oh, when I looked back in my solitary walk of yesterday morning, how much has passed away:—Grandmother,[92] with her passionate temper but wholesome rule, my dear grandfather Lydig whom I loved so very dearly, better than anyone in the world. I cannot think of him now, even after more than twenty years of separation, without feeling the tears come. The love between us was so pure, so disinterested on my part, so reverential, so perfect in its trust. Then my sister [Margaret][93] away in Germany with her new ties! I cannot

---

[92] Maria Mesier Lydig. See *Personalities in the Diary*, page xxii.
[93] Margaret Lydig Otto. See *Personalities in the Diary*, page xxii.

recover from the shock that her selfish treatment of me has given to my whole nature; it seems to have quite changed my character and made me skeptical of women and the religious profession. I who had given up so much for her and been so forgiving, and then to see Mother believe all her hollow professions.

Our church system has had much to do with the annoyances of my life. Our unmarried clergy are great sources of scandal; their egregious vanity is never satisfied, and young women, led away by a sentiment—half-religious, half-sensuous—are doubly intoxicated, confounding the man with his office and looking upon the surplice as not only an emblem, but the evidence of purity. They seem to think that they may be trusted and allowed greater freedom than other men. The clergy, denied many other gratifications, are seldom holy enough to refuse any such delicate offerings to their vanity. Both of our parish priests have lost my respect from their behavior toward my own sisters; and yet, both are held forth in the world as pattern men. One even dared to try me, but I could never forget that the *man* was beneath the surplice. I could feel it in his gaze. Thanks to my sensitiveness, I was always protected from their tender attentions.

The Hatteras expedition, it seems, was principally carried out and owed its success to Commodore Stringham and General Butler, although as usual he [Butler] succeeded in first getting his report into the papers. He did very little, and that very little was badly done. Stringham had no orders to keep the place, but he disobeyed orders, feeling that otherwise the waste of life and expense was useless. Soon an order came from General Scott to hold it.

Mrs. Lincoln has evidenced very bad taste and great want of delicacy whilst in New York in visiting the *Monticello* [a cruiser], which contained state prisoners from Hatteras. The first lieutenant very properly refused to receive her and sent word that they were at dinner.

I see that Albert Sidney Johnston has been given the command of the division of the Mississippi of the Confederate Army. He was much loved by the officers of the army, but when there was first a report of his defection, his intimate friend who loved him as a brother, "C," went to a lawyer and said that there must be arrangements made to arrest him immediately. The government was notified and requested not to accept his resignation, that he might still be held under military rule and ordered here. But instead of listening to the wise counsel, his resignation was accepted and Johnston was freed to work his country mischief. For some time he has been living with a sister in California.

Today there is a victory in Western Virginia. [Brigadier General John B.] Floyd's army is routed.

September 18, 1861

Yesterday we paid a visit to see Madam von Gerolt, who is still at No. 84 [Clinton Place, New York City].

These six weeks at West Farms have passed very swiftly, only I have not enjoyed it quite as much as I expected. Charles this summer has been a carpenter and only a carpenter. He seems incapable of doing two things at the same time, each hobby for a little while.

Cousin Mary Sheaff[94] is staying with us. She is the same as ever. Even at eighty-eight years of age, she thinks and glories in the style in which her nieces and nephews live and in their alliances. It is very strange that they have dared to treat us as they have done. Why, had we all that has been expended upon their entertainment, we would be most materially better off. Their six weeks at Newport with horses and carriages was somewhat balanced by a six weeks here at our expense. I am sure did they show any family feeling, no one would think of it,

---

[94] See *Personalities in the Diary*, page xxvii.

but I suppose their entire selfishness is one secret of their success in the world. We have spent an immense amount of time and money in entertaining those who could never be of any use to us. They never made that mistake—neither they nor their father before them! . . .

The Judge and Phil have gone today to dine at Mr. Gouverneur Wilkins'. Mrs. W. did not have the politeness to invite me. I suppose she had her reasons. A daughter of the patroon Van Rensselaer ought to know what good manners are, but Madam von Gerolt, whom I asked, thought it very remarkable. The Judge thinks that I am sensitive. Perhaps I am, but I'm sure that if the Judge or myself had been a Morris or one of her connections, or any one of the King family, that she would have done differently. Besides, we are only people of moderate fortune from whom little can be expected in return.

October 6, 1861

Once more home at No. 84, Madam von Gerolt finding it very comfortable, has prolonged her stay much longer than I expected, staying until the very last moment so that I am now obliged to clean house instead of having it done whilst in the country. The girls found her a much more exacting mistress than I am. She has, it would seem, a truly aristocratic and German contempt and want of consideration for those beneath her, and the poor souls had their hands full, having to work for six instead of three. I never find any like my father and my own husband. Baron Gerolt himself is considerate, however, in the extreme, and is one of the most lovable men I have ever met. He is the *noble* side of the family too. Madam is not; she belonged to the literary circle.

We have had a most delightful summer. The more Father[95] sees of the Judge, the more he evidently loves and esteems him. The only drawback was the conduct of our Episcopal clergy-

---

[95] Philip Lydig. See *Personalities in the Diary*, page xxiii.

man, Mr. [W.] Rodman,[96] who has been making love to Kate
for the last five years, and, after winning her fancy, tells her
coolly that he never thought of her except as a child—whilst
all the while he had been making almost passionate declarations
to her! So much for our unmarried clergy. They will ruin our
church, and evidently they take advantage of their cloth to act
in such a manner as no poor unfortunate layman, no graceless
worldling would dare to do for fear of a thrashing. It shall not
be my fault if he does not leave the parish in disgrace.

General Shields has married, I see by the California papers,
and married Miss Cahil—Vivian, as I christened her from one
of the heroines in Tennyson's *Idylls of the King,* for her perseverance. She has followed the General now to my knowledge
for four years with relentless perseverance, declaring that she
was engaged to him long before the old gentleman ever thought
of such a thing, as I know from his own letters. I hope that he
will not repent, but such a bold *lover* (when a maid) rarely
makes a very attractive wife. It is likewise reported that he has
declined the brigadiership offered him. I fear that he must be
selfish and I am heartily disappointed. I thought that, to quote
his own words, "the old war horse would scent the battle from
afar and make himself ready." Being alone and having already
done some good service, I should have thought that he would
have sacrificed the last remaining years of his life to make himself immortal. I'm glad that Harriet [Whetten] is not his wife.
She might have lost her illusions.

When I left the city, I hoped by this time the war would
have been almost over, but Missouri seemed as unsettled as ever.
Charles, from the moment that Frémont[97] was mentioned, has
been mourning over the appointment of Frémont in Missouri,
for he [Charles] believed him to be an incapable, obstinate,
selfish, conceited, and unscrupulous man. His wife Jessie is very

---

[96] The Reverend Mr. W. Rodman was rector of the Grace Episcopal
Church in West Farms, New York.

[97] John Charles Frémont. See *Personalities in the Diary,* page xviii.

ambitious, and between them they might be looking to the main chance rather than the good of their country. They would be nothing loath to be the heads of a Western republic.

Mr. Raasloff, the Danish minister, seemed to think that the state of things in Missouri foreboded internal revolution; but Europeans do not make sufficient allowances, perhaps, for the sound practical sense of the common people. Perhaps in the present crisis, when all politicians are all so corrupt, it is fortunate for our liberties that there is no one of very commanding talent, no Louis Napoleon among them to take advantage of our present necessity. . . .

Last night we went to dine with Mr. and Mrs. Thomas Francis Meagher and went with them to hear his oration in behalf of the Irish Brigade now forming. The oration was full of point, full of sarcasm and of wholesome truths, and calculated to do a great deal of good. It was very interesting and exciting. He has thrown himself with his whole soul into this business. I like him better on closer acquaintance. I like people who commit themselves. Charles was called upon to introduce Mr. Meagher, which he did with very appropriate remarks.

October 7, 1861

Passed a great deal of time this morning with Mrs. Gibbs. She was the daughter of General Wolcott of Rhode Island[98] and married at sixteen, being an only daughter. She was very early matured, and having a remarkable mind, she improved the advantages that her father's position gave her. She is now an old lady—nearly seventy—but so full of enthusiasm, patriotism, of mental activity, her mind always running forward, that she will never grow old. One day last spring, just

---

98 This was Mrs. Laura Wolcott Gibbs, daughter of Oliver Wolcott (1760–1833), Secretary of the Treasury under Washington and John Adams, and Governor of Connecticut. She married Colonel George Gibbs, a noted mineralogist from Newport, R.I.

after war was declared and the inefficiency of the Administration began to be felt, she came around here and, stopping herself when about becoming excited, said, "No, I must not speak the word 'our' country, or I shall not sleep tonight. The Doctor has forbidden me to think." Yesterday she told me that her son, Captain Gibbs,[99] had been taken prisoner. She seemed to wish that she was a man to go to his assistance. "Why don't they send away that drivelling Seward?" said she. A gentleman told her, she said, that if he was not drunk with whiskey, he was either drunk with ambition or self-conceit or opium or something always. "Why does not Lincoln send him off and take Holt[100] or Dix? The Democrats," she continued, "have acted splendidly." I told her of Meagher's lecture, which she highly approved of. Oh, if I had had such a mother, how I should have venerated her. How much more I should have been under such an influence.

Poor Laura D'Oremieulx is ill in Germany of typhoid fever. She writes that she only longs to be home again. There are no comforts in Germany; the people live miserably. Indeed, they seem very different from us. A German will live upon what we cast or give away. They are honest, but have no sort of liberality, as we consider necessary in our treatment of our servants. They look upon the lower classes as mere beasts of burden, whom they can do with exactly as they choose.

---

[99] Alfred Gibbs (1823–1868) was one of the three sons of George and Laura Wolcott Gibbs. He became a captain on May 13, 1861, and was captured by the Confederates two months later, on July 8. He was paroled as a prisoner of war until August 27, 1862, then exchanged. Commissioned colonel of the 130th New York volunteers in September 1862, he saw much military action and received many honors before his death on the Kansas frontier. Alfred's brothers were George, a lawyer, and Oliver Wolcott, the noted chemist.

[100] Joseph Holt, the Judge Advocate General of the army who investigated treasonable organizations in Ohio, Indiana, Illinois, Missouri, and Kentucky in 1864, was appointed to that post by President Lincoln on September 3, 1862. He served on various courts-martial and military commissions, reported the alleged Confederate plot to seize the capital in 1861, on the Fitz-John Porter case, and on other sensational cases.

October 8, 1861

The Judge brought home a letter from a friend of General Shields. It seems that we have wronged him; I do not believe that he is married. It seems that he has been waiting and waiting to be called upon and left only when he had given up all hope of an appointment for Mazatlán to go thence [150 miles into Mexico] to visit a mine in which he is interested. So perhaps all may be right after all and he will not disappoint his friends. I wish he were in Missouri instead of Frémont. The Judge seems to fear that before he is superseded, some dreadful disaster may occur. He seems to fear that he will be led on and surrounded—God forbid!

Poor Lyon! "They have left us, boys," said he [Nathaniel Lyon], "to die for our country," when he attacked the enemy at Springfield. He left all that he possessed—$20,000—to his country by will.

> He has slept his last sleep
> He has fought his last battle,
> No sound shall awake him to glory again!

But his name will long be remembered by his grateful countrymen—one bright example, at least! He has bequeathed also his ancestral farm to his country.

Mrs. Gibbs is very busy in furnishing the Sanitary Committee[101] with what is necessary. She is indefatigable, and being

---

101 The United States Sanitary Commission took its name from a commission which the British sent out to investigate conditions during the Crimean War. The principal organizer of the commission was the Rev. Dr. Henry W. Bellows, a Unitarian pastor who brought his committee to Washington on May 16, 1861, and convinced the government of the need for such a group to supplement the inadequate capacity of the Army Medical Bureau. By June 13, 1861, the Commission received the official blessing of the government and began its work of watching over the comfort of Federal soldiers; supplying medicines, bandages, ambulances; establishing hospitals, rest homes, and other facilities; transporting wounded soldiers to their homes; and giving assistance to families of soldiers. The contribution of the Commission in supplies has been estimated at upwards of $15,000,000, and in cash upwards of $5,000,000. Its philanthropic services attracted much attention in Europe.

herself an accomplished nurse, and having some knowledge of medicine, she is an able auxiliary. I have been busy today in assisting to raise some money for standards for the Irish Brigade, three United States' standards and three *green* flags with Irish emblems and mottos and the guide colors. They will cost about $600.

Charles and I have invested all our spare money in the government loan. I feel quite proud to do even that little. Indeed, I will do anything so long as I not be called to give up my dear ones for soldiers. I wish I had more courage, but I cannot do that. Thank Heaven Charles will be forty-five on the 31st of the month and beyond the age of service!

Mr. Schleiden came in during the evening. He says that McClellan does not yet feel strong enough to detach troops to take them in the rear—that he contents himself by slowly advancing as they retreat. He says the army is even now but very poorly disciplined.

October 9, 1861

Today was passed in going to see Madam von Gerolt, who has returned and is staying at the New York Hotel. She says that she was perfectly well served while here, only Ellen[102] was too much afraid that she would spend too much money. Ellen would say that it was hard to get it from her to spend. I know I paid for the bread and milk and butter and potatoes eaten by the two girls and for some other items. So the world goes!

From the hotel, I went to Washington Market and bought enough to last until next week. I think our grocers and uptown butchers must make fortunes quickly if they make such profits as the difference between their charges and those in the market

---

[102] Ellen and Margaret were Mrs. Daly's serving girls at No. 84 Clinton Place, New York City.

would indicate. I wish that the prices and the quality of edibles were fixed by government, as it is in some European countries. Here one must be ever quickly alive to one's own interest, or else be cheated, and it is so disagreeable to be always on the watch.

In the afternoon, Kate came in, and after staying a while, the new britzska stopped for her with Christina Messer, the gardener's daughter, and her baby on the back seat. I was too angry to see Kate in such familiar company with her inferiors. . . .

This evening, just as we were going out to hear Hermann,[103] the great prestidigitator, Mr. and Mrs. Thomas Francis Meagher came in to say a few words. It ended in their spending the evening. A letter from San Francisco concerning General Shields was read and some counsel was asked of the Judge concerning the Brigade.

The Judge related quite an interesting anecdote concerning President Lincoln and General Shields. It seems the General, when in Illinois, sent him [Lincoln] a challenge. A mean and mischievous attack upon the General appeared in one of the Illinois papers, and the General went to the editor and required him either to give up the author's name or to give him satisfaction himself. The piece was really written by a lady, a great friend of Miss Todd, whom Lincoln had vainly wooed, but of whom he was still in pursuit. The editor consulted Lincoln, who said that the lady's name could not be mentioned. Lincoln told the editor to say that he would be responsible for the article. So the General sent Lincoln a challenge. They met on a field which was a great place for duels, but one of the seconds,

---

[103] Professor Hermann's display of magical powers proved such a diversion to audiences in the major cities of the North that General McClellan called upon him in November 1861 to entertain a large gathering in his quarters. This created much criticism, since many people thought the commander of the Army of the Potomac might better be planning for battle than lavishly entertaining guests.

who knew the whole matter, brought about an amicable settlement. Miss Todd, it was said, married Lincoln on account of this act of chivalrous devotion.

It would seem Miss Cahil is in New York, or somewhere North, so I do not believe the General is married.

Someone then related an anecdote of General Patterson. The only exploit he was ever guilty of, except of playing *grouchy* at Bull's Run, was in Mexico.[104] When an attack was ordered upon the enemy by General Scott, Patterson was ill—too ill to mount his horse. A few hours later, hearing that they were in full retreat, Patterson became better and insisted upon taking command. Mounting his horse, he started off, unmindful of his late illness. Unfortunately, however, for the General's health, the enemy at bay turned and offered resistance which looked quite formidable. General Patterson, feeling unwell again, ordered a retreat and did not venture in his infirm state of health to meet them. All the army officers knew of this affair and were indignant at his nomination.

We hear that [James] Lynch, the first of the eighteen who deserted Sherman's battery and left the field at Bull's Run, is to be nominated at the Mozart Hall[105] a candidate for a most lucrative office. I hope and trust the papers will take notice of his conduct as a soldier and prevent him from succeeding.

I mentioned to Mr. [Adam] Badeau,[106] who likewise dropped

---

104 Major general Robert Patterson, who had served under Scott during the Mexican War and received honorable mention for taking Jalapa, blamed his withdrawal from action just prior to the Bull Run disaster on Scott. On July 21, the battle of Manassas was lost; by the 27th, Patterson was mustered out of service and was on his way back to his native Pennsylvania in disgrace. He never lived down what was popularly regarded as personal cowardice.

105 Mozart Hall was a Democratic club organized by Fernando Wood to defeat powerful Tammany Hall, in which he had been a leader until he lost favor with the group. When Wood ran against Tammany and lost in the 1857 election, he set up Mozart Hall, with a membership predominantly Copperhead, and won the mayoralty again in 1859.

106 See *Personalities in the Diary*, page xiii.

in, Mrs. Gibbs' idea of Junius,[107] which he did not seem to think feasible. He thought that he could not be resuscitated here, but it would be a turn indeed to all misdoers if what they did in darkness could be brought to light.

We received a letter from Father O'Reilly, the Irish chaplain of the 69th, from France. He says that all Ireland, even, is against the North, owing to the letters of Russell. He [Russell] has some deadly purpose. I wish he were out of the country and at home. The friends of Meagher thronged around him to know if the account of his flight from the field at Bull Run, as related by Russell, were really true.[108] He had, he writes, to tell over and over again the story of the battle.

October 14, 1861

I have been engaged in raising some money to aid in presenting the Irish Brigade with stands of colors. I have altogether sixty-five dollars, and as that is one-eighth part of the whole, I shall make no further effort.

I do not quite like Mrs. Meagher's manner and think that she rather desires to keep all the glory and renown to herself and her husband. At the meeting which she called at her house, she had a pretty little formula which she had written out about her not having had the blessings (which she deeply regretted) of having been born in the Ancient Faith, at not belonging to the

---

[107] The pseudonym for the author of 69 political letters, published from January 21, 1769 to January 21, 1772 in the *Public Advertiser*, Britain's most popular newspaper at that time. The "Letters of Junius" were critical of British colonial policy in America, and did not spare even the King. Although the true identity of Junius is still undetermined, there is good reason to believe he was Sir Philip Francis.

[108] William Howard Russell's account of the Battle of Bull Run, personally witnessed by the London *Times* correspondent, earned for him the sobriquet "Bull Run Russell" and the hatred of the North. Russell considered the volunteer Union Army rabble, and was openly respectful of the South. Although he was regarded as unfair and biased by Northerners, his pro-Southern newspaper was delighted with the material he sent. Historians have come to regard Russell's news reporting as accurate and responsible.

great warm-hearted, devoted, but oppressed nation whose feelings the Brigade represented. I rather think that she would have
been quite willing that I should have stayed away, as I had so
much to do with the 69th.

I think it was very inexcusable in Meagher to brand those
who chose to stay behind as being impostors, to say that as the
best of the Regiment would be with him, there could be no
regiment with the number "69" on their caps parading Broadway in their absence. He was not probably aware of the force
of his word. Surely no one should say a word even though the
worthy mechanics and laborers who had done such good service in our time of great need should determine now to remain
and work at their trade and leave others to take their place. Had
Corcoran been here to lead them, doubtless they would have
gone, but in Meagher they do not place such reliance. A countryman said of him [Meagher] a few days ago that God Almighty had just made him to step off a scaffold with a big
speech in his mouth. He has a very domineering, arrogant disposition. He is very jealous too, I should think, and both
O'Gorman and Savage began to quarrel with him. The old 69th
are very irate about his attack upon them.

October 17, 1861

.   .   .   .   .

Today Baron Gerolt, who arrived from Washington
last night, and Madam dined with us. And in the evening,
Carlotta and Dorothea came. Mrs. Gibbs dropped in. Then
Mr. Savage and his brother-in-law, [William] Reid, whom I
do not fancy; and then Mr. Schleiden. So we had quite a little
reception! We persuaded Mr. Savage to sing "The Tempta-
tions of St. Anthony," which amused them all very much, and
I sent for some ice cream and cake. So we had quite a pleasant
evening.

Dorothea looked beautifully, but I did not like Carlotta. She is, I think, more self-conceited than others. Madam von Gerolt was regretting that she and her daughters had so little sympathy. She said that being brought up and educated in foreign countries, they have no nationality and don't feel at all as she does. Carlotta, she says, is cold, and yet likes to be petted. She is very susceptible to flattery, but Madam cannot give expression to her feelings in that way. So they are distant with each other.

Children are, after all, not so ardently to be desired. If they live to be men and women, they are not always the companions you would choose for yourself. How dreadful to have a stupid animal for a child to drag about all one's life, or how wearisome and agonizing to have always to combat with a violent or sullen temper. No doubt God gives us what will make us most happy in this life. God be thanked for my happy lot. Sometimes I wish for a child; but perhaps it would not add either to mine or my husband's happiness. . . .

Received a long, affectionate, and homesick letter from poor Mag. I wish she could have married differently and settled near us. I cannot conceive how she can find a husband so much younger than herself companionable. She cannot, since she is so dreadfully homesick. One's husband, I find, is all in all to one. I must confess that when he is with me I want no one else, not even my dear mother and father, still less my sisters and brothers, much as I really love them. To wake up and find him beside me, to wait for him to return to dinner after the day's work is over is enough to live for. But then poor Mag is an invalid; still, she has a child. I'm afraid that she is one of those who will never be content. She has not been true to herself, perhaps, and does not therefore find herself good company. So little do I find myself lonely that I almost regret having invited a dear friend to stay with me, but I must not grow selfish, but sacrifice a little to make others happy.

David[109] has returned from his European travels—I fear with little profit. The dear boy is a fine specimen of the country gentleman, with little appreciation, however, as yet, of art, science or literature. Phil[110] is much the most intellectual and Fuggie [Florence, a sister], had she any encouragement from those around her, would certainly make a very interesting and intellectual woman, but the influence is all in favor of *outward* things, as a German would say. . . .

There is a report that the Federal fleet has been much damaged. One ship was sunk before New Orleans by the Mosquito Fleet, but it is only a false report, probably, gotten up to send out by the steamer on Wednesday to add to the prestige of the *rebel* ambassadors, Slidell and Mason—who escaped on the 12th on the *Nashville*, having run the blockade off Charleston.[111] Three steamers have started in pursuit. I hope they may catch them, but the *Nashville* is a very swift vessel.

November 4, 1861

My diary is very imperfectly kept. Since I last opened it, there has been another disaster at Edward's Ferry on the upper Potomac in which General Baker, whom I last saw at Fort Schuyler, was killed and Colonel Cogswell taken prisoner.[112] It would seem that our troops fought this time, however, and fought bravely.

---

109 David Lydig, Mrs. Daly's brother. See *Personalities in the Diary*, page xxi.

110 Philip Lydig, another brother. See *Personalities in the Diary*, page xxii.

111 The *Nashville* left Charleston on October 17, 1861, with the Confederate ambassadors James M. Mason and John Slidell aboard. They sailed from Havana, Cuba, for Europe on November 7, 1861, on the mail packet *Trent*, a British merchant ship.

112 This was the disaster of Ball's Bluff, October 21, 1861, some forty miles from Washington. Responsibility for the defeat fell heavily upon Brigadier General Charles P. Stone, who had been ordered to make "a slight demonstration." General Edward D. Baker was caught in the thick of an ill-advised maneuver and was killed. Union troops, completely exposed, were slaughtered by the enemy as they attempted to fall back. Lincoln was grief-

After the Bull Run holocaust, the prestige of General Scott suffered considerably, and this increased the irascibility of the aged General-in-Chief of the Army. In the shakeup which followed, McDowell and Halleck took a back seat to a new savior of the Union, the 36-year-old George B. McClellan.

McClellan came to Washington the last week of July, 1861, with the intention of soon replacing the General-in-Chief, and the attentions showered upon him from the moment he arrived in the capital further heightened his ambitions. He could not wait for nature to remove Scott—a matter of months, as was increasingly apparent—and he began a quarrel with the old man almost at once. His pride hurt, the old hero complained to the President of insubordination, and Lincoln stepped in to still the troubled waters.

"Little Mac" chose to ignore Scott and the President, and set about direct dealings with the men he considered to be really running the government—cabinet members Seward, Chase, Blair, and Cameron. His arrogance was later revealed in a letter written to his wife shortly after his arrival in Washington, in which he said, "By some strange operation of magic, I have become the power of the land." So apparent was McClellan's conspiring with Scott's superior, Secretary of War Cameron, that Scott issued an order forbidding his subordinates to communicate directly with the President or the Secretary of War. McClellan ignored the order.

Before McClellan's cruel and unnecessary campaign came to the critical showdown, nature intervened and prostrated Scott. Afflicted with dropsy, vertigo, and increasing paralysis, Scott arrived at the point where he could scarcely endure a meeting. Lincoln took pity on him and wrote Scott on October 18 that he could no longer object to his retirement. On November 1, the cabinet responded to a formal request from Scott that he be placed on the retirement list, and that day Lincoln headed a little delegation to Scott's quarters for a touching farewell.

---

stricken at the loss of his close personal friend and neighbor from Springfield, "Ned" Baker. McClellan did not escape censure for the vague orders, which, added to Stone's indecisive advance and Baker's impetuosity, brought about the tragedy.

That same night, Lincoln visited McClellan and informed the elated young man that he was being appointed General-in-Chief, a "grave responsibility" which McClellan hastened to assure the President he was equal to bearing without difficulty. Early next morning, McClellan joined the delegation headed by Cameron and Chase to see Scott off on the train. McClellan could not resist delivering what he confessed to his wife was a hypocritical eulogy, but Scott's age and vanity dimmed his perception, and he accepted the tribute as sincere.

With Scott on his way to Europe to consult physicians there, McClellan thought all obstacles had been removed from his path for the realization of his ambitions. He was now the man of the hour, the indispensable one upon whom all eyes were fixed.

General Scott has retired from the service. His resignation must have been one of the most touching and dignified ceremonies ever witnessed. His letter to the President was most admirable—faultless, indeed—and the President's reply was infinitely the best thing he has ever done. Dear old General—may McClellan show himself worthy of the trust placed in him! How little Mrs. Marcy[113] ever dreamed that she would be mother-in-law to the Commander-in-Chief of the American Army when I last saw her. I wonder if she would deign now to notice one. I think I shall forget her, unless she remembers me first, should we meet in Washington.

Yesterday the Judge and I drove out with Mrs. and Colonel Meagher to see a grand dress review of Fort Schuyler, dining with the officers. Meagher is not very officer-like. He is tempted to try a brigadiership, and his wife will urge him on. She seems to be very fond of a soldier's life and told me that

---

113 Randolph Barnes Marcy (1812–1887) was General McClellan's father-in-law, and was appointed his chief of staff in 1861. Late in the year Marcy was commissioned a brigadier general of volunteers and was active in military engagements throughout the war. In 1868 he was named inspector general of the U.S. Army.

she hoped she might join the brigade when ordered off. Meagher is very despotic and very ambitious. . . .

Mrs. Captain Dodge, with whom we dined a few days ago at Mrs. Pritchard's, says that there is a great discontent among the regulars, that civilians are placed and ranked over them. She intimated that the officers generally were in favor of a limited monarchy. Perhaps a despotism would develop our country more advantageously than the present system, which brings the worst of the populace only to its surface.

In this last election, the Irish have quite disgraced themselves by electing [James] Lynch for Sheriff and [John M.] Barbour for Judge: Lynch, who ran away from Bull Run, and Barbour, who last summer was a secessionist! . . .

November 7, 1861

Dined last evening with Mr. Phelps,[114] in company with General and Mrs. Foster, Miss Mary Lee of Baltimore, and a Mr. Tucker,[115] her cousin, both cousins of Mr. Carroll and Colonel Cullum.[116] General Foster was second in command at Fort Sumter,[117] and Mr. Foster carried the letters to Washington from the Fort, although dissuaded by Major Anderson, whom I am inclined to think was only great by accident. It seems to me that he should have blown up the Fort and left in boats, joining the fleet outside if possible. I don't fancy either himself or his wife. He is so pious and she has been twice in the lunatic asylum.

---

[114] William Walter Phelps, who inherited wealth and family connections, gained a reputation in his own right after the war as a member of Congress from New Jersey and as minister to Germany. During the war he lived on Madison Avenue, New York City.

[115] Gideon J. Tucker, prominent Copperhead Democrat and former Secretary of State in Albany, was at this time a Surrogate in New York.

[116] George W. Cullum served as General Scott's aide before the old gentleman retired on November 1, 1861. At that time he had the rank of major, but shortly thereafter he was promoted to the rank of colonel.

[117] Mrs. Daly is in error in saying that John Gray Foster was second in command at Fort Sumter. This was the post of Captain Abner Doubleday.

Mr. Phelps has patriotically run for assemblyman and has been elected. Quite a triumph for respectability. . . .

Colonel Cullum gave us a very accurate account of the rise and progress of the *Pathfinder*, the *great* Frémont. His greatness, it seems, began by running away with the daughter of Senator Benton, a lady not then remarkable for her beauty and who was probably won by his outer man, aided possibly by her father's fierce opposition. After the marriage, however, despite this determination to the contrary, Benton relented and pushed Frémont, who was sent by his [Benton's] influence on the expedition to the Rocky Mountains, taking with him a scientific engineer who did all the work and a secretary who wrote without dictation. Benton made up the reports from his documents, for all of which Frémont received the credit. The reports were found in the handwriting of Benton in the Secretary's office in Washington. He was guilty of the greatest ingratitude to Nicollet,[118] who taught him all he knew, and intrigued him out of his place. The papers this morning gave an account of his removal. His address to his soldiers is another instance of his consummate impudence. I suppose his wife wrote it for him, for she is much the cleverer of the two. He takes to himself the glory of having formed the Western Army— ignoring Lyon, Sigel[119] and the other good generals in his command.

---

118 Reference here is made to Joseph N. Nicollet, whom Frémont assisted in exploring the plateau between the upper Mississippi and Missouri rivers in 1838. This was three years before Frémont's marriage to Senator Benton's daughter, and therefore prior to the period when Frémont used Benton's influence to make the explorations which earned him the sobriquet, "the Pathfinder."

119 German-born Franz Sigel had been involved with revolutionary activity and fled to the United States in 1852 to escape punishment. He served as a major in the 5th New York militia until 1857, when he moved to St. Louis. There he organized the 3rd Missouri infantry and was commissioned a colonel in 1861. Sigel participated in the Wilson's Creek fighting which cost Lyon his life, and for his valor during the battle of Pea Ridge, Arkansas, he was rewarded with a promotion to the rank of major general in 1862. Before the war ended, he resigned from the army to become editor of New York's *Deutsches Volksblatt*.

Popular though was the account the diarist offers about Frémont's dismissal, it does not accurately reflect the circumstances. Frémont's career was stormy and reckless, but he did run into a nearly hopeless situation when he accepted the command of the Department of the West.

So much attention was being given by the government to the defense of Washington at the beginning of the war that the West was all but forgotten. The "Department" was created on July 3, 1861, to formalize Frémont's appointment to it, but when he reached Missouri on July 25, he found chaos. Volunteers almost totally lacked training; money and supplies were nonexistent; and the Union portion of the state of Missouri was under the direction of politician Francis P. (Frank) Blair, Jr., and the inadequate military force of General Nathaniel Lyon. St. Louis was a city divided against itself, and the Union position was hopelessly weak.

Frémont worked day and night to establish order, to train and equip troops, to reduce the vast command over all the states and territories between the Mississippi and the Rockies, including Illinois and Kentucky, to something workable and defensible. Not only did he accomplish a great deal along these lines during the few months of his incumbency as commander of the department, but he also managed to salvage for command a man by the name of Ulysses S. Grant.

Perhaps the greatest mistake Frémont made was in offending the powerful Blair family, which had the ear of the President as well as of so many leading officials in Washington. Head of the family was old Francis P. Blair, a former member of President Jackson's "Kitchen Cabinet." Then there was Montgomery Blair, a member of Lincoln's cabinet and his Postmaster General. Finally, there was Frank Blair, the man with whom Frémont came into conflict. Frank Blair had urged Frémont's appointment, and as Frémont came on to Missouri, Blair returned to the House of Representatives.

When Congress adjourned, Frank Blair returned to St. Louis, hoping to be more the source of real authority there than he had been when only he and Nathaniel Lyon were running the show. But Frémont would have no part of this, and *soon they were bitter enemies. Sufficient ammunition was not placed in the hands of the Blair family to destroy Frémont's little empire until the General handed it to them himself.*

On August 30, 1861, Frémont issued a proclamation which startled the nation and changed the entire course of the war. He declared martial law for all Missouri; drew a line across the state and stated his intention of court martialing anyone north of that line found in possession of arms which were not authorized; announced that the property of all enemies of the United States would be seized, and their slaves freed; and added additional punitive measures. This brought the issue of slavery to the fore and ignited fuses throughout the nation— North as well as South.

Frémont had no right or authority to make such a political and policy decision, as President Lincoln informed him as politely as possible. But Frémont was being hailed by his abolitionist friends as a great hero for bringing attention to the real purpose of fighting the war, and he would not retreat when the President asked him to. Lincoln, who was really placed on the spot by Frémont's declaration, merely requested that Frémont modify his proclamation to conform to the recent Confiscation Act, which allowed the seizure of property when it was used for purposes of insurrection. Since most of the Missouri slaves were north of the line Frémont had established, and since the abolitionists were now looking to Frémont to be their liberator, the General felt he could not turn back.

The Blairs descended upon the White House as a delegation, admitted that their judgment had been wrong, and built a strong case for Frémont's mismanagement, bungling, and extravagance, which included testimony by the provisional governor of Missouri, Hamilton R. Gamble, and state senator James O. Broadhead. This, added to Frémont's refusal to relieve Lincoln from the untenable position in which he had placed him over the issue of slavery, was enough to end the matter.

Although it may have amounted to little more than rubbing salt into the wound, Frémont's final stroke of genius in this matter was the sending of his high-strung wife Jessie to Wash-

*ington to plead his side of the case with Lincoln. Mrs. Frémont,
whose Benton blood was not famous for its even temperature,
was exhausted when she arrived in Washington after two days
on the road. She had strength enough to inform the President
of her presence, however, and when Lincoln asked to see her
immediately, she arrived for the interview in poor temper.*

*What followed sealed Frémont's doom, if it was not already
settled. Jessie scolded, vilified the Blairs, and lectured an exasperated Lincoln on abolition. Usually patient and temperate,
Lincoln reportedly lost his temper and Mrs. Frémont went
away insulted.*

*As a concession to the abolitionist element of his party, Lin-
coln appointed Frémont to the command of the Mountain Department. Ordered to cooperate against Stonewall Jackson in
the Valley raid of 1862, he displayed his ignorance of military
tactics and was defeated at Cross Keys. He retired from service
shortly thereafter and became relatively obscure. In 1890,
shortly before his death, his rank as Major General in the Army
was restored.*

This morning, walking up Broadway, the 56th N.Y. passed
me going to the seat of war. I have seen no better regiments,
and the men were singing all the way. It was most inspiring.

Would to God the war were finished. I hate to hear the
women, gentle-hearted ladies, admiring swords, pistols, etc.
and seeming to wish to hear of the death of Southerners. I am
sure, as a matter of feeling, aside from policy, I would much
rather have the life of a red Republican than a Rebel. I hate the
thought of being of service to the arrogant, self-righteous
pharisees of the present age who go about preaching abolitionism and who believe in no creed save their own.

I heard an anecdote of Lincoln this morning which gives a
very good idea of the kind of company he has been accustomed
to. He was speaking of the number of office-seekers about him
and saying how tired he was of hearing their solicitations. "The
fact is," says he, "there are too many pigs for the teats!"

November 10, 1861

Last evening Mr. Raasloff passed with us. The Judge having gone to play whist at Mr. O'Gorman's, Harriet and I had him all to ourselves. Of course we discussed the country. He said that he looked in vain for anything fixed. Nothing but the Catholic Church seemed permanent, and he thought that they would have a great future here. So soon as the commotions in Italy were quieted, the reform of the Church would be attended to—the Pope be made the spiritual head only, the Cardinals chosen from every nation and every department, and every ecclesiastical minutia carefully inspected. We said that we would be only too happy to have unity restored to Christendom. . . .

I, for one, would much rather belong to the Catholic than to our Church, because the former is really an organization that has some hold upon its followers. The Episcopal Church in this country has none. Our clergy are men of light passions and manners, as *ourselves*, and only in this respect resemble St. Peter. They are no better than most of their congregation, and being dependent upon their flock for their sustenance and for that of their wives and generally numerous families, they give soft words and prophecy—deceit! Few of us have much respect for them. The life of the Catholic priest, on the contrary, is one of *self-denial*. They do not in this country, at least, live softly, and if scandals sometimes arise, it is the exception, for which, as they are not allowed to *marry*, there is the more excuse. In the dogmas of the Church, however, there are many things with which I cannot comply. Neither could I allow my baptism to be void and confess myself in error. I do believe in all that is necessary for salvation.

Mr. Raasloff likewise lamented that our American families had not kept up their prestige. They might indeed have done like the legitimists of France and would have been, however poor, a power which would have had some control in society, but they have all bowed to Mammon and have married with rich, unscrupulous nobodys, until their nobility or any title to consideration which their name might give them is an imaginary distinction altogether. A Livingston, a Schuyler, a Stuyvesant would do just as low and unscrupulous actions as the hod-carriers of yesterday, and their families would still receive him if he is successful and rich. We certainly deserve punishment. "When the salt has lost its savor, wherewith shall it be salted?"

Mr. Savage is upstairs, talking over the Irish Brigade. Meagher is evidently double-faced. On Tuesday last, he said nothing would induce him to be a brigadier; on Saturday last, he begged Mr. Savage to push the matter with some influential men in Washington. In the carriage, I saw him exchange a very equivocal glance with his wife when the dear, *innocent*, frank Judge told him his mind upon the subject and dissuaded him absolutely from accepting such a responsibility. "No, Lizzy," said he, "no, I certainly will not. You may look as cross as you please." Then, turning to Charles, he said, "You have no objec-tion, I suppose, to my being colonel of the 5th, have you Judge?" I was afraid that Charles, with equal frankness, would have said, "I don't think you have sufficient military knowl-edge!"...

Saturday, November 16, 1861

On the 9th we have at last gained a great victory and our troops are in the heart of the cotton district of South Caro-lina[120]—that pestilential little state! The poor fellows are feast-ing on sweet potatoes and corn and secession bacon and think of sending cotton forward, fifty bales being on their own little farm which their valor has conquered on Port Royal Island.

---

[120] The Union navy which blockaded the Southern coast was engaged in the fall of 1861 in amphibian operations with the army to reduce, one by one, the Albemarle Sound, North Carolina ports; Hilton Head and Port Royal in South Carolina; Fort Pulaski, near Savannah; and then Savannah and Wilmington. The Port Royal victory was November 7, 1861.

Union camps are forming on the Carolina line, and I feel as if the rebellion is now almost conquered. When that is subdued, we shall have to subdue the enormous, corrupt political mass at the North.

I see that the Union Committee have nominated William B. Astor[121] for Mayor. I hope he may accept, as he is the richest man in the city and therefore the most interested in having its government well and economically carried on. I should think it would be his interest to do so.

This week we passed very pleasantly. Harriet Whetten has been staying here, and Mr. Raasloff came in two or three times unexpectedly to dine. He is always agreeable. One evening we had quite a reunion. Mrs. Phelps and Miss Lee came in. Miss Lee is natural and very clever; I should like to know her better. Mrs. Phelps, a South-American by birth, a warm-hearted, timid, indolent, romantic, yet very judicial woman, a grandmother at 37 doting upon babies and the country, is the wife of one of the richest of our city merchants—a strong, sensible, practical, public-spirited man who has just been chosen assemblyman, a triumph for respectability!

Harriet Whetten is seized with the desire of devoting herself and has done nothing but talk of going as hospital nurse since last spring. On Monday, she's going to Washington to see Miss Dix,[122] who is the general directress of the hospitals, a deaf and despotic maiden lady of uncertain age. Harriet's ideas I

---

121 William B. Astor was educated at Heidelburg and Gottingen and became a partner in the firm of John Jacob Astor & Son in 1815. On his father's death in 1848, William inherited the bulk of his father's $20 million fortune and was the richest man in America. He invested heavily in New York real estate. One of his many philanthropic enterprises was the construction of the Astor library in New York City.

122 In June of 1861, 59-year-old Miss Dorothea L. Dix of Massachusetts, well known for her philanthropic efforts on behalf of the insane, the impoverished, and the imprisoned, was appointed U.S. Superintendent of Women Nurses. The majority of the thousands of applicants who appealed to Miss Dix for the opportunity to serve were rejected, for she considered all persons under 30, or possessing an attractive waistline or a pretty face, to be disqualified.

think are far too impractical. She cannot sit up all night; nor is she strong enough to *lift;* nor does she wish to live in the hospital. So I think she had better stay here and do what she may. I don't believe in dilettante nursing. If I were [one of] the *boys,* I should not want a lady about my sickbed unless she were some motherly person with a snowy-white cap and ample shape. Harriet will never be a motherly-looking person, whatever age she may attain. Her feelings are so very young that she will never know the comfortable feeling of being middle-aged or old. Ten years ago, I felt older than she does now. I think she makes a mistake. Were she more subdued, she would please more lastingly men of suitable age. I love her dearly, for she has very noble qualities. She is generous, affectionate, intelligent, and high-minded, but she would please my taste better if she were less cordial with all. . . .

Poor Colonel Corcoran is kept a close prisoner, reserved for retaliation by the rebels should the officers of the Privateer *Petrel* be executed as was threatened. It is a great compliment to his bravery to give him this sad preeminence.

November 17, 1861

Slidell and Mason have been arrested on the high seas in an English vessel by Commodore Wilkes. [They] soon will be safe in a Northern fortress and the government in possession of the secrets of the Confederates. Providence seems to favor our cause, for everything now seems to succeed. This morning Mr. Swinton,[123] the editor of the *Times,* came to search up in the library cases in point. At first it was feared that England might growl, but there are so many precedents of her own that she will not dare to have the assurance to do so.

---

[123] John Swinton emigrated from Scotland to Canada first in 1843, but by 1856 he had crossed the border, was managing editor of the *Lawrence Republican,* and was in the thick of the "Bleeding Kansas" controversy. Between 1860 and 1870, Swinton was editor of *The New York Times,* and from 1875 to 1883, of the New York *Sun.*

Mrs. Daly speaks here of the famous Trent *affair, about which a good deal more is to be said in the diary. Judge Daly was moved to write a legal opinion on this matter, which was sent on to Secretary Seward in Washington and was later published and distributed by the Judge.*

The facts of the case are well known. James M. Mason, former Senator from Virginia, and John Slidell, former Louisiana Senator, were named commissioners to London and Paris respectively by the Confederacy. They sailed from the Spanish port of Havana, Cuba, aboard a British merchant ship, the Trent, *a mail packet, on November 7, 1861. The next day, their ship was stopped by the Union ship* San Jacinto, *under the command of Captain Charles Wilkes. Wilkes arrested the commissioners and their secretaries and removed them to Boston Harbor, where they were imprisoned in Fort Warren.*

Wilkes was innocent of the implications of his action, as were the vast majority of Northerners. Actually, this was tantamount to an act of piracy on the high seas, and such issues as impressment of persons as contraband of war, the right of search of a neutral vessel, and interference with the delivery of mail by a neutral nation were involved. Britain was outraged by this high-handed act, and active preparations for war with the Union were made.

In America, there was great rejoicing over the Trent *affair. The majority of Northerners could not appreciate the fine points of international law, and thought that Wilkes had outfoxed the pro-Southern British and had captured important prisoners of war. The House of Representatives voted that a gold medal be struck in honor of Wilkes and he was feted and celebrated wherever he went. The South rejoiced because they realized what a colossal blunder had been made, and hoped that the incident would drive the British into the war.*

Henry Adams, sage Minister of the Union to Britain, was appalled by the development. Fortunately, the British government did not desire war, particularly at a time when Louis Napoleon's next action defied prediction. Unpopular though the action was in the North, the Federal government issued

*an apology and an explanation that Wilkes' action was un-
authorized. The Confederate envoys were released and allowed
to continue their journey in late January 1862, and the British
forgave the blunder.*

Charles is thinking over a speech which he is expected to
make tomorrow on presenting a stand of colors to the 69th
New York volunteers, the first Regiment of the Irish Brigade.
I shall go and see the ceremony.

November 18, 1861

Spent all the morning at the Archbishop's residence[124]
waiting for the Regiment to arrive. Poor Charles, who had to
speak, was tired out. Indeed, it was enough to dampen anyone's
enthusiasm. The wind, too, was in such a direction that it carried his voice away from us. What I heard sounded well. He
had to speak first. Dear John Savage was there and aided us
(Mrs. Foster, Miss Lee, and myself) in getting a good place.
I saw the Vicar-General, Father Star, the Archbishop of Halifax,[125] Miss Lane, Mrs. Roosevelt,[126] and a number of prominent *Catholic* ladies. The Avenue was thronged and altogether
it was a very fine sight, the Regiment a fine body of men.

I do not think, from what I hear, that Meagher particularly
enjoyed hearing the Judge compliment Corcoran so highly just
at this moment, for should he regain his freedom, he [Corcoran]
would be entitled to the brigadiership. . . .

---

[124] Residence of John Hughes, first Roman Catholic Archbishop of New
York. Judge Daly helped to raise the funds with which the then Bishop
Hughes constructed St. Patrick's Cathedral and its attendant buildings in
the 1850's.

[125] Thomas Louis Connolly, second Archbishop of Halifax, consecrated
in 1859 and died in 1876.

[126] Probably the wife of James I. Roosevelt (1795–1875), justice of the
Supreme Court of the State of New York (1851–59). He was appointed
U.S. District Attorney for southern New York by President Buchanan and
served in 1860 and 1861. From 1841 to 1843 he had been U. S. Representative from New York.

November 24, 1861

. . . . .

Last evening we were enlivened by a visit from Arabella and Frank Barlow, now Lieutenant Colonel of the 61st. Arabella is either going to have a baby or another abscess like the one she had four years ago, she looked so large. In the face she looked very well. Matrimony agrees with her better than it does with her young husband. It sounded to me strangely and disrespectfully to hear him call her "Belle." She looks so much older (as she is full ten, if not twelve, years) that the woman who opened the door told us there was a young soldier and his mother in the parlor. She [Mrs. Barlow] tried to speak depreciatingly of the fate of a soldier's wife, but I know that in her heart it is just the thing she would choose and has, no doubt, had much to do in urging Frank to return. She was more subdued than usual last evening, but there is always a want of refinement about her, even in the very motion of her hand in taking a cup of tea and in the tones of her voice. She is off to Washington on Monday for the winter. I wonder whether she would not rather be there as Miss Griffith. There is such a field for intriguing, clever women in Washington! These Western politicians might be easily imposed on by Eastern *beauty* and *talent* and *savoir faire*. Arabella says that women rule everything and can get anything—that Emory was indebted to his wife (a pretty little woman who went crying and coaxing to the President and begged him to reinstate him despite his *two* resignations[127]). Charles presented Barlow with his own pet book upon tactics because the young Lieutenant Colonel could not, he said, procure a copy. I hope he will appreciate the sacri-

[127] Probably William H. Emory (1811–1887), who was General Kearny's chief of staff during the Mexican War. As a brevet major he was stationed in Kansas from 1854 to 1858, moved to Utah, and resigned from the U.S. Army on May 9, 1861. He was immediately reappointed lieutenant colonel, and served with distinction until his retirement with the rank of brigadier general in 1876.

fice, for to give away a book of any kind is the greatest self-sacrifice you could impose upon him [the Judge].

After they left, Judge Brady came in and we had a little talk about Kate. If they should like each other, it would be very pleasant for us, but I dare not take any part in bringing it about. It is too great a responsibility.

Charles has received at last a letter, and a most unsatisfactory one, from General Shields. He would come on if the government would make him a major general in the regular army. I should think he might, and his country owes him little thanks for his patriotism. He is probably married to Miss Cahil; *Vivian* has beguiled old Merlin! I do not see how he can expect to be promoted so high before he has even offered his services to the government.[128] He had better stay in California and take care of his health and his girl-wife. We can do without him now. A few months ago, and he could have done his adopted country good service. I don't like his letter. It is disingenuous and savors more of the politician than of the soldier.

There seems little news. General Dix is quietly clearing Maryland and the neighboring counties of Virginia. If the jealous European monarchies will let us alone, we shall not be very long in settling our quarrels, and what then? God only knows. With an army of 600,000 men what may not some ambitious general be tempted to try? The government could not have been more corrupt than under Buchanan, however.

November 25, 1861

Paid a visit to Mrs. Lieber and encountered the Doctor.[129] He told me that he had always said and wished that it

---

[128] General Shields was made a brigadier general of Union volunteers on August 19, 1861. He had offered his services to the Union on the outbreak of the war.

[129] Berlin-born Francis Lieber (1800–1875) fought with Napoleon in 1815, earned his Ph.D. degree at Jena in 1820, and fought with the Greeks in 1822. He migrated to the United States in 1827 and edited the *Encyclopedia*

might be published as history that the causes of this war were first Satanic Pride and Whiskey. Whilst living at Columbia, he said he noticed that when the legislature of South Carolina was in session there was a constant stream of men, like a body of ants, down the courthouse steps to the different drinking houses. And at election time, certain friends of the principal candidates would have what some used to call pews where they would keep men in a constant state of intoxication, sometimes for three days, and then take them up tipsy to the polls to drop in their vote. . . .

November 27, 1861

Had a visit yesterday from Mr. Henry Tuckerman,[130] a man I most thoroughly esteem. He seems so good and so intelligent, there is no *beauish* nonsense about him. He is going to bring Mr. Anthony Trollope,[131] the novelist, who is now in the country here some evening. He wants him to get some sensible view of the state of things in America, and thinks Charles the most able to indoctrinate him with good Union principles. We talked gossip and literature.

December 1, 1861

The weather being unfavorable, we did not go to the lunch at Mrs. O'Conor's given in honor of Miss Lane.[132] Charles said a very clever thing on the subject. James T. [Brady] was bantering him because he asked what kind of entertainment it

---

Americana from 1829 to 1833. From 1835 to 1855 he was a professor of history at the University of South Carolina, and from 1857 until his death he was at Columbia University.

130 An American critic, essayist, and poet.

131 Trollope became an ardent Union supporter after his 1862 visit to the United States, and helped influence British opinion toward the Northern viewpoint.

132 Doubtless Miss Harriet Lane, niece of James Buchanan and his official White House hostess during his Presidency.

was to be. "Why," said J.T., "don't you know, it is a breakfast at midday given in honor of Miss Lane and that is all that
can be specifically said about it. Can you say anything more
than that?" "Yes, I think so," said Charles. "Well, what can
you say?" "That it will be a *Miss Laneous* collection."

These two men, though they see each other so seldom, are
excellent good friends. It is a great pity that James T. could
not lead a more regular life and replenish his gifted mind from
time to time by a little study. What a great man he would be,
did he think more and to his great eloquence add deep, acute
thought and observation. His orations would then live, but now
they will perish with the orator as their chief charm is in the
manner and grace with which they are spoken. As they have
little variety, his speeches will give those who may ever read
them collectively a very inadequate idea of the great cleverness
of their author. Judge Brady has little of his brother's genius,[133]
but all the common sense, judgment, and excellence of character of both. He has, besides, a very clear mind, great imitative
powers, and is very capable in conversation, witty and clever
at repartee.

December 5, 1861

Heard direct from Colonel Corcoran, and the Judge is
going to Washington to try and induce the government to consent to an exchange of prisoners.

This morning I had a very pleasant visit from the Catholic
Archbishop of Halifax and Father Hecker.[134] I had just been
writing to Father O'Reilly, and not having seen him [Hecker]
for two years, in the dim light of the parlour I mistook him and

---

[133] Mrs. Daly refers here to John R. Brady, Judge Brady's younger
brother. See *Personalities in the Diary*, page xv, James Topham Brady.

[134] Father Isaac Thomas Hecker, a convert to Roman Catholicism,
founded the Paulist Fathers, and served as the Order's superior from 1858
to 1888. He was also founder of the *Catholic World*, the *Young Catholic*,
and the Catholic Publication Society.

called him Father O'Reilly. We had a talk upon the Church and the country. His Reverence the Archbishop seemed to think that we could never subdue the South and asked what inducement we could offer to them. I answered that no doubt they would be received on the old terms, but said he, "Both parties have incurred great debts. Will you pay one and *repudiate* the other? How can that be done?" His Reverence seemed to think that we should be responsible for both. I answered that we, the U.S., thought that if any of the old governments of Europe had been so rash as to trust the rebellious states without the sanction of the United States government, it seemed to me only fair that they should lose, just as though we should lose what we had given to favor the Irish rebellion. "But," said he, "what will you do with such a number of traitors, as you call them? Execute them?" "No," I said laughingly, "not all, only the arch-traitors. The rest we will exile to Europe, and a great many to England, where those misguided slaveholders will learn how dreadful a crime it is to hold one's fellow creatures in bondage, where the English, who teach abolitionism so eloquently, may indoctrinate them." It would be a good idea to send their slaves there to be taken care of by the Duchess of Sutherland and other friends of Mrs. [Harriet Beecher] Stowe.

Father Hecker proposes to send me some sermons to read. I agree with him that the Roman Catholic Church organization is the only one that can succeed in America, overrun as the country is by foreigners of that persuasion, and the more we strengthen Her hand and purify Her teachings, the better for us. I wish I had been born a Catholic.

December 10, 1861

The Judge left on Saturday for Washington and I for Staten Island to pass Sunday with Harriet Whetten, but I was soon tired and wished myself back in my own bedroom. The people were all strange, and I felt melancholy. Besides, the mir-

ror in my room was bad, and whenever I looked in it, I looked
so old and ugly that I felt distressed. I find, on my return to
my own [mirror] that I am just the same person that I thought
myself before I left home. I do not suppose that Charles will
be at home before the end of the week. I wish I could have gone
with him to have seen the military pomp. I do not think that
he will feel inclined to make a second visit.

December 19, 1861

Charles returned yesterday and is full of anecdotes of
the celebrities of Washington. Blenker gave him a review by
moonlight of his brigade and sent me many kind remembrances.
It must have been a beautiful sight—their fine band and their
bayonets glittering in the moonlight. Lincoln had a cabinet
council called especially for their benefit and Mr. O'Gorman
and himself spoke at the benefit, and some home-truths. Besides,
he [the Judge] has been asked to write an article in the shape
of a letter to Senator Ira Harris [Republican, New York] on
privateering which is to be published and read. If he were in
Washington he would be very useful, having such a just and
impartial mind and the happy faculty of expressing himself
clearly. He was very much feted at Washington. Evidently
Chase,[135] he says, is the greatest man in the administration, and
a very great man, he thinks.

Phil has almost succeeded, I fear, in getting a commission as
lieutenant in the regular army and a staff appointment. He'll
make a splendid figure, but it makes my heart ache to think of
it. Poor Father cannot hear it spoken of without an involuntary

---

[135] Lincoln's Secretary of the Treasury, Salmon P. Chase, became a leader
of the antislavery movement soon after he finished his studies at Dartmouth
and was admitted to the bar. He was an organizer of the Liberty party in
1841, a founder of the Free-soil party in 1848, a United States Senator from
1849 to 1855, and the Republican Governor of Ohio from 1855 to 1860. In
1864, he resigned from Lincoln's cabinet because of conflict with Seward,
and was appointed Chief Justice of the United States in December, 1864.
As Chief Justice, he upheld most of the Republican party's reconstruction
policies.

shudder, although he tries to look brave about it. David is crazy to go likewise, especially now that General Shields has accepted the brigadiership. Perhaps I have done the dear General an injustice, and perhaps he is not even married, so I shall invite him here as usual.

Charles says that there was a deputation from Indians in the South in Washington who came to see for themselves whether Uncle Sam was dead, as the Southern Confederacy wished them to believe. They were amazingly impressed with the display, and particularly with the review of Blenker's Brigade which they witnessed. One of them, getting very excited, struck Charles on the shoulder, crying "My side, my side," meaning that he was for the Union.

Lincoln is mentally what he is physically, long and loose in the joints. He cannot gather himself up easily for an effort, but all agree [he] is a conscientious, honest fellow, most unfit for his high position, not realizing the peril of the country, content to be President and have Mrs. Lincoln dress herself up and hold levees. Mrs. Lincoln behaves in the most undignified manner possible, associating with Wyckoff and Sickles, with whom no lady would deign to speak; but she seems to be easily flattered. She is not a young woman by any means, but dresses like one and rather bullies her husband, which they say accounts for his meekness. The people in Springfield say that she was often heard crying from her doorstep: "Abraham, Abraham, we want a bushel of potatoes."

December 20, 1861

Went this morning with the Judge to see Colonel Mulligan[136] and his wife, of the courageous defenders of Lexington,

---

[136] James A. Mulligan organized and served as colonel of the 23rd Illinois Regiment, another "Irish Brigade," and assisted in the defense of Lexington, Missouri, from July to September 1861. Fatally wounded in the battle of Winchester on July 25, 1864, he was reported to have said, "Lay me down and save the flag!" when his men tried to carry him off the field of battle.

and liked them both exceedingly. She, although a plain woman, evidently not much used to society, had most easy and dignified, simple and ladylike manners, and did credit to the sisters in the convent at Chicago where she was educated in her good English. He is a tall, fine-looking man and gives a good hearty shake of the hand. They had just come from Washington, where Mrs. Mulligan was shocked by the bad manners of the greatest lady of the land. She says that Mrs. Lincoln was preposterously attired, and says "yes *ma'am*," and "no *ma'am*" like a servant-woman, and has, as she expressed herself, no natural manners.

This is the last evening of the Union Fair for the poor of the city. So many of my friends have tables there that I sent what little I had to give but did not go myself. I was afraid, having no money to spend uselessly. Besides, as they have determined to distribute it all themselves, I did not choose to give much, as the regular paupers will get the greater part of it probably.

Charles seems to have been greatly impressed by Chase, whom he thinks a very great man. The rest of the Cabinet struck him as utterly inefficient, good, respectable, plain citizens, fitted for nothing but a very private station. To do Lincoln justice, they are not rowdies.

I heard a good story of Mrs. Lincoln yesterday. It seems that her husband was in the habit of staying out rather late at political and social meetings and sometimes came home rather mellow. She used to lock him out and call from the windows, "You can't come in *now*; it is of no use, you can't come in." On one occasion last autumn he came home very late indeed, and Mrs. Lincoln called angrily from the window: "You shall not come in at this hour." "My dear," said he, "come down, do. I have something to tell you." "I don't believe it," was the conjugal answer. "I have, dear, indeed," pleaded poor Lincoln, "I have something astonishing to tell you. I have been nominated

President." "Pshaw," answered his wife, "now I know you're drunk, and you shall not come in this night," and so shut down the window and cut short the colloquy.

It is yet very doubtful whether we shall have war with England or not. I feel that we shall not. She has too much at stake.

December 22, 1861

Went last night to hear Colonel Mulligan speak before the 69th Regiment and give his recollections of the siege of Lexington,[137] and never have I heard anything more thrilling. He described first their nine days' march to the city, and then the news came that ten thousand men were advancing towards them; their moonlight labor entrenching themselves; the pickets driven in early in the morning; their attack; their repulse from the hill to the bridge, across the bridge, and then their return to Lexington to breakfast; how they worked all day and night upon their earthworks; the approach of the enemy by the cemetery; the dead below, above the sod; the repulse of the enemy after six hours of fighting; their retreat three miles back, and they thought them beaten. But again, after twenty-four hours they returned; batteries from here, there, before, behind, and a storm of shot and shell burst over and into the works. Colonel Mulligan then told how, in the bright, mellow moonlight, he went out to view the lines and found under a tree six men lying one above the other, not *sleeping*. He wiped the blood and dew from their faces, composed their poor, shattered limbs, and laid them, grim, ghastly, and maimed as they were, under the ramparts. And there, said he, they shall stand at the last day, men who have done their duty.

---

[137] After crushing Lyons at Wilson's Creek, the Confederates advanced on Lexington, Missouri, under General Price. Frémont was unable to reinforce Colonel Mulligan, who was in charge of the Lexington garrison of 3,000 troops. The rebel forces increased to 28,000, encircled Lexington, and cut off the water supply. On September 20, using movable breastworks to advance, they finally compelled Mulligan to surrender.

December 31, 1861

The Judge has just finished his letter to Senator Harris about the privateersmen, entitled, "Are the Privateersmen Pirates?"[138] and it seems to meet with general acceptance. Mr. George Davis of Greenfield, who was here, advises him to publish it in pamphlet form and send it to all the principal men of the country and to Count Gasparin[139] and Mr. Bright[140] and our sympathizers abroad. Captain Kirker insists upon publishing it without expense.

Mr. Barney[141] was here last evening and I read to him Count Gasparin's able letter, as well as the Judge's speech. He came in with Charles, both having been to pay dear old General Scott a visit at the Brevoort House. General Scott sent me a most gallant message and declared that he returned fearing to be caught on the other side and unable to return in the event of a war with England. Napoleon sent his aide-de-camp to inquire of his health daily, and has asked Mrs. Scott often to dine at the Tuileries. Mindful of his [Scott's] attention to him [Louis

---

[138] This concerned the Mason-Slidell incident, and appeared in the public press. Subsequently, his legal judgment on the case was issued in pamphlet form under the title, *Are the Southern Privateersmen Pirates?* and was widely distributed. Daly urged the release of Mason and Slidell from prison, and their freedom to continue to their original destinations; he argued against treating rebel privateers as pirates. Secretary Seward wished the pamphlet to be widely circulated as a means of preparing public opinion for the government's reversal of policy.

[139] Agénor Étienne, Comte de Gasparin (1810–1871) was a French political writer and politician. He wrote *Les Etats-Unis en 1861* and *L'Amerique devant l'Europe* (1862).

[140] John Bright, an English liberal statesman, was a noted orator and a power in the Anti-Corn Law League before his election to Parliament in 1843. His sympathies were strongly with the North in the Civil War, and he was a firm advocate of abolition.

[141] Hiram Barney, Collector of the Port of New York, distinguished himself as a lawyer and affiliated himself with the Free-soil Democrats. Later he switched to the Republican party, but managed to incur the enmity of political boss Thurlow Weed. His appointment by Lincoln to the juiciest political plum the Federal government had to offer in New York was interpreted as an affront to Weed and Seward.

Napoleon] when an exile in America [in 1836], he is a real hero.

General Shields is expected every hour, and I take back all I ever said about him, now that he is really coming on to serve his country in earnest. I hope he will come here as usual.

Mason and Slidell are to be given up. It seems the law of the United States, if not their own law, is on the side of the English. But I wish Seward had stated this fact only and made it both his argument and his apology, expressing his regret that Captain Wilkes, in consideration of private interests, had hazarded public ones so materially. Seward thereby obliged us to thus set two traitors to the government at large in order to prevent a great point for which we have been so long contending from being endangered, namely, the inviolability of neutral vessels. The first part of the letter is very good. I am glad war with England is at least put off for a season.

Phil has just come in to say that he has received a telegraph from General Parke[142] to say that if he [Phil] has his commission he [Parke] would like him to join him at once at Annapolis to go on Burnside's[143] expedition, which is destined for York-

---

[142] John Grubb Parke (1827–1900) helped to determine the northwestern boundary between the United States and Canada prior to the Civil War. In 1861, he saw his first active military service as a brevetted brigadier general. He fought at Roanoke Island and Fort Forest, and in 1862 he was placed in command of the 9th Army Corps. Toward the end of the war, he was made Commander of the Army of the Potomac and participated in the final military engagements. After the war, Parke returned to his surveying activities in the army until his retirement in 1889 as a colonel.

[143] Ambrose Everett Burnside gained national attention by his capture of Roanoke Island early in 1862. Part of his 9th Corps participated in the second battle of Bull Run, and at Antietam he was criticized for poor military tactics. He was relieved of his command of the Army of the Potomac and was assigned to the Department of the Ohio, where he embarrassed the government by the court-martial of Copperhead Clement L. Vallandigham. Late in 1863, he captured Knoxville and was besieged in eastern Tennessee for a month. Again in command of the 9th Corps and with the Army of the Potomac in the Spring of 1864, he designed the Petersburg mine which backfired on the Union forces. General Meade blamed Burnside for the disaster, and Burnside resigned his commission before the end of the war. Thrice elected governor of Rhode Island after the war, Burnside was a U.S. Senator from 1874 until his death in 1881.

town and sails in a few days. May God protect him. I feel that
he does his duty in going, but it is dreadful to have this anxiety.
Dear boy, when I looked at his handsome face I could not but
feel that he was too handsome and too good to make a target
of. This dreadful, unnatural war!

Dr. [George] Potts, who has a son in our army, a brother
and brother-in-law in the Southern, came over this morning to
air his mind and relieve himself by a little converse. He spoke
of the war as a dread delusion sent upon the Southern people as
a scourge. He said that he remembered when in the South that
all spoke of slavery as a terrible evil under which they groaned
and which Christian families deprecated and yearned to be released from. Now, he says, scarcely a generation has passed
away and Stephens,[144] a moderate man, speaks of slavery as the
divine institution. Christian ministers uphold it in their pulpits,
etc. It was cupidity that had brought it upon them. Money was
indeed in the true and impressive words of Scripture the root
of all evil. Were not cotton so valuable, slavery would not be
a divine institution. The Doctor spoke in a very broadminded
and Christian spirit, and I was vexed that the necessity of providing for the household before New Year's Day prevented my
staying to hear it all.

Mrs. Dempsey, the wife of a lieutenant, prisoner at the
South, came this evening to see the Judge about having her husband exchanged. Poor, poor, woman, she looked as though
months of anxious waiting had worn her body and spirit. I am
not heroine enough to wish my love a knight and glory in his
battle cry.

Tomorrow is New Year's Day, 1862. This eventful old year
is nearly gone. May the new be the harbinger of better things.

---

[144] Alexander Hamilton Stephens represented Georgia in the United
States Congress from 1843, walked out with the Georgia delegation when
that state seceded, and was elected vice president of the Confederacy on
February 9, 1861. After the war, he identified with the reconstruction
policies of President Johnson and was elected to Congress in 1866. The
Radical Republicans prevented him from being seated.

We are in the hands of God, and let us take His chastisement humbly, for although afflicted like the children of Israel in Egypt, there is light in our dwellings, although the rest of the land is in darkness. We at the North feel but slightly the inconveniences and witness few of the horrors of war.

Mrs. Leffreys' woman Hannah came today to see us. She has just left Charleston, Kanawha Valley, Virginia, and gave us a terrible account of what the condition of things had been there. For three weeks, she said, everything was kept packed up, fearing that the house would be burned over their heads. Once they fled to the mountains, and the enemy's cavalry came even there and threatened to burn the coal works, but retired without doing so. Then the river rose and inundated the whole valley, the water being as high as the chimney piece in their parlor and people coming in boats over their garden fence. Everything was destroyed when the Federal troops came in the town. Mrs. Leffreys returned ten and twelve times a day to spread the table for the hungry soldiers, and three times a day did they go to take care of the wounded in the hospital where Mrs. Leffreys took a fever, being ill for six weeks. What an eventful life she has led, and what a good, true, noble women she has proved herself in every emergency.

1862

January 4, 1862

General Shields arrived this morning most unexpectedly from California to take his command and finds himself superseded by the crafty Meagher, who has wheedled himself into a brigadiership by making use of General Shields' name and all the Irish influence he could cajole into aiding him. The General, it seems, is married and *not* to Miss Cahil.[1] He won't speak a word to me on the subject. This morning he went to see General Scott, who advised him to go on to Washington at once and report himself.

Phil has received notice to join General Parke, and although he has not as yet received his commission, he leaves tomorrow. May God bring him safely back to us. It makes me shudder and quake to think of the danger into which he goes. . . .

January 6, 1862

The General left this morning. Mr. O'Gorman and Jack Savage spending the evening, or rather the night, with us, for they did not leave until half-past one. I wish he would confess about his marriage. I hope the report that he has married his

---

[1] General Shields married Mary Ann Carr, the daughter of a friend in Armagh, Ireland, late in 1861, and had three children by her.

servant-woman is not correct. He borrowed five hundred dollars of the Judge. I think he seems desperate and will probably scarcely come out of this war. I'm glad my brothers are not with him. Some army officers from Oregon who came on with him came to see him in the evening and they took out the map and planned out the campaign. One lieutenant seemed to me a very able military man and devoted to the General.

A few days ago Mr. Barney and Mr. [George] Harrington, the Assistant Secretary of the Treasury, dined here. They want a meeting called at Tammany Hall[2] of the great Democratic party to act upon the government and, if possible, oblige a retrenchment in the wild extravagance of the army and navy; for the banks refuse to loan any more money and Congress busies itself in doing everything else but what is necessary: namely, provide for regular taxation.

I bade dear Phil good-by today. When Mother kissed him, he said, "Dear mother, don't trouble yourself about me; I was never happier in my life. It is my duty to go." I know the old people, despite this grief, feel very proud of him.

January 8, 1862

Judge Pierrepont[3] stated here this evening that the corruption in Washington was notorious, and [that it] could be proved that Welles[4] gave his brother, a grocer here, $95,000 for what Mr. Moses Grinnell[5] offered to do without expense to the government, namely, buy what ships were needed—a busi-

2 Then located on 14th Street, "to the east of Irving Place." This was the fourth home of this political club, established in 1786.

3 See *Personalities in the Diary*, page xxv.

4 Gideon Welles (1802–1878) served as a Democratic legislator in Connecticut from 1827–35 and then helped to organize the Republican party in 1856. Secretary of the Navy under Lincoln and Johnson (1861–69), he built a fighting force from almost nothing.

5 Moses Grinnell (1803–1877) was the brother of Joseph Grinnell, one of the founders of Fish & Grinnell, the greatest shipping firm of its day. Moses joined the firm in 1825, and from 1839 to 1841 was U.S. Representative from New York, Whig. In addition to other civic posts, he was a commissioner of charities and corrections from 1860 until 1865.

ness which Mr. Grinnell knew something about, but the grocer nothing, of course. What can we do with such rulers?

The Judge wants me to induce the ladies of New York to join in discountenancing calls and entertainments this winter. I don't think that I should have influence enough. In America, the *young* rule; all is subservient to them.

I made my first appearance yesterday at the Council Board of the School of Design for Women. Miss Hamilton,[6] Mrs. Hamilton Fish,[7] Mrs. [Abram Stevens] Hewitt, are of this Council. Mrs. [William A.] Carson was there and told me that she had secured a letter from her father, Mr. Petigru,[8] who would not come north although the only Unionist, they say, in South Carolina. Notwithstanding his sentiments, they have appointed him to codify the laws of state, a great testimony of their respect. I must ask Mrs. Carson to try and send him the Judge's pamphlet.

Mrs. Stanard[9] has proved herself a cold, shallow-hearted woman, notwithstanding the great kindness she has always received among us. She refused to do anything for the Union prisoners, especially for Mrs. [James B.] Ricketts,[10] saying that

---

[6] Miss Mary Hamilton was a granddaughter of Alexander Hamilton, and became the wife of George Lee Schuyler, a noted yachtsman.

[7] Whig governor of New York (1849–50) and U.S. Senator (1851–57), Hamilton Fish was a member of the Union Defense Committee of New York State and a Federal commissioner for the relief of prisoners during the war. He served as Grant's Secretary of State from 1869 to 1877.

[8] James Louis Petigru was the leader of the Union party in South Carolina from 1832 on. While he was a Southern sympathizer, he did not support the Confederate government, and President Lincoln considered appointing him to the U.S. Supreme Court. A lawyer, he remained a staunch Federalist until his death in 1863.

[9] The beautiful and brilliant Mrs. Robert Stanard of Richmond, Virginia, became famous for her "teas," at which she served broiled chicken and hot muffins to vacationing soldiers.

[10] James B. Ricketts (1817–1887) attained the rank of captain in 1852. Wounded and captured in the Battle of Bull Run, he was exchanged six months later. He fought with McDowell at Cedar Mountain as a brigadier general of volunteers, was wounded at Antietam in 1862, fought at Spotsylvania, Wilderness, and Cold Harbor in 1864, and was wounded again at Cedar Creek in 1864. Ricketts retired, a major general, in 1867.

she would do nothing for anyone who had spoken against the Confederate government. All women so fond of admiration are cold-hearted. She could not sacrifice present popularity for anything else in the world. How little men really know of womankind.

January 19, 1862

The Judge's letter is much approved. He is constantly receiving letters of compliment on the subject. They want to call a public meeting to force the government to release Corcoran, but Charles says that it must not be done. It would be bad faith to the Administration, which has promised to do its best. . . .

General Shields turns out to be little more than a politician. He has fraternized entirely with Meagher and endorses him wholesale—calls him an honorable, brave, high-minded man and his best friend and as competent as three-quarters of the briga-dier-generals (a very small compliment to the army generally). What a dreadful thing it is to have to realize that your friend is a politician! How few noble-minded men there are! A major-generalship, I suppose, tempts the General and makes him thus insincere. Pshaw! I never wish to see him, for I shall never again trust him. Mrs. [Richard] Busteed declares that she does not believe he is married, for he has promised to marry women that he would not dare to. So false in one respect, he may be false in others.

January 25, 1862

Received yesterday a letter from the General, a very dispiriting one from Washington. He says that he would pledge his reputation on being able to take Washington, were he prop-erly supported; but I think McClellan probably knows what he is doing, and hopes by cutting off gradually all its resources to oblige the rebel army of the Potomac to surrender. What a glorious day that would be for us! He [Shields] mourns over the place-seeking and want of energy in the government, but at the same time I am afraid the General is somewhat of a politician himself since his wholesale endorsement of Meagher. Perhaps, however, he too has been cajoled by him.

Father O'Reilly answered my letter yesterday; it was a long one and the most beautiful that I have ever received; it was that of a saint. There is something great in that sanctified, religious, virgin life of the true Catholic priest which gives an elevation of character which cannot be reached by any other. It approaches the nearest to the imitation of Christ.

Colonel and Mrs. Ricketts, being released from imprisonment in Richmond, are *starring* it in New York, having parties given for them where Mrs. R. details all the perils and dangers through which they have passed; embellished, perhaps, perhaps not. I do not think it very good taste, but perhaps it is natural to find it very pleasant to be a heroine.

My dear brother! I hope he will return safely. He is always in Father's thoughts. I wish we could hear something from the expedition.

John George Daly, Sir Dominick's son, is married, and wrote me a very pleasant letter congratulating himself and us that war was no longer to be feared between our respective governments. Sir Dominick told the Judge, when here, that his family was a branch of his, the Galway Dalys. A few evenings since, Charles met Colonel Rowan at the club, who knew well the present Earl of Dunsandel, the head of the Daly family of Galway, cousin of Sir Dominick. They had been fellow soldiers together. He describes him as being a great athlete— the best boxer, the best walker, the best rider, the best billiard player, and of great dignity of character. His father had much embarrassed the estate, and this young man, Sir Dennis Daly, had the fortitude and courage, although the eldest son of a peer, to abstain from all expensive amusements. He did not bet nor play, but he was universally respected.

.   .   .   .   .

January 29, 1862

Thanks to God's good providence, Burnside's expedition has arrived after dreadful buffeting by the storms which have been raging ever since he left Fort Monroe at Pamlico Sound.[11] His loss was only two or three vessels and but three lives. So far Phil is safe, but for how long! God will protect him in danger, as in his own home. . . .

Although Seward has been prophesying like Jonah continually, yet thirty days and Nineveh will be destroyed, still the rebel army of the Potomac threatens Washington, and still hopes to take it, whilst our three hundred thousand soldiers lie opposite them, idle and well-fed, with full pay, their families supported by public charity, their officers spending their time in reveling, flirting, and drinking. The old story of Capua[12] may be acted over again. In these days, Washington is the scene of continual gaiety. No one seems to feel the danger in which we stand, or to realize that we are a bankrupt and ruined nation, should this continue longer.

McClellan, they now say, is incapable, and is striving after the Presidency, instigated by his wife. It will not be worth having soon. It seems he found Miss [Mary Ellen] Marcy a difficult conquest, and therefore, I suppose, is all the more deferential to her.

General Shields writes the most mournful letters upon the country. I am comforted to find that although he speaks his piece, he agrees with us about that braggadocio, Meagher.

---

[11] The date of this occurrence was January 13, 1862.

[12] An ancient city of Italy noted for its luxury. The people allied themselves with Hannibal, but the city fell to the Romans and its inhabitants were sold into slavery as a warning to all who meditated revolt.

The Judge came home last night after seeing Pierrepont and Evarts,[13] entirely disheartened. The corruption of every part of the government and the country is so great that he despairs of it altogether. Some hope seems left in Stanton,[14] the new Secretary of War. The paper this evening suggests that the Secretary of the Navy will likewise resign,[15] and be replaced by a man from New York. Should it be Pierrepont, he has, I *believe* and trust, judgment, and is an honest, though a very ambitious, self-seeking man. He is better, however, than Welles.

Hamilton Fish and a Methodist bishop from Ohio have been appointed and left today, commissioners to the South. For my part, if they would consent to yield the border states, the rest of the slave states might go. They would soon revert to us again, in all probability. For what can we do with them if we conquer, or with their black chattels if we free them? I wish I could do something to ease myself of my excitement. We are ruled from beneath. Mediocrity is king, and money our ultimatum, and what can be done with a people who worship these gods? I have been putting some letters in good English for Mr. Peltz which are to be published anonymously. I think they are

[13] William M. Evarts represented the Federal government before the Supreme Court during the war in asserting its right to treat captured vessels as maritime prizes. Evarts was also President Johnson's chief defense counsel in the famous impeachment trial before the Senate of the United States. He served as Johnson's attorney general thereafter, as Secretary of State in the Hayes administration (1877–81) and as a United States Senator from New York from 1885 to 1891.

[14] Late in 1861, a House Committee made public evidence of corruption on a gigantic scale in the War Department, and Lincoln hastily sent the scandal-besmirched Secretary Simon Cameron on a foreign mission. Replacing him was Edwin M. Stanton, a "War Democrat," who took office on January 15, 1862. Ill-mannered, ignorant of military matters, contemptuous toward subordinates, the much-hated Stanton was thorough and systematic and got results. When Lincoln was assassinated, President Johnson kept Stanton on as Secretary of War. Johnson was to regret this, for Stanton plotted with the Radical Republicans against Johnson's reconstruction policies. When the President tried to fire him for his disloyalty, Congress passed the Tenure of Office Act which served as the basis of the impeachment trial of Johnson in 1868.

[15] Gideon Welles did not resign as Secretary of Navy, but remained in that position until the end of President Johnson's administration, 1869.

too sensible to be generally read. I wrote one on my own account this morning to Mrs. McClellan, telling her of the reports about her husband, and urging her to use her influence for great and patriotic purposes. I wonder if it will be read.

February 1, 1862

Attended a reception given by the artists in the studio buildings, Tenth Street.[16] Saw [Sandford R.] Gifford, [Albert] Bierstadt, Ginoux, and [Henry K.] Brown's studios, and had a pleasant chat with Gifford and Bierstadt. Was introduced to young Choate and his bride and to General [Robert] Anderson, who remarked, "I am glad to take your hand, madam," in an old-fashioned, gallant manner—very pleasing. Gifford I like, and were it possible, would like to see more of him.

.   .   .   .   .

Had a letter from Phil, who gives a vivid account of the storm and of the havoc in Burnside's fleet. By this time, I suppose, they have Roanoke Island. He writes in excellent spirits and praises the officers and seems quite contented. Prime[17] is quite devoted to him, always going to visit, and is so kind and considerate towards Mother. He spent last Sunday evening with us. I must ask him some day to dine.

February 5, 1862

Lieutenant Conolly, who has just been exchanged and has been in prison with Colonel Corcoran nearly nine months, came to see the Judge last evening with several other officers

---

[16] Built in 1857 on the north side of East Tenth Street from designs by Richard Morris Hunt, the Tenth Street Studios Building was the first structure erected in New York for the exclusive purpose of providing artists' studios.

[17] Temple Prime (1832–1903) was an intimate friend of the Dalys, active in New York's civic and social affairs.

of the 69th Regiment. So we had some whiskey punch and
some most interesting accounts of his life during that time. He
said that nothing was seen of Meagher after the first charge,
and Colonel Corcoran and himself believed him dead; for
when asked by some kind rebel soldier what he could do for
him, the Colonel said, "Look for poor Meagher's body, and
have it sent through the lines to his wife." How different from
his conduct towards Corcoran! It would seem, from all we
can learn, that Meagher was intoxicated and had just sense
and elation enough to make one rush forward and afterwards
fell from his horse drunk, and was picked up by the troopers,
who he says brought him off the field behind him. So much
for our Irish hero, Thomas Francis Meagher. He has made
bitter enemies in the 69th Regiment.

Colonel Corcoran might have escaped, as he was within the
house and they did not search it. He and seven men, including
Conolly, had gone there and intended to defend themselves to
the last, but one man came up and said, "Colonel, you will not
sacrifice the lives of this brave little band." The Colonel was
moved and said, "Well, do as you like," and went into the
house. But when he found that all the rest, having surrendered,
were leaving him, he came out and cried: "Stop. There is one
man more." They raised a great shout when they found who
he was. He was asked for his sword, but refused to deliver it
to anyone but an officer. The Captain asked then for his belt
and field glasses. "I am ashamed, sir," said he, "that you should
think of asking for my private property. You will have to
take them by force. You are no soldier or gentleman."

Conolly said: "It would break your heart to hear of our
sufferings in Richmond," but in Charleston and Columbus they
were better treated, the *Irish* sentinels always letting them have
information. Had our troops advanced upon Charleston from
Port Royal, he said that they could have taken it without
resistance. There were but 200 men in the city. The officers
of an Irish regiment stationed there had resolved to go over

to the Union cause and Corcoran could have raised a brigade on the spot.

Somewhere about Christmas, Conolly received a letter from his brother in which he told him that he had sent Conolly on his trunk with two pairs of boots, one a coarse pair and one a fine one: "Knowing that your foot troubles you, I have had the heel arranged as you wished on the left boot." Conolly said he knew his foot was all right, so he thought, "Well, there is something else in the heel of that boot." On Christmas eve, three trunks came; one for Corcoran, one for Lieutenant Dempsey, and one for himself. But they had no money to pay for the freight, which was fifteen dollars. At last they managed to get five dollars amongst them and Lieutenant Conolly had his trunk brought in, opened it and took out his boots. He shook first one, then the other. Out of the left heel that so much had been said about, he shook first one twenty dollar gold piece, then another. So he got the other two trunks and then sent for turkeys and whiskey for a Christmas dinner. Corcoran was confined and handcuffed in one solitary cell, Dempsey in another for having sent on letters by private hands to the North. But the officer in command tried to do everything in his power to lessen their misery, and so he let Dempsey's door open into the corridor and Dempsey moved his trunk to Corcoran's door and handed over to him (through the bars) turkey and whiskey and they drank to the health of absent friends. They feasted the prisoners generally.

Conolly mentions a Captain Shriver who, in Columbus, disobeyed orders to oblige them. Instead of shutting them up in solitary cells as commanded, he gave them fine cozy quarters and allowed them what they wanted. Even newspapers reached them. A kind Mrs. O'Reilly sent them excellent dinners. A Mr. Brennan, a German, gave them thirty dollars and his wife sent whiskey and provisions, very good things, the Lieutenant said, the whiskey bottles done up in newspapers. Most of the middle class, he says, are Unionists, and they are kept by fear only to the rebel cause.

Conolly disabused us of any good opinion of Congressman Ely,[18] who, he says, owes a poor fellow to this day $25 who is yet in prison and much want and Ely won't send him the money. Faulkner[19] gave Ely a hundred dollars in gold for the prisoners, which the latter changed into shin plasters before he sent it to them, giving Conolly only a percentage. In Washington, Ely behaved very meanly, promising to take Conolly with him to see the President, but going without him—using his carriage all day and making him pay the eight dollars it cost, although he said his brother has presented him with a fine horse (which made Conolly much provoked) because Ely gave out that he had rescued the Union prisoners and effected the exchange. The story that he distributed five thousand dollars among the soldiers is all bogus. I suppose he thinks that it would help him into Congress again or higher.

February 13, 1862

Several victories at last! Roanoke Island and two thousand prisoners, six gunboats and all the ordnance and munitions of war on the Island, have been won. I trust dear Phil is safe. Fort Henry on the Tennessee River likewise is taken, and our gunboats have run down the river to Florence, Alabama, where the Stars and Stripes were joyously welcomed. This is the best news of all!

Disgusted at last with McClellan's martinet conduct of the war, President Lincoln issued an executive order late in January

---

[18] Alfred Ely (1815–1892) served as a Republican congressman from New York from 1859 to 1863. He was a prisoner of the Confederacy for six months following his capture while witnessing the battle of Bull Run.

[19] Charles James Faulkner (1806–1884) was a U.S. Representative from Virginia from 1851 to 1859, when he became minister to France. In August 1861 he returned to the United States and was detained as a prisoner of state in Fort Warren, Boston, until December 1861, when he was exchanged for Alfred Ely. He then joined the Confederate Army.

of 1862 directing the land and naval forces of the Union to move against the enemy no later than February 22. McClellan had his choice of moving against Manassas in a frontal attack, while protecting Washington, or an insular campaign. While he was making up his mind, good news came from Burnside's expedition, which took Roanoke Island in cooperation with a naval force under Admiral Louis M. Goldsborough, thus enabling the Union to tighten the blockade. In the West, another military and naval expedition commanded by General Grant and Commodore Foote captured Fort Henry on the Tennessee, shortly to be followed by the surrender of Fort Donelson on the Cumberland, opening western and central Tennessee to Union occupation. After so many months of discouragement, these victories lifted the spirits of the North.

The Judge dined yesterday with Mr. Barney, in company with the Prince de Joinville, the Comte de Paris,[20] General Scott, and a number of other prominent men. He thinks the Prince de Joinville a man of much capacity. Charles was called upon to answer some questions in French law, which, as he is well versed in it, he could answer immediately—much, he said, apparently, to the delight of old General Scott. General Stahel was there, and, as we surmised, is of one of the most ancient and distinguished families in all Hungary. He *looks* noble. He has promised to send me his photograph, and would have called today had the Judge not excused him, for which I am the loser. I should have liked to have seen him.

Seward told Mrs. Oakes Smith[21] that the Judge's letter had

20 In 1861, the Comte de Paris, direct descendant in the line of Orleanist pretenders to the throne of France, his brother the Duc de Chartres, and their uncle, the Prince de Joinville, came to America and joined McClellan's army to fight for the Union. The Comte de Paris, who became head of the entire house of Bourbon, wrote a four-volume military *History of the Civil War in America.*

21 Elizabeth Oakes Smith (1806–1893) was an author and lecturer and the wife of Seba Smith (1792–1868), a noted journalist and political satirist. She worked closely with her husband until his death, having taken up a career of her own in journalism after her marriage. In 1842, the Smiths came to New York City from Maine.

decided the action of the Cabinet, so we may now look to see Corcoran, Cogswell, and others back.

What can this be about General Stone?[22] It is too dreadful to believe that he could be another Arnold. McClellan seems to have acted with great sagacity and his delay seems only part of a preconceived plan. General Shields, I am afraid, has destroyed himself. Meagher, like the fox in the fable, has induced him to drop his piece of meal in the Irish Brigade by telling him how much better he would be as a major general, and flattering his vanity. His nomination is still before the Senate. Had he come on earlier, he could have had any position he wanted. So his great prudence, and perhaps his regard for his own interest, has not served him so well, as a little more generous disinterestedness might. He writes very despondingly.

February 18, 1862

> *In February 1862, the Confederate defense line stretched from Cumberland Gap to Columbus. General Grant captured Fort Henry and moved on Fort Donelson on the Cumberland River. His first attack was repulsed, and Commodore Foote's gunboats were badly damaged and beaten off. Grant's force was superior, and as he prepared to launch an all-out attack, General Buckner asked for a truce to discuss terms of surrender. Grant demanded unconditional surrender, and on February 15 Fort Donelson capitulated. Twelve to fifteen thousand prisoners were taken, including Generals Buckner and Bushrod Johnson. John*

---

[22] After the death of the popular "Ned" Baker at Ball's Bluff, Charles Pomeroy Stone was accused by Baker's friends of being a traitor. The Massachusetts Democrat was relieved of his command and thrown into Federal prison for nine months, without a trial, without a shred of evidence to justify the act. When he was released, he was still not able to discover what it was all about, and Lincoln's door was closed to him. Finally exonerated, Stone served with Banks in 1864, but resigned shortly thereafter under the pressure of the same false accusations. From 1870 to 1883, he was a Lieutenant General and Chief of Staff for the Egyptian army, and in 1886 he was chief engineer for the construction of the Statue of Liberty pedestal in New York harbor.

B. Floyd and Gideon J. Pillow turned over their commands to Buckner, so they would not be captured, and escaped.

Fort Donelson taken—fifteen thousand prisoners, including General Albert Johnston,[23] Buckner[24] and Pillow![25] The rebellion is at last beginning to succumb. Good news from Phil, who has had active duty. We see by the papers that he was in command of the naval pickets at Roanoke Island.

On Sunday evening last, we paid some visits. Among others, we saw Mr. [William B.] Astor at home. He has as low an opinion of the Administration as my husband. We freely commented upon the assurance of the wife of a second-rate Illinois lawyer being obliged to choose her company and selecting five hundred élite to entertain at the White House—and then to have the affectation to put on court mourning out of respect to Queen Victoria's recent loss![26] It is too comical; it is too sad to see such extravagance and folly in the White House with the country bankrupt and a civil war raging.

On Saturday last we dined at Mrs. Stout's with Mr. and Mrs. [George Templeton] Strong, Mr. and Mrs. [George] Bancroft,[27] Miss Thayer, and some other gentlemanly nonentities. I had a pleasant enough dinner, but the Judge found it

---

23 Mrs. Daly here confused Albert Sidney Johnston, Commander of the Western Department for the Confederacy, with General Bushrod Johnson, who was in command of Fort Henry when Grant took it.

24 Simon Bolivar Buckner (1823–1914), who surrendered to Grant at Fort Donelson. In August 1862, he was exchanged and became a major general that year and a lieutenant general in 1863. He fought throughout the war; later he became a newspaper editor, and then Governor of Kentucky from 1887 to 1891. In 1896 he was Democratic candidate for the Vice Presidency.

25 Gideon Johnson Pillow (1806–1878) served as a brigadier general in the Mexican War but was a very poor officer and quarreled with Scott. He served as a brigadier general for the Confederacy and was cited for poor tactics and cowardice at Fort Donelson. In 1862 he was relieved of his command.

26 Albert, prince consort of England and husband of Queen Victoria, died in 1861. His last political paper was prepared for the Queen urging that the *Trent* matter be amicably settled. In Britain, Albert was sincerely mourned, and the Queen was inconsolable.

27 See *Personalities in the Diary*, page xiii.

stupid. I should have preferred my quiet dinner at home, I confess. To indemnify himself, the Judge went to the Century Club[28] after leaving me at home. They were all rather stuffy people, although they consider themselves among the intellectuals. American society is only half-civilized. Mrs. Bancroft, for instance, seems to think herself the quintessence of refinement in mind and manner, whilst in reality the *parvenu* shines out everywhere. . . .

One night last week we were invited to an artists' reception on Fifth Avenue. Afterwards we went to supper at Mrs. [Charles] Gould's[29] to meet some artists. Among the ladies were Mrs. Henry Field,[30] the notorious Mrs. H. Delusy in the Duchess de Praslin tragedy. She is a wonderfully clever woman and a fine artist, and I looked in her face and wondered if all the poor Duchess had written in her diary were true. Was that woman, who seemed so earnest to bring up the girls in the Academy of Design for Women now under her charge in the strictest principles of truth and morality, was she the ambitious, lewd woman there represented? Her face is a very hard one, and whilst I talked with her, I know she felt I did not like her despite my politeness.

Little Miss Gould provoked me by her abolition. She would hear of no peace that was not a right peace, no compromise

---

[28] Judge Daly was a director of the Century Club, then located on 15th Street, between Fourth Avenue and Irving Place. Originally devoted to art and called The Sketch Club, the association was reorganized in 1847 with a much broader range of interests. On March 7, 1857, it became incorporated as the Century Club, "composed of authors, artists, and amateurs of letters and the fine arts, residents of the city of New York and vicinity . . . [for] the cultivation of a taste for letters and the arts and social enjoyment."

[29] Charles Gould, a banker, had a business address of 58 Wall Street and resided at 5 East 26th Street.

[30] Henry M. Field, brother of Cyrus W. and David Dudley Field, married Laure Desportes in May 1851. Mrs. Field had been innocently involved in the widely publicized Choiseul-Praslin murder case in France (a story told by Rachel Field in *All This and Heaven Too.*) A Williams College graduate, Henry Field trained for the ministry and received a pastorate in St. Louis, Missouri, in 1842. He traveled extensively in Europe, became owner and editor of the *Evangelist* in New York.

with slavery. She ought to have had her ears boxed for intruding her crude eighteen-year-old ideas upon people older and wiser than herself and misleading some poor boy by her influence, probably, for I believe that every woman can do that with one man in her lifetime at least. We do not sufficiently realize how great our influence is.

Agassiz[31] is going to lecture here and we must go and hear him.

February 23, 1862

We had a glorious celebration of Washington's birthday yesterday. The Judge was invited by the Mayor and city authorities to give the oration, but being engaged in General Term and having only two days' notice, he declined. This was much against my will, for he would have done it well and the occasion was so great a one and the audience such a fine one. The Judge induced Mr. Bancroft to give the address and Bancroft acquitted himself admirably. He spoke of Jefferson Davis doing public penance in his robes of office at Richmond for his traitorous rebellion on the day, for he was to have been inaugurated on the twenty-second, and alluded to the intervention of the alien governments of Europe in Mexico and their intention of placing a monarch in that country. He said, "What mean they by this, braving us and bringing democracy and royalty in collision? Are they not afraid? Do they not fear to stir the mysterious sympathies of the millions?" We illuminated the house in the evening in remembrance of Washington and in honor of the recent victories.

---

[31] Jean Louis Rodolphe Agassiz (1807–1873), the great naturalist and biologist, came to the United States from Switzerland in 1846. Between that year and 1870 he delivered eight series of Lowell Institute Lectures, and was professor of zoology and of geology at Harvard until his death. He founded the predecessor of Radcliffe College in 1855, and several other schools and museums.

Napoleon III entertained visions of imperial grandeur when the American Civil War broke out. He saw an opportunity to restore something equivalent to the New World empire his uncle had sold to finance his European campaigns. Had Britain been willing to join him, as she did in the Crimea, there is little question that France would have intervened on behalf of the Confederacy.

An opportunity presented itself when bankrupt Mexico declared a two-year moratorium on its foreign debts on July 17, 1861. Britain, France, and Spain were the main creditors involved, and at the Convention of London in October of 1861 it was decided to jointly intervene in Mexico until the debts were paid. Britain and Spain were interested only in clearing up the debts, however, and by April 1862 they had made their peace with the Mexican government.

Napoleon III did succeed in establishing an imperial government in Mexico in 1863, and the Archduke Maximilian of Austria accepted his offer of the Mexican throne on April 10, 1864.

Nashville is ours and Tennessee once more is in the Union, so there are but the Southern Gulf states left, which will soon give up likewise. Thank God for His protecting providence! We have heard from Phil since the taking of Roanoke Island, and he is unhurt. He writes that it was a strange feeling to hear the whistling of the balls about his ears and see the men ducking their heads and lying behind the logs as the balls came down the road. I think from his letter that he must have behaved bravely.

February 26, 1862

Heard Agassiz lecture on Monday. How clear, simple, comprehensive! He evidently spoke from a full mind. His voice is sweet and sympathetic. He speaks a little brokenly and draws what he wishes to represent in outline on the blackboard.

Last night I went to the French Theater and saw a lively little comedy founded upon Sterne's story, *A Question of Delicacy*. It was very well acted, and I found that I could understand perfectly well; I wish I could go oftener. Our quartette concerts have begun again. As our purse is rather low, I would rather have postponed them until next winter. The first one was at Mr. [William] Scharfenberg's and very agreeable; the music was beautifully chosen. . . .

March 3, 1682

From the papers this morning, I see that General Shields is appointed to succeed General Lander[32] in Western Virginia. I am glad that he will be able to do something to distinguish himself before the war is over. General Scott told the Judge yesterday that he was sure by May it will all be over; they must submit. Last evening, Mr. Prime was here and we had a very pleasant talk. I could not help but wish that I could have taken shorthand notes. Charles talked so well. He has evidently been thinking very deeply over the present state of things, and the possible ameliorations that might be made in the Constitution. Charles and Mr. Prime differ somewhat. Charles proposed that the members of Congress and the members of the state legislatures should receive no emolument, but that it should be merely an honorary office; that all offices excepting these and the cabinet, which form the advisory council of the President, should be held during good conduct, not subject to such rotation in office as now; that slavery should, by the action of Congress, be confined to those states where it now exists and measures taken to eradicate it gradually, either by declaring all born after a certain fixed time free or else making the slaves serfs, attaching them to the soil, so that this selling [separation]

---

[32] Frederick W. Lander had died of pneumonia early in 1862. A brigadier general, he had been an aide to McClellan, was wounded at Edward's Ferry, and distinguished himself at Hancock.

of families should be avoided and no encouragement be given to the slave trade, African or American.

March 11, 1862

The Union flag waves over Manassas; the scandal of Bull's Run is effaced. McClellan is to be superseded. He has not shown sufficient audacity, but has allowed the Confederates to escape. We had a great fright on Sunday on hearing of the attack of the *Merrimac* on our vessels. Now they are fretting lest she should get out again, despite the *Monitor*, but I have great faith that God means the utter overthrow of the Confederates, for it was the revolt of the few, the gentlemen in broadcloth, against the good of the many in frieze.

Although the South expected early assistance from England and France in breaking the Northern blockade, such help never came. When the Confederates discovered that foreign ships were not willing to risk involvement to obtain cotton, the blockade became more than irksome. What little naval strength the South possessed was rapidly being dissipated by the warships of the North. Meantime, they were in desperate need of supplies from the outside.

When the North evacuated the Norfolk navy yard, the Merrimac, *a forty-gun steam frigate, was fired and sunk so that it would not fall into Confederate hands. But the Confederates raised the hulk, remodeled it into a low-lying ironclad with ten guns and a cast-iron ram, renamed it the* Virginia, *and sent it against the blockading squadron at Hampton Roads in March of 1862. There on March 8, the* Merrimac *(as it is almost invariably called) sank the Union man-of-war the* Cumberland, *forced the* Congress *to surrender, and planned to go after the warship* Minnesota *the next morning.*

While the South was remaking the Merrimac, *the North was busy producing an ironclad in the Brooklyn Navy Yard according to a design by John Ericsson, a Swedish engineer.*

Called the Monitor, *this craft had a flat, heavily armored deck surmounted by a revolving iron turret in which two powerful guns were mounted. Much smaller than the* Merrimac, *the* Monitor *was likened to a cheese-box on a raft or a tin can on a shingle.*

By an odd coincidence, the Monitor *arrived at Hampton Roads on the night of March 8 and was able to engage the* Merrimac *the next morning when the Southern ship set about finishing off the blockading Union naval fleet. Neither ship was able to sink or seriously damage the other, but the* Merrimac *withdrew after a time and never fought again. The importance of the contest lies in the obsolescence of wooden ships in naval warfare. Significant to the war was the fact that the North could manufacture all the armored ships it wished, whereas the South was never able to put another* Merrimac *into service.*

[Charles] Mackay, the [Scottish] poet, is in town and called here yesterday.

We have just received a letter from Phil from Roanoke Island. He writes bravely and seems delighted with his life and with General Parke. The General himself has written to Washington about Phil's commission.

March 22, 1862

Phil has distinguished himself at the battle of Neuberne, North Carolina, and is mentioned honorably in the papers, which I am so delighted at. Father is as proud of him as possible. Baron Gerolt, who is staying here, having arrived last evening, tells us that Secretary Seward has promised to speak to the Secretary of War about his [Phil's] commission. He was told that the subject was under consideration and not forgotten, that anything that Judge Daly wished should be granted, the government feeling under much obligation to him for his assistance concerning the question about the Southern privateers, and likewise, I imagine, about the Trent question, which Seward decided almost in the very words Charles used when he told him in Washington that Slidell and Mason would have to be given up. Charles was the first to recognize the law which, declaring captives on the sea different from those on the land, the sea being the property of all nations, decided that all vessels should be taken and judged by a prize court and not by the captain of the victorious vessel. Charles has received a very flattering letter from Sir Richard Kindersley, a Vice-Chancellor of England, which Baron Gerolt asked me to copy for him, as he wished to show it to Mr. Seward.

.   .   .   .   .

General Shields has the advance of General Banks'[33] division and has fifteen thousand men, the finest troops in the army. I hear he is delighted. I wrote to him to mention the Judge's name as a candidate for the judgeship of the Supreme Court, but he had left Washington, I am sorry to say, before my letter had reached him.

April 1, 1862

General Shields has been wounded, but has achieved a victory—a double one; one over the enemies of the country and one over his own, in which last the Judge and I feel that we have a share. I wrote to him privately about the Judge and the appointment of United States judges, which he answered im-

---

[33] Nathaniel Prentiss Banks (1816–1894) was Speaker of the House in 1856–57 and Republican governor of Massachusetts from 1858 to 1861. When the war began, he was made a major general of volunteers. He succeeded Butler as commander of Union troops in November 1862, and took Port Hudson on the Mississippi in July 1863. Defeated at Sabine Crossroads the next spring, he was blamed for his failure to gain this controlling center in Western Louisiana and resigned his commission. He was reelected to Congress after the war.

mediately, promising his aid (as did also Baron Gerolt). I wrote to him and [N. P.] Willis without Charles' knowledge or consent. I hope I did no wrong. It was done with a good motive. I thought that however foolish Willis might be, still he was a good friend of ours and might be of influence. Sometimes such as he are more than others of greater merit. He wrote me such an answer, enclosing a copy of the letter he wrote to Mrs. Lincoln, in which he magnifies me to such an extent that all plausibility is even destroyed. I am one of the most superbly beautiful women of America, a luminous ornament of society, accomplished, and the Judge! Well, I don't think he can say too much for him.

Hackett,[34] the actor and the conscientious, honorable merchant, dined with us last week in company with James T. Brady and Baron Gerolt. The latter was somewhat a weight upon us, but Hackett is a delightful companion. We gave Hackett a bottle of the "Old House" wine which he greatly enjoyed. He well remembered Grandpapa Lydig and the clique to which he belonged. . . .

April 9, 1862

The news of today is most inspiring: Island No. 10 taken, with 6,000 prisoners, 100 siege guns, etc. etc., three generals, the floating Iron Battery, of which we were so afraid, and all their fleet ammunition, etc.[35] I think the rebels must

---

[34] James Henry Hackett (1800–1871) was known as the father of the American stage comedy.

[35] After evacuating Columbus, Kentucky, the Confederates under Generals Leonidas Polk and Gideon J. Pillow made a stand on a bend of the river called Madrid Bend. Their batteries were placed to command the river from the shore and from Island Number Ten. General John Pope maneuvered his Union army of 20,000 into a position below the bend, thus surrounding and cutting off the Confederates from a possible retreat. On March 14, the Confederates abandoned New Madrid, and on April 7, 1862, Island Number Ten was surrendered without bloodshed. Over 5,000 men, plus artillery, ammunition, and provisions fell into Union hands.

give up. Charles says that he thinks if the Confiscation Act[36] was now put in force, it would have a good effect.

I'm sorry that the letter of General Shields has been published in which he speaks so confidently of himself and abuses General Banks. If published without his knowledge, it was most injudicious in his friends. Vanity, vanity, both for men as for women, is the parent stem of many other vices. The General is by no means free of this mortal weakness. . . .

Dana has been obliged to leave the *Tribune*,[37] and their house is to let. Greeley has behaved shamefully towards him, and most consistently his vanity makes him desire to be head. Dana is too important, so Greeley has made him, as it were, the example and laid upon him the obloquy of the attack upon the government and McClellan.

I have been translating a little French book called *Les Salons de Paris* to which, at Charles' suggestion, I wrote an introduction and Scribner has promised to publish it. What a sensation it will give me. Charles wishes me to put my name, but I would rather not for fear that it might not read as well in print as in manuscript.

Father Peltz is constantly writing to me about our emigration business. I hope he will succeed. The government has begun to consider the question. We have worked very hard for it, and Baron Gerolt has promised to speak a good word for it in Washington.

[36] There were two Confiscation Acts passed by Congress. The first, in August 1861, called for the confiscation of any property that was being used for insurrectionary purposes, including slaves. The second, in July 1862, declared that whenever slaves of "rebel" masters should fall into Union hands, they should be "forever free of their servitude." Approximately 150,000 Negroes so freed under these acts served in the Union army during the war.

[37] The New York *Tribune* was founded by Horace Greeley and began publication in 1841. Charles A. Dana was one of the most able supporters of Greeley's opposition to the expansion of slavery, and this made the two men close friends. Greeley gave Dana much power on the *Tribune* until they broke over Dana's "Forward to Richmond" campaign and Greeley forced Dana's resignation. Dana later refused to support Greeley for the Presidency.

April 11, 1862

Went last night to the Academy of Music[38] to see the reception of the crews of the *Cumberland* and *Congress*, the two vessels destroyed by the *Merrimac* in Hampton Roads. It was one of the most interesting sights I ever witnessed. The speeches of [George] Bancroft and [William Maxwell] Evarts were very inadequate, but Jack himself entertained us. There were some 200 sailors on the stage, and one from each vessel came forward and described the scene. The first was a man named Hayward, who belonged to the *Cumberland*. He said that they fired shot and shell with no more effect upon the *Merrimac* than if they had been peas. At last the *Merrimac* ran her ugly iron prow into their side, hog fashion, and [Franklin] Buchanan, who knew his Captain, called out, "Will you surrender, Mr. Morris?" "No," said [Lieutenant George U.] Morris. Then they hauled off and ran down into them again, and Buchanan said again, "If you don't strike your flag and surrender, I'll sink you." "Very well," said Captain Morris, "I won't surrender, and that flag shall go down with the vessel." By this time the vessel began to sink, but the men stood to their guns still and fired until they were quite under water, and her last volley was fired from her deck guns as she sank into nine fathoms of water. Some sixty of the crew went down with her.

The orator of the *Congress* described their waiting for the *Merrimac*, and when they did see her coming, they were as glad they said as a little boy when his father brings him a top. The *Monitor* he called "that little bumble bee." They too were summoned to surrender, and their commander, [Acting Commander Lieutenant Joseph B.] Smith, cried, "Never, never." "We'll make you," cried they, and they fired away—killed Captain Smith. Hayward said that just as they were going down, however, he saw a marine drop a bead into the hole

---

[38] Founded in 1854, the Academy of Music was the first home for opera in New York. It was built on 14th Street.

where Buchanan was, and that bead, he knew, did something, and Buchanan is not alive now, he knew, although the rebels say he is only wounded. "Who," said the sailor, "went, I am sure, straight up to heaven, God bless him!" At last a shell set the ship on fire and they had to give up. It was a wonderful providence that sent the *Monitor* just at that moment. There was a fearful panic even here in New York lest she [the *Merrimac*] should get out and come and bombard us.

The sailors gave us several songs, two forecastle songs with chorus, and then one of them sang "The Yacht America" with a chorus,

> Where did she come from?
> New York Town.
> Who's her Capting?
> One Mr. Brown.

which was extremely humorous. The sailors seemed to enjoy it as much as the audience. Then there was such shouting and cheering. It seemed really a grand family meeting of brothers, all equally interested, all of one mind and heart, and a really democratic solemnity. It made your heart warm, and you could not but feel that with such a spirit among us, we could conquer the world. I did not like the gentlemen orators addressing the sailors as "these plain men," or as Mr. George Bancroft said, "*My men*." They should have said, "our brave countrymen here," or "my countrymen," for they were superior to their advisors, in my opinion at least. I could see what pleased and what displeased the sailors from where I sat. Thanks to the politeness of a Mr. Kingland, we had seats in a proscenium box.

April 13, 1862

Last evening, Mr. [John] McKeon, who has been to Winchester and seen General Shields, came in and brought me some things—a shell from Manassas, and one from the battlefield of Winchester, some secession letters, and a piece of the shell which struck the General. The General sent the shell on, saying he hoped I would keep it until I saw him again, for he hoped to spend many pleasant evenings in our company. In the morning we went with Mother and Florence to the menagerie. I love to look into the faces of wild creatures. How majestic and calm the lions and tigers are. Their eyes look so full into yours. Charles' eyes are like those of the younger lions we saw yesterday—so clear, fearless, and calm.

Today was Palm Sunday. I went in the morning to church, where the President's request was complied with—thanksgiving for the success of our arms and a prayer for those who had lost relatives in battle were offered. It was very affecting. I did not stay for the sermon, but contented myself with the lessons in gospel, and opened my prayer book upon a picture of the passion of our Lord, a more eloquent sermon than anything which could have been preached to me. . . .

April 14, 1862

Spent today with Harriet Whetten on Staten Island, and induced her to copy an admonition to our pastor at West Farms for me, which I sent by post to him. It being Lent, I thought it would be well to call his sins to his remembrance. Perhaps being a clergyman, he never thought of himself in those respects. . . .

I have just finished my translation of a little book, *Les Salons de Paris*. The Judge thinks that it and the introduction are good enough to publish, so it is to be sent tomorrow. What an excitement it will be to see it in print!

Charles Mackay is in the city. He dined here two weeks ago, and I was to go and return his wife's visit. She is a Spanish woman and so very lively that I can scarcely get on with her.

She is too frank and natural. Mackay the Judge likes, but I find him heavy.

Mrs. General Halleck[39] and Mrs. General Schuyler Hamilton[40] were here to ask us to put our names to a subscription list for aid of the Western Sanitary Commission, which I will willingly do. Never has there been so much done by private enterprise for the benefit of the army of any country before. Nothing seems to be too much for the defenders of the Union.

April 16, 1862

Had a letter from Temple Prime, telling me that he had secured a lieutenant's commission for Phil, so now that matter is over. Received a delightful letter from Father O'Reilly, containing his photograph for Mr. Laing [the artist]. He prophesies war, revolution in Europe, everywhere. He speaks most enthusiastically of the Judge. I would be willing to do as that man thought right. Next to my own husband, I never saw anyone I thought so reliable.

There is no chance as yet of any United States judgeship for Charles. A very kind letter from Baron Gerolt explains the whole matter, so I shall have to have the house put in order a little, as we shall probably stay here.

Some of Charles' cousins by the mother's side, the least in-

---

[39] Henry Wager Halleck (1815–1872) served as a major general, and was in command of the Union Army before and after McClellan. In 1862, in Mississippi, he was found too conservative and was relieved of his command after failing to pursue Beauregard at Corinth. From 1862 to 1864 he was Chief of Staff in Washington, but the job was too much for him though he tried valiantly. In 1866 he served in the Division of the Pacific and in 1869 he was assigned to the Division of the South.

[40] Schuyler Hamilton (1822–1903) served in the Mexican War and was appointed captain for bravery. In 1854 he resigned, but reenlisted as a private during the Civil War. He was made a lieutenant colonel and Assistant Chief of Staff to Halleck. In 1862 he was made a major general. He fought at Kent, Island Number Ten, and New Madrid, and proved himself skillful. He became ill and resigned in February 1863, to work as an engineer.

teresting ones, if we believe Mrs. O'Neill, have found him out, and one of them writes to him. I wish he would make a will more particularly. I am sure he will not want our goods to go to some unknown people in Ireland. Sir Dominick Daly sends him a message begging him to write through Mrs. Roosevelt.

Harriett Whetten has disappointed me. I wished to write an admonitory letter to Mr. Rodman and asked her to copy it for me. She did so, but changed her mind, got it out of the post, and sent it back to me. Because the rascal has been ordained and has sheep's clothing on, she did not dare. She has too much principle to write disrespectfully to a clergyman. Such a spirit as this is the cause that evil always prevails and goes free. How little courage and magnanimity women possess! I should have done it without scruple, if only to oblige my friend.

Went this morning to church at Grace. Heard a very good lecture from Dr. Taylor.[41] Dr. Hawks[42] has resigned at Calvary and is looking out for the vacant bishopric of Virginia, it is said. Our church has disgraced itself in this war. What is truth among all the contending sects of Christiandom? I am often tempted to join the Roman Catholic because they are the *largest* body of Christians, if for nothing else, and because their priests do not marry and therefore have no worldly interests to struggle against. Our clergy seem to me excessively worldly.

Maggie writes that she is coming out next Spring to stay a year. It will be a good treat to see her, but who knows what a year may bring forth. Sufficient unto the day is the evil thereof. I have so much to thank God for, that I ought to be far above such littleness, but she has been always such a hypocrite and I know it now. It will be hard for me to act calm.

---

[41] Thomas H. Taylor (1799–1867), an Episcopal clergyman, was rector of Grace Church in New York City from 1834 to 1867. He was active throughout as a church law controversialist.

[42] Francis L. Hawks (1798–1866) was an Episcopal rector in New Haven, Philadelphia, and Hartford before moving to St. Stephen's Church in New York City. From there he moved to St. Thomas' in New York, and then to Calvary Episcopal Church, where he was rector from 1849 to 1862.

April 20, 1862

Had an unexpected visit last evening (Sunday) from Adam Badeau, who is now aide to General Hunter[43] and has come on with dispatches. He says that the missionaries at Fort Royal are somewhat disenchanted. The philanthropic ladies who went down to instruct Mrs. Stowe's ideal Negro find him a very different article in reality, and a Mrs. Johnson and a Miss Donelson, two of these ladies, told him that they thought it injudicious to emancipate them as yet, that they must have masters and be made to obey them or help themselves. Badeau himself says that he never wants to see a Negro. All the officers have to give their Negro servants $10 a month and find them lazy, impertinent, stupid, thievish, and generally disgusting. "What can be done with them?" said he. I think they should be billeted upon the abolitionists. I wish the Democrats would refuse to assist them, and then they will be obliged to emigrate.

Badeau deems it a great injustice in the government to have recalled General Sherman,[44] who, he says, is a general of great ability and to him is due all the praise for what has been accomplished at Fort Royal and Fort Pulaski,[45] etc. Had Commodore du Pont[46] aided him in any way effectually, Savannah would

---

[43] David Hunter (1802–1886) was rapidly advanced in rank from major to major general in 1861, and he later distinguished himself in the battles of Bull Run, Charleston, Piedmont, and Lynchburg.

[44] Thomas West Sherman (1813–1879) was commissioned a major in the U.S. Army in April of 1861 and rose quickly to the rank of brigadier general of volunteers. He commanded the land forces of the Port Royal expedition from October 1861 to March 1862, capturing Port Royal. At the end of March he was replaced by David Hunter, who was given command of the Department of the South.

[45] Fort Pulaski was erected by the United States on Cockspur Island for the defense of Savannah. It was seized by Georgia troops on January 3, 1861, and strongly garrisoned. General Quincy A. Gillmore (North) was sent in February 1862, to gain back the fort. He landed and set up big guns. On April 9 the batteries opened fire. General C. H. Olmstead was defending. The fort was surrendered on April 11, and as a result the Savannah River was closed.

[46] Commodore Samuel F. du Pont (1803–1865) experienced few naval combats prior to the Civil War. On land during much of his service, he

have been taken in January before it was fortified, for General Sherman, by a reconnaissance, had found Wales' Cut manageable for gunboats and sent to Commodore du Pont to cooperate with him, which he refused to do, saying that the bluffs were high and that there were batteries, that it was too great a risk, etc. Had he done as Sherman wished, they could have approached Savannah and avoided Fort Pulaski. It seems du Pont pleases himself by going about taking small, insignificant places, neglecting the snares which General Sherman knew that if the greater were taken, the smaller would fall of themselves. General Sherman, however, is a martyr to dyspepsia, sometimes very irritable and arbitrary and very unpopular with his officers.

It would seem that Secretary Stanton begins to have his head turned by power, and Wendell Phillips[47] says that by November next he will be an abolitionist.

Badeau speaks despondingly of the feeling for the Union in the South. He says that he talked with the garrison at Fort Pulaski and that all said we might take their forts and seaports, but they would retreat inland and keeping up an incessant guerilla warfare, defy us. Some allowed that they knew the North did not wish to take their slaves, but they did not care. They were fighting for independence. It seems now impossible for them to hold out much longer.

Phil writes to father that Colonel Rodman[48] of the Rhode Island regiment has been made a brigadier for his bayonet

was instrumental in the founding of the Naval Academy at Annapolis. He was made a rear admiral after the Fort Royal victory, but in 1863 he was severely defeated at Charleston and retired from the service.

[47] Wendell Phillips (1811–1884) was a lawyer, orator, and reformer who was associated with William Lloyd Garrison in the abolitionist movement. President of the Anti-slavery Society from 1865 to 1870, he also worked for penal reforms and woman suffrage.

[48] Isaac Rodman (1822–1862), Rhode Island legislator, was made a colonel after the battle of Bull Run. His participation in battles at Roanoke, New Berne, and the capture of Fort Macon resulted in his elevation to the rank of brigadier general.

charge at New Berne, and that he thanked him for it, saying that he was indebted to him. It seems that Phil was sent by Burnside with orders to General Parke to bring up one of his regiments to support the Massachusetts 4th, which was storming the Fort and needed it—as General [John Gray] Foster's could not come in time. The one ordered by General Burnside from General Parke was fast in the march, which Phil knew. Passing Colonel Rodman, whose regiment belonged to Parke's brigade, Phil said: "So charge, Colonel. See, our men are retreating, so charge with the bayonet." "I will," said the Colonel, "if you will take the responsibility and inform General Parke that I have left my position."

Yesterday being Easter Sunday, I went to church with the Judge and heard most beautiful music, though an indifferent sermon. As Dr. Bronson says, in an admirable article in his review for this month entitled *The Church, Not a Despotism—* "the church needs Americanizing." Catholics want American priests who speak our language at least correctly. A little yielding on the side of the Roman Church would almost Catholicize the Episcopal and make us one again.

April 27, 1862

Had one of the warmest letters from the General [Shields], in which he says he prizes—more than all—the true and constant friendship which, in prosperity and adversity, we have shown to him, etc., etc. He is a warm-hearted old fellow.

On Friday the Judge gave his first lecture of the series on "The Origin of the Laws of the Sea." It was deeply interesting. I wish he would write them out and make a little book of them. I cannot bear to see him so lavish of his mental wealth. I see some of his journalist friends supply themselves from his abundant source and weaken and dilute some few comprehensive phrases into an article. . . .

Yesterday, Florence, Maggie Pierrepont, the Judge and myself went to hear a whaling voyage described by an old sea captain named Williams at Hope Chapel, expecting to be only moderately amused, but never were we more diverted. Williams and his boatsmen were men of no mean ability as actors even, and a panorama admirably illustrated his descriptions of scenes, places, and hairbreadth escapes. The Judge laughed until it was painful. He said that it was so natural, so what he remembered when a sailor boy himself.[49] I think I should so enjoy being out at sea. How I love the sea breeze and salt spray—and you seemed almost to feel it. Old Williams was so true and so salt himself.

James T. Brady was here last night. He says he means to turn Capuchin monk after the war because he will never be able to live in the world with so many heroes.

May 7, 1862

Yorktown is evacuated, and McClellan in hot pursuit.[50] Corinth likewise,[51] and New Orleans[52] in our possession. All the

---

[49] When he was fourteen, Judge Daly went to sea for two years, first serving as a cabin boy and then before the mast. He was present off the Barbary Coast when Algiers was besieged and captured by the French in 1830.

[50] Yorktown, though strongly fortified, was a position the Confederates were unwilling to fight for because their line of defense across the Peninsula to the James River was weak. Although they probably would have yielded immediately to a Union assault, McClellan devoted a month to the siege before sending word on May 4, 1862, that "Yorktown is in our possession." Norfolk now fell into Union hands, and the James River was open and exposed to the kind of joint land-sea operations which had been so successful in the East as well as in the West.

[51] Mrs. Daly was a little precipitous here. General Halleck was approaching Corinth at the average rate of a mile a day, at the time of writing, with a huge army which included the forces of Thomas, Pope, Buell, McClernand, and Grant. He spent a week erecting breastworks five miles from Corinth, shelled every patch of woods before him, prepared for battle on May 30, and discovered the next day that Beauregard had evacuated Corinth by rail. He conquered and occupied an empty city with worthless fortifications.

[52] Late in April, the chief Southern commercial port of New Orleans surrendered to an attacking squadron led by Flag Officer David G. Farragut, a native of Tennessee. Farragut had served in the U.S. Navy for over fifty

fighting has been done on *paper* by the mayor, who contents himself by evincing his courage by writing an impudent letter, not firing a gun. This assumption of superiority is too ridiculous.

Last evening the Judge gave the second of his series of lectures upon maritime law and last evening the subject was "Maritime Cities of the Mediterranean." I wrote it out for him and notwithstanding my familiarity with the text, found it extremely interesting. He had a large and intelligent audience. The first was even to me more interesting: "The Origin of the Laws of the Sea," and I shall tease him until he writes that out as well. He shall not, if I can help it, squander his mental wealth and leave no record remaining. We have no children, and his books must live after him, like Lord Bacon's.

Judge Killin came home with us after the lecture, and Mr. and Mrs. Savage after Mr. and Mrs. K. left. I never heard Charles talk so much of his past. It seems that old Captain Williams, when we went to see the whaling voyage, revived all his youthful associations. He, like the little weakly lad he spoke of, had likewise run away to sea and been indebted to an old sailor for preservation in a fearful storm the first day out. He had been shipwrecked off the coast of Holland and, boylike, stopping behind to look at a puppet show, had lost all his companions, only seven in number saved from the wreck. He described his wanderings for ten days through the streets of Amsterdam, sleeping on cellar doors without a crumb to eat, without money, not understanding a word of Dutch. At last, wandering down to the quay, he saw a Dutch galiot, the captain of which, seeing that he looked in distress, motioned him to come on board. Then Charles made signs he wanted something

years, and, though a Southerner himself and surrounded by secessionists when the war began, he remained loyal to the Union. Another man who distinguished himself in this engagement was Commander David D. Porter, who accompanied Farragut's fleet with his own fleet of mortar boats.

to eat. That piece of salt beef and bread he said was the best thing he ever tasted in his life. He went below deck and fell asleep and slept, he said, for twelve hours. When he awoke they were out at sea on their way to Kronstadt. For three years and six months he was at sea. Once he was left at Dundee without money, without resources, but found a place once more in a ship. He was on the coast of Russia, all along the Mediterranean, was at the siege of Algiers by the French, where he received the saber-cut, the mark of which he still bears upon his forehead. Once, he said, he told a Scotchman how he got his scar and the Scotchman said he was making up a story of whole cloth. The Judge then vowed a great solemn vow that he would never tell the story again to living man or woman. He would not even tell me, but I know it was in trying to do someone a service.

The Judge then told us of his life at home, and how, at last, a brother of Judge Hilton[53] was instrumental, hearing him speak in a debating society, to which he likewise belonged, in urging Charles to enter a law office and study law. In two years, by dint of incessant application, Charles prepared himself for examination and was admitted. He interested himself in politics, was sent to the legislature at twenty-eight years of age, was appointed by old Governor Bouck[54] Judge of the Court of Common Pleas, which was then an office for life, afterwards made elective by a change in the Constitution.

May 11, 1862

What splendid news! Norfolk taken, Portsmouth captured, the Navy Yard saved, the *Merrimac* ours, President Lin-

---

[53] Henry Hilton, who served prior to and with Judge Daly on the Court of Common Pleas of the City and County of New York.

[54] William C. Bouck (1786–1859), a lifelong Democrat, was a state senator in New York in 1820, governor of the state from 1843 to 1845, and U.S. Assistant Treasurer in New York City from 1846 to 1849.

coln with the army before Norfolk! All the news seems to come on Sundays. Now there may be truth in what Mrs. McClellan told us yesterday, that the war would be over by the Fourth of July.

I went yesterday with the Judge to see Mrs. General Marcy and Mrs. McClellan. Found the latter very much improved. A really refined, graceful, sprightly woman, and very pretty. Her mother, whom I rather dreaded to meet, thinking that she would be too elated, was likewise very gentle and much less elevated than I expected to find her. We had a very pleasant visit. Judge [Samuel] Nelson of the [U.S.] Supreme Court came in whilst we were there. Mrs. McClellan showed Charles a letter of Professor Mahan[55] of West Point in which he highly complimented her husband upon his avoidance of bloodshed in his great successes. He must be a great man. He has such wonderful moderation and has the gift of silence. When *reviled*, he reviles not again. He writes to his wife that in the army he had just whipped were many of his most intimate friends. He ends his telegraph dispatch, "How is the baby?" His favorite project, Mrs. McC. says, is to take her to Europe as soon as the war is over.

At Mr. Ruggles'[56] a few evenings since, we met ex-President Fillmore and his wife. He has excellent manners; his wife likewise. . . . Mrs. General Dix says . . . Fillmore ought to have been nominated for the Presidency[57]—he behaved so well, selected his advisers so wisely.

---

[55] Dennis Hart Mahan (1802–1871) graduated from West Point in 1824 and in 1832 became a professor of engineering there. In 1838, he was appointed to the deanship of the Academy, a position which he held for the remainder of his life.

[56] Samuel B. Ruggles was a trustee of Columbia University, and did much to advance that institution. He attended an International Statistical Convention in Berlin in 1863, and promoted the Union cause in Prussia.

[57] Elected Vice President of the United States in 1848 with Zachary Taylor to placate the Clay wing of the Whig party, Millard Fillmore succeeded to the Presidency on July 9, 1850, on Taylor's death. He signed the Clay Compromise of 1850 and sought to enforce the Fugitive Slave Act, which cost him much Northern popularity. He was denied renomination

On Thursday last, Mother and I went to Dr. Ward's[58] to see his opera, "The Gypsy's Frolic," performed for the benefit of the woman's hospital. A Miss Mercies sang and has one of the finest contralto voices I ever heard. Miss Read was Annette. After the opera, Mrs. Richard Thomas Winters appeared as *Columbia*, dressed in a white petticoat and the American flag, making herself extremely conspicuous. She is a woman who, I think, would be extremely bold if she did not consider it, and very justly, more politic and interesting to seem retiring. Richard looked into the seventh heaven. Miss Dix was one of the peasants, as well as Mattie Trasbriand. Dr. Ward did very well.

We heard from Phil last week. As Mrs. McClellan said, "I can scarcely believe we are living, and that what we see and hear is not the fantastic action of our brain, as though in dreams." All feel as though God were aiding us to accomplish some great purpose of His own in the economy of the world.

A Captain Applegate, a young Irishman of good family to whom I have been directing and for whom I have been writing letters, all smiles stopped to thank us. He has been in the Papal Brigade, fighting in Italy, and was likewise at the Crimea. He seemed lost in admiration at the stupendous nature of this contest, the means employed to subdue it, and at the wonderful energy of the people. Those who read the history of these times one hundred years hence will be able to appreciate its great historical importance. We are too near at present. I am very anxious to know how much of the praise and how much of the blame is deserved which McClellan receives, and we cannot judge him aright until the end of the contest. Stanton's head seems quite turned by his elevation.

---

by his party in 1852 and ran a poor third as the nominee of the American (Know-Nothing) party for the Presidency in 1856.

[58] Thomas Ward (1807–1873) was a physician, poet, and author. He wrote such musicals as "A Month of Freedom" and "Flora," and the opera "The Gypsy's Frolic." He presented nearly fifty musical entertainments for New Yorkers between 1862 and 1872.

May 14, 1862

Went this morning with Kate to the Park Barracks to see the wounded and sick soldiers brought on by the *Ocean Queen* from Yorktown. I found a number of ladies there already waiting upon them, some bathing their heads, others giving them their food. The soldiers seemed mostly to suffer from exhaustion. Having taken some cologne and handkerchiefs with me, I went around and distributed it; many of them seemed to find it very grateful. The poor fellows were very patient. Some of them looked grey with pallor and weakness. One young fellow of about eighteen, with a skin like a woman's and bright hazel eyes, looked like a gentleman. He much interested me. I think he was a *deserter*, a Virginian. For he said to me, "How my mother would feel if she knew where I was." I said he was young to go soldiering, and I knew how his mother would feel, for I had a young brother in the army. "Where?" said he. "With Burnside," I answered. I gave him some chicken broth. He ate with relish. "That is the first thing that I have had that has tasted good," said he. "It is better than crackers." He ate it and asked for more cologne, and seemed much refreshed.

Another poor fellow of about 50 was dying of consumption from a kick on the breast by a drunken lieutenant. "Oh," said he, "had I died by a blow from the enemy, I could have borne it better. I was not to blame, and had I my pistol in my hand, I should have shot him. But I remembered I am a Christian, and the lieutenant knew not what he did." Then his mind wandered away to the battlefield. He spoke with tears rolling down his face of the scenes he had witnessed of young fellows dying, moaning for one look at their mothers and sisters or someone still dearer. Kate's beauty seemed to give them great pleasure. Several of the poor fellows would let the older ladies pass, but smiled to attract her attention. Oh, the magic power of youth and beauty!

The rest of the day I have spent in gathering things together for them—shirts, sheets, old linen, towels, clothes of all kinds, and thanks to Grandma and some kind friends, I shall have a good bundle to send. Tomorrow night the Judge is asked to welcome Parson Brownboro and go on the stage, so I shall not go. I shall devote myself to the hospital.

May 16, 1862

Went yesterday again with Kate and Mrs. Minturn[59] to the Park Barracks. Found most of the soldiers convalescent. We took some things down with us, among others some old shirts of the Judge's, which gave great satisfaction. All of the soldiers wanted shirts with shining fronts. One Irishman with one eye and a shattered arm was particularly anxious, so I gave him one, and one to a young fellow who seemed vexed to be out of the fight and whose only desire seemed to be to rejoin his regiment. Besides I brought some canes for them, and for one poor fellow who wanted a chicken leg and nothing else and could not get it (as they had none), I sent out and bought him some. I never had so much pleasure before in spending fifty cents, for he ate it with such satisfaction, he and his next neighbor. Both bolstered up on their cots, ate it up between them.

Whilst I was there, two deputations from the ward schools came with baskets full of groceries, liquors, jellies, crackers, which they had begged from the different grocers, one from the girls' school, one from the boys'. It was difficult, however, to do anything. The ladies of the Committee did not seem to like to be interfered with, and Miss Murray, whose day it was, seemed as cross as a bear, did not want any help, whilst the

---

[59] Robert Bowne Minturn (1805–1866) was a shipowner, a partner in Grinnell, Minturn & Co. He was active in the Century Club, and was noted for his philanthropies. He was first president of the Union League Club.

soldiers seemed to want a good deal. I am afraid to be too importunate; they make such fun of us women, so we did what we could. The last two days I have been mending up all the old clothes I could beg for the men, particularly shirts, and a woman is here doing them up. I think I shall have forty, which, when cleaned, I will take to the Sanitary Committee for distribution.

The Judge was relating some interesting things about the taking of New Orleans. When Captain [Theodorus] Bailey went to the mayor with Commodore Farragut's proposals [for the surrender of New Orleans], the mayor asked very haughtily for his credentials. Captain Bailey was very angry. He stuttered in speaking and stammered out, "By God, sir, I led the *van* in here, and there is my credentials." The French and English Admirals said it would not be possible for the fleet to pass those forts. They said it would be madness to attempt it, but our commanders say there was not a captain or lieutenant or hardly a sailor who was not determined to do it—if every man went to the bottom in the attempt. The reason that the *Mississippi* did not get out was that they could not get her off the docks, and after a week spent in trying they at last found that someone, some Union workman probably, had driven in long staples or screws and fastened her to the docks to prevent her from getting out.

Today another boat goes off, laden with comforts for the wounded and to transport them from Virginia here. Harriet Whetten and Mrs. [William Preston] Griffin, Christine Kean that was, are now at West Point on the *Rappahannock*, a receiving vessel. I had almost determined to go, but finding that others of more experience had volunteered, and having little or no experience myself in taking care of the sick, I did not offer myself. Mrs. George [Templeton] Strong went, and I believe she said she washed the faces of seven men. They tell a very good story of the officiousness of some of us ladies. One poor fellow was lying on his back, looking exhausted, and a young lady came up, "Can I do anything for you?" "No," he said. "Shall I wash your face?" "If it will give you any satisfaction to do so, madam," was his answer, "but it has been washed four times already this morning."

May 18, 1862

Went yesterday to the City Hospital, hearing that someone was wanted to read to the sick or to write their letters. Finding that I should have to go among the typhoid fever patients, being of such full *habit,* I gave up my charitable intention. Mrs. Charles Strong is head nurse, it seems. How strange for that fast, worldly woman, but she is clever, and such never can be as frivolous as fools. They feel at times, at all events, a want of earnest purpose—clever women especially! She is of that class who end their lives as sisters of charity or in a convent. Miss Libby Irving and the two Miss Russells are likewise there. There are single women who want something to occupy their minds and hearts. Thank God that mine, by His good Providence, are both satisfied. I trust that if there was pressing need for my services, even in dangerous cases, I should not be found wanting. I shall go twice a week to the Park Barracks and give one day to working at the Central Relief Association[60] in Cooper Institute. I've collected together some 40 shirts, and some dozen sheets, vests, drawers, quilts, etc. I have sent a donation to the Central Relief Association.

May 19, 1862

Had last evening a visit from old Mrs. Colonel [Laura Wolcott] Gibbs, who narrated two or three very amusing

60 In April 1861, the ladies of New York formed the Central Relief Association for the purpose of scraping lint, knitting socks and other items of clothing, making garments, preparing delicacies, and doing whatever possible to aid the war effort.

anecdotes of Commodore McDonough,[61] whom she was accustomed to see when a girl at school at Middletown. McDonough married a Miss Lucy Slater from that place, a merry, witty, audacious flirty young girl who delighted in teasing her reserved, religious lover. On one occasion, she asked him to join a party to go to a graveyard in the neighborhood, a favorite walk of the young people at Middletown on Sunday afternoon because of the strange droll inscriptions on the old tombstones, such as:

> Here lies the body of John Slaughter
> Who, while he lived, did what he ought to
> And the story could not be told any shorter.

McDonough did not fancy the walk. "Won't you go?" said Miss Lucy. "Why not?" "I do not like merrymaking in graveyards on Sunday, Miss Lucy." She thereupon took his hat, tore off the cockade, and trampled upon it. McDonough stopped, picked up the cockade, put it in his breast, and left the room and the house. He went to the inn and left the town, and he did not return until the lady invited him. . . .

The old lady has a difficult life of it at present. Her daughters are away, and she lives with the wife and children of her son, Captain Alfred Gibbs. Mrs. Captain Gibbs is a Virginian, a Blake, connected with the Leighs, and sympathizes with her *steet*, as they pronounce "state." So she [Mrs. Colonel Gibbs] does not condescend to hold any intercourse with anyone here, but keeps closely to her room excepting whilst at her meals. She treats Mrs. Captain Gibbs with the utmost consideration and tenderness and never speaks on the subject.

Old Mrs. Gibbs narrated a very amusing interview between Mrs. Watkins Lee, another Richmond lady enjoying the protection of the Yankees—and abusing them!—and old Mrs. J.

---

[61] Thomas McDonough (1783–1825) began his outstanding naval career by joining the United States service as an officer in 1800 and climaxed it with the famous battle of Lake Champlain against the British in 1814. He died at sea *en route* to the United States from the Mediterranean theater.

Bell. Mrs. Bell remarked that she was sorry not to have seen her when she called. She said yes, but she saw no one. She visited nowhere. She had been used to such a different state in Richmond, such a delightful intellectual society, where her house was the center of attraction. She met no intellectual people here.

"No?" said Mrs. Bell. "Why, Mr. Bancroft is near you, a man of European reputation," and mentioned several others.

"Oh, Mr. Bancroft, yes. He has written a history of the country which they say is good, but I cannot sympathize, you know; I am not accustomed to people in trade."

"Indeed," said Mrs. Bell, "but your son-in-law, with whom you are staying, Mr. Fry, is, I believe, in *trade*, as you call it, and made his fortune."

"Yes, but you know, *he* is not of my *blood*."

"Well," said Mrs. Bell, "I am very proud that my blood has enriched itself by trade and *honest* industry, and consider it a glory to them and to me." . . .

There seem to be plenty of nurses for the transports and for the hospitals. The Park Barracks seem to be a monopoly. The ladies told me yesterday that doubtless in the warm weather they would need assistance. Now the doctors had desired them not to allow the ladies to go into the wards. I hope they will make arrangements for the warm weather. I had no mania for being useful, but had plenty of pleasant occupation and could now go to it with a clear conscience, since I had offered my services. Having no children, I thought it might be more my duty to offer them than some others who had. They say very kindly and charitably that Mrs. George Strong went down with rouge pot, crinoline, and maid to attend to the wounded and came home having washed the faces of seven men.

May 22, 1862

Went last night to see Judge Pierrepont, who has been very kind in interesting himself about Phil's commission. It is now, I think, a certain thing that he will get a captaincy in the regulars. Secretary Stanton had promised it to Judge Pierrepont, saying that he had all along desired to oblige himself to Judge Daly but could not from the army regulation. Judge Pierrepont went on to say that Stanton was much misjudged, that he had seen the correspondence between himself and the President and that they had thought it necessary to divide the army. McClellan was afraid to risk his position by moving, and it was therefore indispensable to change his arrangements and plans. Stanton says that if he could only publish the letters of the generals who disagreed with him, he would be exculpated in the public opinion, that he can afford to wait, however, and leave his reputation to time. These men are now in the field. It will be Stanton's occasion when the war is over.

The Judges discussed General McDowell. Charles expressed his opinion of McDowell's character and behavior at Bull Run,[62] which Judge Pierrepont said was almost word for word what Stanton had said. His first words on hearing of General Hunter's proclamation[63] were, "What a damned fool!" Again what the Judge said! He shall be recalled tomorrow.

Judge P. says the President is rising above all exterior influence and learning to depend upon himself and taking his own judgment, that Seward, even, has little influence with him now.

---

[62] Irvin McDowell (1818–1885), West-Point trained and acting adjutant general of Wool's column in Mexico, did badly in both battles of Bull Run and became so widely criticized that he was transferred from active field duty to a Washington desk job. In 1864 he was placed in charge of the Pacific Department.

[63] In May 1862, Major General David Hunter issued a proclamation of military emancipation in the Department of the South, which embraced South Carolina, Georgia, and Florida. As a result of successful amphibian operations, Union forces occupied the coastal region, which was now under martial law, and the white population left their slaves behind when they fled. Hunter meant the proclamation to apply to these thousands of abandoned slaves, but he clearly exceeded his military authority. When Lincoln read of this order in the public press, he publicly annulled it.

"He is greater than he seems. His manners are so against him, but he is great from being so *good*, so conscientious. His having been no politician and having little experience has been a providential circumstance for the country instead of being a misfortune."

On our way home, we met Mr. [James] Gerard,[64] who was walking about studying out his cases. We stopped him, and Charles told him of his lectures on the "Trial of Causes" before the Law School last Tuesday, a week ago, and said that he should come and ask him for a few more visits as they wished him to publish it. The boys, it seems, were delighted and wanted Charles to continue, although it was already spun out to an hour and a half. I did not hear it as I went to the Academy, where the pictures are quite good—two beautiful ones by Bierstadt[65] and two magnificent portraits by [Daniel] Huntington, one of Mrs. John J. Astor. Bierstadt joined us there.

It seems that Meagher is disgracing himself, being so intemperate as to be a cause of great scandal, according to Judge Pierrepont.

Poor Rose, who lived with us, was here yesterday. Her husband has enlisted in the regular army, having had no work for three months, and she is distracted. I tried to comfort her by telling her that she might be able to join him as soon as the fighting was over and he placed somewhere in garrison, but she could not be comforted. She thought Judge Daly might perhaps get him off, and was quite desolate when I had to tell her that he could not—that no one could get him released.

---

[64] James W. Gerard (1794–1874) was a New York City lawyer and merchant. Born in Scotland, he came to America at an early age, enlisted for the defense of New York City during the War of 1812, and educated himself sufficiently to be admitted to the bar in 1816. A reformer and philanthropist, he was active in the Society for the Prevention of Pauperism, staunchly opposed slavery, and did much for the cause of free public education.

[65] Albert Bierstadt. See *Personalities in the Diary*, page xiv.

May 27, 1862

Went last evening to see the 7th leave for Washington. Found the streets thronged, and as much enthusiasm as at this time last year. We stood on the curbstones and found ourselves next to Colonel Monroe and Mr. Egbert Benson and Sue. The Judge and Colonel M. discussed the affairs of the country. Although a Virginian by birth, Col. Monroe is a rare exception, having no sympathy with states' rights. Jackson[66] is liable to be caught, for this new rush of troops to Washington of the National Cadets will free the regulars there and will give us overwhelming odds. General Banks has done well, made a masterly retreat, and Jackson, having failed in capturing him, is rapidly retreating.

Charles has been made chairman for the Committee for the Relief of Ireland,[67] which is suffering from famine and for want of fuel. He tells me that he has appointed the committee from the rich merchants and left out all the politicians, much to their disgust. I am glad he is so public-spirited, although it does absorb so much of his time.

On Saturday last, we dined with Judge Hilton in company with Judge James T. Brady. The latter gentlemen are severe upon their old-country people.

Went one day last week to see a burlesque opera composed,

[66] Thomas J. Jackson, who earned the sobriquet "Stonewall" at first Bull Run, was a West Point-trained Virginian who served in the Mexican War, taught military tactics at the Virginia Military Institute, and commanded the cadet corps which hanged John Brown. He joined the Confederate army as a brigadier general, was promoted to major general after first Bull Run, and demonstrated brilliance as a field tactician as commander of the Confederate forces in the Shenandoah Valley. He defeated a superior military force under Nathaniel P. Banks at Fort Royal, May 23, 1862, and Winchester, May 24–25, 1862. Despite Mrs. Daly's hope, Jackson continued to outwit and outmaneuver the superior forces opposing him.

[67] The Committee for the Relief of Ireland had been in operation in New York City since 1822. In 1847 alone, subscriptions amounting to more than $50,000 were raised in the city to assist the famine sufferers. In 1862–63, some thirteen vessels carrying food were sent to Ireland, an effort largely directed by Judge Daly.

or rather put together, by a lawyer here by the name of Hayward. It was an amateur performance by young men of our acquaintance. The female characters were acted by them likewise, and it was well done. The proceeds were given to the Nursery. One young William Burd was the princess and made a charming young girl. The queen of the giants was a German gentleman 6'4" high; Davis was one of the guards.

May 29, 1862

Went last evening to walk with Charles. He says the Mesiers have been in the city government from the first settlement of the island, almost as far as he can trace in an old collection of city directories. I saw great-grandmother Lydig's and Mr. David Grim's names listed there.

Scrilles' wife is a South Carolinian, but as she said, a loyal one. She declared that it was the men of Northern descent who had stirred up this rebellion, and not the Southerners proper. Jeff Davis, she affirmed, was from Connecticut. It is a pity these rebels could not be returned to their several states and have their *state rights* as traitors. This is a most extraordinary war. Certainly there seems no limit to the men and money willingly given for its prosecution, and another 600,000 could be found in a few weeks did the government require it.

The 69th goes tomorrow—1,200 strong and had to refuse a thousand. It is hoped that Corcoran will be released by the time they reach Washington, as the privateersmen for whom they promise to exchange him are at Fortress Monroe. Charles saw at Captain Kirker's the buttons in which the letters were hidden. Lieutenant Dempsey on his return had 12 letters in the 12 U.S. buttons on his coat, some from Corcoran. With a knife they opened the buttons at the back, and as they were hollow, inserted the letters written on very thin paper and then put them back on his uniform. They safely passed the line.

May 30, 1862

Charles has been at home for the past two days studying, and home is consequently delightful, I having my desk and being tolerated in the library.

This afternoon Harriet Whetten came in. She has just come on from the Pamunkey [River] 20 miles from Richmond, Virginia, where she has been nursing the sick and wounded on the transports sent by the Sanitary Commission for their relief. She looked very happy. She has been longing for some active employment and would like to have gone soldiering, I think, long ago. She has done good service and returns tomorrow to continue her good works. She gives a touching account of the patience and fortitude with which the men bear their suffering, and saw many who rivalled Sir Philip Sidney in disinterestedness, putting aside the cup of water offered them for a more distressed comrade. She will have a great deal more to tell when she returns, for she was hurried and nervous today.

I have been reading de Tocqueville's letters, which are, it seems to me, exceedingly suggestive and foreshadowing, especially what he says concerning the present attitude of France and England.

The news tonight is that Corinth is evacuated, Beauregard has retreated on the line of railroad towards Mobile, and McClellan is within two miles of the enemy's works. May God grant a speedy end to this war.

The South seems to be desperate, and horrible atrocities are committed. Stragglers from our army are found tied by their feet to the trees with their throats cut, and it seems that what was said of their barbarities at Manassas after the battle of Bull Run was only too true, that they did boil the flesh and carry away the bones of our poor soldiers as trophies, their boasted chivalry rivalling the Indians, exceeding them even in barbarity. How strange that they should take so much trouble to destroy themselves and thus really bring upon themselves the evils they only feared from us at some more distant period. God makes the evil passions of men to do His Will, even whilst they think they're only doing their own.

Harriet W. says that she was at the White House,[68] Mrs. Custis' dwelling before her marriage with Washington. The present owner, Mrs. Lee, left a card upon the door with this inscription: "Northern soldiers: This was the early home of Washington, whom you so pretend to reverence, the scene of his early married happiness; therefore, respect it!" She and her family had left it, leaving the slaves, who seemed rejoiced to be free. One of them showed Harriet a portrait of old Mr. Custis, which was, she said, put up in the garret because he had willed the servants away from them after a certain number of years. "We were to have been free next year by the will," said the woman, "but I guess if it wasn't for these commotions, it wouldn't have made any difference.". . .

June 5, 1862

Judge Pierrepont called this morning with Phil's commission as Captain, U.S. Army, in his pocket. He has been unwearied in his exertions to oblige us, in urging Secretary Stanton to fulfill his promise. It is a great thing for so young a man. Phil is now independent.

Judge P. tells us that Lincoln told him that he alone was responsible for Banks' retreat, that he had ordered General Shields and his command to join McDowell. "The fact is," said he, "that McClellan worried me so for more troops that I sent McDowell to him and then weakened Banks to strengthen McDowell. McClellan is all the time writing for more troops." Lincoln now considers himself commander in chief and orders

[68] The "White House" was the name given to the Custis family homestead in New Kent, a short distance from Williamsburg, Virginia. Before Martha Custis became Martha Washington, she kept open house here as well as in the Williamsburg town house left to her by her late husband, Colonel Custis.

everything now himself, and Stanton has to bear the blame from those who do not know the real state of affairs. It was Lincoln who made the foolish change in sending General Dix to Fortress Monroe and General Wool[69] to Baltimore to their mutual dissatisfaction. However, the Judge says he does pretty well, only occasionally making these blunders.

McDowell has evidently no capacity as a general. He has allowed Jackson to escape him with all the forces at his command. Judge P. says he has too much stomach; the physical overcomes the intellectual man. He has a stupid, brutish face. Judge P. says that the President told him his plan. To illustrate that he was unchanged, Judge P. stated that Lincoln having mislaid his compasses, said, "Where *be* my compasses? Oh, here they *be;* so come on, Judge." He seemed to believe in McDowell. As Charles says, however, no one who *feels a stomach ache* in battle is fit for a general. How many have lost a limb without feeling it in the mental excitement of the occasion. No one knows better than women how much the body may be made subject to the mind.

June 7, 1862

The Leader of today contains a sketch of Grandpapa Lydig and his father. I wonder if Father will be gratified or displeased. It is a most complimentary notice. How does Grandfather feel about it? How much he would have appreciated Charles! How much they are alike. They have the same aristocratic tastes and habits.

We had a delightful drive yesterday in the park. It seems

---

[69] John E. Wool (1784–1869) was commander of the Department of the East when the Civil War began. He superseded Butler at Fort Monroe and was placed in command of the Department of Virginia. In June 1862, he succeeded General Dix at Baltimore as commander of the Middle Department. He was placed at the head of the Department of the East in January 1863, with headquarters at New York City. Dix succeeded him in this post after the draft riots of 1863 had proved too much for him. He retired shortly thereafter.

strange to me to see how little the rich among us understand about enjoying themselves. *One* stylish carriage, *one* pair of horses, *one* coachman, *one* fine house with over-fine upholstery, etc., and every rich man a duplicator and copy of the other. It seems to me that if I were rich, I should indulge myself in some specialties.

June 8, 1862

Yesterday Charles dined with James T. Brady. He was invited by him to meet two Maryland secessionists, one a Colonel Hamilton whom he took a great fancy to. It was agreed that politics should not be touched upon, but as the evening wore on, it was impossible. Mr. Brady endeavored to make Charles out as leaning as much as he himself did to the South, but Charles told them that he felt no sacrifice was too great to prevent the Union from being dissolved, and had voted against his friend Brady [and] for Douglas,[70] who he thought would have prevented all this trouble had he been elected. Mr. Brady began to talk too freely after a while. [Colonel Hamilton] said: "Stop, sir! Stop, sir! Remember, you are touching chords which vibrate painfully. Remember, sir, you are the wind sweeping over the strings, and they will vibrate when they feel its influence. When I think of Colonel Kenney, how we were friends and neighbors, with what a thrill of joy I heard that he was safe, not killed as was reported, I could not but feel that this was a fratricidal war, although, sir, I differ entirely with you. You know nothing here of war. I see your women in silks and satins, your luxurious living. You do not feel this thing as we Southerners do."

---

[70] Stephen A. Douglas broke with the proslavery Democrats in 1857, and by 1860 the breach between him and the Southern Democrats was wide. Brady ran for governor on the "hardshell," or proslavery, Democratic ticket in New York. Though Brady was a close friend of Judge Daly's, and was soon to become related to him through marriage, Daly could not vote for a Copperhead.

I was observing to Charles that of all the men I had ever met, he was the least expressive of his inner thoughts and spoke the least of his own feelings, the least *self-dissecting*, if I may say so. "It is a very natural result of my life," he answered. "At first I had no one to whom I could talk of myself. Then all such demonstration was repressed by those around, and later the judicial life, looking upon both sides of a question, always represses utterance of anything until it is an opinion." *Advocacy* has just the opposite tendency; it induces a man to talk of himself. James T. Brady is an example. . . .

This evening Laing came in to talk about his picture of the return of the 69th Regiment. He means to have it exhibited for the benefit of the Irish volunteers. I was touched by his generous, kindly feeling. He wishes to put our portraits therein.

June 11, 1862

Dined yesterday at Dr. Ward's and took a drive in the afternoon in the Central Park. If one lived there, no country would be more desirable—one would have all the luxury of a country seat without the trouble or expense. A niece of Dr. Ward, a Virginia lady, is staying there and is a violent secessionist. It is a pity that the abolition female saints and the Charleston female patriots could not meet in fair fight and mutually annihilate each other. It seems to me that the Southern women are turned into furies. The truth is that the South is jealous of the North, and hates us for our wealth and enlightenment. De Tocqueville pays a high compliment to us when writing from Sorrento. He says he would give all the compliments, bows, and good manners of the Italians for the intelligence of the Yankee, who, whilst chewing his tobacco, gives you precise, reliable knowledge of everything about him, seeking in return what you may know about your own country and institutions. One grows very tired of *only* good manners. They make an insipid person all the more so because they give no perceptible cause of offense.

June 15, 1862

Charles, in narrating some of the events of his life, mentioned that when a young man, the two men he most desired to see were Washington Irving and Fitz-Greene Halleck.[71] He wondered if he should ever meet them. The first he met at Mr. Astor's. One cold day when he came there to dine, a gentleman stood warming his hands over the fire, a cheery looking stout man. "It is a cold day, sir," said he, "very cold," stretching out his hands. "You are a younger man and do not feel it so keenly." Mr. Halleck, a few weeks ago, stopped him in the street and, thanking him for his pamphlet on the privateersmen, said, "I am deeply obliged to you, Judge, for sending me your pamphlet. It made the question so clear. What to our minds is obscure, you great lawyers seem to see through at a glance," and they walked downtown together, Halleck seeming to inquire of him as the greater authority.

Kate is engaged to Judge Brady. Will it turn out well or not? I do not believe in disparity of age on either side. Either one or the other is too much dominant, and equality should be maintained in marriage. I would rather Kate should have married a richer man, and one of a more determined and dignified but equally amiable disposition. I fear she will feel the economy she will have to practice. She is not desperately in love; he is. Like Maggie, she is not very constant; I do not understand

---

[71] Fitz-Greene Halleck (1790–1867) came to New York from Guilford, Connecticut, in 1811 and worked as a clerk and then as an accountant for Jacob Barker for twenty years. In 1832, he became bookkeeper to John Jacob Astor until the latter's death in 1849. His reputation as a poet began in 1819 with the publication in the New York *Evening Post* of the "Croaker" papers, satires on political figures written by Halleck and Rodman Drake. He wrote little after 1827, when "Alnwick Castle, with Other Poems" appeared in book form.

either of them. We are so different. I am so much more romantic about love and marriage and so much more reserved, consequently, about my own feelings. It seems that I have been the scapegoat; the family ought to raise a votive tablet in grateful memory of the first bold navigator who showed them the way through the shoals and breakers to the shore of matrimony. I do not believe that anyone would object whoever my sisters chose to marry. I must have been something more precious than the others that they should have made so much ado about parting with me. I, too, have made much the most brilliant marriage, the Judge being not only an eminent jurist, but likewise eminent as a writer and scholar and an LL.D.[72]

When I think of those mediocre people *daring* to interfere and judge *him*, I can scarcely now calm myself. I have ever since longed to be something more to make myself more worthy of him and of the deep love and affection which moved him to endure so much for my sake. I know that Mr. Astor would have willingly received him into his family, giving him his granddaughter, Martha Ward,[73] and the Rhinelanders likewise, Mr. Rhinelander his daughter Julia. Had we a fortune, how brilliant might be his career. If Father could but realize how much he had made us lose (some thousands at least) by his sad mistake and unreasonableness, he would make it up; but he does not. That he deeply regrets the part he had in the matter, he takes every opportunity—unlike my mother's near family connections—to show us. A few days ago when Phil's commission arrived, he told me that if his family became distinguished and honored he should owe it all to Judge Daly, to his popularity and worth, and that he felt that Phil's good conduct would not

---

[72] LL.D. degrees were conferred upon Judges Daniel P. Ingraham, Lewis B. Woodruff, and Charles P. Daly, all of the Court of Common Pleas, by Columbia University in 1860. All three had agreed to act as a committee to examine the essays and examination papers of Columbia's Law School and to award prizes at commencement.

[73] Mrs. Daly means Margaret Ward (later Mrs. John Winthrop Chanler), Samuel Ward's daughter by his first wife, an Astor.

have been so early recognized were it not that he was his brother-in-law.

Sunday, June 15, 1862

Arabella Barlow has been here and has been giving me an account of the battle of Fair Oaks, or as the rebels call it, "Seven Pines." Meagher's brigade, as we supposed, had very little to do with it; the 61st Regiment, of which Frank Barlow was acting colonel, was so far in advance that the first news he received was that the enemy was in his rear. He was unflanked and unsupported and kept the advance at bay. General Howard[74] was so impressed by his bravery that he left him acting brigadier during his absence at that time, the youngest colonel in the brigade. General Howard was shot in the arm whilst standing beside him saying, "Colonel, go to the flank; you are too much exposed." At the same time, his brother at his side fell, the lieutenant colonel of the regiment. There was no bayonet charge at all made and none but the 61st firmly stood its ground, losing all but four of its officers and 200 killed and wounded.

The battle of Fair Oaks, or Seven Pines, was a major engagement between the Confederate army under the command of General J. E. Johnston and the Union forces under General McClellan. Johnston's full strength was about 70,000, and the Army of the Potomac had over 100,000 men, but less than half of either army was actually engaged in battle. Although the Northern troops were successful in driving the Confederates back upon Richmond (just seven miles away), the battle ought

---

[74] General Oliver O. Howard, who led the 11th Corps, lost his right arm in the battle of Fair Oaks. His troops were mostly German, one division of which was led by Carl Schurz. Despite the loss of his arm, he continued active with the army, rode with General Sherman, and commanded the Army of Tennessee until he was replaced by the former congressman John A. Logan. After the war, Howard became commissioner of the Freedmen's Bureau.

to have been a decisive Union victory. McClellan exposed a portion of his army to wholesale slaughter, and only Confederate delays and the heroic crossing of the swollen Chickahominy River by a Massachusetts corps prevented McClellan's right wing from being demolished. On the Confederate side, the wounding of General Johnston affected morale, and communications became hopelessly confused—this despite the presence of Jefferson Davis and General Robert E. Lee (without a command position, however) among the Confederate troops. The Confederate loss numbered some 6,000 to the Union's 5,000, but McClellan's reputation as a strategist was permanently damaged. The battle lasted only two days, May 31 to June 1, 1862.

McDowell is supported by all of Chase's influence, although, as Arabella said, *his* camp is Willard's [Hotel], his fighting ground Pennsylvania Avenue; his enmity towards McClellan is intense; and he it is who urges on Chase to oppose him. She said (which would give the animus of the family) that whilst visiting there one day, Nettie, the younger daughter, took up a photograph book and, suddenly tearing out a card, exclaimed, "Who put that horrid thing here?" She threw it away. It was the photograph of McClellan.

Arabella told me a good anecdote of General Kearny.[75] He and his command were ordered to advance to some place near Manassas, and being a brave man, he moved a little nearer and was the first to plant the flag on Manassas. He was standing on the ramparts when a great flourish of trumpets was heard and up came McDowell with his staff, etc. "How came you here, sir?" said he.

"I was ordered so near," said General Kearny, "that I thought I might venture a little nearer."

[75] Philip Kearny (1814–1862), who had fought with the French in Algiers and Italy and had lost his left arm in the Mexican War, became a major general in 1862. Shortly after second Bull Run, Kearny was shot while reconnoitering near Chantilly.

"You had no right to move, sir. I was ordered to take possession of Manassas."

"True," said General Kearny, bowing politely, "I beg your pardon, but I believe, General, you received those orders more than a year ago," alluding to the battle of Bull Run which McDowell's fit of sleepiness lost. Arabella says that her husband has the greatest respect and admiration for Charles.

June 19, 1862

Father O'Reilly dined with us yesterday. He had just arrived in the *Africa*. We waited in vain for the Judge, so I had him all to myself. He had been much grieved at the want of sympathy shown in Ireland for the North, and says that although England publicly disclaimed all interest in the South, that still she secretly aids it, that vessels for the Confederates are fitting out in several ports, that there were three in the harbor of Queenstown ready to receive their armaments. In the *Africa*, one of the Cunard Line of steamers, one of the officers came up to him, thinking him an Englishman, and after some conversation said, "Well, now, we will agree that it is not sympathy with either side that moves us, but you know we shall all feel glad to see the Yankee nation go to pieces. Besides, although they are afraid of us, they don't like us." Father O'Reilly answered that as an American they could not expect him to sympathize with them in any way, but he could assure them that the Americans had no feeling of fear. They only felt for them what every other nation who had ever come in contact with them did; namely, a feeling of the deepest contempt.

The French constitutionalists, on the contrary—Montalembert,[76] Gasparin, the Duke de Broglie,[77] etc.—felt the strongest

---

[76] Charles Forbes René de Montalembert (1810–1870) was a French journalist and politician, and an outspoken opponent of Louis Napoleon.

[77] Jacques Victor Albert, Duc de Broglie (1821–1901), was a statesman, publicist, and historian.

sympathy with the North. The Emperor would probably feel kindly towards us did we succeed in taking Richmond. At present, O'Reilly thought, Napoleon's eyes were fixed upon the Isthmus of Tehuantepec, which he intends to claim as an indemnity for his claims in Mexico. Father O'Reilly thought the Southerners in New Orleans had sold him their share of the railroad interests there. In England he saw Prince Alfred [Alfred Ernest Albert, Duke of Edinburgh, second son of Queen Victoria], who, hearing that he had been in the battle of Bull Run, wished to ask him about American affairs. He said he deeply regretted the ill feeling between the two countries. His brother [Albert Edward, Prince of Wales, later Edward VII] had been so kindly received. Father O'Reilly said that it was strange and incomprehensible to the Northerners that the reception of his brother was rather a compliment to the son of *Queen Victoria*, whom we reverenced as a *woman* as much as her subjects, not to the future king or the son of the Queen of England. The Prince replied that they had so understood it and his mother had been deeply touched and flattered by the personal tribute, for so they had all felt it to be and that the royal family had done all they possibly could to preserve amity between the two countries.

Soon after Father O'Reilly left, Captain Kirker and two returned Union prisoners arrived, one of whom was Lieutenant Dempsey of the 69th. Dempsey said that nothing we had heard of their treatment in Richmond was in the least exaggerated. The Southerners would walk in and say that though they did not look comfortable, Northerners were used to such things— they were nothing but laborers and used to being shut up in shops. For a free Southern gentleman, imprisonment was a much greater hardship. Whilst in some one of the many gaols into which they were lodged, for their place of confinement was changed every two months when they were carried in procession with a hooting crowd round them through the streets, they were badly off for money. One of the prisoners, being an engraver, cut out on a block of wood a very admirable counterfeit of their Confederate notes. Getting hold, fortunately, of some paper, the prisoners, as Dempsey said, issued paper money to the amount of $300 until the paper was exhausted.

Dempsey said that when he left with his regiment, he was not ashamed to confess that it was because he was ashamed to stay at home. Had he been going to fight the Bostonians, it would have been easy and natural. He looked upon the South as the best portion of the people, but his opinion had been changed by living among them. Such a set of ignorant, foul-mouthed wretches he had never met, to use his own words. No one here, he says, has any conception of the ignorance of the Southern people as a mass.

Poor Mrs. Ricketts, Dempsey said, was forced to do everything for herself and her husband,[78] and the shawl hung up to shelter her from the 300 men in the room was often held up by the cane of an impertinent visitor no matter what she might be doing. Mrs. Ricketts told Mrs. Charles King[79] that when she was obliged to go out to relieve nature, two soldiers walked with her, waited at the door of the privy and accompanied her back. At one of the railroad stations where they stopped, there were some well-dressed girls who cried out, "What have you got there?"

"Yankees," they said.

"Yankees, live Yankees? Oh, I have never seen a Yankee; let me see them."

---

[78] When James B. Ricketts was taken prisoner, his wife was permitted to visit and nurse him in prison. A number of Southern ladies, including Mrs. Joe Johnston, visited Mrs. Ricketts and sympathized with her. Mary Boykin Chesnut wrote of this situation, "Mrs. Rickett was offered a private apartment, but she sought a martyr's crown. She said she came to nurse her husband, and to be with him. She wished to look after the wounded, and to share the privations of the prisoners. I should think she has had a fine opportunity of testing her zeal, occupying a room with half a dozen men."

[79] Charles King (1789–1867) was president of Columbia University from 1849 to 1864.

So they put their heads into the car window.

"Why," said they, "they have hair on their heads just like *we*," as if it was a matter of great astonishment to them.

A reporter of a Southern paper visited Colonel Corcoran and then published a lying account of the conversation in the journal, making the Colonel to admit that the U.S. government was falling to pieces from want of credit, want of troops and munitions of war, and expressing himself as sorry he had had anything to do with it. The Colonel wrote him a letter denying his statements, which of course he would not publish. Then the Colonel wrote to the commanding general with no better effect. He said he did not care a jot about it. Then Colonel Corcoran asked if an officer of the army was to be denied by Southern gentlemen the privileges even accorded to a man under the gallows of saying at least what he had to say. The Southerners think Corcoran a man of so much consequence that they will not release him. Besides, they have a spite against him for his brave defiance of them.

I heard an amusing anecdote of the 69th. A party (among whom was Dempsey) went to Fort Lafayette and suddenly one of them said to the officer, "Let me speak to that man there," pointing to one of the prisoners.

"I cannot break the rules, sir," said the officer.

"But," pleaded the man, "he is my brother. Only a few words within your sight. Let me speak to my brother!"

The officer was an Irishman, so he relented. The first thing he saw was the affectionate brother square off and strike the prisoner a blow full on his face.

"Take that, now," said he, "for striking me with your bayonet when you were guard over me in Richmond, you scoundrel. Now we are even."

And the man disappeared suddenly without anyone knowing who he was, those who witnessed it being strangers to him.

June 20, 1862

Mrs. Hilton dined with us yesterday and told me an anecdote of McClellan. A gentleman was about to tell him something said of him.

"Do not," said the General, "I will not listen. I am afraid I should be tempted to resign, and I do not mean to resign, so I will neither read nor listen to anything about me."

June 24, 1862

Went today to the 12th Street Ward School Commencement. The Judge was asked to address the graduating class, which he did very well and with much originality, giving the girls some good, wholesome lessons instead of flattery. The valedictory was read by a young lady named Bishop, and was full of sense and fine womanly feeling. . . .

June 25, 1862

This morning the Judge and Father O'Reilly were speaking of the present struggle. Father O'Reilly says that the Church has forbidden any Catholic to hold or to teach that slavery is an institution ordained by God, or that the slave trade was lawful. The Judge quoted a conversation with Humboldt.[80] He asked him to give him his impressions as a naturalist, for he knew his strong feelings of antagonism to slavery. Humboldt replied that man was raised infinitely above the inferior animals, even the lowest in the scale. Whatever race of man we might mention was on a plane immeasurably beyond the mere animal creation.

"We may be greatly superior in every attribute to the Negro

---

[80] Baron Alexander von Humboldt (1769–1859), German naturalist and statesman, whom Judge Daly visited on one of his three trips abroad (1851), and with whom he carried on an extensive correspondence.

race," said he, "but he stands on that same plane just as surely and firmly as we."

No naturalist could say otherwise. . . .

Father O'Reilly told me that Meagher had forbidden Colonel Corcoran's health to be drunk before Richmond. How very contemptible!

Father O'Reilly gives a lamentable account of the French and says that there is not a particle of virtue or of religion left, that the country people are almost heathens and savage brutes. They laugh at the ministers of religion. Father O'Reilly thinks that a terrible revolution is preparing. The Emperor has had two sphynxes carved in Egyptian marble for the entrance of the Tuileries. On the morning after they were first placed, on one of them was written with some acid which required the chisel to erase them, these words: *Dis-moi ce que je pense.* The Emperor had it cut out, and notwithstanding the watch-fulness of the police, the next week they found written in the same manner on the other one: *Il ne faut pas croire ce que je te dis.* Louis Napoleon is called "The Sphynx." The incident got into the newspapers despite Napoleon's surveillance and made him furious. Father O'Reilly says that nearly all Paris has been rebuilt, only a few of the old buildings still standing. Is this from vanity on the part of Napoleon III or for his security?

June 26, 1862

Met Judge Hilton this morning, who has just returned from Washington. He was able to be of service to General Viele[81] by giving Secretary Stanton a favorable impression, which the General's appearance and manner confirmed. The General reported himself for orders and Stanton told him to

---

[81] Brigadier General Egbert L. Viele (1825–1902), noted for his engineering work on the plans for Central Park, became military governor of Virginia after he led the advance which resulted in the surrender of Norfolk. He served in this capacity from May to October 1862.

meet at a certain wharf at a certain hour. There he found a small steamer, the President, and Stanton. They sailed down to Fortress Monroe, spoke to General Wool about the feasibility of taking Norfolk, which he approved of but which General Mansfield[82] declared an impossibility. "Get rid of Mansfield," said Stanton, and the General was sent on some duty to Newport News. General Viele was then found to be the next in rank and to him was given the command of the troops for the attack upon Norfolk. The President was so sure that there must be a landing place that he took a boat and rowed along the shore, sounding all the way the depth of the water with a long oar. Some Confederate soldiers came down to the shore, and Stanton entreated Lincoln to return, pointing out to him his danger.

"I came here," said he, "to see if there was a landing place possible, and I mean to find out!" And so he pushed on until he found a spot where he gave orders to land the troops, and there they were landed.

Baron Gerolt and his daughters arrived last evening and so with Kate here likewise, our house is quite full. The Baron tells us many interesting things. He says that a million dollars was offered to the man who would destroy the *Merrimac*, Seward saying that it cost us so much from the delay it caused and the destruction of small craft. General Wool laughingly declared that by the taking of Norfolk he had earned the million, as that had destroyed the *Merrimac*. Had his advice been taken, Norfolk would have long since been ours.

The Baron says that our generals and officers are all poli-

---

[82] Brigadier General Joseph K. Mansfield (1803–1862) had some difficulty with personal relations. Early in September 1862, he complained to Secretary Chase that Scott had superseded him by McDowell, that General Wool had abused him at Fort Monroe, and that now he had been called before a Washington court of inquiry. He demanded active service, and Chase yielded to the pressure. A week after he talked to Chase, he was sent to Maryland and placed in command of Banks' former corps, the 12th, and lost his life in battle two days later.

ticians, each one working for himself, that they get up *pretended* encounters which are published in the newspapers in order to get up for themselves some reputations. He dreads the protracted continuance of the war, fearing intervention evidently. He seems to think the government too lenient towards the secession advocates. In Baltimore, he says, it is the fashion to look upon those who are Unionists as low people. They think, he says, in this way to keep on the safe side in case the secessionists succeed, feeling assured that the government will not resent their conduct.

In the paper this morning, there is an incendiary appeal of the women of New Orleans to the Southern soldiers, the burden of which is that they would rather be buried beneath the ruins of their homes than be left to the mercy of the barbarous Yankees—these barbarous creatures who have done nothing but feed their hungry and clothe their naked since they took their pestilent city. I suppose it was suggested by some Southern politician whose neck is in danger.

July 1, 1862

General Shields arrived here yesterday and came directly up to see me. He has come on business of state to raise, if possible, 300,000 men: 100,000 for service against the rebels; 200,000 to answer the Emperor [Louis Napoleon] and prevent the intervention [in Mexico] which the government dreads. He speaks most despondently of the way in which the war is carried on. His plan was to divide his command into three columns to attack Charlottesville, Lynchburg, etc., the railroads which lead west from Richmond, and cut off their supplies. He went to Washington to propose his plan, where he says he was looked upon as a crazy man.

"What," said the senators, "let Jackson come and take Washington?" So Jackson drew off the army intended to flank

Richmond on the west and by sickness and hard work reduced it to one half.

The General's account of the perseverance and obstinacy of the South is disheartening, and he gives many proofs of the demoniacal spirit of the women. On one occasion, he relates, passing through a little town called Rhea [east Tennessee], a Union man invited himself and his staff to dinner and hospitably entertained them. He asked him if he would be safe, knowing Banks to be in the neighborhood. The General said, as he believed, "Yes." Some weeks after he again passed, and the wife asked him to insist upon her husband being released from prison.

"The night after you left," said she, "he was arrested, but he told me not to be alarmed, that he would only have to stay in prison until you returned; they would do him no harm." The General sent for the mayor and the sheriff. Both had fled. Then he sent for the keeper of the gaol, and at last extracted from him the information that the prisoner and another man had been murdered in the woods and had just been buried before Shields came, to hide the deed from him. Haynes, the one Shields asked for, had asked to say a prayer and was so exemplary that some of his assassins felt inclined to relent, but an *old* man, nearly eighty, seeing this, shot him through the head. When the women were spoken to, they replied indifferently, "Why were they not buried? They should have buried them. We bury dogs, but they were said to be traitors. They were rightly dealt with."

July 3, 1862

The General is full of anecdotes. His command were devoted to him when obliged to fall back after the battle of Fort Republic. The guns were all taken, save but two. The horses having been killed, it was impossible to remove them.

When the enemy came up, they saw a man carelessly leaning against one of the guns and were about to fire, but thinking him wounded, desisted. Just as they came up, the man jumped aside as quick as lightning, touched the gun off, and poured a terrible shower of canister balls, etc., into the advancing columns, making a chasm in the ranks. The gunner, a Tipperary man, escaped in the smoke, joined General Shields, and seemed to think nothing of the incident. He thought, he said, he would just touch the guns off for good-by as they were his.

The General does not feel quite so sanguine, indeed, unless there is some guarantee that generals and not members of Congress shall direct our armies; it is of little use to send more soldiers. McClellan has had bloody fighting, and has been obliged to retreat 15 miles from Richmond. He has, however, now a strong position and has shown himself an able general. His army are devoted. As General Shields says, it is not his fault but that of his enemies, who, to ruin him, would sacrifice a whole army. The General seems to think the campaign over for the summer, both parties having lost at least 20,000.

All day I have been employed in writing out an oration which Charles has been asked to deliver before Tammany tomorrow. It is, I think, a very admirable one and very bold. It is time that Democrats should have something to say. Three quarters of the army are composed of them, yet every Democratic general is persecuted, and the Republicans do their best to get them out of the way.

A friend of General Shields told him that a man had told him that he was going to Washington and that it would not be his fault if General Shields in six weeks is not either in the Confederate Army or in Fort Lafayette. The General is not a well-balanced character, but his military talent is unquestionable. Had he been let alone, the disaster at Richmond would not have occurred. Jackson was in his power, everything ready for battle, the position a superior one when a peremptory order came at Fort Royal from the President to retreat and join McDowell. Stanton and the President together are responsible for all this.

King Log[83] is honest, certainly, but that is but a scanty endowment of virtue and talent for a President of the United States. We are paying the penalty of our venality. We have given offices to the highest bidder and the South has placed authority in the hands of brigands. Some change must soon take place. Why the President cannot be made to cease his interference with military matters, I cannot conceive. Nor why is it necessary to be so forbearing to such malignant foes? If they so brave our anger, let them suffer a little.

Mrs. Hilton told me that a lady who knew [A. T.] Stewart's head-man, Fairchild, walked up to him and asked him to look at her brooch. He said it seemed to be nothing very remarkable.

"No?" said she, "No? It is made from the skull of a Federal soldier!"

Now such a demon in female form as that, I think, should have been arrested. I lose all patience when I think of these demoniac Southern women, whose pride and arrogance have had so much to do with this fearful state of things. Southern ladies and gentlemen, or rather, Southern aristocrats like Governor Manning,[84] General Pillow, Mr. Marshall, and so forth, are very agreeable people with very finished and courtly manners, but they are a class utterly unsuited and antagonistic to the principles of our government. We do not want a nobility here of any kind, except intellect; no millionaires with miles of territory belonging to them and an army of retainers. So they must go down, like the old feudal keeps,

---

83 A reference to Lincoln. See Introducton, page xli.
84 John L. Manning was governor of South Carolina from 1852 to 1854.

etc., which were very picturesque but dangerous from their strength to the public weal.

July 4, 1862

The Judge's oration went off admirably and was much applauded and approved. One man said, "What you have said, Judge, is latent in all our thought, but no one before has had the courage to express it." I have a mind to write an answer to the appeal of the women of the South to the Confederate soldiers, but the weather is so dreadfully warm that all inspiration oozes out at the pores. The Judge brought me home a beautiful bouquet which the Committee of Arrangements at Tammany Hall had prepared for their orator's lady. It was very chivalric and poetical in those rough fellows, as people think them. Tammany is waking up and the Republicans begin to tremble. Judge Whili, who owes his judgeship to his wife's enterprising piety, was here this morning to try to induce Charles to join in a meeting to support the Administration, but Charles refused to do anything but to aid in raising men to prosecute the war.

July 13, 1862

Since I opened this, the weather has been so intensely hot that Baron von Gerolt and ourselves went off for a few days to Long Branch to get a dip into the sea. We have come home much invigorated. We saw Mrs. Hoey and Mr. [Charles] Blake, to whom we paid a visit. He has a charming little house half a mile from the beach. General Shields left yesterday for Philadelphia and Baron von Gerolt for Washington. I spent the day at West Farms, which looked very pleasantly even though contrasted with Long Branch. There is to be a grand Union meeting on Tuesday called in Union Square, of which the Judge is one of the chairmen and at which he is to speak.

July 16, 1862

The speech yesterday was a great success. It was the speech of the day and the meeting was almost as large a one as that of last spring a year ago at the beginning of the war. Judge Pierrepont came in in the morning and Mrs. [John] Sherwood.

The Judge is going to Washington. He says that poor Stanton has to bear the blame of the foolish acts of President Lincoln, who, since the taking of Norfolk, thinks himself a general, and goes about with his compasses in his pocket. He is thinking about being reelected. Can our countrymen be so blind, so stupid, as to again place such a clod, though an honest one, in the presidential chair? What may the country be, and whose may it be before that time? Would that God would raise us up a deliverer. McClellan, the Judge says, is only a good workman, but has no power of combination.

Charles' speech yesterday was very bold. He openly denounced the interference in military matters in Washington by Congress and politician soldiers, and advised drafting the 300,000 men. He was very sorry that he forgot to say something commendatory of Stanton, whom General Shields says took an idea more quickly upon military matters than any man he ever met who was not a soldier, and who is the only man of capacity in the Administration. I sometimes feel a presentiment that Charles will be great some day, and have a voice in the councils of the nation. Perhaps it is only my ambition, however, which makes me feel so.

We have been at West Farms a week. Yesterday the Judge received a letter from Judge Pierrepont in which he tells us that [General Henry Wager] Halleck is to be made commander in chief and that vigorous measures are at length to be resorted to. It is but too true, as President King[85] said in his speech at

---

[85] Charles King, president of Columbia University.

the Union Meeting, that we make war as though we were fighting with friends and brothers whilst the enemy seems actuated by the most direful feelings of hate, revenge, and cruelty. Their women and children and houses are protected by us to afford the owner a safe and comfortable retreat after he has been slaughtering our men, and we pay as we go for everything whilst they only employ the money thus given in buying munitions of war to use against us. We shall have to drive them out in self-defense, even though our feelings are against us.

July 24, 1862

Charles received two very complimentary letters about his speech at the Union meeting, one from General Blenker containing a very pretty allusion to the flag he last year received from the Judge's hand with his patriotic words. Blenker has been most unkindly treated by somebody. The other letter was from Mr. Gouverneur Kemble, expressing his delight at the statesmanlike view Charles had taken of the subject and approving of his proposition to *draft*, as the South does, that we may be able to send masses against them. Doctor [George] Potts likewise wrote to the Judge expressing his sympathies in his views.

I have had quite a disappointment. I made up my mind to ask Father to let me have the old house on the hill and four acres of ground, offering to buy it, and he will not let us have it. I am the more sorry because Charles had taken a great fancy to it. Father might, I think, oblige us in so small a matter. It could be taken out of my portion and I, having cost him so little, having been supported by my grandparents, might, as I am so much older than the rest, have a little more privileges. Instead of which, I have fared the worst. But I must not think of the past if I wish to love my relatives. It is all for the best, doubtless, and I will try to remember *who* has permitted it, and look upon the rest as the agents only. . . . The Judge, too, has done so much for all. Had he not had to come home with Phil when sick at the West, he would have sold those western lands and we would have been independent.[86] I am sure Phil would wish Father to do anything Charles asked after the trouble and interest he has taken in Phil. I feel disposed to go entirely away from the neighborhood, though my childhood associations are all here. Grandfather Lydig is still near at the old garden, and that is all the attraction that barren rock has for me.

July 26, 1862

.   .   .   .   .

Judge Pierrepont has just come from West Point, where he had an interview with General Scott on government business. General Scott, he said, seemed in better health, and he never heard him converse more lucidly. Scott thinks that the war now is one of conquest. He says the Southerners are a united people now, which they were not at first. He gave the Judge an account of this rebellion. The original plan was told him and he was asked, he said, to keep quiet and take no part on either side. The first plan was that Buchanan was to be allowed either to *die* or resign. [John C.] Breckinridge was vice president. He was to be inaugurated by ex-President Tyler. Maryland, Virginia, Kentucky, and Missouri were to secede from the Union, thus enclosing Washington, which would thus be in their hands, with the Congress, archives and foreign ministers, and everything would go on under the new state of

---

[86] For a number of years before his marriage, Judge Daly was active in Midwestern land speculation. By 1849 he had acquired tracts in Illinois, Minnesota, and Wisconsin, and in 1855 he visited some of his holdings along the shores of Lake Superior. Up to this time, he had handled all of his negotiations through a number of agents. Mrs. Daly's statement that the Judge would have realized a fortune had he been able to stay in the West is somewhat doubtful, for he could hardly have changed the economic factors which caused the land values to fluctuate.

things as before. The New England members were to be given the same choice as Buchanan, and it was supposed that all the other states would come into the new arrangement except New England, which was not to be permitted to do so. This was the same plan which Slidell wrote Mr. Charles O'Conor. General Scott says that the Administration was fully aware of all this, for it so pressed upon him that he could not sleep. He rose from his bed one night and wrote it all out fully, sending it to the government, which has never made any use of the document, neither will they return it to him; otherwise it would be published. Governor Hicks[87] was the one who wavered. He came to General Scott for consultation, and the General told him to stand firm and arrest this great, atrocious rebellion. General Scott, under God, was the one man who prevented the success of their scheme by keeping Governor Hicks firm in opposition. The Southerners say that to his *cowardice*, therefore, all this bloodshed is to be attributed, for they intended by this *coup de main* to make the North feel that opposition was useless. The Administration have been most unjust to our great old general. Seward, I suppose, could not believe that anyone could be wiser than himself.

August 14, 1862

Just returned to West Farms after a visit to Dr. Gescheidt at Hastings, and a visit home to No. 84. It is pleasanter in warm weather in the country. One can do nothing then anywhere and we have had an unusually warm summer.

---

[87] A Union man with all the patriotism and timidity of President Buchanan, Governor Thomas H. Hicks of Maryland found his state as badly split as the Union in 1860. The militia companies were secessionist, and Baltimore was a hotbed of sedition. For this reason, Hicks refused to convene the legislature to consider the calling of a secession convention, and when, after the outbreak of war, he did convene the legislature, he summoned them to meet at Frederick rather than Baltimore. The legislature asked the President to try to end the war, recognized the right of Southern states to secede, protested the military occupation of Maryland, and stated its intention *not* to summon a convention to consider secession.

David has just returned home from Milford, and as the government has had recourse to drafting, I fear for him. He is so strong. The weak and miserable and mean will get off. Stonewall Jackson has been fooled in his second raid into the Shenandoah Valley and been obliged to retreat in all haste. Phil writes that Burnside is at Fredericksburg, only twenty miles from Gordonsville, upon which place Jackson is retreating. Burnside will do his best to prevent him from again reaching Richmond. Phil will again be in action. May God protect him.

We received a letter from General Shields yesterday, in which he says that Seward pays Charles the compliment of saying that he is not only a man of remarkable talent, but likewise of great practical ability, and this draft was suggested to the government by him. It will have one good effect; the abolitionists and secessionists among us will now have to take their share.

Ellen Naudain, spending the evening here a few nights since, told us much about the hospitals where she attends two days in the week. She had been attending a sick soldier who told her that he and two brothers and their father had all enlisted the same day and that he was anxious to get well to rejoin them. She thinks the army very patriotic from what she has seen and says they are very much attached to McClellan. The government has now determined to follow out General Shields' original plan to attack the railroads and cut off the communications with the South and their supplies.

Yesterday we spent the day with Mrs. Mary Stewart and went over the establishment of the Sisters of St. Vincent.[88] Mother Jerome remembered the Judge's name and knew Dr.

---

[88] Mrs. Daly refers in one place to the Sisters of St. Vincent, and in another to the Sisters of Charity, who were the same order. Its full name was Sisters of Charity of St. Vincent de Paul. The Academy of Mount St. Vincent opened in 1847 on land which was later taken over by Central Park. In 1856, the Sisters purchased the estate of the famous actor Edwin Forrest at the foot of West 261st Street, overlooking the Hudson. These ninety-six acres became the campus of the College of Mount St. Vincent, an institution for women. The old buildings at Central Park were used during the war for a soldier's hospital (also referred to in the diary).

Powers,[89] an old friend of his father's. She told him that his father was an elegant man who did much good, and said his name was inscribed upon the bells of St. Peter's Church[90] as one of the trustees. They talked together of Dr. Powers, whom Charles seems to hold in loving remembrance. Charles used to sit under his preaching when a child. The more I see of the working of Catholicism in this country, the better I like it. . . . Were I not a happy wife, I would like to be a Sister in such an institution, with no cares for oneself but living only for the good of others, following the footsteps of Christ, whom in the world we forget.

August 20, 1862

My diary is greatly neglected, but it is so difficult to write in the country. Grandmother Suydam has been staying with us at West Farms. She seemed uncommonly well, although nearly 85 years of age. . . .

Charles has been speechmaking in Westchester to try to raise the patriotism of the country, and night before last he made a speech in the town hall of West Farms. It seems the speech was very effective, and the town has made up its quota without having recourse to drafting. The people too raised $4,750 for bounty money. Father gave $250; Mr. Malle $250; Mr. Bailey, $250. I was told this morning that half the village had enlisted. Maria Bathgate said the Judge's speech had changed the public opinion formerly *averse* to the new call for troops. From what I hear, it must have been a very able speech.

Yesterday we encountered Mr. Rodman in the village, who

---

[89] John Powers, a priest of the Roman Catholic Church in the early part of the century when Michael Daly (from Omagh County, Ireland) was alive. Judge Daly's father was a New Yorker from 1814 until his death in 1829.

[90] The oldest Roman Catholic Church in New York, St. Peter's was erected in 1786 and rebuilt in 1838 at the corner of Barclay and Church Streets. It was here that Elizabeth and Michael Daly went to church, and doubtless where Judge Daly was baptized.

seemed to be discontented with himself and the world. He is a mad abolitionist and said that unless emancipation was the policy of the government, he would discourage every man from going to keep or help to foster the fetters on the Negro. He thought the Negro had a right to rise and, he intimated, recover his freedom even by the murder of his master. He does not go to the war, nor none of his kind, but seeks every flimsy *excuse*, this among the rest, to escape. Their [the abolitionists'] fine, patriotic, virtuous, philanthropic *principles* stand them in lieu of great patriotic action. How one despises such creatures!

August 22, 1862

Today Colonel Corcoran, at last free, returns to New York where his reception will be that of a conqueror. He is now brigadier general, has been given the freedom of the city, and has been made its guest. What a freak of fortune, some say, but he is a brave, uncompromising soldier and patriot, who has been true to himself. Such men deserve their greatness, should be recognized. I dissuaded the Judge from going on to Washington to receive him, thinking that the judiciary should keep out of such popular excitements as much as possible. The Judge has gone to meet Corcoran this morning.

We have letters from Phil almost every day. He is so near us, comparatively, being at Fredericksburg. He wrote Father an account of his lunching at the expense of the rebels. Father, more distrustful, wrote him to *beware*, he might be poisoned by those *gentle* ladies, who, in preparing his food, might season it rather too pungently.

August 23, 1862

Corcoran was received yesterday most enthusiastically, welcomed by the mayor and the city authorities and conducted in splendid procession through the city. The streets were crowded. I saw him from a window in Captain Kirker's store and was struck by his air of greatness. He stood in the carriage bowing to the crowd right and left, but in his face was none of the consciousness or conceit which a small man would evince. Nor was there any perturbation of manner, but on the contrary, he seemed to feel grateful only, and I think if I read his face aright, he was not in the least carried away. His manner was full of dignified humility. The Judge left the procession and came for me, and when they reached the St. Nicholas Hotel, where he is lodged, Corcoran missed him and sent Captain Kirker up to see where he was, for he expected him to dine with himself, the mayor, and a few friends. Corcoran feared, he said, that the Judge was offended by all the fuss and parade or by something (his affectionate, grateful heart was lonely without his friends amidst all his honors). . . .

Last evening at the dinner Mayor Opdyke[91] called upon the Judge for a speech most unexpectedly. Charles was much amused when the reporter asked him for the speech, saying that his remarks had been so well considered that he supposed that the Judge had prepared himself and that his report would do little justice to them, that he would be obliged for his manuscript. Charles laughed and said that he was mistaken; they had not been considered. A priest, a Father Houlihan from New Jersey, said to Charles, "Who are you, sir? You are a theologian, a philosopher, a statesman, and a patriot." I have been reading Corcoran's speeches along the routes. He seems to be always equal to the occasion.

September 11, 1862

Since I have been in the city, we have been deeply humiliated, Stonewall Jackson having forced our splendid army and our over-prudent civilian generals across the Potomac,

---

[91] George Opdyke, successor to Fernando Wood as mayor of New York (1861), was a former businessman and a strong Union man.

threatening Washington and invading Pennsylvania whilst the pothouse administration in Washington seems as sanguine as ever. McClellan has been deposed and Halleck has been reinstated as commander in chief. A lady went to ask Halleck, whom she knew very well, a favor to aid in getting a ward of her husband appointed. His answer was that he had always been and was still opposed to the Administration and the Secretary of War and would never ask any favor of them. I feel ashamed of being an American now. To think that we should be conquered by the bare feet and rags of the South, fed from our wagons, supplied from our caissons! Stonewall Jackson told a prisoner (a Major Lee now in our hands) that with three brigades in the position of Pope and McDowell's troops he could have captured the whole of Longstreet's advance. A dying soldier writes to his brother in Michigan, "I die fearlessly. I have fought bravely, but I fall a victim to Pope's imbecility and McDowell's treachery."

Weary of civilian direction and a divided command, Lincoln tried a new equation on July 11, 1862, by putting Stanton in his place, bringing General Halleck from the West to serve as General in Chief, and by making the hero of Island Number Ten, West Pointer John Pope of Kentucky, commander of the new Army of Virginia. McClellan was still at Harrison's Landing, calling for more troops so that he could begin his long-awaited march on Richmond by way of Petersburg.

Lincoln favored the direct attack upon Richmond, with the army covering Washington as it advanced, and Halleck withdrew some of McClellan's forces to accomplish this purpose. Pope was to be the man of the hour, and united under him were the combined troops of Banks, Frémont, and McDowell. When Lee saw that McClellan's troops were being withdrawn from the Peninsula to reinforce Pope, he decided to strike swiftly before Pope was ready to move.

Lee sent Stonewall Jackson with 25,000 men on his famous and dramatic march around Pope, during which Jackson suc-

ceeded in cutting the railroad and telegraph lines between Pope and Washington and in capturing a great quantity of food and clothing. With confusion reigning both in Washington and with Pope's army, Lee and Jackson struck at Manassas on August 29 and 30 and overwhelmed Pope's far superior force. Union losses were very heavy, as the Federals retreated to the defenses immediately outside of Washington, D.C., in a rout reminiscent of the first Bull Run.

The tactics and strategy of Lee and Jackson had been perfect, while on the Union side Fitz-John Porter acted very badly, the Union troops and leaders appeared indifferent and demoralized, and everything went wrong. Pope, who had boasted before the operation began that his policy was attack and not defense, complained bitterly to Washington about the inadequacy of the army he commanded. Against the wishes of the majority of his cabinet, Lincoln restored McClellan to command.

This was one of the Union's darkest hours. With Virginia clear of Federal troops, Lee crossed the Potomac above Washington into Maryland, and the heart of the Union was vulnerable. In the West, Kirby-Smith had taken Lexington and threatened Cincinnati, while Bragg was trying to beat Buell to Louisville to secure Kentucky for the Confederacy and open Ohio to invasion. In Europe, Napoleon III was only waiting for Britain to have her fill of Union defeats before joint assistance would be forthcoming to the Confederacy.

Arabella Barlow, who was here last evening, says that the last blow has been given to the spirit of the army by the appointment of Dick Busteed[92] as brigadier general when the brave men who have been in a dozen battles are unpromoted. Busteed has never handled a musket in his life. It is said that when he

---

[92] Richard Busteed (1822–1898) was born and educated in Ireland. A lawyer, he migrated to New York as a young man and immediately became active in the Democratic party. From 1856 to 1859 he served as a corporation counsel for the City of New York. When the war began, he enlisted in the service of the Union, and in August of 1862 Lincoln appointed him a brigadier general of volunteers. After the war, he was appointed U.S. District Judge for Alabama.

showed the President his letters and said he had others, the President said, "Oh, I know your character perfectly well. You need show me no more." Busteed thought it was all over with him. He knew himself, it seems.

Baron Gerolt tells us that fifteen hundred men were lying for five days, still alive, on the battlefield, and that thousands died from mere starvation, no one going to their succour. The wretched heads of departments know nothing of their duties, and the *honest* fool at their head is content playing President. God forgive the authors of all these horrors and enlighten the mind of the poor creature who dared to take upon himself the high office of President in such a time with no ability to fill the office! Better a dishonest but clever man! Honesty, unfortunately, is often an attribute of imbecility—I suppose to fill the law of compensation which seems to pervade all things in this world. I am sure I would not willingly sit at the table of Lincoln or his wife, much less receive them at mine. In the *World* of this morning there was a very bold article against the Administration. I hope it is a sign of public opinion. I wish the army would take Washington and defend it for the nation and drive Lincoln and his host of locusts, like those which infested Egypt of old, into the sea. Phil writes that everyone now wonders that anyone is desirous of entering the army.

September 12, 1862

Charles dined yesterday with General Corcoran, and did not reach home until late. He is going with him on Wednesday to Poughkeepsie and Albany and will have, I suppose, to speak. The news of this morning is not encouraging. Cincinnati is in danger and Philadelphia is threatened.

Madam von Gerolt writes to her husband to come on for her. She wished me, I think, to take charge of her daughters, but I cannot do it. My house is too unsettled, the country too unsettled for me to find any pleasure in amusing three young ladies—foreigners who, of course, have little sympathy with us. Madam must take charge of her pretty daughters herself, which she can do here as well as stay in a Philadelphia hotel. I like her husband, but not herself. . . .

There seems to be a panic at the North at Jackson's success. As far as I am concerned, I would as willingly be ruled by Jefferson Davis as by poor Lincoln, and I suppose many feel the same. Treason, however, should not prosper. Had the Southerners waited four years, this bloodshed would have been spared and they would again have been in the ascendant with the whole Democratic party. But they certainly have the military talent.

An aide-de-camp of McDowell says that whenever it is possible, McDowell keeps out of danger, and so do most of our generals. They sought their high rank to *live* well, not to *die* well in the defense of their country's liberties, and their chief aim is to live.

Poor Kearny! Though a man of little moral principle—as evinced in his elopement with Miss Mansfield, his present widow, during the lifetime of his first wife, who died broken-hearted—was a brave and competent officer to be mourned by the nation.[93]

Generals Shields and Blenker the President leaves unemployed. He so fears the abolitionists to whom they are opposed, and yet they are two brave, able men. Jefferson Davis would be wiser. His danger makes him so. Lincoln and his crew are likewise in danger. They may be displaced sooner than they imagine by an outraged, indignant people whom they have sold out to contractors. McClellan, after all, has most greatness of mind of all. To the thousands of attacks made upon him he returns no answer, but keeps a dignified silence. This is either the result of great intrepidity and calmness or of weakness. His wife told an uncle of mine that he had telegraphed to Stanton after

---

[93] Philip Kearny was killed on September 2, 1862.

his retreat from before Richmond: "In attempting to ruin men, you have nearly ruined your country." I do not like Stanton's face; it is that of a very self-confident, presuming man. Judge Pierrepont says that Stanton declared himself willing to abide by the judgment of posterity.

What is truth? As Pilate once asked so must we do now among the many contradictory assertions we everywhere hear. In truth, Northern men are educated to act individually and are unwilling to submit to discipline of any kind. This begins in the family, thence to the private soldier, who dissents from his captain, the captain from his colonel, the colonel from his general, the general from the commander in chief, and the generals are all rivals—whilst at the South, Jefferson Davis is the head; Lee's and Jackson's orders are obeyed.

September 13, 1862

Had an affectionate letter from General Shields. It is strange how apathetic we feel with the rebels within our borders. Well, Lincoln and suit will go to the *Devil* at all events if they conquer, and that will be some comfort even if we have to go halfway! Harriet Whetten stopped this morning, dear old soul, to see us. She has seen hard service this summer, and says that the rank and file of the army are splendid. She says little for the officers. The soldiers bear all with unmurmuring patience, but she is disgusted by the coldness and delay and want of feeling in the government officers. She related that the day after the last battle of Fair Oaks, the *Spalding* came near enough for them to go and try to feed some of the men on the battlefield. The cargo was taken out and five hundred of the most badly wounded were to be taken aboard. Orders came to replace the cargo and move to Harrison's Landing (seven miles), where the poor fellows were left.

Harriet has met Arabella, who has been living, it seems, very comfortably at government expense at the hospital at Harrison's Landing near her husband's regiment. She has done nothing, comparatively, but lounge on a sofa, for the men told her that there had not been a lady near them to sit beside them a moment for ten days. The hospital, too, is small. Harriet was asked, although she was a stranger, for a night only to give out the linens whilst Mrs. Barlow was sprawling out on the couch. My instincts are right about her. Barlow, they say, is very cruel to his men. He may, however, be only a stern disciplinarian.

Whilst waiting for the return prisoners from Richmond, the rebel officers came on board, drank with Captain Harris and his officers, and to Harriet's disgust dined on board. After dinner, the Captain asked her if she would not give these men some tea. Harriet said she wished she had authority to say no, but she answered that she only distributed things to the sick. He must ask the quartermaster, who she was vexed to see give it. The rebels said it was $16 a pound, and it would be a great comfort. How contemptible to take it! I would not, it seems to me, have touched a leaf. Harriet said the utmost cordiality seemed to exist between them, and the surgeon said: "Our officers told all they knew. The rebels were not quite so bad."

Charles advised Harriet to leave the boat, as so much is said about the nurses who have gone. Some of the men say that they are closeted for hours with the surgeons in pantries and all kinds of disorders go on. The surgeons dislike, as a body, the Sisters of Charity because they are obliged to be respectful to them.

Five days after Second Bull Run, Lee entered Maryland with the confidence that McClellan would be weeks organizing Pope's defeated army. But here he was mistaken, for McClellan had some magical quality which inspired something akin to worship in his troops. Within a week after Manassas, McClellan was on the march with nearly 90,000 men.

Lee's army consisted of between 50,000 and 55,000 ill-fed, ill-clothed, and poorly equipped men, and when they hit the lush Maryland farms at harvest-time, desertions far outnumbered new recruits. Many of Lee's troops were without shoes

when they entered Maryland, but they had many sympathizers
there and were treated hospitably—by many as liberators.

Stonewall Jackson had an early victory at Harper's Ferry,
and then he hurried to join Lee's main body. McClellan, mean-
time, rushed to overtake Lee, and arrived in Frederick, Mary-
land, shortly after the Confederates had abandoned it. It was
at Frederick that McClellan came upon an order of Lee which
disclosed his exact plan of attack.

Thereupon followed the battle of South Mountain and the
battle of Antietam, and Lee's escape across the Potomac and
back into Virginia.

September 19, 1862

The wheel of Fortune has turned around once more and
the rebels seem to be caught in their own trap. The Potomac
has risen and cut off their retreat, being no longer fordable, and
McClellan has been gaining victory after victory. The last news
is that Longstreet is a prisoner with 15,000 rebels, that the
troops of Jackson and Lee are surrounded and will make a desperate resistance, that victory must be ours. One dare scarcely
believe it, so often has the sequel been just the contrary of what
first we heard. I must sincerely trust that McClellan will prove
himself all that was first hoped.

September 20, 1862

The Judge has just returned from Albany and Poughkeepsie, where he has been speaking. He went up with Corcoran and had an ovation. They told him that they had never
heard any speech better suited to the people. Mr. Savage remarked that he had heard [Charles] O'Conor and had never
heard a better speech for him or more adapted to the purpose.
There were 12,000 present in Albany and an immense gathering in Poughkeepsie. In Albany they dined at the old Schuyler
House, now inhabited by Mrs. Lacy, one of whose sons is an

aide-de-camp of General Corcoran. He describes it as a most elegant mansion. Much of the old furniture has been preserved, and it carries you back to the old-fashioned elegance of the time of Washington. Corcoran, Charles says, is always equal to the occasion, whatever that may be, and the better he knows him, the more he esteems him.

Father O'Reilly and Mr. Savage were both of the party. One old woman in the crowd asked Mr. Savage, "Which is the General? If I could just see him!"

So the Judge said, hearing her inquiry, "Here, General, is an old lady who I think would like to shake your hand."

"Yes, indeed I would," said the old lady. "I have given you all I have, my husband and three sons."

"What," said the General, "all in this war?"

"Yes, indeed," said she, "and here," pointing to a fine-looking man, "is the eldest of them sent wounded to David's Island and just come up to see us at home before he goes back again. We thought we would go down to New York with him and see him off. I'll send them all with you, General, and may the great God give you strength to put down those tyrannical rebellions."

Lieutenant Donovan was there likewise. He had lost one eye, shot out at the battle of Malvern Hill.[94] Hearing them read the news of General Hill's capture, he said, "I wonder if there are two General Hills in the Confederate Army?"[95] He then went

---

[94] Fair Oaks had been reported in Northern newspapers as a great victory, but McClellan's forces began to pull back. Then came news of additional battles from hitherto unknown places—Mechanicsville, Gaines's Mill, Savage's Station, White Oak Swamp—and all that people at the North could figure out was that McClellan was making some kind of new approach to Richmond. In the battle of Malvern Hill, ending a punishing week of retreat, the Army of the Potomac drove the enemy back from the slopes. Now the North knew that McClellan's grand army had changed its base from the Pamunkey to Harrison's Landing on the James, some 25 miles from Richmond. Those with maps could not now be convinced that the battles of the Seven Days had been victories rather than defeats.

[95] There were two Confederate generals named Hill: Lieutenant General Ambrose P. Hill, active in the battles of second Bull Run, Antietam, Fred-

on to relate that whilst lying wounded on the battlefield, unable to move from the nerves in his head being so disordered by his wounds, he had made several ineffectual attempts to move when he felt someone touch him with his sword. Looking up, he saw a commissioned officer standing over him. "Why don't you get up?"

"Because I cannot," said Donovan.

"You have got your eye shot out," said he, "and that is all you will get for going into this business."

"May I ask who I have the honor of addressing?" said Donovan.

"Are you a commissioned officer?" said the other.

"I am."

"Where do you belong?"

"The New York 69th."

"Then, sir, you vagabonds are speaking to General Hill of the Confederate Army. You have a bad wound. You seem to have lost your eye. You are an Irishman, I suppose. That's what you've got for interfering to prevent the Southern people from maintaining their rights."

"I lost that eye," said Donovan, "in the cause of the old Union and the old flag, and I am prepared to lose the other in the same cause if I get a chance. And if I lose that, I can go it blind!"

September 24, 1862

Mr. Barney, the Collector of the Port, was here on Sunday last. He seems much discouraged and wished the Judge to go on to Washington. "You," said he, "have the ear of the

---

ericksburg, Chancellorsville, the 1863 Shenandoah campaign, the Wilderness campaign, and Petersburg; and Lieutenant General Daniel Harvey Hill, active in the battles of second Bull Run, Antietam, the first invasion of Maryland, Fredericksburg, Chancellorsville, and Lynchburg. McClellan didn't capture any Confederate generals as a result of Malvern Hill, but General Lee captured two Northern generals in that engagement, George A. McCall and John F. Reynolds.

President, and he needs advice." He spoke about raising Negro brigades, which the Judge disapproved. Charles said that if that was done he would wash his hands of the whole matter; that recruiting was difficult enough now because of the everlasting Negro question; that President Lincoln was sufficiently unpopular. The Judge said he had done what he could to support the government, not because he thought well of it or its measures, but because he feared the consequences if it should be overthrown.

The new levies came in very slowly. Fifty thousand were as yet last week in the field, and the government had neither arms nor clothing for another 50,000 encamped in Illinois. We are heartily sick of the whole business, and in the face of all this, yesterday the President issued a proclamation freeing all slaves in those states which shall be in rebellion on the first of January next. Better wait until we have the power to perform than utter these weak threats.

On September 22, 1862, a few days after the Antietam victory, Abraham Lincoln announced to his cabinet that he had made a compact with God that if the Confederates were driven out of Maryland, he would free the slaves. The decision had been made by God, he continued, on the battlefield at Antietam, and now the time had come for him to do his part.

Lincoln was asking for neither consent nor approval; he was simply giving his cabinet the benefit of advance information as to the course of action he was about to follow. Some members of the cabinet thought the President's timing poor, but the Emancipation Proclamation was issued as Lincoln prepared it. Effective January 1, 1863, all slaves within any state in rebellion against the Union "shall be then, thenceforward, and forever free."

The South felt that Lincoln was presenting all slaves with an invitation to rise up and murder their masters. The Negroes did receive the Proclamation as a promise of salvation, but the full import of emancipation was hardly within their compre-

hension. Undoubtedly Negro enlistment increased in the relatively few colored regiments organized late in the war, but the predictions of Southerners were far from realized.

If the Proclamation lent impetus to the Confederate war effort, it did little to stimulate Northern enlistment or zeal. The Democrats used it as evidence that Lincoln had been the stooge of the abolitionists all along, and the fall elections bore out the propaganda value of their arguments. Although there was rejoicing among the abolitionists, a relatively small but vociferous group, the more radical among them declared that the Proclamation had come too late. The reaction abroad was similar to that of the North; the intellectuals and the liberals regarded it with rejoicing and respect; the masses looked upon it as merely a political device.

Gradually, however, the significance of this momentous document was realized; to many, the Civil War became a crusade, and if anything gave pause to the British government when they were most seriously considering recognition of the Confederacy, it was the Emancipation Proclamation.

Lawrence, our woodman, was among the prisoners at Harper's Ferry. He says that [Colonel Dixon S.] Miles was a traitor and shamefully betrayed his post. He was shot by one of his own men, one of the Garibaldi Guard.[96] The troops were indignant in the extreme, and he would like to go back again even with all the risks he incurs. He says his feelings are shared by all the rest of his comrades. The rebel officers he thought real gentlemen. They treated their men very differently from what our officers did. The rebels told him that we would never succeed, that they had their friends in our midst and knew everything going on in Washington before we did. Stonewall Jackson said, "We had men enough to beat them, but our generals were not quick enough."

I had a beautiful letter from Father O'Reilly from Albany, telling me about the mass meeting there and the effect pro-

---

[96] The 39th Infantry Regiment from New York City.

duced by Charles' speech. He said he felt proud of having such a friend; how proud I must feel of having such a husband!

Sunday, September 28, 1862

Yesterday was our wedding day. Six happy years of marriage. Few can say this in this world of change. I have been six years perfectly happy. Thank God for the blessings of life, health, and happiness.

The Judge had a letter from Phil in which he complained that Burnside has not been noticed in McClellan's dispatches, and yet he owed his victory to him and even his present position. McC. is jealous and has never mentioned Burnside, although it was he who fought the battle of South Mountain[97] and directed all the moves.

Judge Pierrepont tells us that the President told him that the Emancipation Act was his own doing. The Cabinet were not consulted. He told them it was there for them to criticize verbally, not to argue upon. What supreme impertinence in the railsplitter of Illinois! "It is my last trump card, Judge," said he. "If that don't do, we must give up." Father O'Reilly says we are under a worse despotism than they have in France or Russia. There is no law but the despotic will of poor Abe Lincoln, who is worse than a knave because he is a *cover* for every knave and fanatic who has the address to use him. Therefore we have not one devil, but many to contend with. Yet he only stands between us and internal revolution. It is terrible. God help our unhappy country!

Father O'Reilly seems to agree with us that McClellan is

---

[97] On September 14, the Union Army advanced toward Lee's army, couched on the other side of South Mountain, a spur of the Blue Ridge. Union troops made contact with the Confederates on the western slope of the mountain, and savage fighting began. The result was a victory for the Union forces. Mrs. Daly is certainly correct in stating that McClellan wished all the credit for this and any other victory; he was in desperate need of credits at this point.

wanting in good generalship. He stands idly on this side of the Potomac, whilst Lee is recruiting and furnishing himself in Virginia.

Another winter campaign before us and its load of debt. As for property, it has no value. I do not feel that banknotes are safe day by day. As for gold and silver, one never sees such a thing any longer.[98]

October 1, 1862

General Corcoran, Savage, O'Gorman, and Father O'Reilly dined with us yesterday. I was not disappointed in Corcoran. He is a plain, unpretending man, without a shadow of personal vanity; he is really of the *heroic* stamp—most disinterested, tender-hearted, and a man of very few words. He kept a journal which he told Savage he should give to him. "It will pay you for your time," said he.

"But I don't want to be paid for my time," said Savage. "Oh, yes," said Corcoran. "What do I want with the money? I have no one to leave it to." We all laughed and said that we thought the use of money was to spend it, not leave it behind us, when duty obliged us. Savage has no children either.

Savage seems to think that General [Charles Pomeroy] Stone was a traitor, for Colonel O'Meara told him that the officers would allow no boats to come to the rescue of our poor fellows at Ball's Bluff, saying that it was the General's positive orders. He said that a soldier heard the rebel officers ask where they had received their account of our numbers, position, etc., and they said from the same party as before. Then they added, "But our troops did not come up as soon as we expected, and so we missed some."

---

98 McClellan's failure to take Richmond in the summer of 1862 impaired Northern morale to such an extent that the Wall Street market fell to a distressing low. By mid-July, the gold dollar had reached a seventeen-percent premium over paper, and Congress was compelled to authorize a new issue of $150,000,000 in paper money to alleviate the crisis.

October 4, 1862

Judge Pierrepont dined with us on Tuesday last. He seems quite at sea. No one seems to know what now to expect. He gave us a most discouraging account of the conduct of our men in the field, 200 only being the average of those who would fight in a regiment. It is incredible, he says, how many slink to the rear pretending want of ammunition, etc. Some pretend to fall and are carried off by half a dozen other friends and all kinds of excuses are found. So our material is not quite as good as the papers make out! McClellan, Pierrepont says, is popular because he keeps his soldiers out of harm's way as much as possible. "I think, too," he said, "there were 34,000 on furlough at the last battle." No wonder he says McClellan is popular—with 18,000 stragglers! The rebels shoot their stragglers, so they have none. We talked despondently enough of the state of the country. Both of the gentlemen seemed to feel that it would be utterly broken up into four parts at least. New York would be a free city, perhaps, like Hamburg.

Last evening Mr. Raasloff, the Danish minister, came in. He is to sail in a few days to China to make a treaty for his government. He tells us that the President has not even given any satisfaction to the abolitionists, who will press him to resign. He said justly that we have no political sense of honor in this country. In any other country where a cabinet had been similarly treated as Lincoln did his in this matter of the emancipation proclamation, they would have at once resigned. We felt this likewise. It has lowered them all very much and the nation with them, both home and abroad. Seward, he says, is now at sea. He does not know where he stands, or the President either. When Seward went to bid the President adieu, Lincoln said, "Tell them in Europe we are trying. Yes, tell them in Europe we are trying." He was evidently unable to collect himself to say anything more. They frightened him with the governor's convention at Altoona,[99] and to get the upper hand he seized upon the desperate project of this proclamation. Lincoln had declared to the Chicago convention the principle of the proclamation unwise and false only a fortnight before, so that he has lost the confidence of both parties.

Judge Pierrepont told us that the French are watching our November elections with the greatest earnestness, and hope that the government will be so embarrassed if Seymour[100] is elected that they may interfere with advantage. The French Admiral has gone to New Orleans with his ship of war to protect the 15,000 Frenchmen who he says are living there, and to watch if Louis Napoleon can get a foothold. Louis Napoleon fears for his dynasty. Should this *once* great Republic become united once more, it will give great encouragement to the republicans of France whom the Orleanists have begun to court.

I have just received a most interesting letter from Adam Badeau from New Orleans which contains statements as to the disaffection and dissensions in the South, some of which may be useful to the government if they are known. I shall copy the letter and beg the Judge to send it to Seward or Lincoln himself. The government complains that but few Irish, comparatively, volunteer. They have no idea of fighting for the blacks. The abolitionists, they say, tell them that soon they will have good, faithful, colored servants, and that these Irish will then

---

[99] The reference here is to the meeting of governors from eleven "free labor" states held at Altoona, Pennsylvania, in September 1862 to discuss the state of the Union, and to urge that the government accept the services of colored troops and emancipate the slaves. Governor John A. Andrew of Massachusetts prepared the address which was submitted by the meeting to the people of the North, and early in 1863 the Secretary of War empowered him to raise colored troops.

[100] Horatio Seymour (1810–1886), a Democrat, had run unsuccessfully for governor of New York in 1850, but won in the next election and served from 1853 to 1855. He opposed the draft, emancipation, and wartime restrictions on personal liberty. Seymour—consistently a Copperhead—won the 1862 election, and served again as governor from 1863 to 1865, but his conciliatory attitude toward the draft rioters in 1863 virtually ended his political career. He was Democratic candidate for President in 1868.

have to go back to their poorhouses. The Irish believe the abolitionists hate both Irish and Catholic and want to kill them off. The abolitionists always, the Irish say, put them in front of the battle.

October 5, 1862

Colonel Raasloff came in yesterday unexpectedly to dinner. Although the conversation began by a declaration that no politics should be discussed, soon we found ourselves in the midst of them.

Colonel Raasloff thinks McClellan a general, not a man of genius, not very strong-minded, but a capable, practical man of great equanimity and moral courage who probably knows how much (or rather how little) can be done with such soldiers as his army are composed of and who therefore *saves* them as much as possible on that account. Two Swedish officers who were with McClellan at the battle of Antietam were, Raasloff says, much impressed by him. They said McClellan took a stand where he could see everything and where he could be found. When Hooker was wounded and McClellan's presence was needed to rally the troops, he went to the front, rode through the ranks, encouraged and rallied the troops successfully, and then returned to his place. He was calm, collected, took nothing but a little whiskey and water, smoked a cigar, and after the battle rode out on the field to meet and encourage the wounded and praise those who had fought well. It lightened our hearts to hear so favorable a soldier's account of the general in command.

Instead of following up his South Mountain victory, McClellan took more reconnaissance time—enough to allow Lee to move in from Hagerstown, thus preventing the Union Army from keeping Lee's army separated from that of Stonewall Jackson. Despite this error, McClellan had the reunited Army

*of Northern Virginia outnumbered two to one and caught in
a cramped position between Antietam Creek and the Potomac.
The Battle of Antietam, or Sharpsburg, was fought on September 17. Losses were great on both sides, and although Lee's
army was worn down, it was not driven from its position. Instead of renewing the battle the next day, and very possibly
delivering the final blow to the Confederacy, McClellan refused to fight. With the pressure relieved, Lee retired across
the Potomac into Virginia on the night of the 18th, to fight
again. Despite McClellan's failures, Antietam ended all pos-
sibility of recognition of the Confederacy by the European
powers.*

Raasloff says that we are ripe here for a despotism. We stand
so much invasion of our rights that the abolitionists might establish with little trouble a reign of terror. Raasloff thinks some
opposition must be shown if we would avoid this. And then,
what is most disastrous is the enormous debt, the depreciated
currency. He told us that in Denmark after the war $20 in
paper was worth but one in gold or silver, that one sixth of the
whole property in the kingdom was taken by the government
as a basis for the present national bank, which took the government money for one sixth of its nominal value. We shall come
to this! Raasloff thinks peace on any terms would be better for
us than this ever-increasing frightful debt.

Raasloff has a very unfavorable impression of Stanton, who,
he says, is an irritating pettifogger, no statesman, but one who
tries to trip you up by throwing quibbles at you. He says
Stanton and Halleck hate foreigners and that at one time all
the foreign who had come to offer their services to the country
were to have been sent back, and would have been were it not
for the remonstrances of himself and Baron Gerolt. Stanton remarked they did not want any of those gentlemen. As for
[Franz] Sigel, he is so ill-treated that they say he will be obliged
to resign. So the Irish are right in part, supposing they hate
foreigners, Catholics, etc. We are under infidel rule. I could

not but think this morning in church of what Scripture says of the man who believes himself wise and glories in his own thought. "There is more hope of a fool than of him." A submissive spirit and a pure heart and faith in God, Who, as ruler of the world, must do right, is entirely wanting among our modern New England reformers. They have set up human understanding, the most intolerant of all worship, in its stead.

Mr. Savage this morning told us an anecdote about recruiting which is characteristic. Irishmen are seeking to enter American regiments. "Why do you not go with your own people," said Lainor, the recruiting officer, "where you have your own chaplain, etc.?" The Irishman paused and hesitated, and said he would rather go with the Americans. "Would you?" said the officer. "You would rather go with your own countrymen, is it not so?"

"No," said the man, "I want to go in (naming the number of the regiment)."

"Why is that?"

"Well," said the man, "since you push me so hard, I have a wife and family and when the Irish are all by themselves they do a deal of fighting and get killed. Now your Yankee chaps don't fight much, so I'd rather go with them, you see, as I don't want to get killed either."

October 10, 1862

Mr. O'Gorman has been making a very able speech before the Democratic convention, but whether it will do good or do harm in the present unsettled state of affairs cannot be told. Charles seems to feel that any division at the North now will be injurious. The French are anxiously waiting to see if they will have a chance to interfere. Our money is 27% below par; gold is at 20% premium.

Father offers me my residue, for which I am not duly grateful, as I shall have to lose $400 to place it anywhere. So I think

I shall induce him to keep it until better times. The Judge hates even to hear stocks spoken of, having no love of moneymaking, although a very good idea of spending, or rather giving it away.

October 13, 1862

Just returned from a visit to Camp Scott, Staten Island, where General Corcoran and his legion are. The General obliged us to stay last night and we had a very pleasant time of it. His wife is a plain, unpresuming, unaffected woman who does not seem to wish to pass for anything more than she is. She has good sense and good manners and they seem very happy together and much attached to each other. We saw the dress parade, and afterwards the Judge presented a flag to the Judge Daly Guards with a very nice little speech which the Captain answered very well. There were likewise two swords presented. We then went to Corcoran's house, supped and passed the evening talking and singing songs until long after one.

Father Duranquet,[101] who is confessing the men previous to confirmation, a ceremony which is to be performed on Wednesday and which we are going to see, gave me some most interesting accounts of his ministry in the Tombs. He devotes himself to the depraved and says that he wonders to see how these poor creatures meet death—how they prepare themselves, and with what religious confidence they go to execution. God, he says, punishes them in this life to save them in the next. The more I see of the Catholics, the more strongly do I incline towards them.

The General pointed out to me Johnny Owen, who has followed him and would not leave Corcoran during all his imprisonment. Owen was so unhappy when they gave him his

---

[101] Father Henry Duranquet was one of the parish priests of St. Francis Xavier Roman Catholic Church, located at 36 West 16th Street.

freedom that the General was obliged to beg them to leave
Owen with him. "He washed my clothes, combed my hair,
washed my face, did everything. He would have been a father
to me," said Corcoran "if possible." A small boy he pointed
out to me by name, singularly enough Michael Corcoran, was
a sailor boy in a Baltimore vessel. Hearing of the 69th Regiment led by Michael Corcoran, the boy ran away and joined
the regiment because of the name. The General attaches
everyone to him by his great manliness and tenderness of
character, his utter disregard of self. He treated me as if I
had been a princess. One must feel complimented by such
marks of attention from anyone so sincere. We sang some
comical songs and had a right merry evening in the General's room, which had to be cleared for us to sleep in afterwards.

October 19, 1862

On Wednesday last, according to our promise to Corcoran, we went to Staten Island to witness the ceremony of
confirmation. Corcoran sent an officer to escort me there as
the Judge could not go, so Mrs. Savage and I went protected
by a pair of epaulettes. The Archbishop [John Hughes]
was on the boat. When we arrived, we were conducted within
the lines so that we could see everything, and the General
ordered one of his orderlies to hold an umbrella over us during the ceremony. I never saw anything in my life that impressed me so much. There were five thousand men present
with bared heads and bended knees. Corcoran, who knelt
near us, was at their head. The Archbishop, in his splendid
robes, his mitre on his head, his golden crozier in his hand,
and his venerable benevolent countenance, was supported by
Father Hares, in a deacon's dress, a black cassock, and short
white surplice. Another deacon was on the other side, the

banner was flying, the fine band was performing the music
for the Mass, and beyond the heights [Highlands] of Never-
sink, the narrows and the bay were dotted with sails.

It was a picture such as I never saw equaled. Four hundred men were confirmed and as many more took the sacra-
ment. I could scarcely *restrain* my tears, for I felt it was like
a mass for the dead. Corcoran is evidently a very religious
man.

After we returned to the house, dinner was served and I
sat next to the Archbishop, whom I found a most gentlemanly,
agreeable man. After I felt a little at home with him, I had
a very pleasant time, but I confess I was a little embarrassed
and awkward, although Mrs. Savage insists that I never am,
and never forget my *duchess's* manner, as she is pleased to
term it. I made one conquest, I believe, of old Mrs. Henessey,
an Irishwoman by birth, whom I liked very much myself.
She seemed so cheerful and bright. She shook my hand most
warmly at parting. Corcoran proposed His Grace, the Archbishop's, health in a very dignified speech, and then the Archbishop replied. The Judge arrived unexpectedly and we all
returned together, Corcoran and staff escorting the Archbishop's carriage to the boat.

On Thursday we dined at Savage's with Mr. Kingman of
Washington. Kingman is a Union man, although his wife is
a secessionist and all his friends, as he said, are in "Secessia."
He told us that Foot,[102] who will be president of Congress—
and should anything happen to Lincoln, Hamlin[103] will be
President of the United States—told him he wished the army
would take possession of the government. Foot's idea is that

---

[102] Solomon Foot, a Representative and Senator from Vermont elected
as a Whig and as a Republican, served several times as president pro tempore
of the Senate between February 1861 and March 1865. He died in 1866.

[103] Hannibal Hamlin, Lincoln's Vice President during his first term in
office, was little known and inconspicuous in office. The Republicans
dropped him in 1864 in favor of Andrew Johnson of Tennessee. Hamlin was
a former Maine Senator.

we should conquer Virginia, which will insure us the Border States, and then fortify the Mississippi, keeping New Orleans, Texas, and all the territories; we can let those states east of the Mississippi River do as they choose. We will in time be able to make them return. The idea of the Confederate government is to endeavor to induce the Northwest to join them, aid the French in their design on Mexico (and have a share), and then conquer Cuba and form a gigantic slave empire. There has already been a commissioner sent from Richmond to Rio Grande to confer with the French general and arrange the terms.

Day before yesterday I spent at West Farms with Mother. I found Mr. Weston there, who was as gallant as usual, telling Rosalie[104] that it was fortunate for her that I was married as she would now have some chance with the beaux, etc., and shaking hands three times when once would have been enough. Mrs. Clift was likewise there, looking as affected and conceited as usual. I stayed overnight and went over yesterday morning to Fort Schuyler, where the government has erected hospitals to accommodate 4,000 men. We went into the different wards and into the Westchester kitchen where the ladies were preparing the food for the sick.

Rev. M. Jackson, our clergyman at Westchester, has just been administering the communion. We had a little talk over the times, and we agreed that we are now under the rule of worshippers of the human understanding. Rev. Jackson told me something very pleasant about Phil. One of the soldiers at the Fort, it seems, served under Phil. Young Jackson discovered it accidentally. He was asking the soldier about incidents of the last engagement, whom he was with, etc. The man, not knowing that anyone of his connections or friends would ever hear it, said that they had such a gallant

---

[104] Rosalie Lydig, Mrs. Daly's younger sister. See "The Lydig Family," Introduction, page xxxiv.

young officer with them, a Captain Lydig, who was so kind to his men and so brave. The Captain would say, "Come, my men, we must carry such or such a point. I don't ask you to go anywhere where I am afraid to go myself, you may be sure of that." And then he would come, hiding his uniform among them to make himself one with them. The soldier said that Phil was very much loved and respected.

Charles was appointed a commissioner of the draft, but cannot serve, being still surrogate. They seem in no haste to displace him, but seem to think him the best they have had in many years. Baron Osten-Sacken,[105] the Russian consul-general, spent last evening with us.

October 23, 1862

Went up last evening to see General Barlow, as Arabella had desired us. Poor Frank was stretched upon his pallet, or rather upon the stretcher which had carried him all the way from the field of battle at Antietam. He was very earnest in his thanks to Charles for his exertion in procuring him his brigadiership, and Charles was equally earnest in his professions of having done very little. Barlow gave a fine description of the fighting of the Irish Brigade and said that Meagher rode before his troops during *fire*. He then went on to say how much he admired the rebels, what constancy, endurance, and discipline they showed, with what bravery they fought. Their long grey lines, he said, their shaved heads, their lank, emaciated forms and pale, cadaverous faces made them seem like an army of phantoms awaiting you. They were terrible, he said, and fearful from their fierce hate. Frank told us that as prisoners too, the rebels were impertinent and reckless. He does not seem to feel any confidence in McClellan.

---

[105] See *Personalities in the Diary*, page xxv.

October 23, 1862

. . . . .

The whole North seems to be going for the Democrats. What a revolution of public opinion since Lincoln's election. I almost feel sorry for the Republicans, struggling 20 years for power and losing it after one year's possession. . . .

October 24, 1862

Just as I was going to bed last night, the Judge having gone out, the bell rang and Mr. George Davis, our clever friend from Greenfield, Mass., came in. He stayed until after 2 o'clock, and we talked over Balzac, French women, the deceits practiced between the sexes, the dreadful lottery of matrimony, and the state of the country character. The latter induced him to ask me how I happened to meet my husband and get thrown into such a different atmosphere, for he knew something of that *fearfully* respectable circle from which I had emerged, "like a butterfly," I interpolated, "being then in the grub state."

"Well, yes," said Mr. Davis, "it is rather respectable for enjoyment." He then told me something of his married life, which had not been happy. His wife was wayward, excitable, loved him but tormented him. He had married her from inclination. She was very handsome, regal looking, and clever. She was fascinating when she chose to be, but for several years a wall between them had grown up little by little.

Mr. Davis likes Mrs. Ames of Washington very much and seemed to wish me to see her. He wanted to know what I thought of her, so I went this morning to see her and found her very different from what I expected. . . . I confess that although prepared to dislike, I liked her very much. She told me an anecdote about Seward. It seems that he was very jealous at first of [Commodore Charles] Wilkes' popularity after taking Slidell and Mason off the *Trent*. Seward told a friend, who told Mrs. Ames, that he had sent Wilkes instructions to do what he did. The instructions, fortunately for the country and for Seward, did not reach Wilkes, so Seward was enabled then to say that Wilkes acted without instructions and to come out with the letter which gained him so much praise (which I have before mentioned, at that time).

After leaving Mrs. Ames, I went to see Mrs. General Dix. We lamented together over the times. She quoted what Hillard[106] said, that we were drunk with liberty and in danger of a delirium tremens of freedom. She spoke of how the young acted without regard to the experience or wishes of their parents or elders. Someone said that there was no family government in America. The answer was, in no country was there so much, but it was the young who governed.

As an instance of the sudden manner in which fortunes have been made during the war, Mrs. Dix told me that a saddler's wife went to Tiffany and Young's[107] yesterday and ordered the greatest quantity of pearls and diamonds and plate. Before the war began, her husband could scarcely get his bread. These diamonds, if not of the finest water, are of the best *blood* of the country. Would to God these wretches could be exposed! You see magnificent equipages in the street, and if you look at those who are seated in them, they look like the commonest kind of humanity. Old women who might be apple-sellers or fruit-carriers are dressed in velvet

---

106 George Stillman Hillard (1808–1879) was a lawyer and author who became solicitor of Boston and an editor on the *Christian Register* and the *Jurist*. On the latter, he was associated with Charles Sumner.

107 Tiffany & Co. started business in 1837 under the firm name of Tiffany & Young, and introduced its first stock of jewelry in 1845. The firm expanded and erected its own building at 550 Broadway in 1853, its address until 1870.

and satins. Mrs. Farnham told me that she had gone into a confectioner's and there was an old orange-woman, to judge from her face, dressed up very gorgeously, ordering things for a supper party. She evidently knew nothing about what was required. "Sandwiches?" said she. "What are those? Oh, yes, I suppose I must have sandwiches. Send plenty. And salt, shan't I want salt? Send the salt spoons." And thus she went on as if she feared to trust herself to remember any trivia even.

October 31, 1862

This is the Judge's birthday. Mr. and Mrs. Young are coming to dine with us; I did not ask any others. The time is too sad for gaiety. Charles is busy writing out the history of the surrogate court, the question having come before him. I shall be very glad when he is free again, for it seems to me that our life is slipping away so fast, so little enjoyed. I wish one could stop and rest, as it were, by the way.

Mr. Davis sent me an account of the people's convention at Springfield [Mass.] in opposition to Sumner.[108] It seemed to me, as I wrote him, the embodiment of the common sense and judgment of the nation. If Sumner is conquered, it will be equal to an army of 100,000 to the Union cause in the South.

I have been busy writing some letters dictated by the Judge to Seward on emigration, some thoughts upon education in the form of letters. I have begun a story to illustrate the

---

[108] Charles Sumner (1811–1874), Senator from Massachusetts from 1851 until his death, was an ardent abolitionist and an organizer of the Republican party. His "Crime Against Kansas" speech in 1856, in which he denounced Senator Andrew P. Butler and his state of South Carolina, had led to his being assaulted on the Senate floor by Representative Preston Brooks of the same state; Sumner's health was permanently damaged. He supported the Emancipation Proclamation, advocated harsh treatment of the South after the war, and led the impeachment movement against Johnson.

career of a shoddy merchant, but do not believe I can manage it. I shall wait for some dull, rainy day. This Indian Summer weather constantly tempts me away. I wish I were on horseback or on water, away somewhere in the country, and I cannot think or work. I cannot enjoy myself alone, and Charles is so busy.

People are very much afraid of the draft. The authorities here seem to declare that they are not to be governed by any of the rules laid down in August last. Tuesday next is election day.

The relatively new Republican party faced the Fall 1862 elections with considerable anxiety, for its first major victory at the polls was only two years old, Lincoln had come to power in a four-way contest, and the war had been going very badly for the Union. In New York particularly, Copperhead influence within the Democratic Party had grown stronger as critics of the war and the administration in Washington became bolder.

In New York State, the governorship was an open contest, for Republican Governor Morgan had announced that he would not again be a candidate, and the Democrats were united in their discontent over the prosecution of the war. When the Democrats met in Albany on September 10, they nominated an outspoken opponent of Lincoln, emancipation, and the war effort, Horatio Seymour. The Republicans replied from Utica in September by nominating General James S. Wadsworth, who had conducted himself well at Bull Run and who stood for a vigorous endorsement of the war aims of the Union.

The campaign which followed was vitriolic—the Democrats identifying Wadsworth with the despised abolitionists, and the Republicans casting aspersions on Seymour's loyalty as an American. Lincoln watched the contest with more than a little anxiety, for though New York was not the barometer of public opinion in the Union, it was an important state and the gubernatorial contest there was as big a one as was conducted in the North in 1862. Further, England and France would be

close observers of this most critical election, insofar as their
decision about intervention was concerned.

When the returns were in, Seymour had carried New York
by a majority of more than 11,000 votes, a disheartening blow
to all who believed strongly in the correctness of the Union's
position. The New York Assembly was returned with a fifty-
fifty balance, and little could be predicted from that.

On a national level, the Democrats gained strength in such
states as New Jersey, Pennsylvania, and Ohio, and even in
Lincoln's own state of Illinois. But despite substantial gains
in the number of Democratic Congressional seats, the Repub-
licans still retained a majority vote in the House, and their
strong control of the Senate was not in contest. From a prac-
tical standpoint, therefore, Lincoln had received little more
than a reprimand at the polls to spur him on to greater efforts.

November 6, 1862

The election is over and Seymour is the Democratic
Governor; 36 congressmen and senators probably elected.
There has never been so great a revolution of public feeling.
Everything two years ago was carried by the Republicans,
but now radicals have ruined themselves and abolitionism. As
a popular Democratic song describes it: "It has died before
it was weaned, weaned, weaned; it has died before it was
weaned." Seymour, however, is not the man that the Democrats should have nominated. Their nominee should have
been Dix, or someone who exerted himself for the war.
Neither should they have nominated those two scamps, Fernando Wood and his *foolish*, unprincipled brother [Ben-
jamin] for Congress. It is a blot upon the party, and doubtless Fernando has paid the wire-pullers handsomely. He has
a good tool in his brother, and if made Speaker of the House,
as I see is spoken of, may stand a chance of the White House.
He is both so clever as well as unscrupulous that he should
not be trusted with any power, and he is now so rich that he

has great influence. John Van Buren[109] made a very clever demagogue kind of speech in Tammany Hall the day before election period. He mentioned that General Scott said: "If the country wishes to give Lincoln courage, elect Seymour." I seem to feel that there is now some hope of a return of good feeling in the South.

I sometimes wish that Charles were more ambitious. He would shine in public life and be an ornament to the country. Had we a settled competency, I sometimes think he would allow himself to run for a seat in Congress, or as senator. Perhaps, however, we might not be so happy together were he a greater man in public estimation. . . . The Republican press seem more exasperated than the Democratic with the Administration, and attributes their defeat to its incompetency and want of energy.

The Corcoran legion leaves today for the war. Poor Corcoran has been prostrated by fever. I wish to give him something, but do not know what to offer. May he live to enjoy the reputation that his bravery and nobleness of character have made for him! . . .

November 9, 1862

Those whom the gods wish to destroy, they first make mad. President Lincoln has removed McClellan and appointed Secretary [Caleb B.] Smith of the Interior, a poor country lawyer, Judge of the Supreme Court. Burnside succeeds McClellan. I trust that he will not allow himself to be goaded on by the public clamor to do anything rash with the new levies.

We have had a terrible snowstorm, lasting three days, which is very much against the advance of the army. Poor Corcoran has been obliged to leave in the midst of it yesterday. The Judge went to Staten Island to bid him good-by.

---

[109] John Van Buren, son of President Martin Van Buren, was a prominent New York lawyer who was identified with the Copperhead element in the city.

I sent him a little pocket Shakespeare by way of remembrance. He sent his sword, gold medals, and watch to us to take care of for him. I trust he may live to return. . . .

November 16, 1862

. . . . Had two letters from Phil, one directed to me, one to Charles. He does not approve of the removal at this time of McClellan, although he has the highest opinion of Burnside and believes him fully as able as McC.[110] He fears this organization, the enemy being so near and McC. so popular. The army, he says, curse the Administration as the cause of all the reverses of the Union army. . . .

November 21, 1862

Received a letter from Phil containing a vignette. How much he has improved! How handsome he is! His face has lost none of its sweetness, but has much gained in manliness. He was a boy when he left us; he is now a man.

Paying a visit to Mrs. [George H.] Stout, I encountered young Anchinoty, who had come home on sick leave. He had been with McClellan on the James River. He hears the same testimony to the bravery of the rebel soldiers as General Barlow and others. On one occasion, whilst at Harrison's Landing, they had posted themselves to defend the embarkation of the troops. They had 400 guns, 10 and 30-pounders

---

[110] On November 7, Stanton's Assistant Adjutant General, Catharinus P. Buckingham, arrived from the capital with an order ostensibly from Halleck directing Burnside to accept command of the Army of the Potomac. This was the third time that Washington had offered the post to Burnside, but previous to this he had too many doubts about his own capacity to accept such a responsibility. McClellan received the order relieving him of command with aplomb, and wrote to his wife afterward, "Alas for my poor country!" He was ordered to report to Trenton, where there had been no military activity since 1776, and await orders.

ranged in three lines (one behind the other), and the gunboats on their flank. They never dreamed of an attack upon such a formidable front. Anchinoty said a dense column emerged from a wood, and although an incessant fire was poured into the enemy by their guns and the enemy were shelled by the gunboats, they still came on and on. Finally guns had to be sent to the rear to prevent their being captured, and our men had to defend themselves with their bayonets. Anchinoty allowed that McClellan allowed too many Virginians to come prowling about his camp and was too lenient towards stragglers and deserters. He confessed that although he liked McClellan personally extremely, still he thought him too tame and too slow as a general and not strict enough in maintaining discipline. Anchinoty said McClellan's heart was not in the war, but I don't think this.

We had a great discussion afterwards upon the politics of the day. Mrs. Stout thought it such a shame that Wadsworth,[111] *after all he had done*, had been defeated by Seymour, who would now urge a disgraceful peace. I said that it was very strange, for the thing the Democrats most feared was that the Republicans would make peace and divide the country in order to keep the power in their own hands, that the Democrats were totally opposed to peace on such terms.

Mrs. Gibbs, whom I went afterwards to visit, was beside herself with vexation that Fernando Wood should have been elected to Congress. "A rogue, a thief," said she, "whom we were only too glad to get rid of as mayor." I ventured to say that there were rogues on both sides, on the Republican side not as yet so well known (but who had their fortunes yet to make and therefore are more dangerous). Since Fernando

---

111 Major General James Samuel Wadsworth (1807–1864) was a soldier and lawyer, the military governor of Washington, D.C. in 1862, and the unsuccessful Republican candidate for governor of New York in 1862. He commanded divisions at Fredericksburg and Gettysburg, and was killed in the battle of the Wilderness on May 6, 1864.

has already made his fortune, he can now devote himself to making a good reputation for himself. Mrs. Gibbs blamed the Administration. Lincoln was a well-intentioned man, she said, but utterly incompetent; but then the Republicans had been hampered by keeping so many Democrats in office. I asked *whom* they had retained. She could not mention any, but said, "They have; there were many Democrats. They should have been all turned out."

"What," I said, "when two thirds of your army are Democrats? That they would scarcely dare to do! What, let us fight *your battle* at our own expense and give you the spoils? There would soon be an end of the Illinois Attorney and his advisers at Washington!" . . .

Goodwin Berrian[112] has just left me. He came up to tell me how scandalously they were talking about them in the parish. The Dr. invested his property all in Western lands which, being now unavailable, his daughters will be reduced to an income of $450. He therefore begged a temporary provision for his daughters from the vestry. Dr. Berrian being always considered a rich man, I as well as the rest thought it at first very strange. The brothers are quarreling to have the Western property sold, bring what it may, and the son-in-law means to contest the will because, having received a fortune with his wife, his children are left but a thousand dollars apiece. Alas for the ties of affection and blood when money comes between.

November 23, 1862

Went to call today upon Mrs. Marcy and Mrs. Mc-Clellan, who are at the Fifth Avenue Hotel. The General has been most warmly received. John Van Buren, Mrs. Judge

---

[112] Son of William Berrian (1787–1862), clergyman, author, and rector of Trinity Church in New York City from 1830 until his death on November 7, 1862.

Roosevelt, Mrs. Francis B. Cutting,[113] Mr. and Mrs. [August] Belmont, and a number of others were there and I had a very pleasant visit. Wrote to Phil to ask if there was any place for Lieutenant Nolan.

November 26, 1862

On Monday we had a gentleman to dine with us whom I did not at all like, Mr. [Gideon J.] Tucker, the new surrogate. His little turned-up pug nose pronounced him conceited and his speech likewise betrayed him. He is nothing but a politician, has been in the legislature, and sold a lease of Washington Market to certain parties to the disadvantage of the city but greatly to the advantage of himself. He is a needy man and takes the office for hire and will doubtless make more than his salary therein. *Seven* men nominated him and 100,000 obeyed them. So we are ruled by an *autocracy*, not a democracy. If this is not stopped, neither life nor property will long be safe under our boasted free government. I wish to heaven that Charles was independent of public office. I shall do my best to induce him to decline renomination and resume his profession. In a few years he will then have a competency and freedom and can take an office and yet feel quite independent.

Received a letter from Captain Badeau, who deprecates a secession of the West from the East, and one from Harriet Whetten from Portsmouth Hospital. She says the soldiers are like great children, and seem with their oath of allegiance to give up all personal responsibility.

The new surrogate allowed himself to be in favor of letting the South go to govern itself.

---

[113] Francis B. Cutting (1805–1870) was a lawyer and jurist who served as counsel in leading commercial cases from 1840 to 1853, and was a Democratic Representative from New York from 1853 to 1855. He then returned to his law practice.

December 1, 1862

Went Saturday to the theater to see "The Clandestine Marriage," which was admirably performed at Wallack's.[114] John Gilbert[115] played Lord Ogilvy, Mrs. Vernon[116] the old aunt. In the box above were Helen Russell and Lord Cavendish,[117] Mr. and Mrs. Belmont and some others. Miss Helen served the purpose of an entr'acte to us. It was the comedy of real life. She little knew how she amused the parquette by her attentions to my lord. . . .

Went yesterday to see new flags presented to the officers of the Irish Brigade and the old, tattered, and bullet-riven ones consigned to the care of Mr. John A. Devlin. The ceremony took place at his house at Fort Washington. Judge Hilton drove us out in his carriage and I was edified by hearing the two judges discuss politics and politicians. What a state of corruption! Judge Hilton said that he hoped the old gentleman would take Fernando Wood to himself, that was all which could be hoped, that Wood had such demagogic talents that he fooled the masses.

General McClellan was expected to present the flags, but he did not arrive; therefore, the ceremonies went on without him. Captain Magee, on the part of General Meagher, con-

114 James William Wallack (c. 1795–1864) was a London-born actor and theater manager who moved to the United States in 1852 and managed several New York theaters which bore his name. In 1861 he built his own theater at Broadway and 13th Street, where his troupe won the reputation of being the finest theatrical company in New York.

115 John Gibbs Gilbert (1810–1889), an American comedian noted for his wide range of characterizations, was a great success in all the important cities of the United States and in London.

116 Jane Marchant Fisher Vernon (1796–1869) was a British-born actress connected with Wallack's company in England and in the United States.

117 Spencer Compton Cavendish (1833–1908), son of William Cavendish, 7th Duke of Devonshire. He visited the United States in 1862, at which time he carried the title of Marquis of Hartington and was a Liberal member of Parliament. On his father's death in 1891, he became the 8th Duke of Devonshire.

signed in a very soldierly, unaffected speech, the old flags to
Mr. Devlin's care. Mr. Saunders presented the new ones in
a very appropriate and touching address to which Magee
responded admirably well. Magee is a natural orator. The
Archbishop was present, as were J. T. Brady, Mr. Belmont,
Mrs. Meagher, and several other ladies and gentlemen. After
the presentation, we had a splendid collation, the officers and
gentlemen in one room, we ladies in another with about a
dozen gentlemen who were detailed to wait upon us. The
collation was by Delmonico's[118] and excellent, with splendid
fruit. Mrs. Devlin is a very ladylike and I should think an accomplished woman. I was invited because of having contributed to the first standards. It was very touching to see the
old, faded, tattered standards which I had seen in all their
first freshness, and the officers of the brigade, with their
honorable scars, who received the second ones.

The Judge today met a Captain Earle of the English army
who had been with Phil before Fredericksburg. He is coming
to dine with us on Monday next, when I think I will ask
Imogen Willis and Kitty Dick to meet him. I will add the
artist Bierstadt to the party.

Today I have been employed in writing letters for the
Judge to Seward, Baron Gerolt, and Mr. Barney, the Collector of the Port, to endeavor to urge the government to do
something toward favoring emigration to this country. I had
to lend Father Peltz a hundred dollars to go to Washington
with, and had to borrow it to do so. If he succeeds, Chengwatana and Superior[119] will be something, and be worth
something. If not, a hundred dollars will not make me much

---

[118] The elegant Delmonico's Restaurant, which became world-famous
for its elaborate European and American menus, was established about 1834
on William Street by Lorenzo Delmonico and his two uncles. In 1861 it
moved to Beaver Street, and made several subsequent moves.

[119] Chengwatana, in Pine County, Minnesota, and property on the north
shore of Lake Superior were among Judge Daly's fields of land speculation.

the poorer. Besides, it is worthwhile doing it for a patriotic purpose alone, and nothing else can save us but a fresh emigration. The crops are wasting in the fields for lack of laborers to gather them.

December 6, 1862

Mr. Peltz and I have at last succeeded in drawing a letter from Mr. Barney to Seward about emigration, and I think we have some chance of success. If we succeed, the country will soon recover the effects of the war. I think I must for future reference write a sketch of Edward Peltz.

Peltz began life as a bookseller in Berlin. His parents, it would seem (from what he has told me), were strict formalists, very *severe* Christians, and desperate churchgoers and Sabbath-keepers. As he grew up, being always obliged to so much religious profession, Peltz took a disgust to all religions and professes now no allegiance to any faith. From Berlin he went to St. Petersburg, where he was well received by the best society, being not only a publisher but a literary man himself. He must have been a very interesting companion, as he spoke French, German, English, and Swedish, and has a very considerable musical talent. He sang well to the guitar and wrote good verses, particularly satirical verses. He returned to Germany rich and bought an estate in Saxony, went into farming, acquainting himself with all the new ideas upon prepared soils, artificial manures, etc. He wrote, among many things, *Letters from St. Petersburg* and *The History of Peter the Great*, in which he exposes the miseries of the Russian peasantry and the oppression of the government.

On the occasion of a visit from one of his Russian friends, Peltz was asked why he was silent upon the evils of his own country when he had been so severe upon Russia. His attention was called to the distress of the Saxony weavers. Peltz's humanity was at once interested. He wrote a pamphlet upon the subject for which he was imprisoned. He lost his monies by continuing to oppose the government, was afterwards a very influential member of the Congress of Frankfurt [Frankfurt Assembly] and at last was banished to America. No country, as he says, would receive him until he came here, and now he has devoted himself to do what he can for us, for the nation which gave him a home. Peltz is much respected as a writer in Germany and trusted because of his uncompromising probity. He is the greatest living authority upon emigrant matters. To direct a great European emigration to the Northwest is now the master passion of his mind. He takes of this a statesmanlike and philanthropic view, for he does not own an acre of land on the Western continent.

For the last two years, I have been his aider and abetter, and the old man is as grateful to me as though I had done him some personal service. "You encourage me, madam," he says, "in my hobby. It is all I live for." On account of his uncompromising integrity, he was much persecuted by the emigrant runners whose object it was to deceive and plunder the poor emigrants during the years from 1856 to 1858. The Judge first made his acquaintance by a complaint lodged against him which, by investigation, he found was a combination formed against him by the emigrant runners to send him to the state's prison because he hindered their machinations. The Judge personally went to the Justice and had the matter fully cleared up, justifying Mr. Peltz, for which the old man holds him in most grateful remembrance and says it would be well for America were there many such conscientious, wise officials. There are no subjects upon which my old friend cannot give useful suggestions. There is nothing which he has not studied, and although he has some faults of manner, he is always a very satisfactory companion.

Mrs. General Burnside called upon me this morning. She is a pleasant, lively woman, and, I should think, clever.

Paid a visit to Cousin Mary Sheaff, who told me how much [Uncle] Lydig and Gould thought of the Judge. "Maria," said they, "has made a great match. The Judge is known all over Europe."

"Indeed," said I, "have they just found that out? I knew it six years ago."

My own family were the only people to whom he was unknown, which pronounces them to be so. It was very nice, certainly, to be so particular in trying to keep the only great man we have out of the family.

December 7, 1862

Last evening the Judge dined with the St. Nicholas Society. John Van Buren being president, he made an excellent speech. Judge Pierrepont spoke but was so prosy that he groaned into silence. Evarts likewise made a clever speech. . . .

December 9, 1862

Had a very pleasant little dinner company yesterday. An English captain who had been in the Crimea and had been in camp with Phil, Mr. [Townsend] Harris,[120] our minister to Japan, N. P. Willis, two young pretty girls, and Mr. Young. Mr. Harris told me a great deal about Japan. The climate, he says, is perfect, the thermometer never falling below forty degrees, seldom rising above eighty degrees, the scenery unsurpassed, the green lanes about Jeddo affording the most beautiful rides for equestrians. Had it not been for his associations, Mr. Harris would never have returned, but he could not live longer without interchange of ideas. He received the mail only twice a year, sometimes not so often,

---

[120] See *Personalities in the Diary*, page xix.

and until Lord Elgin[121] arrived, had not seen a European for 12 years. . . .

Willis made himself very agreeable. He harped upon his age and growing infirmities, wished he might be buried to the world officially here and taken to Jeddo to live the rest of his days in that calm, terrestrial paradise.

December 14, 1862

A few evenings since, the Judge met Dr. Mac-Gowan,[122] the great Japanese and Chinese traveler and scholar who had been twenty years in those countries, at the Ethnological Society. MacGowan proposed that measures be taken to explore the country north of Canton, the island of Formosa, and the island of Korea, which he said would furnish much useful knowledge as to agriculture and in comparative philology. In the country north of Canton particularly, Mac-Gowan said the people had never been conquered and spoke one of the oldest languages in the world. The Judge rose and seconded the motion. . . .

On Thursday last, Mr. Schleiden and Baron Osten-Sacken dined with us, Charles bringing them unexpectedly to dinner. Mr. Schleiden said that the Emancipation Proclamation was looked upon in Europe as an admission that the government did not consider it possible to restore the Union on the old basis.

Today the papers say a battle is raging at Fredericksburg. It began yesterday and at night neither side had the advantage.

---

121 Undoubtedly James Bruce, 8th Earl of Elgin and 12th Earl of Kincardine, a British diplomat who was special envoy to China and Japan from 1857 to 1859 and became governor general of India in 1862.

122 Dr. D. J. MacGowan, at this time a surgeon in the U.S. Army, was active in American Geographical Society affairs. He delivered a series of lectures on Japan before the Society, and tried to arouse interest in a plan which contemplated diplomatic, geographical, scientific, and economic objectives in Annam, an empire which became a French protectorate in 1884, was named Central Vietnam in 1949, and is now divided between North and South Vietnam.

It was to begin at daylight again this morning. God help us and protect my brother!

They have this winter an admirable German opera. We went on Thursday evening to hear "Fidelio" given for the benefit of Carl Anschütz, the director. We had the three overtures composed for it by Beethoven, one before each act, and the music surpassed even the high anticipation I had formed. . . .

Had a letter from Mr. Peltz. Mr. Seward wants to put him off.

Yesterday the Judge was invited to go on an excursion up the Bay to the Navy Yard and the *Great Eastern*, a revenue cutter. The party consisted of eight Americans and the English noblemen now visiting New York: Lord Cavendish —the son of the Duke of Devonshire, the Marquis of Hartington—and some baronets and officers whose names I do not remember. Charles found them, he said, very simple, unobtrusive gentlemen. He enjoyed his excursion very much, as well as a magnificent collation on board the *Great Eastern*.

October was a bleak month for the Confederacy, after the promising situation at the beginning of September. Lee's Army of Northern Virginia retreated to the Shenandoah Valley in a state of demoralization, and Braxton Bragg was making his way back to central Tennessee after a defeat at Perryville at the hands of Buell on October 8. Not only was Maryland lost to the Confederacy, but so was Kentucky, and both Confederate generals knew that their troops and supplies were not up to renewed invasions. Now it must be a defensive war for both Confederate armies.

In the North, rage mounted again over McClellan's delays and failure to take advantage of opportunities. An exasperated Abraham Lincoln waited until October 6 before ordering McClellan to pursue Lee across the Potomac. True to form, McClellan demanded more troops, more supplies, more food and clothing before he would budge, and when the procrastina-

tion allowed Lee to once more get between the Army of the
Potomac and Richmond, Lincoln fired McClellan. Side-
whiskered, gentlemanly Burnside was placed in command of
the great Army, despite the incompetency he had demonstrated at Antietam, and Halleck remained general-in-chief in
Washington.

Burnside made his advance on Richmond and got as far as
the Rappahannock River, where he took a position on Stafford Heights overlooking Fredericksburg. Lee and Jackson,
meantime, rapidly approached the enemy and took position on
the wooded heights above Fredericksburg before Burnside
could cross the river. On the 12th of December, Burnside
crossed the river, and on the 13th he made a series of frontal
attacks on the Confederate intrenchments.

Six times Burnside sent his magnificently uniformed troops
across an open plain covered by Confederate artillery and entrenched riflemen to the foot of Marye's Heights, and six
times they were mowed down by the Confederates in a terrible slaughter. Burnside's losses were nearly 13,000 to less than
5,500 for the Confederates. Although Burnside accepted entire responsibility for the frightful waste of life, Lincoln could
do nothing but bear with an unhappy situation on the eve of
the national elections throughout the North.

When Burnside retreated from Fredericksburg with his still
magnificent army of 100,000 men, many in the South thought
that the Union would finally give up. But Lee's army was in
no position to pursue, and Lincoln was not about to abandon
the cause despite his failure to find a leader equal to the su-
perb Northern armies in the East. An angry public shifted the
blame from Burnside to Secretary Seward, but the President
rode out this storm, too.

December 20, 1862

I have had no heart to write. Since I opened my diary
last, the battle of Fredericksburg has occurred and our repulse with the loss of 14,000 killed, wounded, and missing.

Burnside hoped to surprise the enemy, but our dilatory government officials kept his bridges and supplies so long behind-
hand they had two weeks to fortify themselves. Poor Burnside will therefore have to suffer.

It is surprising how people spend despite the present distress. The artists say they have never been so busy. Bierstadt is
even offered more than he has asked for his pictures, and every
place of amusement is crowded.

This week we have attended Dr. MacGowan's lectures on
Japan, and learned more in an hour and a half than in a month
of reading. He is an excellent, genuine, clever little man, and
his wife is the daughter of a master in chancery in England,
a superior woman I should think. . . .

Whilst he and Mrs. MacGowan were here, there was a
ringing of the bell, and who should come in but Phil, Captain
Phil, just arrived from Fredericksburg. How glad we were to
see him! It is almost a year since he left, and he looks so
strong, manly, and handsome. We shall have him for Christmas. . . .

There is a rumor tonight that Seward has resigned and
Sumner has been appointed.

Saw Mrs. Tom Gibbs last Tuesday. I called late and asked
for her, and I had a very pleasant visit. In the course of conversation she said, "Don't you think, Maria, that everybody
now is very good and charitable? Dr. [Francis E.] Lawrence,
the clergyman at the Church of Holy Communion, however,
says that he does not think the world any better now than
before. What do you think?"

I was obliged, I said, to agree with Mr. Lawrence that
religion was the fashion, that it was advantageous to people
in this world. . . .

Mrs. Gibbs, when I first remember her, was the lady of
fashion and ruler of it in this city. She had just returned from
Paris and gave the most delightful select musical parties, little
suppers and masquerades, to which Mother sometimes went,

etc. Now she wears a widow's cap and eschews society. She had a very severe tongue, but I always liked her very much. . . .

Peltz returned yesterday, much encouraged by the reception he had met with. The Judge has promised to draw up a bill which Elijah Ward,[123] Mr. C., and Senator [Ira] Harris promised to bring before Congress and the Senate during this session if possible. It is unfortunate for him that Seward has resigned, for he favored emigration. Peltz tells me that Charles' name is of more weight than Barney's or any other man's in Washington. . . .

---

[123] Elijah Ward (1816–1882), lawyer, served as Congressman from New York from 1857 to 1859, and again from 1861 through the end of the war. After the war, he was elected to the Bench of New York.

1863

Almost a fortnight since I opened this. Christmas and New Year both past. I do not feel comfortable about Kate's marriage. I fear both are of uncomfortable tempers, and on knowing Judge Brady more intimately, I find he has some small vanities which Kate will at once perceive and will not humor. Perhaps, however, they may discipline each other. . . .

New Year's Day was very agreeable. We had between 70 and 80 visitors. Florence spent the day with me and we took her home in the evening. There was a great variety in the men who called, and the conversations, therefore, were varied and interesting.

Day before yesterday, Phil dined with us and we asked Mr. Barney, Temple Prime, and David to meet him. We had a pleasant evening. Phil is very modest and talks but little of his experiences. The Judge mentioned that he had met a colonel at Judge Pierrepont's on New Year's Day who said that had it not been for the want of heart in the brigadier generals, they could have carried the entrenchments, but that Hancock[1] and Meagher were the only ones who persevered.

---

[1] Winfield Scott Hancock (1824–1886) distinguished himself at Fredericksburg, Chancellorsville, and Gettysburg. He commanded the Corps in the Wilderness Campaign, and was highly regarded by Grant. As military

Phil then mentioned that they had all agreed with General Burnside that the attack should be made and that it would be successful until it came to the point of who should take the advance. Then one by one they thought they had better not attempt it. Phil did not seem to think so much of Hooker. He said you would find by the returns that his command was very little injured, that he did not put himself at all forward. Hooker hopes, I suppose, to supersede Burnside.[2] It was a noble thing in Burnside to take all the responsibility of the attack upon himself. As Mr. Barney said, it absolutely saved the government. Phil says that Burnside is of a most noble character, indifferent to public opinion, full of energy, tender and humane and generous in disposition.

McClellan has injured himself by too much tampering with the ultra-Democrats. Seeing how the rebels act, it would seem that we might as well accept the issue as they offer it. They have inaugurated the war, declared slavery incompatible with our free institutions, invited the aid of foreign nations against us, and we have therefore little cause to consider them. Slavery may as well be abolished if it is possible. The only question with the Judge was, is it practicable? Mr. Barney said that the Black Brigade[3] at New Orleans was the richest one in the army, being composed of so many wealthy Negroes; that commands in it were eagerly sought by our officers. God

---

commander of Washington in the summer of 1865, he had to order the execution of the Lincoln conspirators, and for the rest of his life was criticized for the hanging of Mrs. Suratt. In 1880 he was Democratic Presidential candidate, defeated by Garfield.

2 Massachusetts-born Joseph Hooker (1814–1879) earned the sobriquet "Fighting Joe" for his performance in the Peninsula Campaign, second Bull Run, and Antietam. After the Fredericksburg disaster, Hooker was so openly scornful of Burnside that Burnside went to Washington and demanded a showdown—either Hooker must go or he would. Lincoln chose the latter alternative and Hooker succeeded Burnside.

3 The "Black Brigades" were all-Negro regiments raised on a volunteer basis from among the free Negroes of the North and liberated Negroes of Southern areas invaded by Union troops. New York City recruited, trained, and equipped three Negro regiments to fight for the Union, the first of which (the 20th Regiment) embarked for New Orleans on March 5, 1864.

overrules the councils of men and makes even their wickedness and weakness means to fulfill His ends.

January 9, 1863

I have read Governor Seymour's message and think it very able and patriotic. I wish New England were obliged to consolidate itself. It does not seem just that New York, with equal population, should be but represented by two, whilst they have 12 senators.

We have had a costly victory at Murfreesboro, been repulsed at Vicksburg.[4] There are rumors of dissent and disunion between the Eastern and Western and Middle states; New England will have to yield if they join against her.

I paid some visits yesterday. It was amusing to hear the political views of the ladies. Such vapid, inconsistent, violent expressions! General Wadsworth's daughter, for instance, declared herself a dreadful abolitionist, Republican, and all that, and in the same breath wished we had a monarchy, hated the blacks so that she could not sit in a railroad car with them, and declared herself for the Administration. But, she said, Lincoln is a miserable creature whose inordinate conceit and vanity make his stupidity and vulgarity unendurable.

Mrs. [William F.] Ritchie is a pretty woman who aids nature a little by art. Her hair was dressed in the modern Phrygian style in two great hills on either side of her head, the center being occupied on full-dress occasions with a bunch of hair full of feathers, birds, or flowers. One lady, a Mrs.

---

4 Shortly after the New Year began, good news came from Murfreesboro, Tennessee, where Major General William S. Rosecrans claimed a victory for the Army of the Cumberland. Rosecrans was hailed as a hero until the appalling cost of the engagement in dead and wounded filtered through. Balancing the encouraging first reports from Tennessee was the news that the Confederates had recaptured the port of Galveston, and on the Mississippi Grant's expedition against Vicksburg had failed.

Ronaldi, who is now the toast of the town, wears a bird's nest with eggs, making her head a hatchery. I doubt if there is enough brain there to hatch anything, even on top. I suggested to some ladies yesterday to study Livingstone's travels in Africa, that I thought they might there find some suggestive wood-cuts for new styles of coiffure in the present fashion.

January 14, 1863

. . . . Spent the morning in Laight Street, and had all my old grievances renewed by the sight of the preparations for Kate's marriage. I tried hard to keep them down, but could not. Poor Mother, nature has given her little brains; she has not one ounce of spirit. Kate, dear child, wishes to give me a handsome present, which I will not receive. I do not wish to be obliged to Judge Brady, nor do I wish Mother to have the satisfaction of knowing that she did wrong. Kate did not. I rather would be *poor* and independent, and have a right to say what I please.

January 19, 1863

Been suffering for the last three days from a pain in the face, having taken cold arranging flowers for the wedding in a cold room. The wedding went off very well. Mother was in the highest spirits, the presents were very handsome, and the bride looked very pretty. I never saw two people more self-possessed. Dear Kate; I trust her married life may be a very happy one. Mother, as usual, knowing that I must feel something at the contrast, kept constantly probing the old wound all day long in her foolish manner. . . .

Although I had unpleasant feelings, still I had many agreeable things said to me on the day of the wedding. Father said before Kate that I was the most dignified and handsomest woman of the family and had the best manner. And Mr.

[Nathaniel] Jarvis told me that the Archbishop had devoted fifteen minutes to speaking my praises. This, I confess, flattered me, for I liked the Archbishop. I do not think I have great self reliance. I never think of producing an effect, and therefore I suppose I am more susceptible to appreciation from those I esteem.

The Judge has been requested to write down his remarks before the board of managers of the dispensary in our ward that they may be incorporated in the report for this year. They were much pleased with it, and it is the first occasion upon which it has ever been done.

Yesterday we passed a delightful morning at the Tenth Street studios. Bierstadt made himself very agreeable. He was at work when we came in upon a very large picture, a scene in the Windriver Mountains, a waterfall, snow-peaked mountains, a narrow green valley with an Indian encampment in the foreground with their horses and dead game which the hunters had brought home. It is the grandest landscape I think I have ever seen. He is going on a most enticing journey this summer, first across the continent to San Francisco via the overland mail, then up the Pacific Coast to Vancouver's Island, when he will have to go on horseback. Bierstadt, I think, surpasses [Frederick] Church as a landscape painter. He gives broader effects. . . .

January 24, 1863

Dined yesterday at Mrs. W. B. Astor's with Mr. and Mrs. C. H. Davis, Mrs. O'Conor, Mrs. Carson, Mr. Hoppin, and a Miss Hunt from New Orleans. Miss Hunt gave us very much the same accounts of the feeling in Louisiana as Captain Badeau, but she says that now all feeling is dead and that no one cares which party conquers. [General Benjamin F.] Butler they hate for his rude manners.

Mr. Astor told me that he thought the Judge had been very

courageous last summer in saying the bold things he did in Tammany Hall. Mr. and Mrs. Davis seemed to try to take Lincoln's part because he has been civil. Mr. Hayes, who with his wife dined with us last Tuesday, says that there will never be another army raised in Illinois, and when Mr. Doyle began to say something about the Illinois legislature, Hayes said, "Spare us! Is it not shame enough for us to have Lincoln to represent us. God knows, when I used to see that *thing* now in the White House, sitting on the old drygoods box in Springfield, just near enough to his house to be able to hear his wife's voice when very angry call him to dinner, telling his indecent, vulgar stories to the crowd of rowdies about him, I used to think, 'Well, I am a better man than you. I could not, if I would, talk such ribaldry. Joe Miller's jokes can be written, but yours no one would dare to write, much less publish!'"

Grant[5] had an interview with General Polk[6] and said, "There is one toast we can drink, General, 'General Washington.'"

"Yes," said Polk, "the first rebel!"

Mrs. Astor related an anecdote that she heard from someone to whom the Marquis of Hartington told it. The Marquis had been introduced and was standing silently looking on beside Mrs. Lincoln at the White House. Mrs. Lincoln, thinking that he ought to entertain her, suddenly turned around, started violently, and said, "BOO!" The Marquis started and looked wonderingly around. "I thought I would arouse you," said the President's lady. We had a pleasant dinner.

On Saturday, Mr. Townsend Harris breakfasted with us, and afterwards the Judge went with him to the different artists' studios, coming back for me to take me with them to Eastman Johnson's, who has many beautiful things on his

---

[5] See *Personalities in the Diary*, page xix.

[6] Confederate Lieutenant General Leonidas Polk played a conspicuous part in the Atlanta campaign.

easel. We saw fine sketches of Indians from Lake Superior, many pleasing scenes from New England life, some fine old cabinets. . . .

Monday, January 26, 1863

Yesterday Mr. George T. Davis dined with and passed the evening with us. As usual he was full of anecdotes. He approved of the Judge's address before the dispensary highly, saying it contained very original matter. In the evening, Father and Mother came in with Mr. Bierstadt and Mr. Coffin.[7] We had a discussion by no means complimentary of "Bull Run" Russell. I wish I could publish that an American lady refuses to be introduced to him because of his repulsive countenance and want of gentlemanly expression, for I did at the St. Patrick's dinner. I felt not the slightest inclination to make his acquaintance and requested (although Charles had, I found, no intention of asking him) that he should not be invited to our house. In his Diary,[8] he makes two false statements about Charles. The first is that he called on Charles with a committee to invite him to the St. Patrick's dinner; the second is that he misstates a conversation with Baron Gerolt, when he dined with the Judge and the Baron, about the *Trent*. The Judge first advised Seward that we were wrong and could not keep the Southern commissioners. Charles could not have said what Russell states. Russell probably added it himself, as I have heard him say before that although the English had the truth on their side and that Captain Wilkes was in the wrong, still he did not believe that had the English found Mitchell and Olgerman on an American vessel, that the English would have hesitated to act but would have seized the commissioners,

---

[7] Probably Charles Carleton Coffin (1823–1896), American author and journalist, Washington correspondent for the Boston *Journal* during the war; he signed his articles "Carleton."

[8] William Howard Russell published *My Diary, North and South During the Civil War in America* in 1862.

and if they felt powerful enough would have kept them; that though the British knew the law they did not always practice it.

The Judge has at last finished writing out his address before the dispensary. It is to be printed Tuesday, January 27th.

I shall paste in my book these bits of newspaper. The anecdote of the President is true excepting, as the paper says, it was Picayune Butler,[9] and I think the paper quite just in its remarks. The incident was told me by someone in Lincoln's company on the occasion. [Newspaper clipping pasted in to which reference is made]:

When President Lincoln visited the battlefield of Antietam before the corpses had been buried, he called upon an officer with a reputation as a singer to step out and sing him a song. . . . The officer sang "Jim-along Josey." Nero's tyranny never slaughtered as many bodies as Lincoln's incompetency. . . . It was not "Jim-along Josey" but "Picayune Butler" that was sung.

February 13, 1863

It is strange to see how apathetic our people are about the war. This last fortnight has been almost like a Saturnalia, and the celebrations will finish on Tuesday with a masquerade ball at Mr. Belmont's. I do not think I shall go, not at such a time. For the Judge to appear at such an entertainment would look, I think, somewhat undignified. Last evening we went to Judge Bell's; the day before to a musical matinee at Mrs. James Brooks';[10] Tuesday to a grand entertainment at Mr. Francis Cutting's on the occasion of his son's marriage.

---

[9] Term of derision applied to General Benjamin F. Butler, much criticized commander of New Orleans. His most infamous order was that any woman who insulted a Northern soldier would be treated as a woman of the town. He executed a Southerner for tearing down the U.S. flag, and Jefferson Davis declared him an outlaw. Charged with personal corruption in his administration of the city, Butler was recalled in December of 1862.

[10] James Brooks was the publisher of the New York *Daily Express* and congressman from New York City at this time.

The beautiful bride and her eight pretty bridesmaids were very imposing with their long white veils.

It is a sign of the popular feeling to see Fitz-John Porter,[11] although dismissed from the service, going everywhere. He seems to feel it no disgrace, and the people seem disposed to make a lion of anyone reprimanded or disgraced by the Administration. I am told that several regiments in the Army of the Potomac declare that they will never fire another shot, that the government can draft men but cannot make them fight, that they will no longer be butchered for political generals, etc. Two regiments at Baton Rouge have likewise laid down their arms on account of having Negro regiments raised. I'm sure that I cannot imagine how all this is to end. It is dreadful. Yet no one seems to think or care. The women dress as extravagantly as ever, and the supper and dinner parties are far more numerous than they have been for several winters.

At Mrs. Cutting's I saw General Burnside and General Parke, and was rather disappointed in both. Burnside has a fine glance, but does not look like a great man. Parke is gentlemanly, and has a broad forehead. But I had such a momentary look at them that I cannot form any just opinion. Corcoran seems to me to have more elements of greatness than anyone the war has as yet brought forward. He does not think of himself or of his own advancement, of what others are thinking of him who can be useful, etc. I think Parke has great sincerity of character from his face.

We have been in a round of engagements lately. My visits are so many that I feel almost hopeless about returning them

---

11 Handsome Fitz-John Porter became the scapegoat for the Union defeat at second Bull Run. At his court martial late in 1862, General McDowell testified that he ordered Porter to advance and engage Longstreet's troops. Porter denied the order and claimed that he retired from the field with his force of ten or twelve thousand men without fighting because the enemy was so strong that to engage them would have meant annihilation. He was cashiered out of the army, and it was not until the historians pronounced their verdict that Porter's name was cleared.

all, and I have engaged in paying what I could of the reception visits. Places of public amusement are crowded. We have the opera, Wallack's, Mr. [Henry] Wood at Laura Keene's,[12] Booth[13] at the Winter Garden.[14]

The city has been greatly amused and excited at the marriage of Tom Thumb and Lavinia Warren, the two dwarfs,[15] and I think our Episcopal Church has disgraced herself by marrying them in such pomp in Grace Church. There could not have been more done had they been some distinguished personages. Poor [Isaac] Brown, the sexton, was so disgusted that he would not be present, and the police took his place. He told us when opening the carriage door for us at Judge Bell's reception that Bishop [Horatio] Potter had asked Dr. [Thomas H.] Taylor for the church. Another lady told me that Dr. Taylor received $500 for the use of the church, which now I think is on a par with Barnum's Museum.[16]

February 22, 1863

My diary is neglected, for I have so many interruptions that I put off writing from day to day. Lent has begun and

---

[12] Laura Keene (c. 1826–1873), an English-born actress, became a theater manager in New York and was the lessee of the Olympic Theater from 1855 until 1863. It was her company which was presenting Tom Taylor's *Our American Cousin* at Ford's Theatre in Washington when President Lincoln was shot.

[13] See *Personalities in the Diary*, page xiv.

[14] The Winter Garden, at 667 Broadway, had been a theater under various names for nine years before the adoption of this name in 1859. Destroyed by fire in 1867, its site was used for the construction of the Grand Central Hotel, later known as the Broadway Central.

[15] Tom Thumb, the famous dwarf promoted by P. T. Barnum, was married to the midget Lavinia Warren in Grace Episcopal Church on February 10, 1863. Best man and maid of honor were the midgets "Commodore" Nutt and Minnie Warren, the bride's sister. The occasion was a real publicity production, and it created a great deal of attention. Tom Thumb's real name was Charles Sherwood Stratton; Lavinia Warren's was Mercy Lavinia Bump.

[16] Located south of City Hall Park from 1842 to 1865. The Museum burned down on July 13, 1865, and a new one was established at Broadway and Ann Streets.

I suppose that Mr. Belmont's masquerade will be the last of the gaiety. Shrove Tuesday we passed at Mr. Savage's. William Reid having returned from New Orleans, he insisted upon our coming to dinner. Corcoran we heard was in town, and on Thursday he came in for a moment but was obliged to leave before the Judge came home. After dinner, as the Judge was about leaving the house to try and see him, General Shields came in and finished the evening. He has been appointed to the Department of the Pacific and sailed yesterday for San Francisco.

The Judge and General Shields talked politics. The General thought that the party in power had acted with consummate art. They had, he said, gradually got everything into their hands and meant, he thought, to keep the government only going through the form of an election in 1863. He thought they had intended it from the beginning. The West, he thought, would not stand it, but would separate and go with the South. The Judge thought that Westerners had no such fixed plan and he said that the Administration could only be convinced by the course of events (God Almighty's logic, as Mr. Hatfield called it), and that it was best that the Administration should be allowed to try its panacea. They would not otherwise yield. . . .

I sat down and wrote a few lines to Corcoran and explained the Judge's apparent neglect, inviting the General to dine with us if possible the next day. Corcoran came in on Friday evening and told us of the action of his troops in the battle near Suffolk.[17] The Pennsylvanians behaved badly. Corcoran does not believe much in German courage, and General Shields agrees. General Shields said too that the Yankees were not nearly as good soldiers as the Western men. Corcoran

---

[17] On May 10, 1862, the Union Army occupied Suffolk, Virginia. In January 1863, the Confederates laid siege to the city, now defended by Union troops under General Michael Corcoran. The Confederates were driven back, but with heavy losses on both sides. The attack was renewed on April 30, 1863, and on July 3 the Union troops evacuated the city.

likewise agreed with this. Colonel [Alfred] Gibbs, Mrs. [Laura] Wolcott Gibbs' son, was dead drunk, and Corcoran was obliged to put him under arrest. . . .

Last evening the Judge went once more to try and see Corcoran but missed him. Then he stopped to see Mrs. [Matilda C.] Wood in "The Fair One with the Golden Locks," and meeting Mr. Savage and Mr. Reid, brought them home. They found me asleep on the sofa in my dressing gown, but we made some whiskey punch and stayed up to a very late hour.

Today no one can stir out. We are having the first snowstorm of the season and the snow is a foot and a half deep.

William Reid confirms Captain Badeau's account of the feeling in New Orleans. He says that the men are generally willing to yield to reason. They feel that the war was unreasonable on their part, but add that the women would not let any man remain peaceably at home. The women sent the slackers presents of petticoats and nightcaps, and so insulted and goaded them that they were obliged to join the army. How strange, how unnatural for wives, mothers, and sisters!

Phil goes off this week again—this time I believe to North Carolina.

Gold is at one hundred sixty-eight; it will soon be two hundred, I suppose. How will all this end? What is to become of the poor?

I have just written to Father O'Reilly for his advice about a project of mine for our poor widows and children dependent upon the Widows' Society. I wish to plant a Catholic colony at Chengwatana, with each widow's family to join a family in which there is a male head. Each family will be given a tract of land to begin upon. I think I should like to feel that I had made a few families comfortable, and since God has denied me a child that some will feel that I have not lived quite in vain. I shall have to beg for money to send them out, however. . . .

March 19, 1863

The great Union meeting at Cooper's Institute ten days ago has occasioned great excitement. Judge Daly, James T. Brady, and John Van Buren, in concert with Mayor Opdyke, Mr. Gould, and Mr. Greeley, have astonished everyone. The Judge made an excellent speech denouncing the corrupt party organization which is greatly responsible for the miserable administration now in power. All these Democratic leaders advocated, however, loyalty to the existing government and the prosecution of the war for the maintenance of the Union. They suggested killing the Copperheads on the one side and the Negro-worshippers on the other, both of whom were for peace and disunion. They formed a great central, conservative party, called the Union League,[18] of which they made the Judge one of the vice-presidents.

Phil has returned to the army and David has gone to the Agricultural College, where he writes he has been employed in unloading the wheat, etc. I hope he will persevere. I hope some day to see him living in the old garden and filling my dear grandfather's place honorably, as he bears his name.

We have been quite dissipated lately. The Judge dined out on Friday and Saturday at Mr. W. [William B.] Duncan's. On Monday we dined at Mr. Astor's to meet Mr. Schleiden. Tuesday was St. Patrick's Day, and Charles went to the annual dinner. Since he resigned his presidentship to Mr. Brady, the occasion was not so interesting to me, nor did I think it was as dignified and orderly as before when the Judge

---

[18] The meeting of some sixty "Union Leaguers" at 823 Broadway on Saturday evening, February 21, 1863, was for the purpose of arousing a more patriotic spirit in New York and of counteracting the ever-recurring pessimism spread abroad by the Copperheads. Those who met were prominent New Yorkers, and from the meeting emerged New York's Union League Club, with Robert B. Minturn as first president and an impressive list of vice presidents, including John A. Dix, Murray Hoffman, George Bancroft, A. T. Stewart, Moses Taylor, and Henry W. Bellows. The Club raised three Negro regiments in 1863–64 and issued many pamphlets on the Union cause.

presided.[19] Mr. Van Buren made a good speech and drew an admirable sketch of General [Andrew] Jackson's character. Mr. [Joseph H.] Choate intended to be brilliant, but said just what he said before two years ago when I had the pleasure of hearing him. Yesterday we had dinner company at home, Mr. Schleiden, Mr. and Mrs. Dailey, Bierstadt and Mrs. Carson, and it was pleasant enough. Today the Judge dined with Mr. William Astor, just to meet McClellan. So there is no lack of entertainment, and the war does not seem to press heavily upon the the rich New Yorkers.

A. T. Stewart has done a very noble act, and I forgive his buying up all the butter and cotton goods in consequence. He has chartered a ship and loaded it with food at his own expense and sent it to the poor, famishing Irish. At the dinner there was $1,600 subscribed for the same purpose.

We have good account from Minnesota; perhaps we may be able to sell some of our land there. I wish the Judge were independent of his office.

April 3, 1863

Yesterday the Judge breakfasted in company with Major General Butler, or as the song calls him, "Picayune Butler." Butler related many interesting anecdotes. When he arrived at New Orleans, he found that in order to retain their slaves without taking the oath of allegiance to the United States, most of the population had registered themselves as French or English, although they had been in America for two or three generations. Before taking any steps, therefore,

---

[19] An organization to which Judge Daly bore a lifelong devotion was the Friendly Sons of St. Patrick, a descendant of the pre-Revolutionary "Friendly Brothers." The Society was chartered in 1827, and Daly joined it in 1835. He was president from 1860 to 1862. For many years, the Judge led the St. Patrick's Day parade up Fifth Avenue on a white charger, and more often than not he was toastmaster for the annual 17th of March banquet given by the Friendly Sons.

General Butler looked up the English law upon slavery and found that the holding of slaves was not permitted to English subjects. Then he consulted the French law and ascertained that it permitted no slaves except such as had been inherited to be held. Thus fortified, he issued his proclamation, setting forth that as the English and French law permitted no slaves to be held except in this latter circumstances, and as all who would not take the oath of allegiance to the United States must be considered as enemies, none but loyal citizens would be protected in retaining their slaves. This showed great sagacity.

Another circumstance Butler related to us showed ability. A letter was intercepted in which the writer offered $5,000 to anyone who would horsewhip General Butler. The latter bided his time and on the occasion of the writer of the letter coming to New Orleans sometime afterwards, he sent for him and asked if that was his handwriting. The astonished gentleman answered that it was. "Well, then," said Butler, "since you can afford so much money for so useless a purpose, I shall expect you to sign a check for that amount for the benefit of the Union soldiers." The man refused, but a threat of imprisonment in the Fort made him change his mind.

Another intercepted letter contained an account of General Butler and described the atrocities committed under his government. The writer went on to describe insults which he had seen offered to women, etc. Butler sent for the writer as before and asked if it was his handwriting. The man acknowledged it.

"Have you, sir, ever seen me before?" said Butler.

"I have not."

"Then," said the General, "this statement (reading his letter to him) is false."

The man was obliged to acknowledge that it was.

"And," continued Butler, "this other statement of outrages committed by Union soldiers which you state you saw, gives the particulars and the names of the offenders and they shall be summarily punished."

The man hung his head in great embarrassment and was at last obliged to confess that that statement was likewise false.

"Now, sir," said the General, "write at the foot of this page that this statement is all false and sign your name to it."

The man declared he would not, and taking up a pistol, he handed it to Butler, saying, "You may shoot me, but this I will not do."

"I will give you half an hour to consider, and if you do not, I will have you hung. And as you have confessed this falsehood to me, I will take the responsibility of the act upon myself and publish the matter."

General Butler then went in to dinner. The man in great agony, at length seeing his imperturbability, consented to sign. "These lying letters," said the General, "are what do us the greatest injury both at home and abroad, and in hanging him I should have felt justified."

The Judge, though much impressed by his capacity and energy, said that he did not like Butler's face.

President Lincoln, on being asked to give Butler the command at Charleston said, "I can't. *That job is let out.*"

For the last week I have been striving to aid in getting names for a ball to be given for the poor famishing people of Ireland. The Judge is Chairman of the Committee for Relief, and has raised one thousand six hundred dollars himself. The people respond most generously.

Last evening Mr. Peltz brought Count Gurowski,[20] a Polish nobleman and descendant of Stanislas, here. Now that there is some movement in Poland, the Count has come on from Washington (where he holds a small office) to create

---

[20] Count Adam de Gurowski (1805–1866) was a Polish patriot and author who played a leading role in the revolution of 1830. In 1849 he came to the United States, and was employed as a translator in the State Department from 1861 to 1863.

a Polish sympathetic movement here. He is a man of deep, acute observation. I tried to catch what he said, but Father Peltz was bent upon making himself agreeable and I had in courtesy to listen to him.

April 8, 1863

Last evening there was a grand gathering at the Academy of Music for the benefit of the suffering poor of Ireland, where famine is desolating the country. The Judge, Mr. O'Gorman, Meagher, McClellan, and Bishop Hughes[21] were present and spoke. It was very bad weather, but the house was filled. I had a box next to General McClellan with Mrs. Meagher. The speeches I thought best were those of Meagher and the Judge. McClellan spoke from the box, and spoke in a very dignified manner, very modestly and to the purpose. The editor of the *Irish-American* sent for a copy of the Judge's speech, so he had to write it out. He began by alluding to the story of Joseph, very appropriate to the occasion. "That early emigrant," as Charles called Joseph, "having prospered in the land of his adoption, sent of the abundance with which God had blest him to preserve the lives of his brethren in Canaan when they fainted by reason of the famine."

April 9, 1863

Last evening I was waited on by a Polish nobleman, a most elegant and agreeable man, who, on the part of the Polish Central Committee, came to entreat me to form a committee of ladies to sympathize with the Poles on their present

---

[21] John Hughes (1797–1864) was the first Roman Catholic Archbishop of New York. Born at Annaloghan, Tyrone County, Ireland (Judge Daly's parents came from the same county), Hughes came to America in 1817. He was consecrated a bishop in New York in 1838 and Archbishop in 1850. The construction of St. Patrick's Cathedral and the founding of St. John's College were among his works.

struggle to free themselves from the [foreign] yoke. I can do nothing, so the entreaty was in vain. I assured him that as we did not entertain and had nothing to give, it was the object of no one to do anything to please or oblige me. He must seek, I urged, those who had wealth and influence. General Frank Barlow and his wife came in and relieved me from my agreeable but urgent pleader from Poland.

Frank Barlow is not fit but will return to active service. Arabella declares that he loves fighting for the sake of fighting, and is really bloodthirsty. I told him that I thought with him that he should be in arms, but that he must not yet shoulder arms except at home. He looks very frail.

April 10, 1863

We had a visit last evening from Mr. Hall,[22] the Arctic explorer, who returned this last autumn after three years' absence. Hall brought with him [Sir Martin] Frobisher's relics, the first accounts that have been heard of him for nearly three hundred years. Hall told us many interesting things concerning the accuracy of the information he received from the Esquimaux women. From an old woman (whom he thought must have been eighty years old), he learned of this Island, which, in the Esquimaux tongue, is called "White Man's Island." Five white men once lived there and built a vessel with two masts, she revealed among many other particulars. On this Island, Hall found the Newcastle coal brought out for mining purposes and some of the iron which had been proved. They built a trench with which to launch their

---

[22] Charles Francis Hall (1821–1871), an American who undertook a search for Sir John Franklin's expedition to find the North Pole in 1845. This expedition disappeared, and so became a challenge to a number of explorers. Hall set out in 1860, and returned in 1862 with no clues of Franklin's party but some relics of Frobisher's expedition of 1577–78. In a second attempt (1864–69), Hall did find evidence of the lost expedition, and in 1871, after reaching the northernmost point yet attained by any explorer—82°11′N.— he died of apoplexy in Greenland.

vessel. On Hall's return, on consulting the accounts of Frobisher preserved in the British Museum, he found that his information agreed in every point with the accounts of the old woman. Hall thinks white men can exist for a long period among the Esquimaux, and he wishes to go again to discover some of Franklin's men whom he still believes to be alive. He said that after six weeks he could eat their raw meat, enjoy their sports, and live in their huts. He represents the women as being much more intelligent than the men. He brought a family out with him, and the woman is his interpreter. The family had been in England and went at Windsor to see the Queen and Prince Albert, whom they remembered. They often talked of the things they saw in England and in the palace. Mr. Hall is a very modest, unassuming, heavy-looking man. He does not look unlike an Esquimaux, but he is very patient, very accurate, laborious, and conscientious; he is very observant and an enthusiast upon Arctic matters.

April 15, 1863

The Irish Ball last evening was a great success. General McClellan, Franklin, Mrs. Meagher, Mrs. and Mr. O'Gorman, and all whom I asked came, as well as many others of our acquaintance. Mr. Meehan thanked me for the interest which I have taken (which they very politely said had added greatly to its success). The Judge accepted an invitation to lecture for the same cause in Boston on the twenty-ninth, and I shall go with him.

Harriet Whetten paid me a visit on Monday last. She has come home (*on a furlough*) from the Portsmouth Hospital at Newport, where she has been since last autumn. She is now a government official, being one of the assistant lady superintendents of the United States Army. She says that if *Punch* could only get hold of the many letters she receives with her military address, what a good thing could be made of it. She wears a uniform consisting of a skirt of blue army flannel, a zouave jacket lined with red with gilt United States buttons, and a round hat and cavalry gloves. Harriet says her life is a very pleasant one, full of occupation. She and Miss Woolsey, the "Colonel" (as she calls Miss Woolsey, their head), agree and have a very pleasant time together. The men, she says, obey them implicitly, but will, like children, hide apples away under their pillows and eat raw clams though ill of chronic diarrhea, which is the most general disease.

April 16, 1863

I hear that General Shields has arrived at San Francisco and has resigned his command, having no further connection with the United States Army. General Corcoran has shot Colonel Kimball, and the papers are talking about it.[23] I fear it will do him harm, although I have no doubt but that he did it in self-defense. I have written to beg him to send us a true account, so that it may be published at once.

I received, a few days since, a present of tea, I suppose from Mr. Townsend Harris. Mr. Reid sent me oranges, and Phil sent us from Cincinnati a box of our native wine. This was a great deal to be sent in one day.

April 19, 1863

Went yesterday with Florence to the Academy of Design; saw many good pictures. The exhibit was the best I have ever seen, although Bierstadt's fine picture of the Rocky

---

[23] Colonel Edgar A. Kimball (1821–1863) joined the army as a captain of infantry in 1847. At the beginning of the Civil War he helped to organize and train a company of New York volunteers. In April of 1863, General Corcoran mistook Colonel Kimball for an enemy and shot and killed him. A question was raised because of bad feelings which existed between the two men.

Mountains is in Boston on exhibition. Gifford had a beautiful sunset in the mountains; the scenery reminded me of Delaware County. Maggie Pierrepont and Florence dined with us yesterday. In the evening, Baron Osten-Sacken and Mr. [James] Day came in. The latter wants me to go and see pictures with him and drive in the park. It would of course be quite proper to go, but I should feel as if I were making myself ridiculous. Osten-Sacken had been in Boston and says that the Judge's name is placarded all over the city on huge bills like those for the theater.

Mr. John O'Mahony[24] came in late last evening and gave us a true version of the death of Colonel Kimball, whom General Corcoran shot. It was done, as I supposed from the first, knowing Corcoran's character, in self-defense. Colonel Kimball was drunk, would not give his name, and stopped Corcoran and O'Mahony as they were riding under General Dix's orders to the front. Since the enemy was about to attack, Kimball was without any right to do so; it was within the lines and he had no right to demand the countersign. Corcoran remonstrated in vain for some minutes and said, "Stop me then at your peril!" General Corcoran had no idea who Kimball was nor that he was killed. I trust it will do Corcoran no harm. That it will distress him, I have no doubt, although it could not be helped, as Kimball drew his sword and cocked his pistol.

O'Mahony is a most interesting man, a fine scholar, a man of great intelligence, well-versed too in the Irish language, very romantic and poetical, devoted to the country, his only thought being how to free his unfortunate countrymen. His family is one of the oldest in Ireland and he sacrificed his

---

[24] John O'Mahony (1816–1877) was born in County Cork, Ireland, joined the "Young Irelanders" in 1845, and fled to France after the Smith O'Brien insurrection in 1848. In 1854 he came to the United States and helped to found the Fenian Brotherhood. He translated and published the Gaelic *History of Ireland by Geoffrey Keating*. O'Mahony died in New York, but his body was returned to Dublin and buried with honors.

estates by joining the popular movement. He is a man about thirty-eight, handsome, melancholy, but impressing you with his sincerity, his dauntlessness of character, and his warmth of feeling.

April 22, 1863

. . . . Mr. Harris and Dr. Gescheidt dined with us. We had much interesting conversation. The Doctor told us how he cured hysteria on one occasion of a wilful young lady. He said to her mother, who was in great distress, whilst the daughter seemed to be unconscious, "Do not speak of this, for should it be known that a lady so young and of such pretension got these attacks, she will never get married." The Doctor said he was never called in again for anything of the kind. Women of weak mind and strong will are the only ones subject, I think, to such attacks. Mr. Harris told us much about his residence in the East. He seems to have been everywhere; he has gathered crystals of sulphur from volcanoes in Borneo, shot anomalous animals in Australia, dined with the tycoon [shogun] in Japan, lived in Ceylon, read the *Mahabharata*. Doctor Gescheidt is one of the cleverest men I know, besides being such an excellent physician. We had a talk over the discoveries of the Swiss lakes and the Irish bogs. Mankind, I found, is some sixteen thousand rather than six thousand years old.

I wish we had a larger income, and the Judge a little more leisure. What a delightful society we might gather around us! Mr. Day wonders that I do not take a greater lead in society. Why should I when I have so pleasant a companion at home? Mr. Gould has sent for us to come this evening and meet Miss Dickinson[25]—the oratress, shall I call her? Miss Dickinson, feel-

---

25 Anna Elizabeth Dickinson (1842–1932) was the daughter of a Philadelphia merchant and active abolitionist, John Dickinson. She was also an ardent abolitionist, and was called upon frequently by the Union League to give lectures during the war. She also advocated woman suffrage, labor reforms, and a severe policy toward the South after the war.

ing she has a mission to speak what she considers God's truth to the people, is going about speaking. Last night she spoke here to a crowded audience for two hours. Had we been disengaged, we should have gone to hear her. Miss Gould thinks she has turned the elections in Connecticut and New Hampshire—that she is a Jeanne d'Arc of the 19th century.

May 5, 1863

On the twenty-eighth of last month, we left home to go to Boston, where the Judge had been invited to deliver a lecture for the Irish fund. We returned yesterday. On our arrival, we were met by a committee with a carriage, furnished with a room and parlour at the Tremont House, a carriage was put at our disposal, a bottle of sherry and of brandy was put on the table for our refreshment, and we installed ourselves—the Judge to look over his lecture, and I to write the concluding pages from his dictation.

We found Mr. George T. Davis already there waiting for us. He went with me to the lecture and the *Committee* took charge of the Judge. The lecture was a great success; it was given at Tremont Temple, which holds about two thousand five hundred persons and which was filled with a most respectable set of people. Mr. and Mrs. Sidney Bartlett,[26] who called on us in the morning, told us that their domestics had all asked permission to go to hear a lecture which a great man was to deliver that evening. I knew but few of the aristocrats would be present, as they would not go where their servants would. However, aristocratic Boston was very respectably represented. The committee waited on the Judge here and wished to give him a serenade, but he refused.

The next morning, by invitation of Judge Russell, we went to see the school ship in Boston Harbor, where vagrant boys

---

[26] Sidney Bartlett (1799–1889) was one of the founders of the Boston Bar Association, and its first president.

are committed and taught navigation. We were delighted with the institution, which is principally supported by the state. When we arrived the boys were engrossed in mathematics and other studies, but later they sang us a number of very amusing songs. Some of the boys had fine, intelligent faces and one of them, an Irish boy, had a delicious voice. The Judge was asked to address them, and he spoke, I thought, very well for fifteen minutes, telling them of his experiences. A son of Mr. Davis who was of our party was an excellent specimen of a young gentleman, such a one as might please a maiden's eye and satisfy her mind. Judge Russell afterwards addressed them very well. . . .

We dined with Mr. Sidney Bartlett, the head of the Boston bar, in company with George Hillard, the author of an admirable book upon Italy, our friend George Davis, and Mrs. Judge Warren. . . . There is much more of the aristocratic element in Boston than here. Many of the old names are still well sustained and respected, and they manage to keep up a sort of fence around themselves, which, whilst it has preserved a good deal of refinement of manner, has somewhat dwarfed their minds. They reminded me of a greenhouse fruit, very beautiful to look at, but somewhat insipid on the taste. I would rather trust the mind of some honest Western man or some honest Irishman, even though he were one of the hewers of wood or drawers of water, on all subjects outside of Massachusetts than these horticultural specimens of Americans.

The Irish do not hold the same place in Boston that they do here. They have no representative men, and there is a great deal of Puritan prejudice. Bostonians must be dreadfully mortified to see how England feels towards even the very English part of America. They have so many English prejudices and manners that they must feel like King David, that it was even their own familiar friend who raised his hand against them. At the same time, they do not fear the war at all, and they may well be patriots for the few dollars they expend in maintaining their quota of troops. They are trebly paid by the work supplies brought to their industrial manufacturing establishment. New England never was so prosperous. New Englanders are the embodiment of Protestant energy, selfish and local in their feelings, and therefore prosperous. I do not believe there will be much taken up for the poor, starving Irish.

A gentleman who ought to have been broader minded thought it not wise to encourage emigration here, although the wide West is languishing and the harvest spoiling in the fields for want of laborers. We were very much touched by the modesty and delicacy of feeling shown by these poor Irishmen a few years ago. They had been disarmed by their state. They now have a regiment who drill, and each man owns his own musket. Only a few years ago, a Catholic church was burned in Boston. The Bostonian Irish showed the greatest possible deference and respect for the Judge, for whom they could not do enough. They were delighted with the high and dignified tone of his lecture, which raised them in their own eyes and placed the condition of the Irish nation before Boston hearers with eloquence, earnestness, and with proper seriousness. This deigning, as they said, was the usual clap-trap.

The next day, Friday, we went to Cambridge. We missed James Russell Lowell[27] and Agassiz, but we went into the museum, the library, and the law school. We saw a solar spectrum which proved by the similarity of the light of the sun with that of every burning substance on the earth that the sun is an igneous mass and not surrounded by a luminous atmosphere. We found that it is a ball of fire, as we believed without any scientific doubts in our childhood.

Young Bartlett is a bright, amiable young fellow who has had every advantage, has a good opinion of himself and a good impression of others. I fear the Judge did not raise himself in Bartlett's estimation by informing him that he had been an arti-

---

[27] In 1863, James Russell Lowell was Professor of English at Harvard and co-editor of the *North American Review*.

san and a sailor in his youth. Mrs. Bartlett is an ordinary, pleasant, amiable person; the daughter is very bright and talkative.
She said she had observed the Judge whilst traveling on one occasion in the railroad with him, that he had such wonderful eyes
—they were so deep-set, so wise and tender. It was the Judge's
eyes which first struck my attention when I made his acquaintance. Miss Bartlett went on to say she had often wondered what
kind of woman Charles had married. Mr. Bartlett, Sr., I like
very much.

Saturday I went to return some visits, and the Judge went
with Mr. Hillard to see the public library where everyone is
allowed to take books home. It is as large as the Astor Library
and admirably managed. . . .

Mrs. Harrison Gray Otis[28] was much vexed at our not letting
her know where we were. She wanted to see the wife of Judge
Daly. She has been devoting herself to the soldiers unremit-
tingly since the beginning of the war. The Judge says she is still
a fine-looking woman, very large, but still full of energy and
enthusiasm. She has some fine pictures. Some of her fine pictures are at the Lyceum, an interior of St. Peter's (which really
gives one an idea of that wonder of art), three pictures of
Washington Allston[29] (which gave me some idea of his genius),
a Greuze, and several others. Dr. Hooker, a gentleman of independent fortune, devotes his time to the institution. Indeed the
gentlemen of Boston are public-spirited as far as regards their
own city and do wise and liberal things.

We met several people at the Lyceum who devoted them-

---

[28] Widow of the Massachusetts statesman who served in the Massachusetts legislature, the U.S. House of Representatives from 1797 to 1801, the
U.S. Senate from 1817 to 1822, and participated in the Hartford Convention of 1814. Otis, a well-known orator, died in 1848.

[29] Washington Allston (1779–1843), artist and poet, was born in South
Carolina and educated at Harvard. He married the sister of William Ellery
Channing, and when she died in 1813, he married a sister of Richard Henry
Dana. He spent a good deal of time in Europe, but returned to America
in 1818 and lived the rest of his life in Boston and Cambridge. Among his
most noted paintings are portraits of Benjamin West, Coleridge, and himself.

selves to the institution. We likewise went to the Historical Society. The rooms looked pleasant and studious, and we saw some very rare valuable books. This institution was much endowed by an old fellow whom nobody knew named Doyce. The professorships at Cambridge [Harvard College, Cambridge, Mass.] are most of them founded by gentlemen and are named after them, as the Parker Professorship, etc. The Judge thought Mr. Hillard the most Europeanlike man he had met in Boston.

May 6, 1863

We returned with satisfaction to our home employment. Received a letter from Phil enclosing money for the Irish fund —$20.00. I think it too much and shall return it to him, as he will be called upon in Cincinnati to contribute.

Went last night to hear a lecture by Mr. O'Gorman upon (as we supposed) Edmund Burke for the benefit of the Irish Relief Fund. The consequence was that the Judge went on the platform. To our surprise, indignation, and disgust, the lecture was an infamous attempt to wrest the eloquence of Burke from its original meaning and make of it an ingenious appeal for the South. I expected every moment to see the Judge get up and leave the stage. Mr. O'Gorman seemed to think himself over Burke. His lecture was very clever, beautifully written and delivered, but most hypocritical. I fear it will destroy our intimacy. The Judge wished to sit down and write to him his opinion, but I think I *wisely* dissuaded him.

May 10, 1863

Caught a dreadful cold at the lecture on Monday last which has confined me to the house and to my bed. [General] Hooker has crossed the Rappahannock, but been obliged to retreat with the loss of ten thousand men, which, after his boastful proclamations and arrogant criticisms of other generals, must be to him a great mortification. He was so sure of victory that he declared that Lee's army was now the legitimate property of the Army of the Potomac, but on going to take possession, he found that the nine points of law, namely, possession, were all in their favor and the legitimacy of his claim was entirely overlooked. There are rumors today which (may it prove true!) assert that Stoneman[30] is in possession of Richmond, and Peck[31] and Corcoran and others are advancing from Suffolk and other reinforcements from the York River. I care not who conquers so that this dreadful waste of blood and treasure be but stopped.

Had a letter yesterday from Phil, who has been acting on court martial, trying deserters and spies. He was one of the court before whom Vallandigham[32] was brought to trial.

The Judge has been asked to repeat his lecture here for the Relief and has been asked to speak on Wednesday in Brooklyn.

May 14, 1863

I have been confined to my bed for a day or two with an attack of influenza. I shall have to take care of myself.

---

[30] George Stoneman (1822–1894) served with McClellan as cavalry commander (1861–62), and later became division and corps commander in the Army of the Potomac.

[31] John James Peck (1821–1878) was brevetted major for bravery in the Mexican War, was made a brigadier general of volunteers on August 7, 1861, and distinguished himself at Williamsburg and Yorktown. As a major general, he was at Suffolk, Virginia, from July 1861 until May 1863, and defended it successfully. He then went on duty on the Canadian frontier. In 1867 he organized the New York State Life Insurance Company, of which he was president until his death.

[32] Clement L. Vallandigham (1820–1871) served in Congress as a Representative from Ohio from 1858 to 1863, and became a leader of the "Peace Democrats," or Copperheads. Failing reelection in 1862, he was arrested and tried by the military authorities in Ohio in 1863 for making a speech openly sympathetic toward the Confederacy. Lincoln commuted the sentence set by the military court, and instead sentenced Vallandigham to banishment behind the Confederate lines. He made his way to Canada shortly afterward, and returned to the United States in 1864, unmolested, to speak in support of McClellan's candidacy for the Presidency.

Night before last, we had a visit from a Captain Reilley who has been in the Papal Brigade and in the Crimea and who has been chief of General Shields' staff. He is a most interesting, intelligent man. He was wounded and has lost a part of his right jaw. He is now going to the Southwest with General Stone, whom the government has at last reinstated.[33] Captain Reilley, in answer to some questions with regard to the government, answered, "Were I not in the service of the United States, I might criticize its actions." It gave us great respect for him; he has observed much. He gave us a lamentable account of the condition of the priests in Italy and said that he feared to bring his Irish soldiers whose faith was so pure and fervent into the towns, lest they should witness the ill conduct and loose lives of the inferior clergy, who mostly kept coffee houses, etc. He mentioned that everyone in Italy was educated —too many to find employment.

May 26, 1863

Baron Gerolt and Carlotta arrived here on Thursday last, and will leave, I trust, tomorrow. I do not much care to have young ladies with me, although I like young girls very much. Carlotta is going to be married in the Spring and goes to India to live.

Good news from the Mississippi. General Grant has gained several great victories and Vicksburg must soon fall. On Sunday there was a report that the Federal flag was floating from its defenses, but it was a report got up to send out by the steamer or for some financial operations. I wish something might soon occur, for everything is so expensive. Coal is at eight dollars per ton, and other things are in proportion. Yet there is no increase of salary. . . .

---

[33] Charles Pomeroy Stone was officially reinstated in August 1862, but he was not made use of again until May 1863.

June 17, 1863

. . . . Today there is news from Pennsylvania that Harrisburg is in danger from Lee's army, which (just as they did last year) has crossed the Potomac and is laying waste the Cumberland Valley. It is dispiriting in the extreme. Sickles, it is supposed, may be the next military experiment. If he gets influence over the army, he may try to *coup d'état* and supersede Lincoln. It would be a fine satire upon the morality of "democratic institutions" to see Daniel Sickles and his wife in the White House, the representatives of the American nation.

Phil is at Vicksburg with the Ninth Army Corps. It is not taken yet, though the flags were hung out in honor of its capture six weeks ago. David has returned from the agricultural college, as little settled as before he left. How wrong it is to bring up young men so idly, to consult only their own wishes! How much happier are they who are early disciplined to labor and economize; how much easier life is made by it. I am thankful for every hardship I have ever had to endure.

June 18, 1863

Another rebel raid into Pennsylvania by Lee has been more successful than the last. Our wretched Administration have allowed all the three-years' men to return without making any provision whatever to replace them. Truly God has a controversy with this people. He raises for us no deliverer. There is not one honest, clever man left; at least such are not permitted to have influence. One would not admit the men who rule us in Washington, with the exception of Chase and Seward, even into the drawing room. The Republicans who place them where they are are equally disgusted. It saps all patriotism! Vicksburg is not yet taken, and our *civilian* General Banks blunders still before Port Hudson. Poor General Sherman and our friend Badeau have been badly wounded. I must write to the latter as soon as I have leisure. No one seems to take any interest in the war any longer; it has become chronic.

June 29, 1863

How virulent Republicans are against McClellan. Mrs. D'Oremieulx was here last evening and inveigled most violently against him. Today the news is that Hooker has been removed at his own request and Meade[34] has been placed at the head of the army. It is wonderful to see the apathy which prevails. Whatever troops can be raised will be but state, not United States troops. None will consent to put themselves at the disposition of the Federal government. It is extraordinary to hear the violence that the Republicans indulge in against the Democrats. They hate them worse than the secessionists. . . .

A lull followed Fredericksburg and Bragg's retreat to Tennessee, while both sides recovered from losses and defeats. Late in December 1862, Bragg moved out of Chattanooga towards Nashville, and Rosecrans came out to meet him. On December 26, the two armies met at Murfreesboro, or Stone's River, and a bloody battle ensued. Although the Union losses were over 13,000 to Bragg's 10,000, Rosecrans claimed the victory, for Bragg was so crippled by his loss of manpower that he was unable to prevent the Union army from taking Chattanooga the next summer.

In January 1863, at Grant's failure to take Vicksburg, demoralization overtook the North as the true losses of life at Fredericksburg, Murfreesboro, and Vicksburg became known.

---

[34] George G. Meade (1815–1872) was made a brigadier general in 1861. Second Bull Run and Antietam proved Meade's military capabilities, and he succeeded Hooker in command of the 1st Corps in 1862. He became a major general of volunteers in November 1862, did brilliantly at Chancellorsville, leading the 5th Corps, and was appointed Commander of the Army of the Potomac in June 1863—the position he held until the end of the war.

Hooker, now in command of the Grand Army of the Potomac, did what he could to bolster the spirits of his troops, and by April 1863, he was prepared to go on the offensive. His 130,000 troops faced Lee's 60,000 across the Rappahannock, and by the end of the month Hooker took up his position at Chancellorsville.

Meantime, Grant in the West was only waiting for dry weather before resuming his attack on Vicksburg. By April 1, McClernand was on the march, with Sherman and McPherson soon to follow. Since the "Confederate Gibraltar" was impregnable to assault from the river, and since Grant had already failed to get at General Pemberton through the jungle of the lower Yazoo, he determined to bring his army to dry ground below Vicksburg and attack the fortress from the rear.

On the night of April 16, 1863, Grant loaded his troops on the fleet of Flag Officer Porter, and floated downstream toward the Fort until discovered. Porter went full-steam ahead, directly under the guns of the Fort, and all but one boat made it past the Fort. Without waiting for Sherman or any other reinforcements, Grant met Pemberton's army with only about 20,000 men, took the important railroad junction at Jackson, Mississippi, before Joe Johnston's force coming from Chattanooga could arrive, and then turned and bottled Pemberton up in Vicksburg. The siege of Vicksburg began on May 22, and by this time Grant's force had built up to 75,000 men. Joseph E. Johnston was on one side of him at Canton, but he had only 25,000 troops, and communications were severed with Pemberton's force of 30,000 men inside the Fort. The siege continued until July 3, when Pemberton surrendered. Port Hudson, which had been under siege by General Banks, surrendered on July 9. Now the entire Mississippi from St. Louis to New Orleans was in Union hands.

Back on the Eastern front, one of the bloodiest battles of the war took place at Chancellorsville in the beginning of May. Hooker outnumbered the Confederates better than two to one, but he began to retreat the moment he met stiff resistance from Lee's army. This surprising movement encouraged Lee to make the daring decision of dividing his small army into two parts, with Jackson taking half Lee's army around the right flank of Hooker and striking fiercely at General Howard's Eleventh Corps. Howard's men broke and ran, and soon Hooker's huge army was utterly demoralized. The Union army retreated back across the Rappahannock and left Lee and Jackson in possession of the field. Union losses were nearly 5,000 more than Lee's—17,300 to 12,500.

As great a loss to the Confederacy as the men who died on the battlefield at Chancellorsville was the loss of their beloved leader Stonewall Jackson. Jackson had been riding with his escort back along his own lines when they were mistaken for enemy cavalry and fired upon. Jackson was seriously wounded, pneumonia set in, and he was dead within a matter of days.

After his crushing defeat of the Union army at Chancellorsville, Lee was eager to strike the North in its own territory once again, and Jefferson Davis went along in the hope that a successful invasion would at last bring foreign aid. By June, Lee's forces had been built up to 76,000, and Hooker's discouraged force had been whittled down to 105,000. On June 15, Lee crossed the Potomac in the direction of Harrisburg. Hooker followed cautiously, keeping between Lee and Washington, D.C. On June 27, Lee's entire army was in Pennsylvania, and some of his troops under Ewell were only twenty miles from the capital at Harrisburg. The next day, ostensibly over a quarrel with Halleck, Hooker resigned his command over the Army of the Potomac, and the more reliable General George G. Meade took over.

The site of the great battle of Gettysburg was quite accidentally chosen. Confederate General A. P. Hill wandered into Gettysburg for boots and supplies and ran into a Union cavalry division under Buford. Fighting began on July 1, with each military unit from either side taking position upon arrival. The first day went to the Confederates, for they drove the Union forces out of the town to Cemetery Ridge. On the evening of July 2, Early and Ewell broke the Union defenses on Cemetery Ridge, but they could not hold their advantage be-

cause the expected reinforcements did not arrive. Longstreet
had also driven Sickles' corps back with great losses to the
Union. On the 3rd, Lee attacked the strong point in the Union
lines, and met withering fire.

Lee held his position on July 4, though he had seen the best
of his army torn to pieces the previous day. That evening he
began his retreat, only to find that the Potomac was flooded
behind him. Lincoln had begged that the Union commander
take advantage of Lee's trapped situation, but Meade failed
to deal the crushing blow. Instead, he called the council of
war Lincoln had urged him to omit, the Potomac receded, and
Lee's army escaped on the 14th of July.

July 4, 1863, was, therefore, a double celebration at the
North—Vicksburg had fallen on the 3rd, and Gettysburg was
won except for the ceremony of withdrawal. On the evening
of July 3, Lincoln called for a day of thanks—"He whose
will, not ours, should ever be done, be everywhere remembered
and reverenced with profoundest gratitude."

July 12, 1863

.   .   .   .   .

Much has occurred since I opened this book last.
Hooker has been displaced, and General Meade has led the
Army of the Potomac to victory, driving Lee back to the
Potomac where they are now probably fighting the decisive
battle of this war. Vicksburg was at last surrendered on the
fourth, on which day Meade likewise defeated Lee, so that
there has never been a Fourth of July kept before so grandly
by the nation. God seems to have at last sent us a leader. General Meade is a native of Spain, but his parents were Americans.
Now if Lincoln had but the sense to publish a general amnesty
and annul his emancipation act, we might once more be a
united nation, for we have great reason to be proud of the
courage and talent exhibited on both sides. This last battle has

never been surpassed by any in history. The North and South will now have learned to respect each other.

We met some Kentuckians at Long Branch. One of them knew Mrs. Lincoln intimately when a girl. He quoted the Spanish proverb, "Set a beggar on horseback and he will ride to the devil," when I asked him what he thought of her. Old Mr. Sayre[35] was a fine specimen of a Kentuckian. He invited us to his house and any of our friends we chose to send. They were both strong Union men and talked more justly and moderately than anyone except the Judge that I have met. "We must keep the country together," said old Mr. Sayre, "whatever it may cost." The old man has no children, but has raised and educated twenty, I believe. He has lost $300,000 in this war, but is willing, he says, to lose as much more to keep the nation entire.

I am so happy to be at home again. The Judge's public position exposes him to so much company. I enjoy the solitude and silence of my own home. I was so tired of the common crowds; they even troubled me on the seashore with their vulgar show and noise. Frank Leslie[36] we found a very gentlemanly, agreeable man. He was at the Branch; likewise Dr. and Mrs. Hutton,[37] the Dutch Reformed clergyman, with both of whom we had much doctrinal discussion. Though very excellent people, their doctrine makes them necessarily narrow-minded. They could not argue with either of us as we began from different premises.

---

[35] David Austin Sayre (1793–1870), a philanthropist, was born in Bottle Hill, New Jersey, but at an early age moved to Lexington, Kentucky. Successful as a merchant and banker, he gave about $500,000 to benevolent causes during his lifetime, and founded Sayre Institute.

[36] Frank Leslie (1821–1880) was born in Ipswich, England; his real name was Henry Carter. Leslie came to New York in 1838, became noted for his engraving skill, and founded *Frank Leslie's Illustrated Newspaper* in New York City on December 14, 1855. He also published a number of other papers and magazines which enjoyed considerable popularity.

[37] Dr. Mancius S. Hutton was at this time the minister of the Washington Square Dutch Reformed Church at Wooster Street and Washington Place.

July 14, 1863

The draft began on Saturday, the twelfth, very foolishly ordered by the government, who supposed that these
Union victories would make the people willing to submit. By
giving them Sunday to think it over, by Monday morning there
were large crowds assembled to resist the draft. All day yesterday there were dreadful scenes enacted in the city. The police
were successfully opposed; many were killed, many houses
were gutted and burned: the colored asylum was burned and
all the furniture was carried off by *women:* Negroes were hung
in the streets! All last night the fire-bells rang, but at last, in
God's good mercy, the rain came down in torrents and scat-
tered the crowds, giving the city authorities time to organize.
Today bodies of police and military patrolled the city to prevent any assembly of rioters. A Virginian, last evening, ha-
rangued the crowd.[38] Fearful that they might attack a Negro
tenement house some blocks below us, as they had attacked
others, I ordered the doors to be shut and no gas to be lighted
in front of the house. I was afraid people would come to visit
Judge Daly, ask questions, etc. I did not wonder at the spirit
in which the poor resented the three-hundred-dollar clause.

*Although the Union optimistically began the war with
ninety-day recruits, it soon became apparent that longer-range
service would be required, and that a volunteer army was not
adequate. The Federal government, therefore, adopted a com-
pulsory draft system in 1863 and set Saturday, July 11, as the
date for the drawing of names. The new Draft Act contained
a provision whereby a man could hire a substitute for himself
for the sum of $300, a considerable amount of money in those
days.*

The foreign-born element in New York City, and especially

---

[38] The story that "a Virginian" incited the rioters was a baseless rumor,
according to later historians.

the Irish, were day-laborers who were unable to accumulate $300, and deeply resented this clause which favored the rich. Their menial occupations also caused them to resent the Negro, for the influx of free Negroes from the South in ever-increasing numbers represented serious economic competition. Further, they had become convinced by Democratic politicians that the Republicans in power were responsible for all their grievances, and that this war was being fought by the abolitionists for ends that would only increase the competition. In addition to all this, prices outdistanced wages while the value of money fell, and the poor and foreign-born were the first to suffer.

On Saturday, July 12, the names of those selected to serve in the armed forces were published in the newspapers. On Monday morning, July 13, a crowd of malcontents gathered before draft headquarters at Third Avenue and 46th Street. By noon they had begun an attack upon the building, and it soon spread to all the buildings in the block. Fires were set, buildings were sacked and looted, and when the police arrived on the scene, they were attacked and driven back.

The initial successes of the mob resulted in increases in their ranks and the spread of violence to other parts of the city. Drink added to their courage, and soon they were roaming the streets in search of trouble. They hunted down Negroes as the cause of their woes, attacked and hanged them. The Colored Orphan Asylum on Fifth Avenue and 43rd Street was invaded and burned, and before long the mob had complete control of the upper East Side.

Since the situation was soon beyond the control of the city police, troops were called. General John E. Wool managed to gather almost 1,000 men from various military installations around the city, including West Point, and they supported the city's 2,000 policemen. Groups of private citizens armed and organized themselves to help repress the mobs which terrorized the city for four whole days—looting, burning, destroying life and property without discrimination.

Pitched battles took place on Broadway, on 42nd Street, in Gramercy Park, on 29th Street, and it was not until the 16th

*that order was restored to the city. Estimates vary as to the
number of lives lost on the streets of New York during these
four days, but it was certainly somewhere between 750 and
1,000. The only victory the rioters won was a temporary delay
in the drafting procedure, for it was resumed in August without incident.*

The news from the army is most encouraging. It is thought
that Lee will not be able to escape. It would seem as though
this war might now be brought to an end, but this news of the
riots here will give the rebels encouragement. The principal
cause of discontent was the provision that by paying three hundred dollars any man could avoid serving if drafted, thus obliging all who could not beg, borrow, or steal this sum to go to
the war. This is exceedingly unjust. The laboring classes say
that they are sold for three hundred dollars, whilst they pay one
thousand dollars for Negroes.

Things seem quiet this morning. People are returning to their
homes, though the tops of the stages are crowded with work-
ingmen and boys.

Mr. Leslie at Long Branch told me that he was in disgrace
with Mrs. Lincoln for having published in his paper a likeness
of her taken at Springfield by a skillful photographist sent there
for the purpose just after Lincoln's election. At the time she
was entirely satisfied with the likeness, but after she had been
dressed by city mantua-makers and milliners, she considered it
a libel. It was certainly the likeness of a very common looking
country body, whilst now she looks like a vulgar, shoddy, contractor's wife who does not know what to do with her money.
Mr. Leslie likewise told me that the clerk at Tiffany and
Young's had told him that their present largest buyers were the
common people, that a common-looking woman came into
the store a few weeks since and asked for diamonds. She picked
out a necklace, earrings, brooch, and bracelet and ordered them
sent to her house. The clerk did not like to do so and asked her

name (which he did not know). Then he said that it was against the rules of the store to send things out of such value without payment.

"Oh, my old man will pay for them," said she.

"Then," said the clerk, "will you write something to that effect?"

"Write what you please; I will sign it," said she, and she made a cross. "He'll know that.". . .

I was told that Admiral du Pont's share of the prize money[39] is $200,000. It is thought that he is in no haste to take Charleston.

July 23, 1863

At last the riot is quelled, but we had four days of great anxiety. Fighting went on constantly in the streets between the military and police and the mob, which was partially armed. The greatest atrocities have been perpetrated. Colonel O'Brian was murdered by the mob in such a brutal manner that nothing in the French Revolution exceeded it. Three or four Negroes were hung and burned; the women assisted and acted like furies by stimulating the men to greater ferocity. Father came into the city on Friday, being warned about his house, and found fifteen Negroes secreted in it by Rachel. They came from York Street, which the mob had attacked, with all their goods and chattels. Father had to order them out. We feared for our own block on account of the Negro tenements below MacDougal

---

[39] The United States had failed to subscribe to the Declaration of Paris of 1856 which outlawed privateering, and although Seward wanted to sign it by the time the war broke out, the European nations felt that since war had begun it was too late to do so. The usual arrangement was for the privateers to receive all but five percent from the sale of prizes captured (ships and cargo). Enterprising Southerners took advantage of this arrangement until the blockade made it impossible for them to deliver their prizes at home ports. Mrs. Daly's reference here is probably to Southern vessels captured in the Charleston harbor or trying to enter the harbor during the siege of that city.

Street, where the Negroes were on the roof, singing psalms and having firearms.

One night, seeing a fire before the house, I thought the time had come, but it proved to be only a bonfire. The Judge sallied out with his pistol, telling me that if he were not at home in five minutes to call up the servants. This mob seems to have a curious sense of justice. They attacked and destroyed many disreputable houses and did not always spare secessionists. On Saturday (the fifth day) we went up to see Judge Hilton, who thought me very courageous, but I felt sorry for Mrs. Hilton upon hearing that she had been so terribly frightened. She gave me such details that I came home too nervous to sleep. In Lexington Avenue, houses were destroyed. One lady before whose house the mob paused with the intention of sacking it, saved her house by raising her window, smiling, and waving her handkerchief. Mr. Bosie's brother was seized by a rioter who asked him if he had $300.

"No," said he.

"Then come along with us," said the rioter, and they kept him two hours. Mrs. Hilton said she never saw such creatures, such gaunt-looking savage men and women and even little children armed with brickbats, stones, pokers, shovels and tongs, coal-scuttles, and even tin pans and bits of iron. They passed her house about four o'clock on Monday morning and continued on in a constant stream until nine o'clock. They looked to her, she said, like Germans, and her first thought was that it was some German festival. Whilst we sat there, we heard occasional pistol shots, and I was very glad that I had ordered a carriage to take us home. The carriage, it seems, was very unwillingly sent since the livery-stable keeper was so much afraid.

Every evening the Judge *would* go out near eleven o'clock, to my great distress. But he threatened to send me into the country if I objected (which I dreaded still more), so I kept quiet. [James] Leonard, the Superintendent of Police in our neighborhood, said the draft could not be enforced; the firemen are against it, as well as all the working classes.

Among those killed or wounded have been found men with delicate hands and feet, and under their outward laborers' clothes were fine cambric shirts and costly underclothing. A dressmaker says she saw from her window a gentleman whom she knows and has seen with young ladies, but whose name she could not remember, disguised in this way in the mob on Sixth Avenue.

On Sunday we went to see Mrs. [Nathaniel] Jarvis and Mr. James T. Brady, who had just arrived from Washington. I saw Susanna Brady, who talked in the most violent manner against the Irish and in favor of the blacks. I feel quite differently, although very sorry and much outraged at the cruelties inflicted. I hope it will give the Negroes a lesson, for since the war commenced, they have been so insolent as to be unbearable. I cannot endure free blacks. They are immoral, with all their piety.

The principal actors in this mob were boys, and I think they were Americans. Catherine, my seamstress, tells me that the plundering was done by the people in the neighborhood who were looking on and who, as the mob broke the houses open, went in to steal. The police this morning found beds, bedding, and furniture in the house of a Scotch Presbyterian who was well off and owned two cows and two horses. The Catholic priests have done their duty as Christians ministers in denouncing these riotous proceedings. One of them remonstrated with a woman in the crowd who wanted to cut off the ears of a Negro [who] was hung. The priest told her that Negroes had souls. "Sure, your reverence," said she, "I thought they only had gizzards."

On Sunday evening, Mr. Dykes came in. He had seen Judge Pierrepont, who had gone to Washington with others to see what can be done. Mr. Dykes thinks that New York, being a Democratic city, may expect little indulgence from the Administration. The Judge went up to see General Dix, now in command here, who says that the government is determined to carry the draft measure through at all costs. Yesterday we went to the wedding of Lydia Watson in Westchester County. Mr. [James] Adie told the Judge that there was a secessionist plot to burn all the houses in the neighborhood on Thursday night, that he had heard that his had been exempted by vote, and that the principal instigator and mover in it was one of the richest and most influential men in the neighborhood. The purpose of the plot was to intimidate the government and prevent conscription. Mrs. Harry Morris, who I hear has been very violent in her invectives against the North, wished to know if the soldiers could be relied upon. I told her entirely so, that they declared they would rather fight these traitors at home who made this fire in their rear whilst they were risking their life to preserve order and the laws than the rebels. For her comfort, I told her that the mob had destroyed the houses of secessionists. I frightened her, I think, not a little.

July 25, 1863

Went last evening to see Uncle John, and met Mr. Turner on our walk home. He had just returned from Nassau, where he went to meet his brother-in-law. We learned much from him. The Richmond people were averse to the war—tired to death of it. Everyone was ruined, but each individual was afraid to act because of the army. Mr. Turner did not think if Charleston was taken that it would be possible for the rebels to hold out any longer. Twenty million dollars' worth of goods (contraband of war) had been sent from Nassau, where there was not a man who was not engaged in the trade. Mr. Turner is from Richmond. . . .

September 10, 1863

Chattanooga is taken without a blow by Rosecrans![40] Good generalship! Charleston, we think, must soon be restored to the U.S. Phil came in most unexpectedly on Thursday last week. He will soon, however, be obliged to return and go on perhaps to Lexington, if not with Burnside to Tennessee.

September 20, 1863

Saturday last the Judge went to a clambake at Manhattanville, a singular kind of entertainment. The clambake is indigenous, I think, to this country. It was given by Devlin Shill and others, and the company was mixed as the entertainment. General Meagher was present, and said to the Judge, "By God, Daly, it seems to me that I see all the enemies of the country here." (There were so many of the "New Gospel of Peace" present.) Brady made an admirable speech. The Judge got out of the way when they called for him, feeling that that was no place for a Judge to speak. A large hole was dug in the ground and it was filled with large stones. A fire was built in it until the stones were heated red hot, and then a large quantity of seaweed was thrown in, upon which was placed clams, lobsters, chickens, sweet potatoes, potatoes, oysters, ducks, geese, etc., with pans in which were butter, salt, peppers and lemon to be mulled into sauce. This was then covered over with seaweed and a tarpaulin. Tin plates were handed around. These different articles were distributed in tin basins, and the Judge says everything was admirably cooked.

[40] William Starke Rosecrans (1819–1898) became volunteer aide-de-camp to McClellan on April 19, 1861, and was subsequently commissioned a brigadier general in the regular army. He was commander of the Department of the Ohio, then of Western Virginia, then of the left wing of Pope's Army of the Mississippi. On September 9, 1863, he forced Bragg to abandon Chattanooga. In the meantime, Burnside's army occupied Knoxville in eastern Tennessee. Bragg gathered all the reinforcements he could muster and attacked Rosecrans on September 19 in the bloody battle of Chickamauga.

It is an Indian practice. The guests were seated at tables under the trees and had champagne, lager beer, etc., in abundance and had a very jolly time.

Rosecrans has been repulsed in his advance upon Atlanta, Georgia, but holds his ground at Chattanooga, and our minds are relieved of anxiety about him for the present.[41]

England is becoming a little more friendly, and hope once more for this distracted country seems possible. A letter from Father O'Reilly to the Judge says that there will be no danger from France; that owing to the late and excessive droughts, the crops have suffered severely; that water is so scarce that the peasantry of the land are killing and salting their cattle to preserve them; that war between France and this country would at once raise the price of bread one third.

The Russian fleet of six vessels in our harbor is quite an event. It is the first time a Russian vessel of war has ever been here, and is a token of good will to the United States government. There is to be a complimentary reception to be given by the city and a public banquet to the officers. The difficulty will be, what can they do with the English Admiral [Sir Alexander] Milne likewise in the city? Will it do not to invite him? Baron Osten-Sacken has promised that we shall go and see mass performed on board the Admiral ship, which, as it will be according to the ritual of the Greek Church, will be very interesting.

When Czar Alexander II of Russia freed the serfs in 1861, his act was highly acclaimed in the North, and many Americans

---

41 The "repulse" which Mrs. Daly refers to here was the Union's near disaster of Chickamauga which began on the 19th. Despite his excellent troops, Rosecrans was struck with panic when Southern troops rushed through a hole which accidentally opened up in the Union lines, and the result was a rush for the safety of Chattanooga twelve miles away. Union hero of the day was General George H. Thomas, who won the sobriquet "Rock of Chickamauga" for standing his ground and allowing the troops which fled to secure themselves behind the Chattanooga defenses. Had it not been for Thomas, a defeat would have been a complete disaster.

interpreted his timing as an act sympathetic with the Union cause. A second basis for the popular belief that the Federal government enjoyed the good will of Russia was a common antagonism to England. Then, when Russian fleets visited New York and San Francisco late in 1863, Northerners were convinced that this act of friendship was a pronouncement to the world of where Russia stood on the issue of the Confederate rebellion.

Actually, however, the Czar probably would not have acted differently had the Civil War never begun. When Alexander II came to power in 1855, he had first to sign a humiliating treaty of peace with Britain, France, and the Ottoman Empire to terminate the Crimean War, and then he had to deal with widespread discontent and criticism within Russia. As a concession to an important and vociferous group of Russians who believed that only through the westernization of Russia could another disaster like the Crimean War be averted, he pronounced the emancipation of the serfs. Concessions were made by Alexander during the 1861–1864 period to other groups within Russia to quiet opposition and unrest brought about by Russia's defeat and poor economic conditions.

In the matter of the two fleets which entered American waters in 1863, Alexander seriously expected war with Britain to be renewed, and he wished to have his fleet situated where it could make a quick attack upon British commerce the moment war broke out. When the crisis had passed, the two fleets made their departure, but the American public was not disabused of the fiction it wished to believe. When, a few years later, Americans were chagrined at the fantastically high price Secretary Seward paid for Alaska ($7,200,000), many Americans consoled themselves with the conviction that such a "gift" to the Russian government was well deserved for the contribution the Czar had made to the Union during the war.

The Judge had an interesting letter from Sir Dominick Daly yesterday, and I received one from Captain Badeau in which he relates a conversation with the Austrian minister, who evidently is on the side of the North. It is doubtful if Maximilian will accept the heavy and vacillating crown of Mexico.[42] Badeau has done well, has been wounded, and will be very interesting when he returns. He is very observant and thoughtful.

October 2, 1863

Yesterday the Russian admiral and his officers had a public reception. All the militia were called out. The crowd was almost as great as on the occasion of the arrival of the Prince of Wales. It was a good test of public feeling. The French and English vessels of war are in the harbor and the English admiral is in the city. Lord Lyons is likewise staying at the Brevoort, over which the English flag is flaunting.

October 3, 1863

Corcoran came in yesterday and went with the Judge to see Dr. Gescheidt, who pronounced the General very unwell and in need of rest; so the Judge has invited Corcoran to stay with us. He is coming today to be fed upon oatmeal and barley water for a few days. I like him but not his train, who, though good, warm-hearted fellows, are somewhat uncouth in manner and language, with the exception of Captain Kirker. Last evening we had a visit from Mr. Schleiden, as sleek, as gentlemanly as ever, and as agreeable. I wish I could remember all the anecdotes of the persons now before the public which I hear, but one crowds the other from my memory. Dr. Gescheidt says that Corcoran's sickness is the result of miserable food and the bad air during his long imprisonment which he now begins to feel in his system.

---

[42] The thirty-one-year-old Archduke of Austria was formally offered the Mexican throne in October of 1863, but he did not accept Louis Napoleon's offer until April 10, 1864.

October 8, 1863

Yesterday Mr. Schleiden and Baron Osten-Sacken dined with us. Osten-Sacken sent us a box for the opera, and we went. We heard Medori in "Roberto Devereux." Her shoulders are so beautiful that I suppose she could not sacrifice so much to the *mise-en-scène* as to wear the ruff and farthingale, the costume of the period. It did not appear well before an audience who spoke English. The opera is a new one by Donizetti, and so like his other works that it produced little impression. Coming out, we met Bertinatti, the Sardinian minister, who stopped to tell the Judge that his article on "Naturalization" had enabled Bertinatti to decide two cases, etc. We went all together to the *Maison Dorée* and took an ice and jabbered away in French to Bertinatti. I think he has a very bad face. . . .

Monday [*October 12*]

Baron Gerolt arrived here and is now writing in his room. We want to go tomorrow to the wedding of Miss Mary Jay, but I do not know whether it would be proper to leave the Baron home alone. I will have my dress, however, prepared and be in readiness for either alternative.

Tuesday [*October 13*]

Last evening Baron Osten-Sacken and Mr. Schleiden dined with Count Piper and spent the evening with us. The Judge went out to see Judge Hilton, who has lost his nomination, and I was left to entertain them as best I might. I have but little confidence when left alone. We talked over the country and mutual friends. I must try to correct my turn for satire. It is not only a disagreeable, but ill-natured trait, and I find it growing upon me.

The Judge came in late and gave our guests a description of the excursion of the morning—an invitation of the city to its guests to visit the public charities. The Russians, for whom it was designed principally, did not go, but sent a regret at the last moment, probably because the English and French admirals attended. The Spanish governor of Morro Castle was likewise of the party, and Admiral Farragut,[43] to whom the Judge was introduced. Farragut speaks four languages perfectly and is a good type of the American character. Five hundred boys were drawn up to receive them in military uniform and went through the echelon movement admirably, after which the little lieutenant colonel made a capital speech. He concluded by saying, "And tell your governments, gentlemen, to leave us to settle our affairs in our own way," after which the Colonel said, "We will now go through our drill, but we beg you to remember that the best of our troops have been lately drafted."

October 16, 1863

.   .   .   .   .

The news from the army is encouraging; the Confederates were foiled in both attempts to turn our position at Chattanooga and in Virginia.

October 20, 1863

The Judge went last night to the banquet given to the Russians, and brought me the *carte* painted on yellow moire

---

[43] David G. Farragut (1801–1870) was made a rear admiral after the capture of New Orleans in the Civil War, and in that capacity he opened the Mississippi to navigation. Congress created the new ranks of vice admiral and then admiral (1866) for him, ranks never before held in the U.S. Navy.

antique. He thought his speech was a failure, but on reading it in the paper this morning, I think it very good for an impromptu. He had to speak on the eagles of Russia and America, and his speech was therefore somewhat ornithological.

October 23, 1863

Baron Gerolt returned to us today after an excursion to the mines of Mr. Detmold.[44] He says the miners get three and four dollars a day, work very short time, and defy the government to draft any of them. The company has been obliged to ask for some troops to prevent the disorders which go on among them. . . .

October 24, 1863

A few evenings since, we had a visit from Mr. John O'Mahony, the Irish patriot and scholar, and we had a long talk upon Ireland and the Irish. He said he was sorry to see them come out here. He would rather that they should fight—or starve—at home. Here they were degraded mostly into hewers of wood and drawers of water. He did not approve of this demonstration in favor of the Russians. He thought we should sympathize with the Poles, of course, but as an American citizen, he would do nothing against the policy of the government at such a time. Mrs. [Claudius E.] Habicht [wife of the Swedish consul] says that the liberal party in Europe will be greatly disheartened. Baron Gerolt asked the Judge this morning what he should say, that he had to write a dispatch to his government. "Say," he replied, "that as yet our expenses do not exceed the income of our national wealth, which is always increasing despite the war."

---

[44] Christian Edward Detmold (1810–1887), civil engineer, emigrated to the United States from Germany and built the New Jersey Zinc Company in Newark, New Jersey. He died in New York City.

Miss Cushman[45] and Booth have been playing for the benefit of the Sanitary Commission. It has done a great deal of good, and allowed many rascals to enrich themselves at the expense of our poor soldiers without their suffering so much. It is almost a disgrace to get rich by this dreadful war. Rosecrans has been removed from jealousy of the government, I suppose.[46]

November 6, 1863

Since I opened this, I have had a most severe cold and inflammation of the chest, which, thank God, I am now relieved from. It prevented my going to the Russian Ball. The Judge was one of the committee with the Mayor to receive them at the wharf. It was a magnificent entertainment, more elegant than any before given, even that to the Prince of Wales, and much better managed. It is the last of the Russian civilities, and although we are now in mourning, still I am glad to see us show such recognition of the national courtesy which Russia has shown us during this tedious, unnatural, and dreadful war. In distress, sympathy is ever more welcome than assistance. When deserted by those we supposed friends and we receive it from strangers, it is the more gratefully recognized. Therefore, perhaps, we have somewhat overdone our welcome.

More interesting even than this war, however, is the state

---

[45] Charlotte Saunders Cushman (1816–1876) was an American actress who achieved great success in the United States and England, making frequent trips between the two countries. In 1863 she came to America to give benefit performances for the Sanitary Commission.

[46] On October 17, 1863, Stanton placed Grant in command of the entire area between the Alleghenies and the Mississippi and directed the replacement of Rosecrans by George H. Thomas as commander of the Army of the Cumberland. As Thomas became the new leader of Chattanooga under Grant, Rosecrans went into temporary retirement. Rosecrans was able and a good strategist, and he distinguished himself the next year as commander of the Department of Missouri by a victory over a Confederate army under Sterling Price.

of things in this city as evinced by the last election.[47] Two judges have been bought and sold by Tammany and Mozart, making it a disgrace, almost, to be popular. Judge Hilton, who has lost his election, was unpopular on account of his arbitrary manner, but he told us he could have bought his office last summer and that someone advised him to invite Sweeny[48] to his house to dinner or he would lose his election.

"What," said he, "invite a scamp to my house? I'd be d—— first."

Judge [Joseph S.] Bosworth, a most exceptional judge, lawyer, and gentleman and an old Democrat, was quietly set aside by his party for that rascal John H. McCunn, who ought to be in prison, who released the rioters last summer and professed himself a friend of the poor.[49] But Fernando Wood wanted a judge, and Peter B. Sweeny was one who would attend to his interests. The Judge's turn comes next. Oh that he were rich enough to be able to refuse any nomination by such a corrupt set of *oligarchs*. We are ruled by an aristocracy of public cheats and swindlers and have no right of choice but of two perhaps equally inefficient men for any office. I wish

---

[47] Many Republicans and Union Democrats voted against Governor Horatio Seymour in 1863 because he was tinged with Copperheadism and because of his failure to support the Federal government with troops when the Draft Riots hit New York City. The Union ticket carried the state by some 30,000 votes and the Democrats suffered greatly in New York City. The Union Party won 21 out of 32 seats in the State Senate, and 82 of the 128 Assembly seats. Similar Republican victories occurred throughout the North in 1863.

[48] Peter B. Sweeny (1825–1911) was probably the best educated and ablest of Tammany Hall leaders at the time when William Marcy (Boss) Tweed was in power. Tweed became chairman of the general committee of Tammany Hall in 1863, gained control of the city's finances, and succeeded in robbing millions of dollars before he was arrested in October 1871. Sweeny was appointed comptroller of New York City by Mayor John T. Hoffman in 1867, and when Tweed was apprehended Sweeny fled to Paris. Tweed went to prison.

[49] Joseph S. Bosworth was a justice of the Superior Court of New York, Chambers and Center Streets, at the same time that Judge John H. McCunn was a justice of the General Sessions Court at the New Court House, 32 Chambers Street. McCunn was impeached and removed from the bench in 1871, in the public reaction against the Tweed Ring.

the Judge were free and could go into politics untrammeled to smash right and left into public abuses. I think he would be both troublesome and useful. I dreamt he made a parting speech to Tammany the other night and said that he refused any nomination by a party that had disgraced the dignity of the bench as they had done in the last election, that he should return to his profession, where at least a reputation for honesty and impartiality would not be *injurious* but perhaps a source of income and profit still.

These last three weeks we have been overrun with company. One Sunday we had ten persons in the evening, the next a half-dozen, and someone came every day to dinner. Baron Gerolt left on Friday last, and Mr. Davis from Greenfield came in his place. Then Mr. Schleiden came in his place, then Osten-Sacken, then General Meagher, who told us a very capital anecdote of Gurowski.

Gurowski was talking in his usual manner of the nobility and his disgust of common people, etc.,[50] when dining with some Irish gentlemen, one of whom agreed with all he said. At last Gurowski said, "Vat do you know of counts and nobility?"

"Oh," said the Irishman, "I have been for four years at the Court of St. James."

"Vat, you? Vas you dere?"

"Maid of honor to her Majesty," said he.

"You d—— blackguard," said Gurowski angrily.

Mr. Harris brought with him last Sunday evening a very curious mussel shell (which he himself, he says, caught and opened) which contains nine images of Buddha. They are sold as curiosities in Japan, and Mr. Harris, hearing of them, went to the lake and monastery where they were to be found. After much persuasion, he was allowed to try to catch one himself.

---

[50] Count Gurowski kept a diary from 1862 to 1866 (*My Diary: Notes on the Civil War*) in which he denounced almost everyone and everything. Among others, Lincoln, Stanton, Seward, and McClellan felt the sting of his whip. Each of the three volumes became available as soon as completed, and Gurowski became exceedingly unpopular as a result.

It is, of course, the effect of art, but the image is incrusted with nacre and fastened to the back of the shell as though it were a natural formation. He told us some curious things about the sultans of Java, their glass houses in tanks of water as a refuge from the terrible heat of the climate. He had seen the remains of them, one being still nearly perfect. Java once, he says, had a high degree of civilization. He found a coin of the reign of Antoninus there. Mr. Harris met Rajah [of Sarawak, Sir James] Brooke, whom he described as an enthusiastic romantic Englishman, fond of adventure—a sort of modern sea king. Poor Harris, however, has been ruined by his philanthropy and by his mining operations in Borneo. One never sees him without hearing something new and strange. . . .

November 12, 1863

The Judge's address last evening before the American Institute [of Architects] was a complete success. He is much complimented in today's papers. I was very sorry that I was too unwell to go and hear it. He was thanked and a resolution was passed to print one thousand copies for distribution—a very great compliment.

Received a letter from Mr. Davis enclosing an extract from the journal of Mr. [Samuel Richard] Thayer, our consul-general at Alexandria, who had a very interesting conversation with Prince Napoleon on America. The Prince is, he says, a tall, stout man, the magnified image of his uncle, the Little Corporal.

"I said," said Mr. Thayer, "on being introduced, 'J'éprouve, Monsieur, un vif plaisir d'avoir l'honneur de voir un prince le bien-aimé de mon pays.' He thanked me and said he had visited my country two years ago and was greatly interested in it. It was the finest country in the world, and with such a future." Thayer enjoyed the dinner at Boston, especially the speech of Mr. [Edward] Everett and the poem of Dr. Holmes.

Mr. E. was a very distinguished statesman and a finished orator. He hoped our war would soon end. In France, they were very little acquainted with the merits of our cause, though Laboulaye[51] had written excellently well upon it. In England at the great Exhibition of last year Mr. Thayer had been surprised at the misconceptions on the American question prevailing there. He had talked much with Mr. [John] Bright, whom he knew very well, and who he thought had the best appreciation of the subject, better even than Cobden.[52]

"At the dinner given by the Viceroy of Egypt on this same day," Mr. Thayer continued, "his [Napoleon's] conversation with me was principally upon America. He thinks President Lincoln a sagacious and moderate man, and doubts if any man in his position would have done better. The two great men of the government are Messrs. Seward and Chase, and he thinks this the sentiment of the American people. 'J'aime beaucoup M. Seward,' said he. 'Il est vraiment homme d'état capable et philosophe.' Mr. Chase, whom he had seen much, gave him a favorable impression for ability and comprehension. General McClellan he considered capable, 'quant à la guerre,' but on talking with him, he was surprised at his narrow political views, his inadequate appreciation of the slavery question. Burnside he knew better and liked. The prince applied to Mr. Seward for permission to visit the rebels. Mr. Seward saw no objection. He accordingly entered the rebel lines but did not go to Richmond or see Davis. He saw Generals Lee, Beauregard, and Stonewall Jackson. As for Beauregard, he regards him as very pompous, a man of more show than performance. Lee is capable but ambitious. Jackson

---

51 Édouard René Lefebvre de Laboulaye (1811–1883) was a French jurist, politician, and historian. The work referred to here is very likely his *Histoire politique des Etats-Unis,* published between the years 1855 and 1866.

52 Richard Cobden (1804–1865) was an English economist known as the "apostle of free trade." Like John Bright, he was a power in the Anti-Corn Law League and a supporter of the Northern cause in the Civil War.

pleased him greatly in some respects as a brave, disinterested man. He was the only one of the rebel leaders who seemed to regret the rebellion or retain his patriotism in any degree. Some of his remarks, considering his position, were decidedly patriotic." Something more was said by the prince about the commerce of America with Egypt and his visit to the West and the magnificent future he thinks in store for us. He liked the American fancy drinks, mint juleps, sherry cobblers, etc. He spoke of the great cheapness of ice in America, how everyone had it in abundance, apropos of a remark of the viceroy that ice cost there (even that manufactured at Suez) twc francs for two and one half pounds.

November 24, 1863

I am happy to begin another book with the account of Grant's victory over Bragg at Chattanooga, and the release of Tennessee. As the Judge says, he is indeed U. S. Grant, United States Grant, his interests being those of the country. It has been most brilliantly done. Dr. Gescheidt told us that he heard his wife always accompanied him to prevent his taking intoxicating liquors, that she and his chief physician were the only ones who had influence to prevent him. Lincoln is reported to have said when he heard of his failing, "I would like to know what the brand of whiskey he drinks is, to send it to the other Union generals." It is lamentable that drunkenness is so common among our officers.

Phil is at Knoxville with the Ninth Army Corps. He gives a sad picture of his accommodations (five in a tent), and when he is thus uncomfortable, what must be the condition of the private soldiers? This victory over Bragg, however, will release Burnside, since Longstreet will be obliged to raise the siege. The news came on Thanksgiving Day. It is quite remarkable how often good news has arrived on festival days.

After the near-disaster of Chickamauga, Rosecrans retreated to Chattanooga and allowed himself to be bottled up there by the Confederates under Bragg. With his supply lines cut off, Rosecrans' situation became critical. He had never proved himself much of a leader or military strategist, but he now reached such a state of helpless inaction that Lincoln realized he must be replaced quickly.

General George H. Thomas had proved himself equal to the challenge, but his Virginian birth had made him suspect by many in Washington, so Lincoln called upon Grant to rescue the besieged Army of the Cumberland. He replaced Rosecrans on October 24. Grant's first act was to reestablish the lines of supply, and his second was to summon Sherman's army to Chattanooga.

Sherman arrived on November 15, and by the 23rd Grant was ready to move. The odds were now all in favor of the Union, with a total of over 100,000 men under Grant, Sherman, Sheridan, Hooker, and Thomas, including the armies of the Cumberland and the Tennessee and some men from the Army of the Potomac. Bragg had less than 70,000 men and no such combination of proved military leaders.

Fighting began on the 23rd, and on the 24th, Union troops beat the Confederates back in the battle of Lookout Mountain. Missionary Ridge was the Union objective on the 25th, and when it was taken, the Confederate army broke and fled the field. This victory finished the military career of Braxton Bragg, and Joseph E. Johnston was given command of the defeated army.

Not only did the great victory of Chattanooga boost the morale of the North, but it ended the South's hopes for ultimate victory. The line between the Confederate armies in the East and those in the Mississippi Valley was now broken, and the deep South was exposed to mighty Union forces. Only Johnston and the remnants of Bragg's army (65,000 men) stood between Sherman and Atlanta, Georgia. With this situation well in hand, Grant went East to take personal command of the Army of the Potomac.

Captain Badeau, who dined with us a fortnight ago, told us that Dr. Duncan, a landed proprietor in Mississippi, told him that Louisiana, Mississippi, Arkansas and Missouri, Kentucky and Tennessee would be glad to return to the Union with or without slavery, that the rebels were effectually conquered and knew it. Dr. Duncan has been a consistent Union man. He has lost everything, and from having an income of $100,000, he could not get enough money to live from day to day. What he had, his gardener, who had saved up some, gave him. He sent to a man to whom he had loaned $12,000 some years before and who had made a large fortune on that capital to say, "Give me enough to go to the despised North. I have a nest-egg there which will support me and I shall leave this miserable country and people forever." He is now here and the Judge intends to pay him a visit, as is the duty of all.

The Bostonians have raised $12,000 for Mrs. Carson, who is to enjoy this income during her life. After she dies, the money is to be appropriated towards raising a monument to Mr. [James Louis] Petigru,[53] her father, the only Union man in South Carolina. Notwithstanding the miseries these secessionists have brought on the country, there are still men and women in this city who sympathize with them.

December 2, 1863

Besides the great Union victories, we have achieved a great moral victory in this city, having elected a mayor in opposition to Mozart Hall.[54] Tammany is united and has

---

[53] James Louis Petigru died on March 9, 1863.

[54] On December 1, 1863, a new mayor of the City of New York was elected. The contest was between Charles Godfrey Gunther, who won with some 28,000 votes; Francis Boole, who received some 22,000 votes, and Orison Blunt, who received approximately 10,000 votes. Gunther was a Peace Democrat, a Copperhead, who had belonged to the Anti-Abolition State-Rights Association. Boole had been a "Ring" alderman and had the reputation of being a grafter. In appealing for the Negro vote, he lost the New York Irish vote. Blunt was the Republican candidate. Evidently the Dalys supported Gunther as the best of three poor choices.

broken the power of the Ring, as the *close* corporation of scamps who have for so long ruled our city politics is called. Sweeny, the leader, some years ago [in 1857] got the office of district attorney and was always ill. Dr. Gescheidt told us that he was sent for from time to time. At last the Doctor told Sweeny that he was not sick at all, but wanted an excuse for neglecting the duties of the office which he was too ignorant to be able to fulfill. When Sweeny's term of office expired, he got well. He does not drink himself, but encourages others to drink. Sweeny treats others to drinks while he keeps sober; thus he's somewhat respected by his low associates.

This year there has been violent electioneering. A young and quite pretty woman came with her husband to call upon the Judge to solicit his vote for her spouse, who was ambitious of a police justiceship. The Judge was fortunately out.

Today we are invited by [William H.] Webb, the great shipbuilder, to a banquet. The Judge has gone, but my cold kept me at home. Last evening he went to Mr. [Simon] Bernheimer's[55] to a soirée musicale in honor of his father-in-law's birthday. I stayed at home and read again *The Lady of the Lake* with as much interest as the first time I read it; I much prefer it to Homer. (Pardon, illustrious seer!) Today I have been much favored with visitors.

A few evenings since, Mr. Harris came in and we had a nice gossiping talk before the Judge came in. I related the rise and progress of Mrs. Smith Clift, which seemed to amuse him. He told me some stories about Fernando Wood, who has outwitted his mother-in-law in her marriage settlement, securing his wife's dowry of $100,000 on real estate already mortgaged beyond its value. Mr. Harris also told me about a Miss

---

[55] Simon Bernheimer, head of Bernheimer Brothers, importers and clothiers, 320 Broadway, was a personal friend of the Dalys and at one time collaborated with the Judge in a real estate investment, an apartment house on 59th Street.

Wolfe, who was robbed of a magnificent diamond ring by a fascinating Polish count. This is the present talk of New York. The Count, by the aid of a miraculously swelling and shrinking finger and a jeweler, hoped to realize a nice little sum from a magnificent jewel Miss Wolfe wore. She was foolish enough to trust it for one moment on his finger to satisfy him with a nearer view.

December 26, 1863

I have been again unwell and confined to my room. Christmas I left the house for the first time in ten weeks and dined in Laight Street. Today I have taken a walk in the open air on the back piazza and hope now I shall be able to go about soon as usual. The Judge has been very kind and indulgent. Has anyone so good a husband as I have, or so loving a one? We have been eight years married, and he is the same now as on our wedding day. May God give me grace to keep and deserve his continued affection.

December 29, 1863

Christmas was unusually pleasant, notwithstanding the presence of [Uncle] Lydig Suydam, whose hypocritical face always acts as a wet blanket upon any pleasure to the Judge. Lydig Suydam is always bringing up unpleasant memories. Father seems to think Lydig much attached to him, but I do not know how he has ever shown it except in riding Father's horses, breaking his wagons, and once offering to go to Savannah with him when Father was unwell. Lydig made a great merit of this, telling Maggie (who likewise went on the most disinterested principles, although I would like to have gone) that he wanted a sea voyage because he was suffering with dyspepsia. Father, the poor, deluded, grateful soul, paid all Lydig's expenses to Savannah and back again in consequence of his disinterestedness. Maggie said I should not go as I was stronger than she, and she thought the sea would make her stout again. So she likewise went from the purest filial devotion, whilst I, from choice of course, remained at home *alone* to take care of the younger children. Which was the pleasanter duty? Who was the most disinterested? . . .

On Christmas this year we had some speeches. Mr. Weston, the two Judges, and Uncle Lydig rose to answer. Phil was affectionately remembered.

December 30, 1863

On Sunday the twenty-seventh poor Corcoran was buried. His foolish, inconsiderate marriage has been one of the causes of his death. He was in a weak habit of body when he left us seven weeks ago, and the exposure and the hard duties of the camp were enough without a young wife to humor for one in his state of health. General Meagher was on a visit to him, and riding his horse home, Corcoran fell (it was supposed in a fit) and never spoke afterwards. He had had one or two fainting fits before, it seems. Meagher sent the Judge a telegraph, most eloquently worded, expressing his own distress and appreciation of Corcoran. The telegraph containing no information, however, that had not been in the papers the day before. Meagher supposed the Judge would send the information to the newspaper, of course, and Meagher would have the benefit of it.

Meagher's telegraph ran thus: "Dear Judge: You have by this time heard of the lamentable and sudden death of our gentle, gallant friend, General Corcoran, the Colonel of the valiant 69th, the leader of the Irish Legion, the brave and consistent Union prisoner. We hoped to have had him long with us to have shared with him the festivities of Christmas, but it is a black Christmas for us. Yours, Thomas Francis Meagher." Of course, the telegraph was not paid for, and it cost the Judge five dollars and thirty-eight cents. At my instigation, however, it did not go to the paper.

Meagher was first pallbearer, and in the paper of yesterday, I saw a paragraph from Fairfax saying it is already talked of that the command will be given to General Meagher, but that Meagher has too high a sense of the merits of the deceased, too delicate a regard for his memory for him, to listen to such a proposal (for the present). When I remember how useless he thought it in Mr. Savage and the Judge to do so much to release this brave Union prisoner two years ago and remember his desertion of him on the field of Bull Run, I cannot but marvel. Truly *Reinecke Fuchs* [*Reynard the Fox*] is a genuine story. Meagher is cautiously frank, prudently *reckless*, and brave enough to risk his life when reputation actually requires it. He wears a swashing and martial outside with an appearance of whole-soulness. His generosity and liberality are very taking, but he pays no one. He is the fox all over, as anyone might see by watching his small bright eye. I confess I do not want him to come near us. In his neighborhood, there can be no good luck for others. He ruined General Shields, covered him with flattery, licked him all over, like the anaconda, and swallowed him whole. Now that Corcoran is gone, he is the representative of the Irish brave—what he has all the time been aiming at!

Had a pretty little gift from Davis, a box of Johannisberger from Mr. Bernheimer, a beautiful book from Mr. Jarvis, a ring from Rosalie, some cups from Florence, and some sweets from David and Mother with some money.

1864

We received yesterday seventy visitors. This was not as many as we received last year, and I missed many familiar faces.

Perhaps many did not come because they knew that I had been unwell and thought that I would not receive. The Judge stayed at home to do my talking. We had a visit from Meagher, who has not been appointed to the command of poor Corcoran. I received a little volume from Mr. Savage of his poems, dedicated to the Judge. It was a most complimentary dedication, of course. I think it all deserved. It is very disinterested in Savage, who is the best specimen I have yet met of a native Irish character. He has less of the desire of display and the conceitedness of the race than the other prominent men I have met. Corcoran was even getting a little spoiled and wanted a major-generalship, whereas he had as yet done nothing to deserve it. To be sure, he could not get active service from the government.

Bierstadt arrived and gave us a most interesting account of his eight months' journey to the Rocky Mountains. He has promised to show me his sketches and curiosities.

January 5, 1864

Had a very pleasant little breakfast party yesterday with Mr. and Mrs. Dana, Mr. Young, and Bierstadt. Mr. Dana[1] had seen Phil and spoke of him with the highest commendation, as did Burnside when here. General Burnside said that Phil made the best mounted officer that he knew. He was never weary, never shirked any duty or any danger, was obedient, cool, ready-witted, brave and a thorough gentleman. This he told James T. Brady, who told the Judge. . . .

January 8, 1864

Today Archbishop Hughes is buried. The Judge has gone to the funeral. For the last two days the body has been lying in state in the Cathedral on an elevated bier with the Archbishop in his full robes, his purple boots, his gloves, mantles, and mitre. The Archbishop's loss is regretted by all classes. All denominations regarded him as a patriot and a man of sense and moderation.[2] The Common Council have officiously attended his funeral—I suppose to seek Catholic favor!

February 16, 1864

My diary is much neglected, and I shall not have the satisfaction in my old age of reading over the events of the past.

The experiment of paying my visits by sending cards has been quite successful. My Friday evenings have been very well

---

[1] After Charles A. Dana broke with Greeley and left the New York *Tribune* in 1862, he became Assistant Secretary of War under Stanton, a position he held until the war's end. In 1868 he reorganized the New York *Sun.*

[2] Archbishop Hughes' last public address was delivered during the Draft Riots in July 1863 in response to Governor Seymour's plea, and his influence was believed to have helped quell the riots. He had also, in response to Seward's request, undertaken a mission to Napoleon III to dissuade him from recognizing the Confederacy.

attended. Many of the artists have attended, and some of the notabilities have visited us. Mother has been deeply grieved because I would not ask those of my uncles who treated us differently from Maggie and Kate to our reception, but the Judge was obdurate. They were shallow, conceited men, he said, who must be taught that he would not endure any impertinence. As I was thus treated for marrying him, the Judge felt he owed it to his own self-respect to show that he noticed it. I am afraid I have left out many whom I intended to ask, but I must remedy that another time.

We dined with Father [Thomas] Treanor, a great friend of Father O'Reilly, down on North Street on Sunday and had a most agreeable day. These Catholic priests are like great intellectual children. So natural and so simple-hearted are they that they do not do things for effect as our clergy do. I shall join them some day. It is touching to see how much affection the Judge seems to call forth from them. He resembles them in much of his character. Heaven forgive me, I fear I teach him distrust of his fellows. I do not think his experience with respect to my connections has raised his opinion of human nature any.

Father Hasson, Vicar-General of Georgia and Alabama, dined with us. He is waiting to be able to return to the South. He went out on a mission to Europe just before the war broke out, and having unfortunately gone in a vessel with which there were a number of blockade runners, they were all photographed without their knowledge. The photographs were sent to the government, Father Hasson's face with them, and this has prevented him from getting a pass for the South. So he is now working here.

We find Mrs. Raasloff and her daughters a great addition to our social circle. Through Baron Gerolt, who stayed with us the latter part of January, we have made the acquaintance of General and Mrs. Frémont, and her sister, Madam Boileau, the wife of the French consul-general. Mrs. Frémont, I am convinced, is the enterprising, ambitious woman. The General is very gentlemanly, talks little but well, has a soft, tender, blue eye, and is, I am sure, rather a shy man. He seems to have a chivalric devotion for his wife and is, I feel certain, a brave soldier. Although much prejudiced against him, I liked him very much. The Frémonts have a beautiful house and live very elegantly. Madam Boileau, or Madam la Baronesse Gauldieu Boileau, is a very intelligent, piquant personage, with a rather handsome Indian physiognomy and beautiful arms and shoulders. She is a very zealous Roman Catholic. Both ladies are exceedingly busy about the Sanitary Commission Fair, for which the ladies are giving weekly concerts (at two dollars a ticket) in their respective homes. I shall not often be able to go. It will, besides answering a charitable and patriotic purpose, employ their time and give them a little amusement during this Holy season of Lent. Mr. Young, in the *Albion*, calls it the "Carnival of Charity."

March 11, 1864

I have quite forgotten my diary. Mr. Davis from Greenfield has been here again, leaving for home on Tuesday last, and on Monday we had a very pleasant merry time. Mr. and Mrs. Savage and Miss Harriet Whetten dining with us and we had a great deal of nice music in the evening and some whiskey punch. Mr. Davis told many amusing stories. I do not know what is the matter that I can never remember the good stories. One which he told of Mrs. Howe[3] is worth noting. She was talking with Charles Sumner about some individual cases of misfortune and distress. After a pause, he

---

[3] Mrs. Julia Ward Howe (1819–1910), poet, biographer, and reformer, was born in New York City, but moved to Boston after her marriage to Dr. Samuel Howe and became the mother of four daughters and two sons. She won national fame when "The Battle Hymn of the Republic" appeared in the *Atlantic Monthly*, in February 1862. The first woman admitted to the American Academy of Arts and Letters, she was an abolitionist and a leader in woman suffrage and other social movements.

said, "I have concluded no longer to think of individuals; I can now only consider mankind in masses." Mrs. Howe wrote it in her diary, adding, "I believe the Almighty has not yet come to this conclusion."

I went to Mrs. Viele's last Friday evening and enjoyed myself very much. I saw General Burnside, talked about Phil, had a chat with McDonough about Mrs. Gibbs and radicalism. The old lady would like to gibbet everybody who does not agree with her. [Charles A.] Bristed came up and spoke to me and we talked about Cleveland Coxe's[4] sermon against the Catholics a few Sundays since. Bristed took his part, saying that he had provocation enough. Did not some Irishmen threaten to burn his house because he had brought a decent colored servant from Baltimore with him? He made a capital sermon. Of course, I took the part of the Irish and Catholics. I reminded him that the Catholic priests had saved the city last summer,[5] and said I thought it most indecorous of a Christian clergyman to abuse two thirds of the Christian world because of the conduct of a handful of ignorant men who had proved themselves no Christians at all by their behavior. "We had better drop the subject," said he shortly. "We shall never agree upon it. Let it drop."

"I shall say what I have to say," replied I. "Mr. Coxe's statements are false!"

March 12, 1864

I was very sorry to have been prevented by the damp weather from going last evening to Mrs. Viele's. My cold is still continuing. Whilst we were still at dinner, Dr. Wilson,

---

[4] Arthur Cleveland Coxe (1818–1896) was a rector in Hartford and Baltimore before being called to New York's Protestant Episcopal Calvary Church on Fourth Avenue at 21st Street. In 1865, he was made Bishop of Western New York.

[5] Mrs. Daly is referring to Archbishop Hughes' instruction to New York's parish priests to try to quell the Draft Riots, which were perpetrated largely by Irish Catholics.

the Sachem of the Cayugas, and Pierce, the Chief of the Seneca Indians, came in. They are part of a delegation from the Iroquois (or Six Nations) who are going to Washington. I invited them to sit down and dine with us, which they frankly consented to do. Dr. Wilson told us many interesting things. Most of the Indians still adhere to the old-fashioned religion, as he called it. He quoted Red Jacket's answer to the missionaries when asked to allow them to teach his people: "Go among the white first," he said, "and when we see that you keep them from cheating Indians, we let you come and teach us."

. . . . Dr. Wilson is a man seven feet high, but proportionally broad; therefore his height does not at first strike you. He seemed to be a very cultivated man. He is a full-blooded Indian and speaks, the Judge says, admirably well in public. His tribe once owned from the St. Lawrence to the Ohio, Kentucky and Virginia; now they have a small reservation in Chautauqua County.

It was a very interesting and a very touching sight to see the first colored regiment from this city march down the street for the front. They were a fine body of men and had a look of satisfaction in their faces, as though they felt they had gained a right to be more respected. Many old, respectable darkies stood at the street corners, men and women with tears in their eyes as if they saw the redemption of their race afar off but still the beginning of a better state of affairs for them. Though I am very little Negrophilish and would always prefer the commonest white that lives to a Negro, still I could not but feel moved.

The financial resources of the Sanitary Commission in New York were rapidly diminishing during the active military year of 1863, until by December they dipped below $50,000. Immediate replenishment of funds was vital to the war effort, and the answer determined upon was a grand patriotic fair. The idea had actually been borrowed from Chicago, which raised nearly $75,000 for the cause with an October fair, topped in December by a Cincinnati fair which raised over $200,000.

Two executive committees, one of men and one of women, were established early in 1864, and an effort was made to involve as many industries, businesses, professions, and organizations as possible. A building was constructed on Fourteenth Street to contain numerous exposition booths, and it even contained an art gallery, a restaurant, and a bookstore. Another was built on Union Square for children's things and international products. A block away, provision was made for an animal show, and the animals—all domestic animals—were for sale.

Everything on sale had been contributed by merchants, manufacturers, patriotic citizens, and even friends abroad, and New Yorkers had never before witnessed such a rich or varied display of items. One could find ponies, oil paintings, autographed books, original manuscripts, and curios from all over the world, in addition to all the ordinary things one normally found in the stores of New York. The grand opening was held on April 4, 1864, with speeches, bands playing, and all the fanfare that accompanies so gala an affair.

One of the innumerable features of the Metropolitan Fair was the "Knickerbocker Kitchen," which Mrs. Daly discusses. Here, prominent New York ladies were dressed up in colonial costume and sold everything from foodstuffs to trinkets. Another special attraction was an Indian wigwam erected by the artist Albert Bierstadt, and here Indian products were sold while the public was entertained by Indian war dances.

The New York Metropolitan Fair continued for most of the month of April, and over a million dollars was raised for the Union cause, a sum that dwarfed the proceeds from any of the other fairs held in the North.

March 17, 1864

I went today to the Knickerbocker Kitchen Committee for the benefit of the Sanitary Fair. Mrs. Judge Roosevelt is chairman. She wants us to wear the old Dutch costume. Hers is already being made, she said. It is too far from the Fair, being in Union Square, and too few, I thought, were interested. Having a sore throat and being afraid of too much work and exposure, I backed out and promised to get Mother to send all that she could. I do not think I have any vocation for public life. I am too knickerbocker to be sufficiently democratic and did not particularly fancy the idea of being seated in cap, short gown, and petticoats, pouring out tea for all the rabble that (in such a great city) would come to give their mite to the Sanitary Commission. They would be gratifying their curiosity, and I would be part of the show. My name, too, being so public a one, would be sure of being in the papers.

March 18, 1864

All day I have been receiving company. I had an amusing talk about the degeneracy of modern manners with old Mrs. Webster and Mrs. LeRoy. Mrs. Webster is shocked at the song figure introduced by Pierre Marié into the German cotillion. It consists of a gentleman driving round with reins and whip, married ladies supping with gentlemen at Delmonico's without their husbands, and the rompishness of the younger ladies. Mrs. Ronaldi, who sometimes has good manners, sometimes not, and who receives seated on a kind of dais two steps high, said to me: "What do you think of that, Mrs. Daly?"

"I should never take those steps," said I.

"Nor I," replied the old lady. Then the ladies who were so undignified and so fond of novelty as to join with her (with Mrs. General Wadsworth, who went to her fancy ball, allowed her daughters to go in the midst of Lent—although a churchwoman—and who gave a leap year party) asked the gentlemen to dance and waited upon them. Some of the ladies were quite mortified that they had so little attention paid them. Mr. Hutton, a young married man not on good terms with his wife, carried seven bouquets, at which those good old-fashioned ladies were most naturally shocked.

There is a clique of fast young married women in New York who are very much loosening the reins of good and decorous manners. In one family, there has been a great scandal—that of Mr. Austin Stevens, one of the most respectable men of the city. His daughter, Mrs. Peter Strong, has behaved most shamelessly with her brother-in-law, and her outraged husband is seeking a divorce.[6] Society seems to have gone mad, giving itself up to every kind of extravagance and dissipation.

This Fair for the Sanitary Commission is a good excuse to many, not but that it will do much good and that many of those who are very busy in it would do nothing otherwise. I have taken no active part in it, though I have expended a good deal of money upon it (although it is not yet open) in tickets for concerts, raffles, etc. Mrs. Stout came to me from Mr. Luckerman and Mr. Rutherford to ask me to personate Katrina Van Tassel.[7] I would wear the costume of Huntington's picture and sell Washington Irving's books at the Fair. There was to be a façade of the house in New

---

[6] In May of 1853, Peter R. Strong married Mary E. Stevens, daughter of the prominent banker John Austin Stevens. They were happily married and had three children when Peter Strong's brother, Edward, came to live with them after his wife died. An illicit relationship ensued between Edward Strong and his sister-in-law, and in January of 1862 Mary confessed the two-year-long relationship to her husband. They separated immediately, but there was no talk of divorce until the wife demanded exclusive custody of one of the three children, Alice. Mary Strong disappeared with the child when Peter would not yield to her wishes, though he was able to communicate with his wife through the Stevens family. Peter sued for divorce, and the trial began on November 25, 1865. Mrs. Strong never appeared in the courtroom, but was represented by her father and a brother, John A. Stevens, Jr., as well as by the family attorneys. On December 31, the trial ended in a hung jury because it was felt that Peter Strong had not cleared himself of the counter-charge of adultery.

[7] The village beauty in Washington Irving's *Legend of Sleepy Hollow.*

Jersey where *Salmagundi* was written, and in that I was to sit to complete the picture. Mrs. Stout said that I looked like an old Flemish picture, and that no one else would do. As Katrina Van Tassel is represented as a blooming girl of 18, and I am more than double that age, I think it the part of modesty and patriotism to decline. My refusal will spare me just and critical remarks and a great deal of trouble.

Sunday, March 20, 1864

Went today to St. John's and stayed with Mother to communion. Mr. Dix,[8] the rector, preached. Coming in, I saw Harriet on the bench on the aisle, so I made her come with me. The church was very full, since Mr. Dix has a great number of admirers who follow him—"a company of faithful women." He is like Mr. Weston some years ago, when I in disgust left off the profession of godliness (which is, in unmarried women, so often a hunt for a hubsand when the object of admiration is a bachelor). I once told my sister Maggie that she might better worship the images of saints (as she insisted the Catholics did) than a mortal man like Mr. Weston. I told her that it would not be more idolatrous but much more convenient. When we were coming out of church feeling subdued from the solemn service, old Mrs. Henry came up to me. "What a delightful morning we have had," said she. I thought she spoke of the weather and answered indifferently. She looked disappointed and it occurred to me that she might be one of the faithful women.

"Are you," said I, "one of Mr. Dix's great admirers?"

"Oh, yes," said she fervently. "He only needs age to make him lovely."

I looked at Dix's face this morning. It is one of a good

---

[8] The Reverend Morgan Dix, son of General John A. Dix, was elected to the rectorship of Protestant Episcopal Trinity Church, Broadway at Rector Street, in November 1862 upon the death of the Reverend William Berrian.

deal of strength, though somewhat of a mask—as if he kept much control upon a disposition somewhat impressionable. His general subject is "peace." I thought he had gained some since I last heard him. Perhaps he likes his present position, one of responsibility and activity. The Dixes are a remarkable family. I would like General Dix to be our next President. He is wise, just and brave. The other son [Charles Temple Dix] is the General's aide-de-camp, and a very fine artist. The daughters are both clever, the mother is a very clever, agreeable woman, slightly disposed to satire (which makes her all the more fascinating to me). I often wish that I had had a clever mother.

When I came home, I found Mr. Ayres and Judge Hilton had been here. Judge Hilton has just come from Albany. He told the Judge that the legislature was going to appoint the First Judge of the Common Pleas to choose commissioners to try the heads of the city departments for frauds they are charged with.

"Why that court?" said the Judge.

"Because," said Hilton, "all agree that Judge Daly, the head of that court, is the only man to whom such power can be trusted."

It is a great compliment, but it will make many enemies.

March 22, 1864

Last evening the Judge presided at a meeting for the protection of workingwomen.[9] I am sorry I did not go, but I was afraid of colds and drafts. James T. was to have been there, but he was detained in Washington. All the burden fell upon the Judge, who, however, got through it exceed-

---

[9] The Workingwomen's Protective Union was founded in 1863 for the betterment of working conditions and for the protection of the rights of workingwomen. Judge Daly was a leading light in the organization almost from its inception, and remained chairman of the board of directors of the group for thirty years.

ingly well according to Mr. [George Washington] Matsell (who came in with him) and the papers. Matsell was for 15 years chief of police. He is a broad-shouldered, great-hearted, stout man of fifty-five years. He told us several touching and some terrible cases in his experience of the depth to which women could fall. The Judge and he had known each other in early life; they had both been sailors. It is consoling to see what large charity and trust in human nature those men who have had much experience in life attain to. We children of fortune lose much of what is noble and true by being so shielded. The working classes are the best classes among us in this country. They are the most appreciative, the most intelligent, patriotic, and disinterested. What are called our better class is only the richer and better clothed.

March 30, 1864

Sunday last was Easter. I went to St. Xavier's Church[10] with the Judge. The music was delicious. Mr. Townsend Harris went with us. We have decided to keep our pew, even at eighty dollars. Everything is increased thirty percent because of our depreciated currency. Beef is selling for thirty cents per pound, butter at fifty-five cents, coffee at sixty-five cents, and tea at one dollar and a dollar and twenty-five cents.

Phil unexpectedly dropped in upon us just before dinner, having just arrived with General Parke from Knoxville. The Judge asked him to visit us on Tuesday to meet Mr. Harris and dine on our last dish of sauerkraut. He came yesterday and to our great satisfaction brought with him General Parke. Anna Raasloff was here, so we had an impromptu dinner party. Baron Osten-Sacken came just as dessert was served, and we opened a bottle of doppel-kümmel, of which he had sent us four bottles as a present.

Mr. Sanders unfortunately came in likewise and brought

---

[10] St. Francis Xavier Roman Catholic Church, 36 West 16th Street.

himself and Libby Prison, from which he has just been released on parole. He is much too much forward, thus making himself offensive, particularly before his superior officer, Major General Parke. Sanders is in the commissary department and only a lieutenant colonel. He says nothing deteriorates a man more than prison life, that everything is disregarded—cleanliness and decency. He says they treat our prisoners dreadfully and remarked that they had no right to attempt things on so grand   scale as that of a nation without an adequate means to support it. Since the rebels had neither accommodations nor food for so many guests (their prisoners), they should not have attempted to entertain so many.

I never met General Parke before. I think that he has a face in which there is great coolness, capacity, and judgment. It is one which at once inspires confidence, and he has that usual accompaniment of merit and modesty, which I suggested to Sanders, hoping he might apply the reverse to himself.

Rosalie is very anxious to officiate in the Knickerbocker Kitchen at the Sanitary Fair. All the city will be crazy for the next week, but it tends to keep up a spirit of patriotism. It is to open on Monday next.

April 3, 1864

I received yesterday a letter from now Lieutenant Colonel Badeau, Military Secretary to Lieutenant General Grant. I am glad to hear of his promotion. I think it very pleasant of him to write to me under these, brilliant circumstances. I am so accustomed to be overlooked by those whom I have perhaps lent a hand so soon as I can be of no further use, that I am always agreeably surprised when it is not the case. Badeau, however, is genuine and appreciative and very kindly. Indeed, I always liked him very much despite his natural disadvantages of person and manner. I was agreeably surprised to find him remembering his former friends in prosperity when they were no longer useful. I answered his letter at once in consequence.

Baron Gerolt is staying here. We had a long, serious conversation over the breakfast table about the country. He predicts a terrible financial crisis and anarchy so soon as the war ceases, and he is very far-sighted. He says the members of Congress are a disgrace to the nation, they are so ignorant and corrupt. Mr. Chase is so little a minister of finance that he allows himself to be governed by the gold-brokers of New York. Instead of regulating the gold market, he makes a pact with them.

Tomorrow the Fair is to be opened by Bishop [Horatio] Potter, with prayer and a grand flourish of trumpets. It is the apotheosis of fashionable and cheap patriotism on the part of many, particularly the lady portion (those who have given excepted). My Uncle Lydig, for instance, has given nothing —not even a hundred dollars—to the war, but his name is flourishing in all the papers.

April 5, 1864

Baron Gerolt, who is staying with us, insisted upon presenting us with tickets for the grand opening last evening, so we went. I was agreeably disappointed. The picture gallery is very beautiful. In it are Bierstadt's beautiful picture, "The Rocky Mountains," Church's "Heart of the Andes," Leutze's "Venice Triumphant," "Washington Crossing the Delaware," and many other specimens of these three great artists. There are also exhibited paintings by Kensett, Laing, Gifford, Ginoux and others. The gallery is beautifully proportioned, the pictures well hung and well lighted. The gallery was full of agreeable people, including General Burnside, General and Mrs. Frémont, Bristed, Leutze, Bierstadt, Miss Gray of Baltimore and a great many fashionables.

Then we went into the Indian Department and saw the

Indians dance. The Indians danced several characteristic dances to their own curious chant and their own musical instruments. Three of their instruments were a kind of drum with bells, a species of jew's-harp, and a fife. I thought their dance was graceful and dramatic, especially the scout dance, and the dance of the women, which I thought graceful, dignified, modest and touching. The "Feather Dance" reminded me very much of the country dance. Dancing is evidently a natural impulse of man. These Indians are of the Iroquois or, as we know them better, the Six Nations. The flower department was very beautiful. I have not half seen all yet and shall get a season ticket and go as often as I feel inclined.

April 7, 1864

I went to the Fair yesterday and visited the Knickerbocker Kitchen. I saw Mrs. Roosevelt in her dress. It was quite effective, but made her look like an old woman. There are about six ladies in costume. One man last night said to Mrs. Roosevelt, "If you will come and wait upon me, I will give you two shillings extra."

"I will," said Mrs. Roosevelt, and she did and took the two shillings. Had I been there, I suppose I might likewise have been asked the same, and they would have gone and boasted that they had been served by Mrs. Judge Daly, and my portrait would have been in every newspaper. I saw them sketching the ladies for Frank Leslie's paper. The Kitchen is very fine with its deep iron fireplace, high mantel shelf, and old colored people and furniture. I went again to the Fair today, but could not get in because the crowd was so dense. The Fair was crowded again last evening when I went up with the Judge, Florence, Baron Gerolt, and Temple Prime. Mr. Prime escorted me everywhere and laughed at the devotion of the Judge and myself. I like Temple Prime, but I would rather have had the Judge's arm.

Mother was very amiable and kindly today. We went together to the Fair and then I went home with her. Then we went together to see Mrs. Burnside, whom we found at home and whom I thanked for her prompt answer to Mrs. General Viele on Monday night. Mrs. Burnside congratulated us upon Phil's return and upon his promotion, for which I said, "He is greatly indebted to the General." Mrs. Viele, with a toss of her head, said, "The General, I hear, is very good to those under him and gets them all kinds of good appointments." Of course, I could not have said anything, but Mrs. Burnside very promptly answered, "When they deserve them."

To this I emphatically said, "Thank you, Mrs. Burnside."

She said this morning that Mrs. Viele was rather extraordinary, and I added, "Somewhat peppery." She said her husband had retired from the service because he could make more money than in the office. I told her of what Tiffany showed us yesterday, a magnificent set of silver presented by some brokers to a Mr. Brandhead, a broker who had made their fortunes. The handles were bulls' heads, richly carved. On the top of the tureen was a bear.

Tiffany said, "What do you think of the design, Mrs. Daly?"

"You have forgotten something, I think, have you not?" I answered. "You have forgotten to put a gold crown on the bulls' heads as a sign of royalty, as money is the only sovereign among us." It was the apotheosis of speculation.

Everybody asks of us to give or to buy at the Fair. I answer that, as the Judge gives forty percent to the government and the soldiers by the depreciation of paper, we can afford to do no more.

The Judge is dining out, and in the parlor Baron Gerolt is shut up with Mr. Boileau and a broker who deals in mining stocks. Hackett, the actor, came in and paid me a visit of half an hour. He wanted to see the Judge about a Shakespearean celebration on the twenty-third, which will be the third centennial of Shakespeare's birthday. This Fair swallows all other interests. I met Miss Gray of Baltimore, Mrs. [Anthony] Kennedy's sister, at the Fair. She told me that so early as the summer (we were at the White Sulphur Springs two years before Lincoln's election) this was fermenting, that they had called a congress there to which Mr. Kennedy had been invited. She said that I had been *denounced* as having spoken against slavery, as having said it was injurious to the whites. She said that she told them that they might as well denounce her, then, as she thought so too. I do not remember to have said it, as I was on my guard.

I called this morning to see Mrs. McClellan.

April 17, 1864

The Fair is still crowded, and will be held still another week. Yesterday I went to Niblo's [Theatre] to see "Cinderella" performed by children. It was admirably well done. [Jasper F.] Cropsey the artist's daughter took the part of Cinderella and acted it with all the aplomb of a grown person and with great naturalness. The court ball was beautiful. I think there must have been some 200 children on the stage in fancy dress and they danced the cotillion as well as any *corps de ballet*. Young Frémont was the prince. The house was crowded so that there were not even places to stand. It was amusing to hear the clapping of the many little hands, like a sort of treble clap, at whatever pleased them particularly. The play will net some $2,500 for the Sanitary. Booth gave a performance for it last night.

Next Saturday is the tercentennial anniversary of Shakespeare's birthday, but I fear it will not be particularly honored. This Fair has swallowed all other interests. The different theaters will give Shakespearean entertainment, the proceeds of which go towards making a fund for a monument to be erected to the poet's memory in the Central Park. Mr. Hackett has been here several evenings to confer with the Judge about the matter. He will, I suppose, subscribe liberally.

I do not know what is to become of us; everything is so expensive, and the calls upon the Judge are unremitting. This last fortnight contributions have amounted to one hundred dollars. If this is to continue, we shall have to ask charity ourselves. I have a great mind to try to get a movement among the ladies, the old aristocracy of the country, to give up buying any imported goods whilst this war lasts.[11] They should especially give up buying expensive silks, laces, shawls, wines, etc., to stop the wild extravagance which seems the fashion by making it vulgar. All foreigners look at us with astonishment (I should think too with disgust) to see how little we as a people seem to feel the dreadful state of the country. Its finances are crazy and its government is crazy. When I hear sensible men say that it will be better to have Lincoln again than change, it gives me indeed a feeling of despair. What? Not one great man, not one honest-minded gentleman left among us? It seems to me we have no moral conscientiousness. The emigrants who come over here without our education soon lose their virtue and adopt our vices. This on top of their ignorance makes them worse than ourselves. The Irish particularly have a reverence for learning; they send their children to school and then trust them because they have learned to govern both them and themselves.

Phil returned to the army yesterday. He goes to Annapolis, thence, I fear, to the South. But he has been until now preserved and we can trust the same Providence for the future. I met with an old proverb a few days since: "Be of good cheer;

---

[11] On May 16, 1864, the Women's Patriotic Association for Diminishing the Use of Imported Luxuries was formed at 694 Broadway, New York City. President of the Board of Managers was Mrs. Charles P. Daly; Mrs. Ogden Hoffman was elected treasurer, and Miss Anne S. Edwards secretary. Members of the "Committee for the City" included Mrs. Marshall O. Roberts, Mrs. Francis Lieber, Mrs. Laura W. Gibbs, Mrs. Augustus F. Smith, Mrs. Benjamin Nathan, and Mrs. William Greenough.

God is where He was." This is a most needful reflection for us now.

April 21, 1864

The Fair is nearly over. I sent my three women to it today, giving them money, and have to open the door myself.

On Tuesday last, poor grandmother Suydam was buried at the age of eighty-six. She died full of years and will be lamented by all of us. She was a gentle, harmless nature with a good deal of character but little enthusiasm. She died with great composure and was in perfect possession of her faculties to the last. The family will now scatter. . . . I was very sorry not to have been able to go to the funeral, but I took cold and have been two days confined to the house by the doctor's orders.

The Sunday *Times* was sent to the Judge. It contains a tribute to him; I wonder who has written it?

Judge Daly, considered a leading Shakespearean scholar in New York in his day, proposed that the city pay tribute to the poet on his tricentennial by erecting a statue in Central Park. His friends and fellow-devotees James H. Hackett, Grant White, and actor Edwin Booth agreed, and funds were solicited for the purpose.

On April 23, 1864, the cornerstone for the monument was laid by Hackett; Judge Daly delivered the dedicatory address. The New York Herald *offered the gloomy prediction that "all festivals tend more or less to the absurd and the extravagant, and . . . the Shakespeare Tercentenary will be no exception to this rule on either side of the Atlantic," but* The New York Times *spoke the next morning of the "cordial, though only moderately demonstrative tribute," and mentioned that Judge Daly's address "could not well be improved upon in its structure, its tone, or its admirable brevity."*

April 23, 1864

I spent the day delightfully. I went to Central Park to see the cornerstone of the monument to be erected to the memory of Shakespeare laid, this being the three-hundredth anniversary of his birthday. The Judge, being chosen chairman, was obliged to speak. He spoke very well in well-chosen and appropriate language. Hackett laid the cornerstone and Mendelssohn's "Wedding March" from the "Midsummer Night's Dream" was beautifully played by [Allen] Dodworth's band. [William] Wheatley [the actor] then spoke. He and Hackett were here last evening and I heard the matter of today rehearsed. Wheatley is full of enthusiasm, though very theatrical. As for dear old Hackett, I could not but feel the greatest respect for him for the perseverance he has shown in this matter. A few nights since he came in here looking so wearied that I was afraid he would break down, and I plied him with all kinds of restoratives. The ceremony was very impressive and poetical. The park looked so beautiful, the sun shone so brightly, and the music was so inspiring. . . .

After the ceremonies were over, Mrs. Frémont, who came over to see me (she is always present wherever there is any artistic or literary gratification to be found), and I went to see the cornerstone. How I wished I had brought a wreath of fresh spring flowers to place upon it, for are not Shakespeare's works as immortal as those of nature, since they revive and live again with every new generation of men? Bierstadt was likewise there. How much I like him. How modest and unpresuming, how good a friend, how he loves and admires the Judge! Mrs. Frémont insisted on bringing me home and we had a pleasant drive together. . . . After we returned, we went to the Shakespearean matinee given at the Opera House for the monument. Booth played Romeo for the same purpose, and Hackett played Falstaff at Niblo's for the same. After the matinee, we went to the sculptor's, [Daniel] Draddy, who is taking a bust of the Judge. It is a great likeness. Not finding Mr. Draddy at home, we wandered down to the river and sat for some time on some lumber on a wharf which stretched far out into the river. We inhaled the fresh breeze from the bay and looked up into the bright haze into which the steamboats and sailing vessels which passed us disappeared. Then we went home to dinner.

The Judge has just gone out to open the ballots for the sword at the Fair which is to be given, according to the majority of the ballots, to either Grant or McClellan. It seems they wanted someone whom everyone would be sure would be just (so one of the committee told us). *Die New Yorker Sonntags-Zeitung* has a very laudatory notice of today's ceremonial. It speaks of the Judge as "Ein durch gründliche literarische Bildung und hohes Interesse für Kunst und Wissenschaft rühmlichst bekannter Mann, derselbe welcher beim Schillerjahrlaum [*sic:* -jubiläum?] eine der englischen Festreden hielt." Then follows the address in German.

I learned today of the death of Mrs. Dudley Field. This Fair has probably killed her, as it is said it did poor Mrs. Kirkland.[12] I talked with Mrs. Kirkland only a few hours before her death and thought how well she was looking, what a delightful person she was, and how delightful age was in her person. They were both members of the executive committee of the Fair and very active and enthusiastic about it. I liked Mrs. Field too. She was an amiable, genial, intelligent old lady.

---

[12] According to the newspapers, Mrs. David Dudley Field and Mrs. Caroline Kirkland, both members of the executive committee of the Metropolitan Fair, sacrificed their lives to the cause through overwork. Mrs. Kirkland, widow of Professor William Kirkland of Hamilton College, was stricken at the Fair on a particularly crowded evening. Mrs. Field, wife of the distinguished lawyer and jurist, took ill at the Fair and died about ten days later. Field married three times; this wife was the former Miss Harriet Davidson.

On March 9, 1864, Grant had been promoted to the rank of lieutenant general, the highest military rank then existing in the United States Army and one held previously only by Winfield Scott, and was given command over all the Union Armies. He determined that the backbone of the Confederate resistance was Lee's Army of Virginia, and that he must engage it.

Grant, at the head of the Army of the Potomac's more than 100,000 men, prepared at Culpeper for his advance southward. The plan called for support from General Butler, whose 36,000-strong Army of the James was to make its approach along the south bank of the James River and cut off Lee's retreat to the South. General Franz Sigel was to come up the Shenandoah Valley and take Lynchburg.

Lee had a total of 60,000 troops, plus a supporting army under the command of General Beauregard with 30,000 men in the Richmond-Petersburg area. But the Confederates had the enormous advantage of choosing their site for battle, and they knew well the tangled jungles between the Rapidan River and North Anna. Grant and Meade crossed the Rapidan on May 4 and entered the Wilderness, where Lee's men lay in wait.

In the three-day Battle of the Wilderness which followed, the victory was first with one side and then with the other. The outcome was actually indecisive, but unquestionably Lee outmaneuvered Grant and frustrated his aim of a knockout blow. Lee was surprised that Grant did not fall back as Mc-Clellan, Pope, Burnside, and Hooker had done before him, for Grant marched his troops to Spotsylvania Courthouse—an announcement that he was merely changing his battle station. This maneuver required that Lee's tired troops immediately fight another defensive battle where such natural protection as they had in the Wilderness would not be found.

Although Grant lost 17,000 men to Lee's 10,000 in the Battle of the Wilderness, Grant could afford his losses and Lee could not. The battle of attrition had begun, and Lee was confronted with a determined fighter who didn't care what happened to himself so long as he conquered his opponent.

May 8, 1864

Once more news has arrived from the Army of the Potomac, and it looks as though we should be victorious. Butler is at City Point within 30 miles of Richmond on the James River, and Grant is driving Lee back from the Rapidan, which has been successfully crossed. Phil is with Burnside, who was, I see, in yesterday's battle. May God preserve him! I had another letter from Badeau and it was full of confidence. He seemed pleased with my answer.

Alice and Anna Young are staying with me. They are cultivated, ladylike girls and in every way congenial. Mr. Harris and Temple Prime paid us a visit on Tuesday last. . . . General and Mrs. Meagher were here last evening. Indeed we have not been alone this week. The Raasloffs have been here two or three times, so I hope the girls have been amused.

Since Mrs. Daly's brother Phil had been with the army of N. P. Banks, one-time Speaker of the House and Governor of Massachusetts, it is strange that she did not refer to the military developments which proved disastrous to Banks and resulted in his return to Massachusetts in disgrace.

Early in April 1864, Banks was ordered to proceed with the Red River expedition, aimed at crossing northern Louisiana and capturing Shreveport, and from there launching an invasion of Texas. At best the scheme was hazardous, since it meant cutting deeply into Confederate territory where the only certainty was stiff resistance. Seward's notion was that an immediate restoration of authority in Texas would give pause to the large French army which had landed in Mexico.

With 30,000 men and a fleet of gunboats under Admiral Porter, Banks approached Shreveport, but the Confederates attacked him before he arrived there, and the battles of Sabine Crossroads and Pleasant Hill were fought on April 8 and 9. In the first, Banks was badly defeated, and in the second he retreated after a fierce engagement because his supply lines had broken down. When they returned to Porter's gunboats, they were very nearly trapped by the sudden drop in the water level of the Red River, and it became necessary for dams to be built before they could float away.

Upon hearing of the defeat, Grant angrily recalled Banks and ordered ten thousand of his troops eastward. Alexandria, Louisiana, had to be given up as a result, and it was evacuated on May 13. This was the end of Banks' military career; he was replaced by General Edward R. S. Canby.

Meanwhile, on the eastern front, the battle of Spotsylvania followed on the heels of the Battle of the Wilderness. Grant had moved his forces to Lee's left flank, and Lee was compelled to remove his men from the Wilderness and take up a new defensive position. Lee's men entrenched themselves for the five bloody days which followed, May 8 through the 12th. Again Grant threw his troops against the well-protected Confederates, and again Union losses far outnumbered Lee's. It was on this occasion that Grant made his famous statement in a message to Halleck: "I propose to fight it out along this line if it takes all summer."

At last Grant withdrew and took time out to reassemble his forces, now minus another 12,000 men. Lee took up a new defensive position at Cold Harbor to await the next assault, but his much smaller casualty list represented a far greater loss than the Union's.

May 18, 1864

Eight days of fighting in Virginia have been without any definite result, except that of driving Lee nearer Richmond. Most of the lines of railroad are cut, however, and the old chieftain will find it difficult to get away. Grant seems confident of final success, but says he may have to fight all summer. Phil is in the midst of it all, and as yet unhurt. He says that our prospects are far from brilliant. Gold is at 180. There is a battle going on today, and both armies have been reinforced. 40,000 are wounded, killed, and missing on our side. Among the killed are Generals Wadsworth and [Alexander] Hays. The Wadsworths have been the guests of the gay and the most wildly extravagant. I have wondered at the heartlessness it showed when the land was thus in mourning under God's chastisement. On Tuesday last there was a women's meeting at Cooper's Institute to take some measures to put down this extravagance in dress and entertainment which has been the rule for the last two years. The first year of the war our imports were less than our exports by fifteen million dollars from our great harvests, the scarcity of grain in Europe, and the general economy of our people. Last year, our imports exceeded our exports 50 million dollars, and this year the amount will be greater still.

On Sunday last, to amuse the girls, I asked half a dozen people here, the Raasloffs, Temple Prime and his sister, Mr. McDonough, Baron Osten-Sacken, and Bierstadt, and we had a very pleasant evening. Chocolate, a glass of sherry, and a sandwich was the only entertainment. Last evening Mr. Harris came in and told us some incidents of his eastern life. . . .

Afterwards Mrs. Gibbs came in and talked country. She has been made president of this woman's movement. She agreed with me that the elderly men called in to give advice have prosed fearfully. I left when I heard Dr. Vinton in full flow. They patted us on the back and said they were sure we would be good little dears and give up our laces, French bonnets, and sugar plums, if we knew how well the gentlemen would think of us. He said that they would think us just as pretty in homespun. Mr. Charles King then addressed us as females, a word suggesting, as Mrs. Delafield said, a cat with kittens.

Maggie is expected in the steamer on Saturday. Heaven grant me patience!

Cold Harbor was located between Richmond and Hanover Town, close to the Chickahominy River, and there General

Grant foolishly tried to break the well-entrenched Confederate line by a frontal assault. On June 3 alone, the last of the three days of battle, Grant lost 12,000 men, bringing Union losses in the single month of May 12 to June 12 to 60,000 men, a number equal to Lee's entire Army of Northern Virginia. Confederate casualties during the same period amounted to less than half that number.

Lee's tactics from this point forward in the war were purely defensive and designed to conserve his diminished and irreplaceable force. Two-to-one or even better odds were not good enough, for the Union reserves seemed endless. It was only a matter of time, of delaying the inevitable day of surrender.

The failure to break Lee's army at Cold Harbor did result in a new strategy on Grant's part, however. He decided to move his army to Petersburg, twenty miles below Richmond, and attack that Confederate capital from the rear. He transported his troops south of the James River, and engaged the enemy in the four-day battle of Petersburg, June 15 through the 18th, 1864. Grant lost another 8,000 men in a futile attempt to take the city, and he dug in for a nine-month siege. On July 30, the famous Petersburg mine was exploded in a costly effort to break into the city.

Meantime, the attention of the North was shifted to General Sherman, who was advancing into Georgia from the West, driving Confederate General Johnston's small but valiant army before him. On June 8, the three-weeks' battle for Kenesaw Mountain began, but the action was only a delaying one on the part of the Confederates, and Sherman's advance upon Atlanta pressed forward.

June 8, 1864

I have so much to do and think of that I forget my diary, which, in such momentous times, is a *crime* against myself. Should I live to be an old lady, I shall deeply regret this.

Grant's success has been certain but slow; the enemy has been fighting every inch of the way. I had a letter from Badeau from the front, written in pencil, breathing the utmost confidence in the army, its leader, and the final success which, as he speaks from accurate knowledge, cannot but give us the greatest confidence. Both armies fight with the greatest bravery. Frank Barlow has again greatly distinguished himself, and Grant has recommended him to a major generalship. We have lost some of our best generals—Wadsworth, Sedgwick,[13] [James Clay] Rice, and thousands of heroes whose names are known but to their sorrowing families. Our nationality will be born anew in blood and tears, but we trust it will rise purified and ennobled. On Saturday last, a meeting was called in Union Square in which the Judge took a prominent part to thank and encourage our soldiers and General-in-Chief. It was crowded and enthusiastic. The Judge wrote the resolutions and read them, making very judicious opening remarks, full of point and very practical, counseling moderation and good statesmanship.

I have been very busy lately in the Women's Patriotic League [Association] for Diminishing the Use of Imported Luxuries. I think it will succeed, although some of the ladies wish to push it forward much too fast. The manufacturers say they have not enough hands to fill the orders they already have, so we cannot now force people to buy what is not to be had, but must go to work gradually and systematically. I shall have some trouble to subdue the zeal of Miss Mary Hamilton and Miss Schuyler.[14] I plainly see they have made me president but wish to rule themselves. I shall have to give

---

13 Union Major General John Sedgwick (1813–1864) distinguished himself in the Peninsula Campaign and at Antietam, where he was severely wounded. He fought valiantly at Chancellorsville and Gettysburg, and was killed by a Confederate sharpshooter at Spotsylvania.

14 Louisa Lee Schuyler (1837–1926) was a prominent social worker active in the Sanitary Commission and various New York charities and philanthropies.

my opinion officially, and I am afraid of Miss Mary. I must try and write out my views upon the subject.

Yesterday the Judge came home after being treated by some Irish gentlemen fresh from home who, it seems, were enthusiastic about him, telling him that no one in Ireland is so popular as himself. The poor Judge was almost abashed by their praises and compliments.

Maggie is at home. We are polite to each other and no more. She is sweet upon the Judge.

August 10, 1864

I have been on the wing for West Farms. We had a delightful month of July divided between Greenfield and Mr. Davis and Peach Lake. The Judge would like to buy a few acres at Peach Lake, but I fear it may not be as healthy as we would wish. There is so much vegetation beneath the water, and the shore in many places is marshy. Today the Judge was asked to be one of the four presidents of the McClellan meeting, but not being well enough, was obliged to decline. We met Mr. and Mrs. William T. Lee at Peach Lake, where we enjoyed ourselves very much. . . .

At South-East, about six miles from our hotel, Chancellor Kent[15] was born, and as the Judge proposes to write his biography, we went to look at his birthplace. Mrs. Lee took us to Miltown, but we were unsuccessful in finding it. . . .

September 11, 1864

Returned from West Farms. We are home once more for the winter, and I have been very busy the last week in housecleaning. My poor little cook died in the house of typhus

---

[15] James Kent (1763–1847), a brilliant jurist, was chancellor of the New York Supreme Court, Master in Chancery, and from 1814 chief justice of the New York Court of Chancery. Kent's *Commentaries* are still highly regarded by legal scholars.

fever, and I have had to clean it twice over, whitewashing nearly the whole house. This is a very expensive and a very troublesome process. I sent Margaret off for a holiday to spend her month's wages amusing herself.

I was glad to be with Maggie for a while. We got on very pleasantly, even affectionately, together. She confessed to having acted selfishly, saying I was the only disinterested member of the family. I begged her not to think me so any longer (or to act upon it), for I meant to insist upon having every atom to which I was hereafter entitled, whether of attention or of more material goods. Her little boy is a fine little fellow to whom one becomes easily attached. The little girl did not please me as much.[16] The country about West Farms is not healthy this summer, and I came home with something like chills and fever. The Judge put on his frankincense and I believe it protected him from becoming ill.

On June 7, 1864, the Republican National Union Convention met in Baltimore, and on June 8, Lincoln was renominated on the first ballot, unanimously, after Missouri switched its twenty-two ballots from Grant. War Democrat Andrew Johnson of Tennessee, Lincoln's choice for Vice President, was also nominated on the first ballot. The convention platform called for a continuation of the war to an uncompromising end and for the complete abolition of slavery.

On August 29, 1864, the Democratic National Convention met in Chicago and nominated General George McClellan for President and George H. Pendleton of Ohio for Vice President. Copperheads were in control of the convention, however, and the platform contained a plank inserted by Clement L. Vallandigham which called for an immediate cessation of hostilities and a negotiated peace. In his letter of acceptance, McClellan immediately repudiated this peace plank, stating, "The Union must be preserved at all hazards."

---

[16] Later Mrs. Emy Otto Hoyt, Mrs. Daly's favorite and the person to whom she entrusted her diary.

In New York State, it was expected that Copperhead Governor Horatio Seymour would step down, but when he was renominated by acclaim he allowed himself to be drafted. Thus began immediately a rift within the Democratic party itself, for many of the delegates later proclaimed that they meant the initial vote to be a compliment only, and that they wouldn't have voted for Seymour had they not been assured that he would decline on the basis of poor health and business reasons.

Opposing the weak wartime candidate Seymour was Reuben E. Fenton of Chautauqua County in western New York. Fenton was a businessman with a good record and a flair for politics, and he was generally conceded to be a strong candidate.

The great event of this last week is the nomination of General McClellan to the Chicago platform and the General's letter. The Judge was president of the ratification meeting. It is difficult to determine who will be more successful, Lincoln or McClellan. In his speech at the meeting, the Judge interpreted the platform (as McClellan since has done in his letter of acceptance). Being deeply interested, the Judge wrote to the General, expressing his desire for an interview. Charles said that he thought he might be able to give the General some important information. McClellan answered the letter, appointing an interview very privately at his own house. The General read his letter to Charles some four or five days before it was published, no one but one other person having seen it or knowing McClellan to be in town. McClellan's letter made a great commotion, frightening the Republicans, dissatisfying the peace men, but contenting the moderate people.

September 19, 1864

I went on Saturday evening, the 17th, to look at the Democratic ratification meeting in Union Square. As Mrs. Young's room overlooks it, I was very glad I went. I never saw so dense a crowd. There were ten stands set up, and each one was so crowded that the war clubs, which were numerous and carrying lanterns, could scarcely make their way around the Square. The park, too, was crowded, and the gates had to be opened. The fireworks were very fine, and each club had some beautiful or amusing exhibition. Tammany had her Wigwam and sachems in full war paint, carried by six horses. Another group had a large ship with sailors coiling ropes and making ready for sea. The ship was *The Constitution*. The affair created great enthusiasm. The Judge presided at stand No. 4. The Republican press say there were 25,000 persons present. The Democratic papers say 100,000. Their slogans were amusing. One was, "God forgive them, for they know not what they do." Another was a picture of Lincoln splitting rails, reading "Abe at home, March 3rd." Another was entitled "A Jester," and the Judge brought home a clever caricature of McClellan in the character of Hamlet, the grave-digger a jolly Irish soldier. Hamlet holds Lincoln's head in his hand and says, "A fellow of infinite jests, where be thy jibes now?" It is very uncertain who will conquer, but the Judge knew who he thought should conquer and took his part before it was a settled question. Many of our friends are waiting to see the outcome.

I left Father a McClellan man yesterday. I found him un-certain, and he told me that so many of our friends were sorry to see the Judge take so active a part in the election. But they said his was an elective office and they supposed he must vote with his party. I wonder what they thought he meant when he stepped out of party ranks two years ago to do his best to induce his party to go in for the war and support the administra-tion? Then he was in danger of losing ground with his party, but gets no credit for that now.

Confederate General Jubal A. Early made a series of sorties into Northern territory, from the second to the thirteenth of July 1864, known as "Early's Raids." From Winchester, he crossed the Potomac into Maryland, forced Hagerstown and Frederick to pay him tribute, and then descended upon Washington, D.C. General Grant, completely absorbed with the siege of Petersburg, spared two divisions for the defense of the capital, but did not consider the threat serious enough to do more than this.

Early, who had come within five miles of Washington, was driven back into Virginia territory on July 13. On September 19, General Philip H. Sheridan defeated Early at Winchester, and again on September 22 at Fisher's Hill. A third victory for Sheridan at Cedar Creek on October 19 broke the back of Confederate resistance in the Shenandoah Valley, and it was opened up to the same kind of devastation as Georgia received at the hands of Sherman.

September 25, 1864

I have forgotten to chronicle Farragut's exploit before Mobile. He had himself lashed in the rigging of his vessel with his trumpet in hand and his lieutenant below. He fired directly into the portholes of the forts, killing the gunners. This, however, was a month ago, but Mobile is not yet ours. Sheridan, too, has gained two victories over Early which are a great gain to the country. They will stop the raids into Pennsylvania which have been so successful for two summers. These events seem to have much lessened the chances of McClellan's success, although it is not fair that it should be so, for he is as much for the preservation of the Union in its integrity as anyone of the nation. His father-in-law [Randolph Barnes Marcy] is very unpopular; his mother-in-law is an ambitious woman. These Marcy influences, therefore, are most unfavorable. D. Marcy, the brother, I feel to be a charlatan; I often met him at grandmother Suydam's. . . .

Today I have been writing out all the bad things I have heard of Lincoln and his wife, hoping to get them into the papers. They [the Lincolns] so falsely and abominably abuse the Democrats and McClellan that I would like them to have what they deserve.

Mr. Sermon, a friend of the Judge, who, when in England, gave him [the Judge] a supper at the Inner Temple and who was then a rich man, is now settled after many adventures and misfortunes at St. Louis. He has been all through Illinois and tells us that Lincoln's partner has made three million dollars, having had permits for buying cotton, sugar, tobacco, etc., and that it is well understood that Lincoln goes shares.[17] The bill for the *manure* dinner, as it is called (given to Prince Napoleon) was added to the gardener's bill for manure when the Treasury Department refused to pay it. The set of china bought for the White House from a china merchant in the city, for one thousand five hundred dollars, appeared in the bill as costing three thousand dollars, Mrs. Lincoln pocketing one thousand five hundred dollars.

It is humiliating to all American women who have to economize and struggle and part with their husbands, sons, and brothers in these sad times, to see this creature sitting in the highest place as a specimen of American womanhood, and "Uncle Ape," as he should be called, the specimen of man. People seem to think boorishness and ignorance an evidence of honesty and sincerity. Surely it is much more likely that [a person having] courtesy, consideration for others (another word for politeness), disregard of self—all qualities which, if not possessed, must at least be feigned to constitute gentlemanly behavior—should be virtuous and honest, than one left to his natural brutish instincts. Lincoln is a *clever* hypocrite under the mask of honest boorishness, else he would not stay in a position for which he is so eminently disqualified.

This year has been a remarkably fine fruit year. Peaches and

---

[17] Lincoln's partners were John T. Stuart, a business partner in 1837, Stephen T. Logan in 1841, and William H. Herndon, law partner from 1841 until 1865. Mrs. Daly's reference is undoubtedly to Herndon, and Mr. Sermon's story is typical of those being circulated about the President and his associates during this campaign.

melons have been most abundant and of very fine quality. The weather has been exceedingly hot, and we had a long drought of six weeks during July and August. Since then we have had abundant rains which will make potatoes and the later crops better than at first anticipated. All articles of consumption except fruit are double the usual price. A five-cent loaf of bread 10¢, milk 10¢ per quart, potatoes $5.26 per barrel, beef 28¢ and 30¢ per pound, butter 65¢ per pound. We have almost discontinued the use of the latter article, as the dealers are holding back for high prices. The only means to lower their demands is non-consumption.

I find in my inquiries as president of the Women's Patriotic Association that our manufacturers are very little worthy of our patriotic assistance. Not content, as manufacturers abroad are, with a certain percentage, they at once raise their prices to as high a mark as will enable them to undersell the foreign article. And having no pride in making a good article, they make it as flimsy as possible, compatible with its sale. Home-made ingrain carpets are $3.75 per yard; the single ply $2.75.

October 30, 1864

The times seem to me so out of joint that I can scarcely bear to write. It seems to me that the country is mad. Lincoln is cheating as hard as he can, and good Democrats are helping him. Judge Pierrepont, who is, however, Stanton's lawyer, says that General Dix is disappointed at not being nominated for President or Governor by the Democrats; he comes out for Lincoln. Who can be the worse? If McClellan would be the experiment, what was Lincoln?

John Van Buren made a very clever speech in Columbia courts in which he shows what an unsuccessful one [president] he [Lincoln] has been. *He* [Van Buren] has been consistent. When two years ago he, with the Judge and James T., spoke at Cooper's Institute in favor of supporting the administration, he was sent a thousand dollars retaining fee by Stanton as counsel for the government. The same was done to James T. Brady. Mr. Van Buren returned it, saying that he did not feel at liberty to accept it. James T. accepted it, and has had many cases from Stanton. Perhaps this may account for his patriotic scruples against Pendleton[18] and the Chicago platform, which the Democratic candidates and their principal supporters have overthrown.

We are at present ruled by New England, which was never a gentle or tolerant mistress, and my Dutch or German obstinate blood begins to feel heated to see how arrogantly she dictates and would force her ideas down our throats, even with the bayonet. And such a boor to represent our great nation! I would rather have a bull set up, like the Egyptians worship; he would do little mischief; he would not pretend to brains. *Illiterateness* is the fashion. Lincoln, a rail-splitter, and his wife, two ignorant and vulgar boors, are king and queen for now and candidates for election. Andy Johnson, who boasts that he was taught to read by his wife, is to be Vice President. It seems that statesmanship is much less of a trade than rail-splitting, shoemaking, or tailoring. The two last can be learned only by practice, but statesmanship comes of itself. Even the savage is careful that only the greybeards and those who have *proved* themselves wise in council shall be allowed to decide matters of state policy. We know less than the savage, it would seem.

November 6, 1864

Last evening we went to the Century Club, which gave a festival in honor of [William Cullen] Bryant's seventieth

---

18 George Hunt Pendleton (1825–1889), Representative and Senator from Ohio, was minister to Germany. In 1853, he was nominated and elected by a large majority to the State Senate as a Democrat. He was elected to Congress in 1856 and was nominated for Vice President on the Democratic ticket with McClellan in 1864.

birthday. The poets of the country were all invited. Boker[19] from Philadelphia; Street[20] from Albany; [Oliver Wendell] Holmes and Mrs. Julia Howe from Boston; [Charles A.] Dana, [James Russell] Lowell, and Longfellow did not appear.

Emerson gave a discourse which we arrived just in time to hear, having come too late to hear Mr. Bancroft's address and Bryant's reply, which, I am told, was very dignified. Emerson disappointed me. I never had much respect for him, but his face irresistibly reminds you of the figure of *Punch*—the long inquisitive nose, peaked chin, small intense eyes and meager lank frame. I had no desire to be presented to him. He looks like a man of no convictions. After a long, disjointed, wearisome, hesitating utterance, he said something about Bryant's writing his name on the ridges and mountains and engraving it on nature's shield like Phidias, who wrote his upon that of Pallas Athene. The idea was a good one when you at last got at it.

Mrs. Howe read her poem with too much affectation. I think, however, that it will read very well. Boker was long, prosy, and I think, fulsome. Holmes was very fine. There was a birthday ode, one which sounded very much like a dirge; then we went to supper.

I was presented to Miss Hosmer, the sculptress, to Holmes, and talked with Mrs. Howe, asking Miss Hosmer about Miss Cushman and Emma Stebbins.[21] She told me she had seen them a few weeks ago and hoped soon to see them again.

[19] Poet, dramatist, and diplomat George Henry Boker (1823–1890), a Princeton graduate, published his first play, "Calaynos," in 1842. His best-known play was "Francesca da Rimini" (1855), and he wrote over 300 sonnets. A Union supporter, he founded the Union League of Philadelphia in 1862; in 1871 he was appointed U.S. minister to Turkey.

[20] Alfred B. Street (1811–1881) was a Poughkeepsie-born poet who also worked as a lawyer and as a librarian. He settled in Albany in 1839 with a modest law practice, but spent most of his time writing. He is best known for the poems "The Burning of Schenectady" and "Frontenac."

[21] Harriet Goodhue Hosmer (1830–1908) was an American sculptor of international reputation who became friends with Emma Stebbins (1815–1882), a New York–born sculptor, in Rome in 1857. Charlotte S. Cushman, the actress, was a member of the same American colony in Rome, and she and Miss Stebbins became lifelong friends.

"This happy being [Miss Hosmer]," said Mrs. Howe in a sentimental voice, "is the butterfly of art. She flits from one lovely thing to another, merely stopping to rest her wings."

"I should rather say the grub," said Miss Hosmer in her decided gruff tones.

Saw Gifford, Stone, Eastman Johnson, Thompson, the sculptor, Mr. Evarts, who after supper made a clever speech, Willis, Parke Godwin,[22] Mr. Bancroft. It was a poetical thought to give the festival, and Bryant behaved in a very dignified manner. He is essentially of a dignified character, and though a cold, undemonstrative man, has ever been consistent. Doctors Bellows and Osgood[23] were both there—*humble, retiring Christian men.* It seemed to me that the New Englanders would make good Robespierres, not bloody minded, not unkindly, but who sacrifice remorselessly their best friend for an opinion, and these Unitarian divines, these priests of human reason, would act as high priests on such an occasion.

At the Historical Society[24] a few nights since, the Judge read a paper on "The Ancestry and Early Life of Chancellor Kent" (which, by the way, was very much praised). . . .

November 7, 1864

Sunday evening last we went to the Poet's Tea Party at Mrs. Bancroft's, where were Emerson; Bryant; T. Buchanan

[22] Editor Parke Godwin was on the staff of the New York *Evening Post* from 1837 to 1853 and again after 1865. In the interim he edited *Putnam's Monthly.*

[23] Henry W. Bellows (1814–1882) and Samuel Osgood (1812–1880) were pastors of Unitarian churches in New York City, Dr. Bellows at First Unitarian (later All Souls) and Dr. Osgood at the Church of the Messiah. In 1846 Dr. Bellows helped to found the *Christian Inquirer,* a Unitarian paper, and Dr. Osgood collaborated with him as editor between 1850 and 1854. Dr. Bellows organized the U.S. Sanitary Commission in June of 1861 and was its president.

[24] The New-York Historical Society was founded in 1804, and was at this time located at the corner of Second Avenue and Eleventh Street.

Read;[25] Godwin; Bayard Taylor; Ripley;[26] Boker; Miss Hosmer; [Professor] and Mrs. [Vincenzo] Botta; Street; the Unitarian clergymen before mentioned; and several other ladies and gentlemen. Buchanan Read read us a spirited poem called "Sheridan's Ride," in too artificial a manner, however. Then Bryant was made to stand up and listen to his votive offering, which the supper had interfered with the night before and which Mr. Read would not read afterwards, objecting, as he said, to being served up on the half-shell. Read is too conscious of what ability he has. He is a painter as well as poet, and comes from the Northwest. The address was poetical, very complimentary. I pitied poor Bryant, whose "Druid locks" he several times alluded to. The Century celebration, after all, struck me somewhat as a premature burial service, a foretaste of coming bliss, and an admonition of approaching death. Flowers too were plentifully put into his hands as he left.

Tomorrow is election day and all good citizens must wish it over. To the great discontent of the public, especially the Democrats, General [Benjamin F.] Butler has been put in command here and no one can tell what may not be done to secure Lincoln's election. Republicans are now most unscrupulous. I shall order my doors shut and open to no one after ten o'clock on any pretense of business, as the Judge is one of the electors of the electoral college and for McClellan. They may try to get him out of the way *pro tem.*

Judge Pierrepont and General Dix have disgraced themselves. They ought to be well paid by Lincoln for the sacrifice of character they have made for him. General Meagher too

---

[25] Artist and poet Thomas Buchanan Read (1822–1872) was a Pennsylvanian, but spent most of his time in New York, Boston, and abroad. Among his works are a painting of Longfellow's daughters, a portrait of Mrs. Browning, and "Sheridan's Ride," which illustrates his best-known poem.

[26] George Ripley (1802–1880) was a Harvard-trained Unitarian minister until 1841, a founder and leading member of "Brook Farm" from 1841 to 1847, and a literary critic with the New York *Tribune* from 1849 until his death. He collaborated with Dana on the *New American Cyclopaedia* and was a founder of *The Dial*, a Transcendentalist quarterly.

(whom I myself heard say that as a matter of choice he would prefer Jeff Davis for President), having a brigade given him a few weeks since, comes out for Lincoln. What a lesson in human nature McClellan has learned!

A pious Republican told me a few days since a fabrication concerning the last hour of Judge [Roger B.] Taney, whom he says confessed at the last that the Dred Scott Decision[27] had been forced upon him by his party. I exclaimed, "What a shame to attack an honest man's character when he is no longer here to defend himself!" He was a good Catholic, and had he had anything to confess would have done it long ago to his confessor. He is said to have died in the arms of a favorite slave, to have given them all their freedom and to have ordered his body to be laid out and watched by his house servants only. Judge Taney decided according to the laws of the United States. I suppose they [the laws] were in the wrong, perhaps, but not the Judge.

Throughout the summer of 1864, Republican chances for victory at the polls in November seemed to become less and less hopeful. Grant was halted before Richmond and Petersburg in the longest siege of the war; the Confederates were still in control of the Shenandoah; and Sherman's march to Atlanta appeared to be bogged down. The President became more and more depressed, as Thurlow Weed of New York reported to him that the Democrats were gaining strength every day, and National Republican Chairman Henry J. Raymond, editor of The New York Times, *confirmed that report.*

When, on July 4, Lincoln pocket-vetoed the Wade-Davis Bill, the Radical Republicans' proposal for a harsh reconstruction policy toward the South, Horace Greeley published a denunciation of this action in the pages of the New York Tribune *and followed it with a call for a new convention to*

---

[27] In his *obiter dictum* on the *Dred Scott Case* (1857), U.S. Supreme Court Justice Taney declared the Missouri Compromise and the Compromise of 1850 invalid, and thereby furnished an important cause of the Civil War. Taney died on October 12, 1864.

replace Lincoln with another candidate. By September 1, it looked as though Lincoln had no chance whatever for victory, and he felt despair because he believed his opponent was running on a platform which could only mean the end of the Union.

But on September 1, something happened which changed the entire picture. Confederate General John Bell Hood, Johnston's replacement as head of the Confederate forces defending Atlanta, evacuated the city, and on September 2, Sherman's army occupied Georgia's capital. Following this was Admiral Farragut's occupation of Mobile Bay and a series of victories by Sheridan in the Shenandoah Valley. The morale of the North rose sharply with these victories, and Lincoln's chances for success rose with it.

The state elections in Vermont and Maine in September, and those in Ohio, Indiana, Pennsylvania, and Maryland in October showed Republican strength in these states great enough to keep them from Democratic control. After these elections, Lincoln's triumph in November was taken for granted, and the only question was whether or not Seymour would be successful in New York.

In the national elections, Lincoln won overwhelmingly, with 212 electoral votes to McClellan's 21, and with a popular majority of nearly half a million votes. The only states McClellan carried were New Jersey, Kentucky, and Delaware—and he was a native son of New Jersey. In New York State, Fenton won over Seymour with an 8,000-vote majority.

November 15, 1864

The election has taken place. Lincoln has been reelected. *Vox Populi, vox Dei.* So it must be for the best. All now left us is to put the shoulder to the wheel and do our best to draw the governmental machine out of the slough. There was some ill feeling about General Butler's being sent here to overawe the election. However, there seems to be little ill feeling on either side—a hopeful sign for the country. It is well that Lincoln has so large a majority, as now there will be no one to lay the blame upon.

I wish our political parsons could be done away with together with slavery. What autocrats they are! Beecher, a few Sundays since, before he began to preach, announced: "I am going to preach a political sermon, and if anyone does not like it, he can leave the church." A man rose up and gave three cheers for McClellan.

Poor McClellan! What a lesson he has had of the instability of popular favor and of fair-weather friends. None of his old companions-in-arms, hardly, have voted for him, and the reason is clear—it would not be the way to promotion. A lady said to me a few days since, "What, your husband votes for McClellan and you have a brother in the army?"

Yesterday, Mr. Theodore Fay[28] from Bremen, our former minister to Prussia, came in. He is for Lincoln and quoted what he called "Mr. Lincoln's very appropriate though homely saying that a countryman in crossing a dangerous stream or ford would not willingly change horses." I answered very mildly that Mr. Lincoln was very happy in these little sayings, that like in Scripture, you could always find a story or text to suit the occasion. Now those who, like my husband, voted for McClellan, could quote another of his aphorisms as their excuse. When removing some General (Rosecrans, I believe), he said, "They that made the mess are not exactly the ones to finish it." Mr. Fay, however, is a perfectly sincere and conscientious man.

Butler has been serenaded and feted as though he had saved the country, whereas he did nothing. It was the policy of the Democrats to keep the peace, as they wanted to poll as many votes as possible, whereas the policy of the others was to institute, if possible, martial law. The Judge was asked to meet

---

[28] Theodore S. Fay studied law, but later entered journalism and worked for the New York *Mirror*. He was secretary of the American legation at Berlin from 1837 to 1853 and U.S. minister to Switzerland until 1861. Thereafter, he made Berlin his residence.

him on Saturday, but he did not go. Beecher, at the Loyal League Club, proposed him [Butler] as the next President. In Butler's speech, he adopts McClellan's ideas and thinks everything should now be done to make peace.

Darley[29] and his wife spent the evening with us. The Judge got out his theatrical portraits, I brought forward some doppelkümmel and cake, and we had quite a pleasant time around the blazing woodfire until twelve o'clock. Sunday likewise we had company: Mr. Hackett, Mr. Young, and Mr. Dykes. Tonight I am alone. The Judge has gone out with a great friend of his, a bookworm like himself, to see another of their species, and I shall write up all my letters. His "Chancellor Kent," I think, will be a great success. He has been much complimented on the opening chapters.[30]

I have been writing an article explaining the reasons that we cannot find American goods and exposing the tricks of the manufacturers and shopkeepers, which Mr. [Henry M.] Field has promised to publish.

Mrs. Dana came in to bid me good-by, and very kindly invited us to come and stay with her in Washington. Her husband is Assistant Secretary of War. I thought it very kind of her but declined. If I go at all, it will be only as the guest of Baron Gerolt. The dear old gentleman has just left us after a stay of a fortnight. I like him every day more and more. He is so good a Christian, so wise and observing, and so amiable and generous.

November 17, 1864

Tonight the committee of the Shakespeare Monument Fund[31] meets here, and having made the punch [I] excused the

---

[29] Probably Felix O. C. Darley (1822–1888), American artist who illustrated works of Washington Irving and Dickens, among other writers.

[30] The first three chapters of this manuscript are deposited with the New York Public Library, but the Judge never completed his biography of Kent and no part of the manuscript was ever published.

[31] Judge Daly was chairman of the Shakespeare Monument Fund. The unveiling took place on May 23, 1872.

Judge to the first comer, Mr. [William H.] Appleton. I have retired, not being a member of the committee, to the library, where I shall take a good sleep or read.

On Sunday evening, Mr. Daykink came in with us to Mr. Moreaux's, bookworms and print-lovers all, and Mr. Harris. Mr. D. told me an anecdote of the way in which the Sanitary Commission squanders. A merchant who deals very largely in arrowroot was asked by the ladies to give, which he did very liberally, of that article. Sometime afterwards, a man came into his store and asked for arrowroot and what the price was. The merchant told him. "You've raised, I guess," was the answer.

"I never have but one price, sir."

"Then why is your brand of this article selling so far below cost price round Washington and Richmond?"

The reason was obvious to the merchant, who will give no more sanitary stores. Besides, the funds have been used for electioneering purposes. And after having swallowed within six months all the proceeds of the Fair, they are now crying for more and propose to raise means by taking donations in the churches on Thanksgiving Day, taking the bread out of the mouths of the old and infirm clergymen, to whom it has all along been given.

The Republicans may deny it as they may, but the soldiers were not allowed to vote for McClellan. Kate and Judge Brady heard two [Republicans] conversing in the cars who said they would not give a fellow McClellan tickets, that a great many wanted to vote for Little Mac if they could, but that he meant to be up with them; he would not vote at all if he could not for him.

There was a grand ovation to Butler at the Loyal League Club.

The *World* has such a good name for the Lincoln War Democrats. It calls them "cowboys," probably because they stole so much cattle.

Lieutenant Conolly and a friend have been here to ask me to see Mrs. Dix concerning a prisoner in Fort Lafayette suspected of being a blockade runner. The charge is quite false. The poor fellow has been six months in prison and his wife has been dying of consumption. I shall go tomorrow. They told me that Judge Pierrepont is all-powerful in this commission, that he makes a great deal of money out of the prisoners, and is very mercenary, but that one word from him would be all-powerful. So, I shall write to him.

In the meanwhile, our real blockade runners are staying at our hotels and one of them confessed that he had got off by paying $15,000. The details I hear of the corruption of our office-holders and others are so shameful that I cannot bear to record them.

A few days since, a pretty woman who has collected large sums from the city and from wealthy citizens for a school for soldiers' children has been accused of having embezzled it for her own benefit. She is living in a fine stone house uptown, has three horses, while the school is without a teacher. The institution is managed without a president, board of managers, this lady being the president, board, and treasurer. The few children in the rooms lack even a sufficiency of food. How many crimes are now committed in the name of charity and patriotism!

November 28, 1864

On Friday last I saw Edwin Booth and his two brothers[32] in *Julius Caesar*. It was given as a benefit for the Shakespeare Monument Fund. The seats were double price and it must have realized between three and four thousand dollars. Edwin

---

[32] Junius Brutus Booth (1821–1883) and John Wilkes Booth (1838–1865) were the elder and younger brothers of Edwin Booth. John, who won considerable success as a Shakespearean actor, retired from the stage in 1863 because of a bronchial condition, and made only a few subsequent appearances.

Booth's "Brutus" was faultless. The elder brother played Cassius too admirably. In the midst of the performance, there was a cry of fire. Fortunately we did not know the extent of the danger. The performance was interrupted, but the tumult was soon appeased. When we read the papers the next day, we read of the plot to burn the city and of the many fires which had been discovered and of the inflammable substances strewn in the different hotels and shipping.[33] This [is the] work, it is suspected, of rebel emissaries, alas, some of those, perhaps, whose houses have been burned in the Shenandoah Valley or in Georgia. War! How horrible are its consequences, how brutalizing its effects!

Last evening, had a visit from Dr. Ward, David and Hannah, and Mr. and Mrs. Lucius Luckerman, to whom I spoke of the Women's Protective Union, in which I am interested. She [Mrs. Luckerman] sent me this morning thirty dollars for a particularly hard case of which I spoke, and said how glad she was to find Judge Daly so particularly moderate in his views. She was glad that honest men could agree in the social circle. However, they were obliged in public to consider party. I wrote her a grateful answer and said: "Par parentheses, that God permitted different minds to worship Him under different forms, and difference in political opinions, like difference in religion, served to ventilate and purify party spirit." My husband had been twenty years upon the bench, obliged to listen to both sides of an argument, and I thought by this time felt the truth of Solomon's proverb concerning the man wise in his own conceit.

Last Thursday, Thanksgiving, William Reid and Mr. Harris

---

[33] On November 25, 1864, fire was set to eleven large hotels and Barnum's Museum with its attached theater. The plot to burn the city was organized by Jacob Thompson, onetime member of Buchanan's cabinet, who was then living in Canada. Eight men were sent from Canada to cooperate with the Knights of the Golden Circle (an organization formed to help Confederate prisoners escape) for this purpose. The effect would have been devastating had their incendiaries worked, but they counted upon phosphorus combusting with camphene and it does not.

dined with us. We had a very pleasant day. I did not choose to go to church and listen to a clergyman talk politics. I do not put any faith in their judgment on such matters. The Gospel, not the law, is their province. I am told that in most churches, while you listened to them, you would have thought that these were the palmiest days of the Republic, that war, rapine, and murder were things to be thankful for, not as *discipline* and the judgments of God upon us, but for their beneficial effects. For the first time too this winter, our new rich drive four horses. There were six such turnouts a few days [ago] in the park. The theaters and opera are crowded. Such things have no parallel but in the days of the French Revolution and are, I feel, ominous.

General William T. Sherman set out from Chattanooga on May 7, 1864, with 100,000 men upon his famous and terrible march through Georgia. His progress had caused Confederate General Joseph E. Johnston, who replaced General Bragg after the Chattanooga defeat, to be replaced by General John Bell Hood on July 17. Hood, after two unsuccessful attempts to stop Sherman with offensive action, retreated behind the entrenchments of Atlanta. On September 1, 1864, Atlanta fell to Sherman's forces and Hood retreated further before the enemy.

Sherman's "March to the Sea" began on November 14. He split his army, placing 40,000 men under Thomas to foil Hood's new strategy of circling round and attacking Sherman's extended supply lines, and marching forward with an army of 60,000 toward the sea. Everything in his path, beginning in Atlanta, was either destroyed, confiscated, or rendered useless to the enemy, and his path was a broad one—sixty miles wide and three hundred miles long! Looting and pillage was the order of the day in this orgy of devastation unparalleled in American history, and Southerners would be slow to forgive or forget the "damned Yankees" who perpetrated it.

Since Hood's depleted army of 26,000 stood before Nash-
ville waiting for General Thomas to act, Sherman's army had
virtually no opposition in the march to Savannah. On Decem-
ber 10, Sherman reached Savannah, and after a feeble defense
the city surrendered on December 22. In the meantime, on
December 15, Thomas emerged from Nashville with his army
of now close to 50,000 troops and smashed Hood's army with
a single crushing blow. Fewer than 15,000 of Hood's shattered
troops made it across the Tennessee River, but they ceased to
exist as an army.

December 3, 1864

Had an interesting visitor yesterday, one of Sheridan's
cavalry officers, Captain Coppinger, a handsome, gallant young
fellow of 28 or 30, who has served in Italy and the Crimea.
I asked him if he were one of those dreadful men we read of.
"Yes," said he, "I am one of the 'barnburners,' destroyers of
homes, etc. I don't like such work, Judge," said he. "It is not
civilized war. Although much is military necessity, much could
be avoided. Harshness is never of any use. We lose by this."
Mosby[34] takes ten men of ours where we get one of his.
Sheridan has had three of his staff shot; one escaped from
Mosby by staining his face in a Negro hut and reported himself
in his camp with his face blackened. He was taken with another man and they were obliged to draw lots which should
be shot. He was the fortunate one and came up all along the
Blue Ridge thus disguised, and aided everywhere by the
Negroes. [The] Captain said, however, that this present policy

---

[34] John S. Mosby unnerved the people of Washington with the daring
raids of his Partisan Rangers in Fairfax County. Major Mosby had been a
scout for General Jeb Stuart, and his rangers were in the pay of the Confederate government. The Union government considered these guerrilla
fighters as highway robbers, since they were permitted to retain their spoils.
Noted for their horsemanship, Mosby's raiders attacked isolated pickets,
threw trains off tracks, and captured Federal supplies.

turned every neutral into an enemy, every enemy into a friend. . . .

The Judge has gone to the Century Club, where there is a meeting in honor and in memory of General Wadsworth and Colonel Peter B. Porter.[35]

Paid a visit a few days since to Mrs. Barlow. Had a long talk upon McClellan and his fair-weather friends. She told me some anecdotes very characteristic of President Lincoln, such as saying "Are you a lady?" to a gentlewoman of his acquaintance who wished her son to enter the naval school.

December 6, 1864

Went on Monday night to Mr. Bancroft's, a party given in honor of Goldwin Smith.[36] It was very agreeable, invitations being generally confined to persons of mature years. I saw General Dix, who at once came over to speak to me about the prisoner in Fort Lafayette in whom I had interested myself. I had a talk with Bryant, Mr. [William B.] Astor, and a number of worthies. We heard Miss Read sing Mrs. Howe's battlesong to the tune of "John Brown." Mrs. "Fifth-Avenue-Hotel" [John Austin] Stevens was there, of course, with her sister. I would rather dispense with the music than to have to take Mrs. Stevens with it, and it was no place to sing the "Battle Hymn" and bring John Brown, the *source* of all our woe, in a mixed company. . . .

---

[35] Peter Buell Porter (1773–1844) was John Quincy Adams' Secretary of War in 1828–29. He had served as a congressman from New York from 1809 to 1812 and from 1815 to 1816, and distinguished himself in the War of 1812 at Chippewa and Lundy's Lane (1814).

[36] Goldwin Smith, professor of law and of modern history at Oxford, was highly instrumental in winning British sentiment to the side of the North during the Civil War. With speeches, pamphlets, and articles, Smith argued the Union cause with conviction and persistency. He toured the North in 1864, and was received with gratitude and acclaim wherever he went.

Today there were two morning receptions and we are to
dine at Mr. Henry Grinnell's.[37] I shall be glad when I get home,
as three days of company are almost too much. I am glad, however, to have the Judge go out with me and see him so much
appreciated.

The citizens seem determined to amuse themselves, *coûte
que coûte.*

Sunday evening last, the 3rd, Mrs. Frémont came just as
dinner was put upon the table. She stayed until nine o'clock.
She is very brilliant and original, has somewhat the manner of
one accustomed to rule and direct others, fond of gentlemen's
society, as most clever women are, has some affectations of
thought and idiosyncrasies of taste and feeling, but no affectation of manner and no hypocrisy. I'm afraid she is too positive
and truthful to be popular in New York. Nobody likes so much
fresh breeze and so much sunlight; it disturbs the lazy and
frightens the hypocritical. She can compliment judiciously,
however. What I have seen of her, I like very much. . . .

Sunday, December 11, 1864

A very stormy day. Stayed at home, wrote to Phil,
said my prayers, read a little, pondered much upon the present
condition of society. It is a bad sign when women become lax,
and what I see and hear of *le beau monde* suggests this to be
the case, at least in that circle.

Ellen Strong came in painted like a wanton at Mrs. Bancroft's
with a huge bouquet sent her by one of her little *beaux,* with-

---

[37] Henry Grinnell (1799–1874) was a partner in the whale-oil shipping
firm of Grinnell, Minturn & Co. from 1825 until he retired in 1849. In 1850
and 1853 he fitted out expeditions to search for Sir John Franklin's party,
and Grinnell Land, near Greenland, was named for him. He was first
president of the American Geographical Society, organized in 1852, and its
vice president from 1854 to 1872. Judge Daly joined the Society in 1856
and was its president from 1864 until his death in 1899.

out her husband. What must he think? What can he mean by thus leaving her so much to herself? Mrs. Dr. [John Charles] Peters was in church last Sunday afternoon with one of her little lovers. What was the use of going to church? Could he not sigh just as well and more comfortably at home? Or would the Doctor have been in the way? I was malicious enough to think of going up and congratulating her upon having her son at home, but the idea pleased me so much that it relaxed all my muscles and I felt I could not keep my countenance.

I heard an amusing story about Mr. Bancroft. He was in the habit of riding a good deal with Helen Russell and of going to see her of a morning. Growing sentimental, he objected to her formality in calling him Mr. Bancroft.

"What shall I call you?"

"Call me George," said our historian. So, at a dinner party some time afterward, where Miss Russell and he were, some question was asked by Miss Russell which could not be answered by the gentlemen and she appealed across the table to Mr. Bancroft: "George," said she, "can you tell me, etc., etc.?" Mr. Bancroft has since been heard to remark that Miss Russell was somewhat wanting in tact.

Mr. James Gerard dined with us some time ago and we had a long talk over old times in old New York. He is now a man near eighty, I should think, but as brisk and bright as possible. Having heard grandmother talk so much of all those people and times, I was quite familiar with them all (to his great satisfaction and surprise), and he said: "The style of the present day was nothing in comparison to that in my grandfather's time. Mr. Cadwallader Colden gave dinner parties with twelve liveried servants belonging to his house serving, who were, like in England, always in the hall. And in their plate and wines and loaded tables and their courtesy and elegance of manner far outshone anything their descendants can show." I can feel the difference.

On Monday last, we went to Mr. Charles Butler's,[38] where we met Goldwin Smith. He is a quiet, gentlemanly man who says very little but looks intelligent and modest. I have not, but must read his books in order to judge him. I said something about being sorry that he should be here whilst we were in the confusion of cleaning house (nationally), but feeling that it would be charity to him to leave him alone, soon turned to talk to someone else.

Tuesday, the Women's Protective League held an anniversary meeting. The Judge presided. Beecher, Oakey Hall,[39] and James T. Brady spoke. The first is a very suggestive speaker, full of point and illustration, humor and pathos. If I had not known anything about him, I'm sure I should have thought him very liberal, but that he is not, except in words. James T. made a very amusing, witty speech out of nothing, at which he is very clever. After the meeting, we went to a party at Mr. Miller's, a very beautiful entertainment, handsome house, handsome people, fine music and fine supper, and reached home about two o'clock, having enjoyed myself very well. Had a long gossip with John Van Buren. I felt I must tell him what satisfaction his speeches during the election had given me. Saw Judge Robertson,[40] and ventilated my dislike of Long Island Smiths and Suydams. He promised some time since to look up

[38] Charles E. Butler (1802–1897), lawyer and philanthropist, was deputy clerk of the State Senate in 1822 and was admitted to the bar in 1824. He played an active part in establishing Hobart College, and was one of the twenty-four "founders" of Union Theological Seminary in 1836.

[39] District Attorney in New York City at this time, A. Oakey Hall was infamous for his corruption as Boss Tweed's mayor in 1870. In 1872, Judge Daly presided over the first two of Hall's three impeachment trials, the last of which resulted in acquittal ten days before his term of office expired. While mayor, Hall earned the sobriquet "The Elegant One."

[40] William H. Robertson (1823–1898) served three terms in the Assembly of New York and eight terms in the State Senate. From 1854 to 1866 he was a Westchester County judge, and from 1867 to 1869 he was a U.S. Representative from New York. President Garfield appointed him Collector of Customs for New York against the wishes of Senators Conkling and Platt, and he served in that capacity from 1881 to 1885.

the pedigree of Tangur Smith, as the founder of the family was called, and prove that he was one of Kirke's lambs in Charles II's reign.

Wednesday Miss [Margaret] Gelston sent for us to go with her to the opera to hear "Don Sebastian." We were delighted with it and had a very pleasant time. Miss Gelston is, we were saying, like a piece of old silver, never seen but in the very best company, whilst we are a serviceable service of plate seen in many different circles. Miss Sylvia Grinnell, who went with us, said to me: "Oh, Mrs. Daly, how happy you are. You know everybody from the Catholic priests to—" I laughingly interrupted her, "the buffoons of the theaters." We have a wide circle, certainly, and a very pleasant one therefore. We don't travel in any respectable ruts. . . .

December 22, 1864

James Davis left us yesterday. The day before we got up an impromptu dinner party composed of Judge Brady and Kate; the Youngs—Alice and Anna; Anna Raasloff; Kensett; Bierstadt; Temple Prime; and McDonough, and had a delightful time. Davis seemed delighted and much pleased with Anna Raasloff.

Yesterday we went together to the Cooper Institute through the Bryan Gallery, etc. and old Mr. Cooper[41] showed us all over the building. I think our young friend got some new impressions of life whilst in New York and thought it a greater place than Boston. His father wrote me a letter of thanks, telling me how much James had been pleased.

---

[41] Manufacturer, inventor, and philanthropist Peter Cooper (1791–1883) founded Cooper Union in 1857 "for the advancement of science and art." Cooper had designed and constructed the first steam locomotive, "Tom Thumb," and was the chief supporter of Cyrus Field's Atlantic Cable project. In 1876 he was the Presidential candidate of the Greenback party.

December 26, 1864

Spent a very pleasant Christmas in Laight Street. No one of the Suydams except James, who is a passive member of society, present. Hannah dined with us, so it was strictly a family party. We did not give or receive handsome presents. In truth, the times do not admit of it.

Tonight, we are going to see Booth in "Hamlet." The scenery is very beautiful and characteristic of the Polonius and Ophelia. [It is] very good, and Booth, everyone admits, is as great a Hamlet as ever died upon the stage. The scenery and architecture are old Gothic. It looks like an old Scandinavian stronghold, and the effects of moonlight are admirable in the scene with the ghost and the gravediggers' scene.

Dined yesterday at Mr. Charles Gould's, where we met the Admiral and Mrs. Farragut. I was seated between the Admiral and Dr. [Isaac] Cummings and had a good talk with the hero. He is a simple, direct man, says what he thinks, with little polish but much originality, and no doubt often expresses ideas as he thinks out new methods of attack when excited by the occasion. He does not believe in *long*, unwieldy ships, whether of wood or of iron; believes in all the new inventions; in new ways of reefing the sails, which now by means of ropes are made to reef and open themselves; in the sewing machine (without which he thinks we should never have been able to clothe our armies, which are the best clothed and cared for that ever were known— who want nothing); does not think the Sanitary Commission longer needed [by] the government; thinks the soldiers of the army favored more than its sailors by the ladies. But we don't complain; when we want luxuries, we buy them. I suggested that if the Sanitary would leave the soldiers to the government, they would do well enough. He said he thought it could have been more equitably managed. . . .

1865

January 3, 1865

As New Year's Day came on a Sunday, yesterday was kept as the visiting day. I had 100 visits. The day before, I saw Adam Badeau, now in the city recovering from camp fever, [who] sent to ask permission to sit and receive company with me for two or three hours. He stayed most of the day. Poor fellow. He was weaker than he thought, and I was in constant dread that he would faint outright. Then, he is so extremely ugly and insignificant looking; I think I never realized it so much as yesterday. I would never do for a Sister of Charity, for I felt the greatest repugnance to nurse him up or touch him. How he has reached the responsible position of secretary to Lieutenant General Grant I cannot imagine, but from his manner yesterday, I think it must be that he can *creep*. He does not flatter, at least not me. Perhaps he knows too much for that or only gives it where he is sure it will please and be swallowed. He did not allow an acquaintance of either long or short standing to escape recognition. I wish I were not given so much to dissecting character. Among the visitors were Generals Frémont and [Robert B.] Potter, Colonel Zagoni, Mr. Charles O'Conor, Mr. Harris, Baron Osten-Sacken, Charles Gould. William Reid came in dressed in black velvet from head to foot, white cravat and diamond sleeve buttons. He looked well, but ridiculously; it's sort of shoddy.

January 5, 1865

Yesterday I was alone, so I went down and spent the evening with Mother, paid visits all the morning, and astonished some Loyal Leaguers by my dislike of the fuss made over Gold-win Smith. I said that if we showed so much substantial grati-tude for being well spoken of by a college professor (as there were many others in Europe wise enough not to despair of this continent), we might be in danger of an invasion of professors—large and small; that I thought it unnecessary to be so gratified for the good opinion of any Englishman—the rest would glorify themselves over it at our expense.

The Judge dined yesterday at the Athenaeum Club,[1] a dinner given to Major General Potter, and made, they tell me, two or three clever speeches. Mr. Barney said something about his recollections of those early days when, under the care of Professor Potter (afterwards Bishop, and father of the Gen-eral[2]), he had pursued his studies, etc. etc., to which the Judge alluded as that time when Mr. Barney alludes to himself as "clay in the hands of the Potter, whence he had been made and baked into a vase worthy of the attention of any collector." When coming home to dress for the dinner, he [the Judge] told me he had received a present. "A book, I suppose," said I indifferently.

"You don't care for a book, then, and don't want to hear about it?"

"Yes, I may as well know if it is a pleasant or a handsome one."

---

[1] Judge Daly succeeded George Folsom as president of the Athenaeum Club in 1866. This men's club was located at 108 Fifth Avenue.

[2] Alonzo Potter (1800–1865), the father of Major General Robert B. Potter (1829–1887), became bishop of Pennsylvania in 1845. His brother, Horatio Potter (1802–1887) became bishop of New York in 1861.

"Well, I have had an increase of salary given me of a thousand dollars." This will make things easy, for, from the high prices, we were much straitened.

January 6, 1865

Last evening Bierstadt paid us a long and pleasant visit. I like him as well as anyone we know. This evening [I] went to the Geographical Society with the Judge [and] heard a paper read on Siam, which was very interesting. . . .

January 8, 1865

Paid a visit yesterday to General and Mrs. McClellan, whom I at last found after following them from one magnificent house to another until I [located] them in Mr. Randolph's,[3] the coal merchant's, palace, the third I went to. I did not like to have them leave the city a second time without calling on them, particularly since McClellan was defeated as President. McClellan himself came down to see me. He is trammeled, I think, a little by the ladies of his family.

Mrs. Marcy looked harassed, as though she had indeed been through a campaign. Mrs. McClellan herself had an excited expression, and it was a sore subject to her still to think of Lincoln in the White House. It was shown in her observation about Baron Gerolt. It was time, she said, for his family to come and join him; he was getting into evil courses.

"Yes?" I said, "What, our dear good Baron?"

"Indeed, yes," said she. "He is much too intimate with Mary Lincoln."

The General himself looked as serene, amiable, thoughtful, and self-contained as though he had never been out of his

---

[3] Franklin F. Randolph, head of Randolph & Skidmores, coals, lived at 287 East Broadway. The firm was located at various places in the city, but made its business headquarters at 14 Wall Street.

library all these four eventful years. His wife said they were going to Europe. Why did I not go? "Because the Judge has to make his bread day by day."

"Oh, don't think of that," said she. "No one will give us anything to do and we have no bread to make, so we are going to Europe on nothing."

The General thinks he will turn consulting engineer and become a rich man, but that he never will.[4] "He would give everything away," I interposed.

"Yes," she said, "and if he did anything and charged a reasonable fee, if they should say, 'I think that a great deal,' he would say, 'As you please; give me what you think proper.' " The General smiled and shrugged his shoulders, as much as to say, "I can't help it." I think I know what kind of man he is from my own husband.

Mrs. Gelston, Mr. Harris, and Osten-Sacken dined with us today.

January 9, 1865

Dined today at Father's with Phil most unexpectedly. He is home on leave for ten days. I was glad to hear him speak of Butler as he did before Father. He thinks that Fort Fisher was lost only because Butler lost courage.[5] The story is that the Confederates supposed it taken. They had withdrawn most

---

[4] After his defeat in the election, McClellan spent three years abroad. He then went into shipbuilding, was chief engineer of the New York City Department of Docks from 1870 to 1872, and served as governor of New Jersey from 1878 to 1881.

[5] Wilmington, North Carolina, was the last Southern port open for supplies from the outside by the end of 1864. In December, General Benjamin Butler and Admiral David D. Porter moved against Fort Fisher, which protected the harbor. Troops were landed and the fort was bombarded for a day, and then the amphibian force returned home with the pronouncement that the fort was impregnable. In January of 1865, the same troops and the same fleet returned, but this time they were under a new commander, General Alfred H. Terry. After a heavy bombardment from Porter's ships, Terry's 8,000 troops attacked and the fort fell on January 15. All blockade running to the South was now effectually ended.

of the garrison, leaving only a picket, and were greatly surprised to see Butler rein back his soldiers. The story is not true
that Grant is responsible for maintaining him in his position,
Phil thinks from the fact that when he came up in the boat to
City Point some of Grant's staff officers present said: "There's
the *Beast*." Officers generally in their likes and dislikes are apt
to agree with their commanders.

January 11, 1865

Went out last night to a ball at Mrs. [John W.] Hamersley's, an old New York party. Rosalie, Phil, the Judge, and
I noticed the great preponderance of New Yorkers, very few
New Englanders or new people of any of the new aristocracies
of coal, petroleum, or shoddy. I had quite a pleasant time, having
heard some ill-natured things and said some myself. It is very
amusing to go about once a year into Vanity Fair. There was
the whole Ruggles family, father, mother, two old people
(who would have been better in their beds at one o'clock when
I left them), old Mrs. Ruggles,[6] with her poor neck and arms
bare, with only an imitation white lace scarf carelessly thrown
over her shoulders, a bit of lace and bright pink roses in her
scanty and faded hair instead of a nice matronly cap, and a
tawdry necklace round her throat. Papa Ruggles in a newly
curled wig, white cravat, making himself agreeable to such as
like his style, but saying how tired he was. Of course, he must
have been; he is as old as papa. Mrs. O'Conor, bare to her
waist, dressed for show. She asked me why I wore a high-
necked dress. I was afraid, I said, of getting cold, and dreaded
she would say, "Oh, no danger; look at me," and that the
gentleman near me would laugh. Mrs. Paum came with red
roses in her hair which her nose, cheeks, and chin rivalled, and
a flashy, low-necked silk dress. She must be fifty-five at least.
Ellen Strong painted as usual, looking, as Temple Prime said,

---

[6] Mrs. Philo Ruggles (Ellen Buckley), who died on February 25, 1865.

however, very pretty and very young looking. "It is well done," said he. "I can't see it."

"Put on your glasses and thank Providence you are near-sighted, then."

January 15, 1865

It seems really to be true that Butler has blown himself up with his powder boat. Grant's dispatches to him show that he acted without and contrary to orders. The *Beast*, therefore, is conquered and caged for the present. It was very amusing to read the remarks of the Richmond papers, their comic laments over his loss as of a general that had never done them harm, etc.

Phil dined with us on Wednesday with David and Temple Prime.

Read over this morning the list of the incomes of our private citizens. Stewart, the dry-goods merchant, is the richest man in the city, richer than Astor.

Been devoted all the week to paying reception visits. Having made my own bonnets, I managed to be dressed very hand-somely. I don't think that my Dutch prejudices will ever en-able me to pay forty and fifty dollars for the few scraps of silk and velvet that they charge this price for and call a bonnet. I do not think my dress this year has cost more than two hun-dred dollars. But then, I have worn my old things.

January 19, 1865

Last evening the Judge dined at Mrs. Devlin's in com-pany with Major General Hancock. He [the Judge] is very much pleased with him, represents him as a handsome man, six feet high, like Farragut, brusque, manly, with no personal vanity about his own personal exploits. He remarked he had never lost a friend, but was constant in his friendships.

"You," said Mr. Brady, "love your friends and hate your enemies."

"I do not say that. The enemies of my country and my government are to be met in open fight in the field and conquered, if possible, but I have no personal enmity to them whatever as have soldiers led astray by a mistaken sense of duty. I respect them."

His wife and himself are deeply attached to each other. Speaking of the war, he said the battle of Antietam was the heaviest disappointment the rebels had met with. They then felt certain of success and felt that they should carry the war so far into the Northern states that the recognition of the Confederacy would have been a necessity.

Colonel Badeau dined with us on Sunday last. He said that Grant was one of the purest and most disinterested natures he had ever met with—social, unostentatious, affable, and fatherly with the officers of his staff—dining with them, talking a good deal (sometimes on the most trifling subjects, sometimes on the most momentous); having no jealousy of the fame of others; taking no credit to himself for every movement ever planned by him; and unwilling to be praised or flattered. His contribution of five hundred dollars towards a house for General Sherman and his letter of commendation would prove this. Sherman is perhaps more brilliant than Grant, Badeau said, but has not his moral courage in emergencies or in assuming responsibility.[7] Grant's publication of his dispatches to old Butler shows his moral courage, and the taking of Fort Fisher by [Alfred Howe] Terry in the face of Butler's assertion that it could not be taken must, I think, finish the *Beast*.

---

[7] After Sherman distinguished himself in the Vicksburg campaign and at Chattanooga, he was made head of the Western armies when Grant became commander-in-chief in 1864. Then came Sherman's famous march to Atlanta and north through the Carolinas. Sherman succeeded Grant as a full general when Grant became President, and he retired in 1883. In 1884, he refused to allow his name to be placed in nomination for the Presidency when approached by the Republicans.

Phil returned yesterday to his post.

Judge Cardozo[8] has just paid the Judge a visit, the first social intercourse between them being the return for one on New Year's Day from him and Judge Brady. He is not a man to be afraid of. He does not look like a strong nor shrewd man, and would be no match for my husband if opposed to him. He says, when asked for letters for the Administration, he sends all applications with a line to his friend Judge Pierrepont. When the *World* published his speech directing all the Irish to his house, he [Cardozo] furnished himself with two or three hundred dollars in one-dollar bills and fifty-cent pieces, etc., meaning to give to all that came. He [Judge Daly] spoke of him as a very shrewd man.

As 1865 opened, the Confederacy found itself in desperate circumstances and quite incapable of resisting the devastation being wreaked upon it daily. Both the military and the civilian population suffered a lack of food, clothing, and supplies of all sorts, for with the capture of Fort Fisher, North Carolina, and the closing of the Wilmington port, the Northern blockade was now completely effective. Added to this was a breakdown in Confederate transportation and communications, and Federal occupation of principal productive areas which they had not already devastated.

On the military front, Lee's army was still bottled up in Petersburg, and Grant stood without the city on the banks of the James—increasing his army every day. Sherman, after a brief pause at Savannah, prepared to advance northward through the Carolinas to meet Grant's army and attack Rich-

---

8 Judge Albert Cardozo, father of the famous jurist Benjamin Nathan Cardozo, had been a justice of the Court of Common Pleas before advancing to the State Supreme Court. He was one of the corrupt judges who helped the Tweed Ring perpetrate their frauds on the public. Cardozo was a learned man and a gentleman who doubtless could have made a brilliant reputation for himself, but he sold justice and went along with the naturalization frauds in 1868 which shocked the nation when they were exposed.

mond from the rear. On January 21, his reinforced army of 60,000 began its northward march, looting and burning at will in a holocaust even more destructive than Georgia had known. General Johnston's army of some 30,000 badly equipped and poorly supplied troops could do little more than retreat before Sherman's superior force.

While all this was happening, President Lincoln met with three Confederate commissioners aboard the Union transport River Queen *off Fortress Monroe on February 3. The meeting had been arranged by Francis P. Blair, Sr., a great friend of Lincoln, who thought to terminate the war by getting the North and the South to join hands and drive Maximilian out of Mexico. In an interview with Jefferson Davis at Richmond on January 12, Blair got Davis' agreement to send commissioners Alexander H. Stephens, R. M. T. Hunter, and John A. Campbell to meet with Lincoln and Seward.*

The conference failed, for the Southern emissaries insisted upon the recognition of Confederate independence, and Lincoln insisted upon full and unconditional restoration of the Union. When the Southern commissioners returned to Richmond with the results of the conference, Jefferson Davis publicly announced that the South would fight on to victory. Thus passed the South's last opportunity for a negotiated peace.

February 8, 1865

Since I opened this, we have had the Southern commissioners at Fortress Monroe, who have left without anything being decided upon. It seems they wished an armistice (to gain time and get away, perhaps). It was, I think, properly denied and they have gone home again. Active operations recommenced upon Richmond, whilst Sherman is advancing North again, shutting up Charleston by taking all the points upon the railroads, etc., which command it on his way to join Grant.

Phil has gone back a fortnight since. I must write to him.

We have been very gay, having been at a great many dinner parties. One was given by Mr. Jarvis to his brother-in-law, Major Lowry, who unostentatiously has done great service to the Union cause. He possessed lead mines in New Mexico, and the Confederates offered him a pound of cotton for every pound of lead he would furnish them, which would have given him millions. He refused, knowing the lead was to be used against his country and his flag. Finding that one of his staff (the Confederate general nearest him) could be bought, he paid him regularly, sending the information to General [Edward R. S.] Canby. This enabled him [Canby] to anticipate the invasion into California and New Mexico and defeat it. He [Lowry] has succored and fed Union refugees at his rancho by thousands. Over the bed in the guest chambers always hung the United States flag. He says delicate women and children, people once of ample means, came to his house clad in sheepskins, flying to the coast to avoid the rebel conscription and to get North. The dinner was not pleasant. Judge Brady was so very noisy and the dinner French, which I never like.

The next day we dined at the English consul's, Mr. [Edward M.] Archibald. I had a very pleasant time. . . .

As Sherman set out on his march northward, he seemed to threaten both Charleston and Augusta, but proceeded directly to Columbia, South Carolina, through swamps and muddy roads and across swollen streams. On February 17, the Union forces entered Columbia over a pontoon bridge as the Confederates retreated out the other side of the city. A great fire began that night, and a large portion of the city was destroyed. Each side blamed the other for starting the fire, but Sherman maintained to the end of his life that his troops were never given orders to fire the city. More than a dozen towns had already been burned to the ground, however, on Sherman's northward march.

When Columbia fell, Confederate General William Joseph

Hardee withdrew his small army of 14,000 men from out-flanked Charleston and evacuated the city. Charleston fell on the 21st of February and was occupied by Union forces under General Quincy Adams Gillmore. In the meantime, the American flag was raised over Fort Sumter on February 18, and Sheridan continued to devastate the Shenandoah Valley. On March 5, Sheridan crushed the last remnant of the Confederate Army there, and nothing stood in his path.

Sherman fought his final battle with General Johnston at Bentonville on the 19th and 20th of March. Although the weaker Confederate force was brushed aside, it was not destroyed, but it would not fight again. On the 21st, Sherman entered Goldsboro and joined forces with General John McAllister Schofield. At this point, the South's resistance was reduced to the army of General Lee at Petersburg.

February 26, 1865

Charleston and Wilmington have both been evacuated, and a letter from Badeau tells us that a few more successes and the rebellion is conquered. It will be a long time before peace and order be established, but it must come.

Met Major General [Orlando B.] Wilcox a few nights ago at the theater. Went to see his wife yesterday, but missed her.

Saw "Much Ado About Nothing" played for the Shakespeare Monument Fund by Mrs. General [Frederick W.] Lander, Miss Davenport as Beatrice, and [William] Wheatley as Benedict. It was a great treat.

Heard at Mrs. Dunlap's last week all the amateur *prima donnas:*—Mrs. Moulten; Miss Read; Mrs. Arthur; Mrs. Sampson; and Adelaide Philips. Mrs. Moulten is very handsome and sings with great expression and enthusiasm. She has a horrid little husband whom she will, however, have to mind. I called upon her some days ago at the request of her mother. Met Mrs. Grenough, a thorough New England woman interested in every new thing, president of the Medical College for Women—where last evening she conferred the degrees, it being the anniversary. She wanted the Judge to speak and wishes me to be one of the trustees. I had rather not, as I am not wise enough to judge in such matters. That women should be enabled to understand their own sex and be able to minister to them, I fully agree to. That matronly women should preside in out-dispensaries to watch that the young women who come to seek relief there should not be tampered with is likewise necessary, but I do not think the first movement can be carried out without the aid of learned, experienced medical men. At all events, I must know something more before I join them.

They are to have a grand procession and display and speechifying on Saturday in honor of the capture of Charleston and other victories. The Judge advised the putting of it off until it was known that Sherman was safe, for as he approaches Richmond, he comes nearer the danger. Lee must do all he possibly can to prevent his [Sherman's] joining Grant. Besides, as Saturday would be the 4th of March, it would look like a compliment to Lincoln instead of to the army and navy.

March 2, 1865

The Judge has gone to read "The Early Years of Chancellor Kent" before the Long Island Historical Society. The night was too stormy for me to venture, although I had a particular invitation.

Baron Gerolt has just left us to go on to the inauguration. We had a little party for him on Monday: General Dix; Mr. and Mrs. Bancroft; the Dutch minister and his wife, Mr. Limburg; Mrs. Frémont; Doctor Lieber; the Raasloffs; and a Mr. and Mrs. Weld, with whom he had been staying in Cumberland—very pleasant people to whom I think he was pleased to have me pay some attention. I did not ask one of my own family, as they always laugh at my foreign friends. There were about twenty in all. We had an oyster supper and the party was very sociable and pleasant. I was glad to be able to do something to please the dear little man [Gerolt]. He is so unpresuming and so grateful for kindness; so wise and yet has so much real Christian humility.

March 3, 1865

Had a visit last night from old Dr. Mathews,[9] an old beau of my mother—a fashionable clergyman in his youth and chancellor of the University, dining with the Patroon, Philip Hone,[10] Chancellor Kent, etc.; now driven to all kinds of shifts to get money; now over eighty years of age. We were playing backgammon when he was announced. I said, knowing he had come for money, "Now, don't yield," knowing that it had been said of him [Dr. Mathews] that he could coax the skin off your back. The Judge received him courteously.

"I saw your name in the papers," [said Dr. Mathews]. "I came to say how glad I was to see your protest against this celebration, in which I perfectly agree. It was so well urged by you," etc. etc.

The Judge bowed.

"Are you a New Yorker?"

"Yes."

"Of Irish parentage?"

"Yes, on both sides. My parents were both natives of Tyrone."

"Like myself," said the Doctor, "from the north of Ireland."

---

[9] Reverend James M. Mathews (1785–1870), the first chancellor of New York University.

[10] Famous diarist Philip Hone (1780–1851) was a New York merchant and banker who retired from business in 1821 to devote himself to travel and politics. Instrumental in the formation of the Whig Party, Hone was elected mayor of New York City in 1825.

I, feeling the art of all this, said: "How came you to be a Catholic then, Charles?"

The Doctor then went on to speak of the little difference between true Christians. For his part, he had never made any [distinction]. Some of his most esteemed friends had been Catholic priests.

"Dr. Powers, you knew him, Judge?"

"Yes, he was an intimate friend of my father's" etc., etc., and then there was a discussion of him. Then the South Church and all its old, respectable members were brought on the carpet and the Doctor said, "I have a long acquaintance with Mrs. Daly through her mother—a great pet of mine. I was very intimate in your grandfather's family," etc., etc. I thought if he knew all, he would not elaborate that subject if he wanted to gain his object.

At last he said, "Judge, you are a man of literary tastes; I always see your name foremost in such matters, and I would like to submit to you this little paper which I wish you would read."

Whilst the Judge took it to read, the old fellow turned towards me and kept up the conversation about my family. He had dined with my grandfather Lydig, etc., etc. It was the finest and most consummate piece of acting I have ever seen. The Judge looked amused and I could scarcely keep a bland smile from my own face. At last I heard the Judge say, "Certainly, Doctor, I will subscribe myself and try to aid you in it," taking out a five-dollar note.

"Ah, Judge, your name will be of great value."

The Judge said, "Doctor, the value of names in such a case is in their number." Then followed other compliments and as he spoke of Chancellor Kent, the Judge thought he might pump him a little upon him [Kent] and Egbert Benson, but here the Doctor showed little disposition to yield. He had mentioned such and such things in his book (which the Judge has just been so obliging as to put his name down for), and resisted the pumping process very gently but surely. Seeing that he could make no further use of us, and his time being precious—although I had tea brought up purposely to assist the Judge in his pumping process—he declined a cup and took his leave.

"Oh, the venerable humbug!" said I. "It was worth five dollars to have seen this."

"Did you ever see such an artist?" said the Judge. "The old fellow got my five dollars very willingly. It was quite worth it, but the book will never be published."

March 4, 1865

Last night the Judge came home from the committee about the celebration [of the Charleston victory]. He said the reporter told him that he had read a speech of his in prison at Macon which contained the most convincing arguments for the war founded on physical geography he had ever seen. It was published in a Macon paper with an editorial saying that these were the views of so prominent a Northern Democrat that it showed what the South might expect, coming as it did from such a source from the Democratic party. The Judge has been working very hard. As it rains today, the celebration will be put off until Monday.

Had a pleasant, affectionate letter from Phil and one from Colonel Badeau in answer to one asking if he could do anything for Mrs. Young's stepmother, Mrs. Wilmington, who is still somewhere in South Carolina. General Grant promises me a pass for her. My letter seems to have pleased him. I think Badeau fears that Grant may be overshadowed by Sherman whilst Grant, he says, has planned all these great movements and deserves the credit as the head does which directs a skillful hand. The resolutions which the Judge has written will do him justice.

March 7, 1865

The celebration yesterday was a great success. I never saw such a crowd gathered together ever before in this city. The procession was six miles long, a very fine show of the military and of the firemen. Some wounded soldiers and the orphans of soldiers walked as a little company in the procession. There were too many trucks and advertisements. The Judge read the resolutions, which were thought admirable. General Dix spoke first, Judge Pierrepont spoke next. He [Pierrepont] had the coolness to ask the Judge to put his name first. Why? He has not been patriotic in his expenses, and I learned from Mrs. Cardozo today that he was very intimate with her husband; that she liked him so much. I wonder what he is aiming at, conciliating all these politicians. He professes now to be returning to his Democratic opinions.

"What, is he not a Republican?" I said. "Only in not voting for McClellan does a man belong to your party who does his best to defeat you and put the opposition in power?" I asked, but finding they were intimate, I did not ventilate my mind concerning him. He told the Judge, apparently as a friend, that this celebration was very unpopular with the Democrats. It would be better not to take a prominent part. I wonder what he was so disinterested for. Was it that he might not be overshadowed by a more eloquent speaker?

General Dix spoke first; then Pierrepont; then the Judge read the resolutions; then John Van Buren [spoke]; then [David] Dudley Field, and a number of others. The crowd then reassembled for the fireworks, which were very fine. Fort Sumter was attacked by gunboats and the *Monitor* sent forth shot and shell; Fort Fisher was captured and set in flames; our army and navy and the names of Grant, Sherman, Farragut, and Porter in letters of fire, showering balls from every letter; a figure of victory with Savannah, Charleston, Wilmington, etc., on her shield; the Arms of New York, and stars, wheels, trees, fountains, snakes, rockets, etc., etc., numberless—whilst from the upturned faces of the crowd came a roar of delight.

We read this morning the account of Andy Johnson's drunken speech in the Senate on taking the oath of office. He walked up and down saying that he was a plebeian; our president was a plebeian; the people were all [plebeians]. "You owe everything to the plebeians," etc., etc., thrusting out his fist almost into the faces of the diplomatic corps. It will be a great scandal; perhaps it may cause a reaction. The inauguration ball was likewise more like an orgy than anything else. Lincoln's inauguration address was like a sermon—Beecher and Lincoln, as some papers said, having swapped places.

Vice President-elect Andrew Johnson was just recovering from a serious illness when the inaugural rolled around on March 4. He also had a bad cold and was suffering from exhaustion and shaky nerves. That morning, he attended a stag party given by Colonel John W. Forney at his chambers on Capitol Hill, and took three glasses of whisky to steady his nerves. Normally a very temperate man, and certainly not a person addicted to whisky, Johnson became drunk. When he entered the overheated and already crowded Senate Chamber shortly before twelve noon, the whisky, the heat, and his illness turned his face crimson.

Led to the podium by Hannibal Hamlin, Johnson began a long and confused harangue which embarrassed everyone present. He dwelt upon his lowly origin, lectured the assemblage on his patriotism, and indulged in gibberish which evoked expressions of dismay from cabinet officers and Supreme Court justices alike. Finally the humiliating diatribe came to an end with the Vice President bawling, "I kiss this Book [the Bible] in the face of my nation of the United States."

After Johnson was sworn in as Vice President, Abraham Lincoln delivered his famous address, "With malice toward none; with charity for all . . . let us strive on to finish the work we are in; to bind up the nation's wounds . . . to do all which may achieve and cherish a just and lasting peace."

Johnson's much-publicized intemperance at the inaugural
cost him dearly when he began to have difficulties with the
Radical Republicans once he was President. Men like Charles
Sumner were not averse to indulging in whispering campaigns
designed to misconstrue Johnson's frequent intemperance of
speech as drunkenness. Although the charge was not true, the
damage to Johnson's prestige was the same as if it had been.

On Sunday, when the Judge came from the committee, he told me that a reporter there, on hearing the resolutions read, said: "Those are the views of Judge Daly. I read a speech of his whilst I was a prisoner in Macon, which was more convincing to me than anything I have seen before or since about the necessity for carrying out this war. It was an argument drawn from the physical geography of this country. It was published in the Macon paper with an editorial to the effect that these were the views of a prominent Northern Democrat and one who had always been on that side. It showed, therefore, how little the South could hope for any sympathy from the Democratic party at the North." . . .

March 10, 1865

Judge Pierrepont joined us this morning as we were walking up Broadway. He was full of virtuous principle and virtuous indignation at the manner in which our rights were outraged at Colonel Baker[11] arresting honest, inoffensive men,

---

[11] Lafayette Curry Baker (1826–1868) came to Washington, D.C., shortly after the outbreak of the Civil War and was engaged almost at once by General Winfield Scott for secret service work. Such feats as slipping through the Confederate lines to Richmond, obtaining important information, and returning safely to Washington resulted in his appointment in 1862 as special provost marshal of the War Department. In 1865, he was promoted to the rank of brigadier general, and it was he who planned and led the operation which resulted in the trapping of John Wilkes Booth. President Johnson dismissed him for operating a spy system in the White House, whereupon he retired and wrote *History of the United States Secret Service* (1867).

sending them in chains to Washington, etc., etc. Colonel Baker, he said, was a notorious scoundrel, well known in California. We had been congratulating ourselves that he was getting hold of these bounty-jumpers and public thieves. Why was the honorable Edwards Pierrepont so eloquent upon the abuses of the government? Was he acquainted with any of these honest men?

March 12, 1865

The city is much exercised over this shameful trial, the "Strong Divorce Suit." Poor Peter Strong, the plaintiff, is much to be pitied, and has, I believe, done what he could to keep his grief a secret, but his wife and her relations seem utterly shameless. The scandal is all the greater that Mrs. Strong and her paramour, Edward Strong, were both communicants of the church and all this wickedness went on coming or going to evening church. It is most horrible. The Stevenses seem determined to brazen it out. They go everywhere and even entertain company at home instead of bending with true show of humility to this terrible chastisement until at least this scandal is somewhat forgotten.

March 26, 1865

Had a visit a few days ago from General Barlow. He had poor Arabella's ring on his finger. He will now marry some young woman who will share his glory and prosperity. Poor Belle, how little I ever thought of so short a life for one so full of energy, so untiring.

I have just heard that Booth is engaged or half-engaged (that is, the parents know nothing about it) to a young lady of good family in this city. He too was inconsolable, and held spiritual conversations through mediums.[12] Alas, how slight is human

---

[12] Edwin Booth's wife, Mary Devlin Booth, died suddenly and unexpectedly on February 9, 1863.

love. What a suggestion to us women to place our affections upon things above! I always felt this, but I succumbed, like all the rest of my sex, to that weakness of our sex "to be loved best," to be first with one and to devote ourselves. Women, however, are not in this country to be outdone in inconstancy, though fashioned marriages seem to me a most immodest and extraordinary thing for a woman. Few seem to agree with me. . . .

Events seem hastening on to end this rebellion. Victories every day, and all our neutral friends are coming to shake hands with us on our success. How much the Union men at the South have suffered! Governor [William] Aiken [South Carolina], like Mr. Petigru, held out against them and they had too much respect for him to confiscate his property. He has freed his Negroes and set them to work for wages. One man has had his country house burned and a trench carried through his dwelling house in Atlanta by Sherman's order. "But I do not complain," he said. "It was unavoidable. I saw it all when those benighted people acted as they did, and I told them so. I was among them, and I must share the calamity they have brought upon us all. I do not complain."

Booth has played Hamlet a hundred nights to crowded houses, and they are going to present him with a Hamlet medal, which the Judge is asked to present. All the women are crazy about him. He is, as Stewart, the manager of the Winter Garden, said, "so silent and dark and Gawain-looking and so delightfully indifferent and so distressed (I might add, 'so they think') for the loss of his wife that each and every one would like to do something to console him." He would lose half his popularity if they had heard what I heard this evening of his new love. I believe I have too much reason ever to be amiable or interesting. I hate to do interesting and romantic things. Two girls came to ask me if we would not go with them to the theater, and then Judge Daly go and get Booth to come and talk with them in the box, as they saw him with Mrs. Murray and Mrs. Hoyt. I never could consent to pay a man so great a compliment. Yet, to be popular with men, you must flatter them. The Judge often tells me that I would rather say some severe little thing that would prick or sting than do anything else. It is a most unamiable trait which I will try to conquer, as it may even alarm the vanity of personal friends. I like satirical people, and do not care if I am attacked, so it be done well and not maliciously.

Stewart, the manager of the Winter Garden, told us today that Booth was engaged to a young lady of good family and fortune in Philadelphia. He likewise told us several amusing stories. Among other things, President Lincoln thinks that as he carried on this war so finely and got us through, as he says, he ought to have another four years. He thinks that General Washington (to whom he seems to think himself quite equal) would have run again if he had a chance.

March 30, 1865

Mrs. Young has reached Charleston. She gives in her letters a mournful account of the state of the city; not a pane of glass in the windows; the houses burnt, torn down, or battered by the cannon; no whites to be seen—only a few blacks hovering around to see if anything would turn up for them to do; [Confederate] General [Jeremy F.] Gilmer (despite the letters) showed her, she says, scant courtesy. Mrs. Petigru and Mrs. King had been given a house in which Mrs. Young was staying. They give a dreadful account of their privations. They were reduced to a cracker apiece for dinner and some cornmeal and no meat. Sometimes as a great treat, they would get once or twice a week a small bit of fat bacon.

General Lee's army had been besieged by Grant at Peters-
burg since the summer of 1864, but the Confederates had been
able to hold out only because the Union did not control the

railroad lines west and southwest of Richmond and Petersburg and supplies continued to enter Petersburg in ever-diminishing amounts. Now, however, with Sherman's army rapidly approaching from the south, Lee realized that he would have to break out of Petersburg or be completely cut off and surrounded.

On March 25, Lee attacked Fort Steadman to the east of Petersburg, but his 50,000 troops were no match for Grant's 115,000, and he was beaten back. On April 1, Sheridan engaged the Confederates at Five Forks, southwest of Richmond, and defeated them decisively. The next day, Lee quit Petersburg and headed for Lynchburg, where he hoped to remove his army to North Carolina by rail and join forces with Johnston. Sheridan was too fast for him, for in capturing the railroad junction at Burkesville, he cut off Lee's retreat by rail and stood as a formidable obstacle to a Confederate westward march.

Surrounded, out of supplies, and reduced in number to some 30,000 men, Lee's army had little choice except a final surrender. On April 7, General Grant sent Lee a message requesting his surrender and Lee replied with a request for terms.

April 2, 1865

Today comes news of the taking of three brigades by Sheridan. All the army is in motion and there has been fighting these three days at the front. Lee must either break through our lines or surrender. . . .

April 5, 1865

Richmond is ours! Lee is retreating! 28 locomotives, all his guns, and 25,000 prisoners taken—his line of retreat strewn with arms, knapsacks, etc., thrown down! It [Richmond] was entered on Sunday last, the 2nd, by General [Godfrey] Weitzel, whose command is mostly Negro troops. Phil has been actively engaged, as the Ninth Corps have taken Petersburg. The streets are brilliant with flags. On Saturday when the news came, there was an impromptu meeting in Wall Street. All business adjourned, a few speeches, and then the multitude sang the Doxology and the 100th Psalm in Wall Street, the seat of the money-changers; it was a good augury. When I got the extra containing the great news, the tears rushed to my eyes, my heart to my throat. I could not speak. A few days more, and God be praised, it would seem as though this great trouble will be past. There will be a day of thanksgiving appointed and peace will descend upon the land. May God's blessing come with it and make us less a money-loving, selfish, and self-sufficient people, purified by this great trial.

Sheridan is a splendid officer; what good deeds he has done! Captain Coppinger will tell us about him when he returns.

April 8, 1865

Captures and victories every day! Lee is so surrounded that he must either disband his army or surrender. Grant at last reaps the reward of his long, patient waiting. Jeff Davis received the news in church that the left flank of the rebels had been turned by Sheridan and that the city must be evacuated. He decamped forthwith, his wife having left the Saturday before for Galveston (showing where the rebels hoped to go). Lincoln writes dispatches from Jeff Davis' house in Richmond.

A young woman here of eighteen is lecturing before large audiences upon reconstruction—another Joan of Arc inspired by self-conceit versus patriotism! I suppose she, fired by Miss Dickinson's success, wishes to make a nice little sum by giving advice. Advice worth nothing is generally given gratis. These young Yankee ladies are sharp enough to charge for it. What fools people are to go and listen! . . .

The Capitol at Richmond is uninjured and that fine statue of Washington by Houdon, therefore, which gave me so much satisfaction, still exists. When six years ago I stood beside it, how little did we anticipate the dire events so soon to take place. . . . The White Sulphur Springs are in ruins, and so are the dwellings and the fortunes of those we met there. Poor Mary Lincoln; I wonder where she now is and how she lives. What a change!

April 9, 1865

The Judge is busy upon some important law business which will take him to Washington. Mr. Evarts told him that no man could go to Washington that would have more confidence with the President, for that he [the President] had not only a high opinion of his [the Judge's] abilities as evinced in the case of the privateers in the beginning and in the Trent Affair, but likewise the greatest confidence in his integrity. Mr. Ashburne, Mr. Davis, and Mr. Bernheimer have all been here this morning to talk the matter over. I am not to know it as it is a secret. It is better, and I am not curious.

I have forgotten to mention a visit we paid to Ward Beecher. The Judge was obliged to go to his house on some business, so I went with him. It was Sunday and communion day, so we waited until he came from church, which he did, opening the door with a "Hurrah, hurrah," flinging down his hat, rushing at his little baby grandson, not knowing any stranger was in the house. Truly muscular Christianity! Beecher is no hypocrite; thoroughly wise, however, in his own conceit and confident of his own ability to direct the universe. He would not speak at the meeting, he said, because the cause was doing well enough. "Call me up only on some forlorn hope, some utopian unpopular project" (as I could not but think most men do the Almighty). When everything human fails, they seek the supernatural.

Mr. Davis is to be married on the 26th. I shall send a pair of bronzes.

In the exchange of notes between Grant and Lee, the Confederate chieftain realized that only a total capitulation would satisfy the enemy, but he could not indulge in further and futile dissipation of his already exhausted and shrunken army. Unconditional surrender was the only recourse, and when Grant arranged a rendezvous for the village of Appomattox Courthouse on April 9, Lee commented, "There is nothing left me but to go and see General Grant, and I would rather die a thousand deaths."

Lee arrived first at the little house on the outskirts of town, and shortly after noon Grant and Sheridan entered. After a polite exchange, Grant sat down and wrote out terms which Lee had not expected, terms influenced by Lincoln's policy of "malice toward none." Confederate officers, as well as troops, were paroled with the promise that they would not again serve against the United States of America; military stores and arms were to be surrendered, but officers were allowed to keep their side arms; all Confederate soldiers were to be allowed to keep their privately owned horses and mules. When Lee read of these provisions, he commented that the side arms concession would have "a happy effect" upon his troops.

Even more merciful than all this was Grant's order that rations for twenty-five thousand men be immediately sent to Lee's starving soldiers. Thus was begun a policy of charity and mercy toward the vanquished which would soon be obliterated, upon the demise of its author.

The small Confederate armies under Johnston and Kirby Smith surrendered shortly thereafter on the same terms that Lee had accepted, and on May 10, 1865, Jefferson Davis was captured. Thus ended the Confederate States of America.

April 10, 1865

Last night at midnight we heard an extra called. The Judge rushed to the door, "Surrender of Lee's army, ten cents and no mistake," said the boy all in one breath (a true young American). It was Palm Sunday, and hosanna may we well

cry! Glory be to God on high; the rebellion is ended! Phil,
my brother, is uninjured, and peace soon to descend to bless
the land again.

Lee surrendered to Grant. The officers and privates [are]
to be allowed to go to their homes on their parole, not to be
disturbed by the U.S. government so long as they keep the
peace and behave as loyal citizens. I hope the animosity that has
so long reigned will now pass away. May God comfort and
change the hearts of our so long vindictive foes! They will
have much to suffer for their folly and ambition.

Mr. Harris spent last evening with us. He says we must give
a general amnesty—even let Jeff Davis go. If we execute him,
we should make him a martyr. Let him go and he is only a
miserable failure whom no one will care for, from whom we
shall have nothing to fear. Mr. Harris has always something
interesting to tell us. Last evening he described scenes he had
witnessed in Siam. He must have great powers of adaptation.

A Western man said, speaking of the Union victories and
our indifference hereafter to public opinion in Europe, "The
United States," said he, "will now be bounded by the Atlantic,
the Pacific, and the Aurora Borealis."

*President Lincoln had been warned of threats upon his life
since before his first inaugural, and the only one he took seriously was on the occasion of his entry into Washington following his election. With a feeling of personal shame, he allowed the Pinkerton guards to spirit him through Baltimore and
into Washington like a fugitive. He vowed that such a thing
would not happen again, despite the innumerable rumors of
threats upon his life throughout the war years.*

*Secretary of War Stanton had advance word of the attempt
upon Lincoln's life on the night he was murdered, but he could
not get the President to accept his offer of a heavier guard.
After all, Lincoln had visited the enemy capital, Richmond, on
April 5, and had returned safely.*

The play was Our American Cousin, *and the President was*

not in his lace-and-flag-decorated box at the Ford Theater in Washington when the curtain went up at eight o'clock. At 8:10, Lincoln took leave of his callers, and by 8:30 he entered his box. At 10:15, John Wilkes Booth—hardly a suspicious figure around Washington, or in the theater in which he acted so often—shot the President, jumped to the stage, and escaped from the theater. Lincoln's unconscious body was removed to a lodging house across from the theater, and he died there at 7:30 the following morning, April 15. By 11:00 A.M., Andrew Johnson had been sworn into office as the new President of the United States.

That same evening, and at approximately the same time, one Lewis Powell (alias Payne), a fellow conspirator of Booth, entered the house of the ailing Secretary Seward, forced himself past a protesting servant, and slashed the throat and face of the sick man in his bed. On his way out of the house, Powell managed to cut everyone who tried to intercept him. Seward survived the attack.

Booth had planned the simultaneous assassination of others in high office, but for one reason or other the murders did not come off. Booth himself escaped to Virginia, but was trapped in a barn near Bowling Green on April 26. The barn was set on fire, and Booth either shot himself or was hit by a bullet from the gun of one of his pursuers. Nine others were implicated in the plot. Four of them were hanged on the 7th of July; four were sent to prison, and one was acquitted—John H. Surratt.

April 15, 1865

What dreadful news! President Lincoln assassinated; Secretary Seward's throat cut! Just as we were rejoicing over the return of peace, everything once again in confusion. Poor Lincoln! The Judge is in Washington. He left on the twelfth, and fortunately dined out yesterday in company with Sir Frederick Bruce, the new English minister, and Senator Sumner. He was not, therefore, in the theater. The President was shot through the head through the door of his box. The assassin jumped on the stage and escaped, crying, "*Sic semper tyrannis!*" The assassin is supposed to have been J. Wilkes Booth. The assassin of Secretary Seward (for he is dangerously wounded), forced his way in, saying he had a prescription from the physician, and under pretence of showing it, cut his [Seward's] throat from ear to ear. The Secretary is old already, weakened from having broken his arm; he will scarcely survive. God save us all. What may not a day bring forth!

April 19, 1865

Had letters from the Judge. The last thing the poor President did was to write on a card an order to admit him and Mr. Ashburne on Saturday morning. The Judge dined on Friday with Sir Frederick Bruce, Mr. Geoffre, the French minister, and Mr. Raasloff, at Baron Gerolt's (where he, the Judge, is staying), and as they did not separate until late, he heard nothing of the dreadful news until he went with his papers to see the President at the hour appointed. The shock was very great, he writes; all were paralyzed.

Booth is not yet caught, but it is said it will be impossible for him to escape. Several arrests of men in female attire have been made. It would seem that it is a plot in which many are inculpated. It will make a martyr of Abraham Lincoln, whose death will make all the shortcomings of his life and Presidential career forgotten in, as Shakespeare says, "the deep damnation of his taking off." People had been arrested in the streets only for saying, "Pity it had not been done before," and the Loyal Leaguers are in a furious state of patriotism. The houses are all draped in mourning, each house striving to outdo the other.

Easter morning, instead of the Resurrection and Christ has Arisen, the clergymen began with Abraham Lincoln, mentioning that he was sacrificed on Good Friday, and it seemed to me that they gave Our Lord only the second place in his own house. I suppose that I would do as much for the country as anyone. I was the first to give a flag to any regiment, but I must feel that all the glory of our success must be ascribed to God alone, who makes use of the foolish things of this world to confound the wise and the weak things of the world to bring to naught those who are mighty. The poor rail-splitter, who in these four years of severe schooling had at last learned that only a military man could carry on military operations; whose vanity and self-sufficiency lost us Chancellorsville and Fredericksburg; whose political jealousy kept one of our ablest generals unemployed for two years and at last sent him to Europe because nothing could be given him to do on this continent; whose indecent speeches and stories made him and the nation a byword; whose weakness allowed unlimited plunder by those around him, even members of his own family; whose undignified haste in going to Richmond in the rear of a conquering army and placing himself in the seat, still warm, of Jefferson Davis, sending for Mrs. Lincoln and receiving the visits of his rebellious subjects, was the regret of all noble-minded people! All this will be forgotten in this shameful, cowardly act of his assassination, whilst his heart was full of forgiveness of his enemies, and whilst he was planning for the good of all, having only now just begun to understand the work which four years ago the *South*, by their rebellion, by their desertion of the Democrats of the North, thrust upon him. For it was the rejection of Douglas by the Charleston Convention four years ago that elected Abraham Lincoln and Jefferson Davis, and it was not any fault in Abraham Lincoln. Nor can we blame him that when elected by a legal majority, he accepted the Presidency. Every American feels competent for any place. It is a wise man indeed who feels that he knows but little, and as President of the United States, his government as that of right and law was the one to be sustained by all lovers of their country. As the old proverb says, "God still lives, and the present [is] exaggerated."

We have, as a nation, a very low estimate of merit; so low a one that it is not difficult for many to attain to. Were the standard higher, we would have wiser men and more able rulers and not political trucksters to run the machine of government with the intent to make for themselves so much percent out of the business.

From April 15 until Lincoln's burial in Springfield, Illinois, on May 4, the nation was in mourning. The President's body lay in state for seven days at the capital, first at the White House and then in the Capitol. From there, it went to Union Station to be placed on a train bound for Springfield, along the circuitous route which touched New York City.

When the funeral train reached New York, business came to a standstill and the whole city appeared subdued. Quiet and orderly crowds gathered to pay their respects or satisfy their curiosity, many colored people among them. Before the train continued on its 1,600-mile journey to Springfield, even Mrs. Daly was infected by the universal sorrow—at least temporarily.

Sorrow over the President's death soon turned into rage against the South, however, and the diarist fell into this mood along with most Northerners. Insofar as the Radical Republicans were concerned, fate could not have dealt them a better hand. Not only had a difficult chief executive been removed from the path they wished to take, but the stage was set for a vindictive policy toward the Confederacy. Though Mrs. Daly was far removed from being a Radical Republican, she shared many of their attitudes toward the South and reconstruction.

April 25, 1865

Today President Lincoln's funeral procession passes through the city. The body lies in state in City Hall and some three hundred thousand people, they say, have visited it. I shall not go out to see the show, as the Judge is not at home. I will let the servants go instead; I am sick of pageants. Both yesterday and today all business has been suspended and I read that the

25th of May is to be another fast day. Poor Mrs. Lincoln! Circumstances, verily, make the man. A house a few doors nearer Fifth Avenue opposite to us, having not been put in mourning, was tarred and for two days men have been at work at it. Tomorrow the theaters reopen and then, I suppose, all will be over.

I am very anxious to see the Judge to know what all these reports about and against Sherman mean. He is a Democrat and has many rivals, but I cannot think that after his great deeds he can have been in any way a sympathizer with the South.[13]

The Judge has succeeded in getting Captain Nolan a furlough. He has been twenty-two months in Southern prisons, he said modestly. As he had suffered, he did not like to enlarge upon their sufferings, but [he said] that no account that we had read could give us any idea of them; that he was enabled to draw his pay through underground ways, else he would not have been alive; that five pints of meal and one of molasses were the rations for five days; that they were recklessly shot at by their guards, insulted, and pinched with cold, their garments taken, and in every way [they were] barbarously used. The captain is a young Irishman who held a lieutenancy in the British army. He sold it for the support of sisters and came here with just enough to support him until he could get some appointment. Before he did, he spent all, and the Judge assisted him in getting his outfit and lieutenancy in a cavalry regiment.

Mrs. Young tells me that we have no idea of the destitution of the South; that most of the men (even the Union men) were driven into the Confederate Army because their families would else have starved, and told me several heart-rending examples in cases of our own acquaintance.

---

13 After Lee's surrender, Joseph E. Johnston asked terms of Sherman, whom he had been fighting in North Carolina. Sherman's terms of surrender were so generous that many Northerners were indignant at his "softness" toward the recent enemy.

April 26, 1865

I did go yesterday to see the procession, and it was most imposing. It brought to mind Gray's "Elegy." How little did Lincoln dream of such an end when he used every possible engine of power and influence to secure his reelection, and how little did the friends of McClellan dream that they should ever have felt so much interest in him and so mourn his untimely and cruel death. The catafalque was drawn by sixteen white horses, caparisoned in black to their feet, adorned with silver wreaths, crosses, and festoons of natural flowers; General Scott and the foreign consuls, judiciary and city councilmen, etc., in open carriages, three abreast; a fine show of military trailing their arms. Very fine dirge music, and fifty thousand men of different societies, clubs, etc., and a few colored soldiers with "Abraham Lincoln, Our Liberator," etc., on their breasts, guarded by a police force (because the City Council opposed their joining the procession), marched. It was very, very sorrowful.

An old clergyman at the house began talking politics, abusing General Sherman, who, although he may have transcended his powers, certainly had no sympathy with the Southern cause which he had done so much to destroy. Although these radicals and Christians did not scruple to assert, the Judge writes me that the clergymen, the women, and particularly religious people were the most vindictive and unrelenting of the population. . . .

April 30, 1865

The Judge returned last night after an absence of twenty days. He has had a most interesting visit to Richmond and the different places of interest in its vicinity. He has sent me a very full account of it in his letters, which I have marked and put aside. They will be very interesting hereafter. He will have seen the last of this war as he saw its beginning, the year we were together in Washington, the year I began this diary.

Mr. Harris came in last evening. The Judge related to him some of the things he had seen. He feels that these people have still to be taught humility. They must be convinced that they have been guilty of a crime and not be allowed to feel that they are heroes and martyrs. He said the Confederate parole officers of Lee's army thronged the Spottswood house in their Confederate uniforms as haughty as though they had not been worsted, and that our men almost felt that they were the intruders. An order was issued, however, that they should leave that hotel and go to an inferior one, and since then they have been ordered to take off their uniforms.

A gentleman on the boat offered to introduce the Judge to General Lee, but the Judge refused, saying he did not consider him a man of honor. "Not Robert Lee?" said the indignant Virginian. "I thought everyone thought well of him, whatever his views were of the Cause. I should like to know your reasons." "Well, then," said the Judge, "I will give you them. Six days before he left for Virginia he said that nothing would induce him to desert the United States flag, that he owed everything and all that he was to the United States. He was adjutant general, and in the confidence of General Scott, who believed him." "Well, sir," said the Virginian, "perhaps he changed his mind." The Judge answered ironically, "Perhaps. That would be no compliment to his intellect." He is in Richmond subsisting upon United States rations. What a future for a descendant of Washington!

Booth was tracked, found in a barn, and on his refusal to surrender and attempting to fire [his gun], the barn was set on fire and Booth, attempting to escape, was shot through the head. His last words were that he had done it for the good of his country. Poor, mistaken young man! He killed the best friend of the benighted Southern people. The plot will soon be discovered. It was to assassinate all the heads of the departments;

a fiendish scheme! Poor Edwin Booth is ruined by his brother's
act. His engagement of marriage is broken, his future as an
actor blasted. Many go as far as to declare he should never
again appear, and that he should suffer for his brother's fault.
I said that he suffered doubly already, first as much as any of us,
as a loyal American citizen, and secondly as a son and brother.
I thought nothing should be added. The melancholy Dane: he
will look and act more naturally than ever! This blow has
fallen upon him in the height of his fame.

The Judge has come home with a strong feeling against an
aristocracy. He says nothing of that kind can be tolerated in
this country when he saw how infinitely superior the rank and
file of our army were in spirit and feeling to the Southern
gentry, and how selfish their Northern representatives were
among us, etc. I hear Mrs. Detmold say in the hall, "This country will never be settled whilst anybody has a grandfather."

Among the few Union women were a Mrs. Van Lew, who
stood up valiantly and was ostracized. She had nothing to do
but attend to our prisoners. The gentlemen mean to send her
a flag. "Will you indeed remember it?" said she. "You cannot
tell what it is to me to feel that anyone has sympathy with me,
for it has been so long since any has been shown me. It brings
the tears to my eyes, you see, gentlemen."

Grant's last act of magnanimity in giving Sherman all the
credit of Johnston's surrender, ignoring himself, has won him
the admiration of all. Mr. Harris has a sword of honor presented to him by the Tycoon which he has always intended to
present to whomever should prove the greatest man in this war.
This last act has, he says, decided the question.

May 5, 1865

In the papers today is a telegraphic communication to
the effect that a price has been set upon the head of Jeff Davis
and several Confederate leaders, charging them with inciting,

plotting, and encouraging this assassination. It would seem too dreadful a thing to credit to any American, unless a savage, in this century, but as Baron Gerolt says (who is staying with us), "A man is only the outward case of some animal and a desperate, disappointed, ambitious, selfish schemer, goaded by his utter failure and blinded by incessant churchgoing and unpractical religious profession. What may not Satan tempt him to do!" It is said they have found proof enough to convict them upon the body of Booth.

Went to the Academy of Design (although it lacks some of the effect produced by the lights) the evening of the opening on Thursday a week ago. The light is admirable for the pictures. The building is very tasteful, Venetian style, but it wants an open space around it and a lake to admire itself in. The evening of the opening it had a beautiful fairy effect, its fine marble stairway and the door opening upon another broad marble stairway leading to the galleries, brilliantly lighted, with well-dressed women ascending and descending. Bierstadt took charge of me as the Judge was still away. Bierstadt has two beautiful pictures there, "The Yosemite Valley" and a marine piece, "The Golden Gate at San Francisco." I met a great many acquaintances.

May 6, 1865

Baron Gerolt, who came the day before the Judge's arrival, left us today. Consequently, we have seen a good deal of company.

Last evening, a merchant from Savannah came to get the Judge to take his affidavit about some cotton taken by the government. He had had hard work to keep out of the Confederate Army. He had been a great deal older, he said, jocosely, some months ago. He was not quite so old now. They suffered very much, for food and necessaries. He looked like an honest old fellow. Mr. Bernheimer, who came with him, brought us some information about Bedford Springs, where we propose going this summer, and we hope to get rooms in a private house about a mile from the town.

On Sunday evening, April 2, Jefferson Davis and most of his cabinet departed by train to Danville, leaving the capital of Richmond to fall into the hands of the enemy. The next day, Union troops under General Weitzel occupied Richmond, much of downtown Richmond was destroyed by fire, the city was placed under martial law, and Weitzel occupied the mansion just vacated by Davis.

After a week at Danville, Davis made his way further South, and on the 10th of May he was captured by Federal cavalry in Georgia. From here he was removed to Fort Monroe, where he spent the early part of his two-year imprisonment in chains. Soon his health began to suffer from the close confinement, the chains were removed, he was given better quarters in Carroll Hall at the fort, and his wife, his attorneys, and physician John J. Craven were allowed to visit him.

At the conclusion of his period of imprisonment at the fort, Davis was handed over to civilian authorities. He was indicted for treason, but was released on bail of $100,000 and never came to trial. The reason for the continuous delays was that the courts could not agree upon the matter of jurisdiction, and finally the case was dismissed by the general amnesty which President Johnson issued in December of 1868. Davis spent the last two years of his life on a Mississippi country estate writing his two-volume The Rise and Fall of the Confederate Government.

May 15, 1865

Yesterday came the news of the capture of Jefferson Davis. He was surprised and first attempted to escape in one of his wife's dresses to the woods, but his boots, which he had forgotten to take off or to hide with a sufficiently long petticoat, betrayed him. He did not show any dignity, said he thought the United States government too humane to hunt women and children (as though his female attire had made him a woman!), and Mrs. Jeff said they had better not irritate the President—he might hurt some of them! Poor wretch! I have no sympathy with his cause nor his ambition, but I cannot but feel sorry for him. What torture of mind he will suffer until his end comes! The death of a traitor, though it may not be proven that he sanctioned the death of poor President Lincoln.

The Judge is busy writing an address to the graduating class at the law school. It is to be the "History of the Common Law." It reads to me very well. He has as usual left himself very little time in which to prepare it. I always fear for him when he works so hard.

Had Mr. Lincoln lived, the Judge would have succeeded in the business that took him to Washington. Lincoln told Mr. Evarts that he had the greatest respect for Judge Daly, first as a man of strictest integrity and reliability, and next as a lawyer, for the government had been much indebted to him in two cases, in the matter of the privateers, delivering them from a great embarrassment, and in the Trent business.

Phil is engaged to Pauline Hecksher. I was very sorry not to see her this morning when she called. I think we shall like her very much. I'm glad Phil is engaged. Now that he has left the army, he would have felt restless and unsettled.

June 2, 1865

The Judge has been away again in Washington. He saw the great review of the Army of the Potomac and Sherman's army. It must have been a magnificent, spirit-stirring sight. He enjoyed himself very much and wrote me a long and eloquent account. He made the acquaintance of General Sherman and General Phil Sheridan, both, like Grant, men of great simplicity and sincerity. Sheridan has a splendid face and Sherman looks like a man who did not easily forget; he has a strong fighting face. He [the Judge] likewise saw much of Sir Frederick

Bruce, the British minister. They seem to have taken a mutual fancy to each other.

The spring has gone very fast. The roses and strawberries have come and I do not seem to be ready for summer and for the country. . . .

Extract from a passage from the diary of Mrs. Van Lew, a native Richmond lady, one of few in that city who sympathized with the North, who visited our prisoners and who dared to brave the insults and the ostracism of her fellow citizens and friends in this exercise of Christian charity and patriotism:

Richmond, February 27, 1864: Never shall I forget my visit this day to Belle Isle. It surpassed in wretchedness and squalid filth my most vivid imagination. The long lines of forsaken, despairing, hopeless-looking beings, who, within this hollow square, looked upon us, gaunt hunger staring from their sunken eyes. The crowds within this little space, the wretched, smoky, tattered tents, the holes in the ground, and men lying on the ground, some without a thing over or under them, some picking the vermin off their legs, some looking for them in their clothing, and the prospect to render doubly wretched their wretchedness, within a few, very few steps, the entire length on one side, the newly made graves of their late companions, separated only from them by this low embankment and the walk. Oh, ground of unopened graves, how the eye of hope grows dim and the heartbreaks look on you, for this month-extended, hope deferred, despairing prison house! Oh weary, longing, dying eyes—day of deliverance, will you never come? It may be brave to meet death on the battlefield, but months and weeks and days of dying, a forgotten, uncared for unit of a mighty nation! Surely this is the test of bravery and patriotism! Oh what a test to put bravery and patriotism to! Surely this ought not to be! Hear them! Rouse up, ye men that are at ease, ye who are mighty with your eloquence, ye who are mighty with your intellect, ye who are mighty with your money, ye who are mighty with the youth and strength which God has given you! We think of, we look to you all! Let each do something. Oh put each one something—if you have only a mite—in the glorious army to redeem us from death! Oh think of our prison, such a prison as you could never dream of, among a people practiced in prisons; aye, slave prisons and jails of the most loathesome and degraded character! Prison houses, in which no eye of justice but God's ever looks, always full of innocent victims, sold for convenience, for avarice, for lust. Oh God, hast Thou forsaken us that we are abandoned to the merciless, pitiless tyranny of such a people? The singled few of millions, the martyrs for this glorious cause! I had but an outside view under strict surveillance; what must the inside be!

June 18, 1865

Edwin Booth dined with us on Thursday. His face is much finer than I thought it. His manner is refined, his bearing gentlemanly, and his conversation that of a cultivated man. He speaks very pure grammatical English and uses no slang.

I heard today McClellan was the author of the project of emancipation as a war policy. He spoke of it to Mr. Lincoln when on a visit to headquarters, who thought it worth his while to publish it as a proclamation.

Left home for Bedford Springs in company with the Judge and Mr. Townsend Harris.

July 10, 1865

We had a delightful journey by the New Jersey Central to Harrisburg. From Harrisburg we went to Huntington, thence by the Broad Top Railroad to Bedford. The latter railroad looks most dangerous, being carried over valleys and across mountain streams on wooden trestles. [Over the] Juniata [River], the trestlework is 86 feet high and 250 feet long. We found ourselves most comfortably lodged in a brick farm house belonging to Mr. William Cheneworth, who owns 200 acres of beautiful bottom land watered by a branch of the Juniata. The scenery was exquisite, the view just below the house where the river runs through a gap as beautiful as any landscape I ever saw, the walks romantic, the country sparsely inhabited, but by a very kindly people, some of whom still speak Pennsylvania Dutch. Mr. Townsend Harris we found a most delightful companion. . . .

After a week or two, the house was invaded by a Confederate Navy officer, his wife and two sons. He had been with Mosby. We had to define our position, and Mrs. McBlair was at first disposed to be quarrelsome. She was very violent. She would say she hated to be an American citizen: "Who could ever wish to be an American?" Mr. Harris would answer, taking off his hat with courtly grace, "Madam, I never was so proud of my country as now." And the Judge would say deprecatingly, "You must not hope for us to agree with you. What other nationality can be compared to ours?" She would argue with me and would maintain that the South was justified in all its barbarities because the Yankees were the invaders of *their* country. I said that was the new gospel, I heard it often preached North as South, and as a Christian woman I could not but grieve and feel ashamed to think how by women even the old adage, "Love your enemies; do good to those that hate you," etc., had been overlooked, that it was the part of women to soften men's passions, not inflame them, etc. Poor lady, I thought her very foolish and irrational, though quick of apprehension and affectionate. She thought [me] "a person without prejudice, without character," and was constantly saying crude things. The highest compliment she could pay me, she thought, was to say that no one would ever take me for an American woman, either in look or manner. We grew, however, to be good friends.

An aunt of hers, Miss Eckleburger, came later. She was a good Union woman whom we liked very much. The Judge sang old English songs in the evening which greatly delighted her. She told me she thought my husband one of the most delightful men she had ever met. We parted at last with regret, she insisting upon my accepting a gold thimble, saying we might never meet again in this world. She was past sixty years of age, but most intelligent, accomplished and witty and a perfect lady. . . .

We were seven weeks at Mr. Cheneworth's, went several times to Bedford Springs proper, which was once so fashionable a place of resort and now much frequented in June and July by Philadelphians and Baltimorians, a rambling collection of houses, reminding me of the Virginia Springs. The people were generally Southern sympathizers, the county being settled principally from Virginia and Maryland.

The Judge and Mr. Harris played innumerable games of old sledge and I played bezique and euchre at night with the Confederate captain, who was a very gentlemanly, reasonable, amiable man. One of the sons was a *cub* of 17, the other a promising boy of 15. Both had been with Mosby just before we left Bedford. We (Confederates and all) went to a harvest home dinner in the great farm wagon over roads which in our neighborhood would be thought impracticable.

We returned home by way of Altoona, which we reached after a break-back drive over the beds of torrents, so the roads seemed, of twelve hours. From Altoona we took the railroad to Harrisburg, where we drove around the environs, admiring its beautiful position on the Susquehannah and the comfortable-looking dwellings in the street facing the river. The Judge met a brother of Dr. Dewitt, a clergyman in Harrisburg, sweeping his doorway. He and Mr. Harris paid him a visit.

On our return we went to West Farms. Was shocked to find Father so unwell and concerned about having to go to Phil's wedding. He seemed overjoyed to see us again. . . .

Went to Orange to see Phil married. The bride looked very

lovely, dignified, and serious. She is a winsome little thing. The Judge and I devoted ourselves to Father. Went down and came back with him. He would not go back to the country. [We] kept him [with us] in Laight Street over a fortnight, when I had to dragoon Rosalie and the rest in town to take care of him. I did not see why he should be at double expense, especially as all had the fever and ague. . . .

October 15, 1865

Badeau came in on Sunday night. He has some absurd ideas of the value of blood, which we combated. He appealed to various examples. In this country, everyone, anyone may boast of even noble descent, as many younger sons of noble houses are now among our farmers, mechanics, etc. We instanced an example near us at West Farms [and] the Judge's own case. The O'Dalys were the Irish tribe from whence the Feni (the judges) were always taken. The chief of the O'Dalys was always the chief judge. His family [is] the same as that of Sir Dominick Daly. Badeau said, "There, Mrs. Daly, that shows what blood is!" "It only carries out my argument, Colonel; the Judge does not belong to an old New York family. They call him, and he is, a self-made man.". . .

The Judge and he talked about the propriety of giving General Grant a public reception. The Judge wanted a hundred gentlemen to meet him [Grant] on horseback.

October 20, 1865

General Shields suddenly made his appearance. He looks very well, but I do not feel towards him as I did. He stayed all night, much to my astonishment. As he ignores his wife and child, we do so likewise. His manners have very much deteriorated. He chews and spits in a most disgusting manner. His conversation interesting as usual. He has new, ambitious schemes, had been to see the President [and] told us many anecdotes of his [Lincoln's] magnanimity. When first elected, he said he felt a sensation of joy and vindictive satisfaction that he could now avenge the wrongs [and] insults heaped upon him by his secessionist neighbors, etc. He had been hunted by bloodhounds, [a] price set on his head, assassins sent to waylay him, his wife beaten because she would not reveal his hiding place, but he said thank God this bad feeling had gone. A lady from Tennessee with whom he had been long acquainted (but a rebel sympathizer) called upon him to ask for a pardon for Hunter, with Mrs. Hunter, which he granted. Then he called her aside and said, "Bring me the names of such in Tennessee that you know of. You know those I mean: bring them all. I do not want to see them nor can they wish to see me. I will sign all you bring me." This was as great as anything in history.

General Shields seemed to forget how much he owed to the liberal system of education and easy government of the country. Though a poor boy himself once, he seems now to think that education of the lower classes is rather an evil-maker. A great intellectual, he thought this excitement and march of events had not developed one thinker or poet, etc.—no great men. I ventured to suggest that they were to come. America, the United States, was still a schoolboy, cramming now for futurity. We shall have great thinkers, great writers, great artists, and I hope great statesmen. General Shields criticized freely—by no means blameless himself, neither a disinterested person nor a *pure* moral man.

October 25, 1865

The Judge's election comes again about a fortnight hence. All shades of the Democracy have renominated him. The *Tribune* pays a high compliment to his unquestioned probity. . . .

October 30, 1865

The Judge went to Washington. Mrs. Kent has given him the Chancellor's papers [and] I have my hands full in copying extracts. . . .

November 7, 1865

. . . . .

Judge Hilton came in last evening, told us some anecdotes of Fernando Wood. Mr. Wood wanted a house of his in the lower part of the city which Judge Hilton would not let to him when he discovered who it was who wished to rent it. Some time after, he [Hilton] received an anonymous letter saying that it was a shameful thing that a man, a *reformer* like himself, should be guilty of letting a tenement to a club of gamblers and a house of ill fame (the first floor was let to a literary association, the upper part to a lady, a friend of his wife's of long standing). The Judge looked at the paper: it had "H.C." on it. He thought over the matter, and during the morning, looking over A. T. Stewart's papers, whose lawyer he now is, found a note on the identical paper. He found it signed by Henry Cranston. He went at once to him, showed him the note. He [Cranston] said, "That is my paper, but I never wrote the note." "When was Wood last here?" said Hilton. "A few days ago. He came in, asked me for paper to write a note." "This is the one," said the Judge. "The scamp, I will lock my papers up hereafter," said Mr. Cranston. The writing, though disguised, was plainly Fernando's.

They are instituting a Democratic Club in opposition to the Loyal League where gentlemen may meet [and] political measures [may be] discussed privately. They wish to reform the party, get rid of the Ring, and try to rid us of the vampires sucking the life and marrow of the city. They have a spy in the Ring who will inform.

November 15, 1865

Went yesterday with the Judge to call upon General and Mrs. Grant. He is exactly like his portrait, most positive, honest looking. He looks as firm in keeping his personal base as he was before Lee in Virginia with his army. She is simple, natural, not handsome, but pleasant looking, a slight cast in the eye but fine teeth, and a pleasant, honest smile. She received me very graciously. The General and Mrs. Grant are to have a grand dress reception at the Fifth Avenue Hotel on Friday next. The Judge went to ask him if he will accept it. They are going to the opera tonight and Badeau wishes me to go up to their box, as we are going likewise. I would rather not, as it might make us conspicuous.

Baron Gerolt arrived last evening. Mr. Harris and Mr. Hackett came in.

The night before we had a very interesting visitor, Mr. Herries, a Frenchman, a littérateur. The Judge read him part of his first chapter of Chancellor Kent's life, which he liked, and then gave him some valuable hints for the making of a book. He struck me as a very gentlemanly, very *clever*, astute, *learned* man. Dr. [Robert O.] Doremus came in to see the Judge, as chairman of the Shakespeare Monument Fund, in behalf of a young sculptor. Had a very pleasant chat about art, music and literature. Mr. Herries stayed until past twelve o'clock. . . .

November 16, 1865

Went last night to hear *Fra Diavolo* at the opera. The Baron preferred going to Mr. Detmold's. General Grant and Mrs. Grant, with their suite, were in one of the proscenium boxes. Badeau saw us and came down with an invitation from Mrs. Grant to come to their box, so I had to go up on the arm of the aide-de-camp. I asked Mrs. Grant how she liked the opera. She answered in the simplest, most honest manner:

"Very well, but I know nothing about music. Perhaps you do not know that I have lived always at the West at the backwoods and that everything is new to me. Jesse and Ulysses (alluding to the children) are enchanted." The General said that nothing was a greater bore to him than an opera, but he too was pleased to see his children enjoy it so much.[14] Mr. Robert Cutting, who kept his place in the box although it had been offered to the General's party in a *cavatina* by Miss Kellogg, said with a dreadful lisp, "She is a thweet creature—lofely. She things this tho beautifully. You must lithen, Mrs. Grant." It had a great many trills in it and roulades and the General looked puzzled and uncertain. "It ith ferry difficult," said Mr. Cutting. I asked the General, *sotto voce*, if he had ever heard the anecdote about Dr. Johnson when asked to listen to a very elaborate sonata on the piano. The lady said, thinking it was not sufficiently appreciated, "It is a very difficult piece to play, Doctor. You cannot appreciate how difficult." "Madam," replied the Doctor, "I only wish it were impossible." The General laughed and seemed to think the anecdote very apposite. The General looks as if much given to persistent deep thoughts.

November 17, 1865

Yesterday Mr. and Mrs. Samuel Barlow, Mr. Townsend Harris, Bierstadt, Baron Gerolt, and General Dick Taylor, the *Rebel General*,[15] dined with us and we had a very pleasant dinner. Mr. Harris is such a thoroughly refined and gentlemanly person! Bierstadt was a little stiff with the *rebel* at first, but he won upon him by the charm of his manner and conver-

14 The Grants had four children, Frederick Dent, Jesse, Ulysses, and Nellie (Ellen).

15 Richard Taylor (1826–1879) was the son of Zachary Taylor. In 1862 he served under "Stonewall" Jackson in the Shenandoah Valley and the Seven Days' battle. He defeated Banks at Sabine Crossroads and was defeated by him in 1864 at Pleasant Hill. General Taylor died in New York.

sation. He [Taylor] paid a high compliment to Grant, whom he knew and had lately seen. He said he was not only a very able military man, but that he had also great judgment, moderation, humanity, that he was glad to see these demonstrations of approbation, that he deserved them and would be received at the South with the utmost kindness by the people who appreciated him.

Mr. Detmold came in afterwards. He is a thoroughgoing Republican; did not like rebels; could not pardon them unless they confessed themselves *wrong* and asked pardon for an error of judgment as well as of action. They are willing to allow that as we have beaten them, they were in the wrong, as they found their aims unattainable. It seems to me that is all we can ask. He [Detmold] believes in universal suffrage to the farthest meaning—I suppose the Negro, so I proposed in that case that the women should vote. . . . He is very kind and generous. He sent me $30 for a poor Union soldier the other day. It was so hard a case that I wrote one or two begging letters and succeeded in getting a suit of clothes for himself and mother and a small sum of money.

The Grant reception is postponed until Monday. As the Judge is to escort General and Mrs. Grant, I have asked Mr. Harris to escort me.

Mrs. McClellan, although the immediate cause of putting $1,200 in the hands of the Sanitary Commission at the Fair by what she presented, collected, and sold, has had no mention whatever made of her name in their report. This is very *contemptible*.

November 18, 1865

Spent yesterday morning in Bierstadt's studio. Went with Baron Gerolt and his new secretary of legation, Von

Cuserov. We were delighted. His [Bierstadt's] last picture, a storm on the Rocky Mountains, is even finer than the others. I was introduced there to [former] Governor [Edwin Dennison] Morgan, who introduced me to his wife, a great stout dressy matron of fifty-four or five. He is a heavy looking man who looks as if he were an unfinished sketch. I spoke of Mrs. Grant and her entire freedom from pretense, [telling] what she said to me at the opera. "It is best," said the Senator's [Morgan's] wife. "Everybody knows it and can see it, and it is as well to acknowledge it." I think Mrs. Grant as much of a lady as herself. The Governor is a good friend of the Judge. I have never called, but now that I have been introduced, I suppose it would be as well that I should.

On November 20, 1865, New York gave an elaborate reception to Ulysses S. Grant, and Judge Daly was one of the prime movers in the Committee on Arrangements. This celebration provided Mrs. Daly with another opportunity to cement her relationship with the hero and his wife, and she was delighted when Julia Dent Grant invited her to be one of her ladies in waiting.

The reception was held at New York's Fifth Avenue Hotel, and crowds began to gather early in the evening to see and cheer the man who was credited with winning the war. Among the many well-known generals present were Winfield Scott, John A. Dix, John C. Frémont, Joseph Hooker, Ambrose E. Burnside, George G. Meade, and Robert Anderson. Other prominent guests included Admiral David G. Farragut, William Cullen Bryant, Horace Greeley, Samuel J. Tilden, and Thurlow Weed.

William B. Astor and General Hooker escorted Grant into the hotel; the crowd nearly crushed him to death. Some three thousand people officially attended the reception. The celebration, which was a great success in spite of cold, rainy weather, included a fireworks display in front of the hotel. Grant left for Washington, D.C., the following day.

November 21, 1865

Went last night to the Fifth Avenue hotel to the great reception given to General Grant which has been in preparation for the last week and in which the Judge has taken an active part. In truth, had it not been for his persistency, I do not believe it would have been given. They gave him [the Judge] too conspicuous a place: such things make enemies! They wished even to make him chairman, which, however, he declined, and allowed A. T. Stewart to take that place (which I thought very unwise and injudicious, as he is only a successful retail merchant at the best). Mrs. Grant kindly invited me to [be] one of the four ladies who were to accompany her, and gave me the first place, assigning to me Major General [Cyrus B.] Comstock as my escort, the highest officer on the staff, and placing me next to her. The other ladies were Mrs. George Strong; Mrs. Wetmore; and Miss Mary Hamilton, but as it is to be in the next world, so was it on this occasion—the last shall be first and the first last—for Miss Hamilton quietly ensconced herself into a place on Mrs. Grant's right, upsetting all the arrangements, so that people bowed occasionally to her for Mrs. Grant. I stood back to give room, for Mr. Detmold brought his daughter, uninvited by Mrs. Grant, occasioning confusion. The General was escorted by the Judge; Mr. [Henry] Clews took Mrs. Grant; Mr. Detmold Mr. [Frederick] Dent, the General's father-in-law (a very gentlemanly old man who seemed delighted).

There was a shower of fireworks at the General's arrival at the hotel [and] the music struck up "The Conquering Hero Comes." The crowd was dreadful. It was with difficulty that the police and master of ceremonies could make way for the party—I nearly had my bouquet dragged out of my hand and my lace torn. As soon as we reached the presentation time, the presentations thick and fast came on. I think there must have been 2,000 persons present. Major General Parke looked splendidly in full regimentals. Generals Barlow, Hooker, Hancock, a hundred others [of] whom I did not hear the names, Mrs. Frémont and daughter, Mrs. Meagher, Mrs. Hooker, etc., etc., foreign consuls in their uniforms, the navy dignitaries, church dignitaries, Archbishop McCloskey,[16] Bishop [Horatio] Potter, H. Ward Beecher, Dr. [Henry W.] Bellows, etc., Bancroft, Greeley, Thurlow Weed, General Dix, etc. It was very amusing. I only thought once how many of these people will say, "I wonder what Mrs. Daly does there. How did she get herself there?" Certainly it was greatness thrust upon me, for I had asked Mr. Harris to accompany me before I was invited.

Badeau is fussy [and], I am afraid, not too popular with his brother officers. There is an element of littleness in his character, but he is very kind and thoughtful about the Judge and myself and very gentlemanly. He has many virtues, though some weaknesses.

General Grant, after his health was drunk, thanked the ladies most heartfully for the very great compliments they had paid him in a few very sincere words. Mrs. Grant's health was likewise drunk. Mr. Thompson, Beecher, and John Van Buren made appropriate speeches. It was interesting to watch the shade of *shy* embarrassment which crossed General Grant's face when any direct praise was given him. He has a mild-firm eye.

Mrs. Grant was dressed very simply but richly and in excellent taste and looked ladylike. She is very natural and unaffected and has a ladylike self-possession which is pleasing. I think the General must have been gratified at the demonstration both within and without, for the crowd without, despite the rain, was assembled to see him. He stood a few moments upon the balcony where a Drummond light, cast full upon the building,

---

[16] John McCloskey (1810–1885) was president of St. John's College (Fordham) and bishop of Albany before becoming Archbishop of New York in 1864. He became the first American cardinal in 1875.

brought his face into full view. It was an event in my life—the first time I had been on any platform.

November 24, 1865

Last evening Baron Osten-Sacken came in just as we had finished dinner. He wants a book to be written upon America showing how the remarkable growth is produced, how towns are formed from settlements, etc.; in fact, the whole organism! He asked Dr. Lieber, but he [Lieber] said that the difficulty would be that no European could be made to believe that an American was born with all this organism *in* him and developed it as naturally as he breathed. The work would require great labor.

The Grant reception is much criticized. It was too crowded. Many were asked who should not have been, and many omitted who should have been asked. All the artists were omitted and are inclined to sulk. The Recorder[17] expected to have been invited, and would not pay his hundred dollars after having had his name in the paper as one of the subscribers. Neither the Mayor nor the City Council were asked, nor did they call on the General.

As an instance of Grant's capacity, Colonel Hilegard told the Judge that at the siege of Fort Donelson, the commander made a sally and broke the left wing all to pieces, capturing half our men. Colonel Hilegard reported it to Grant. "Have we taken any prisoners?" asked Grant. "They have taken a great many from us—half the corps." "I did not ask that," said he. "Have we taken any?" "A few, perhaps," said Hilegard.

---

17 This was John T. Hoffman, a city judge who handled the cases of those involved in inciting the Draft Riots. He was mayor of New York from 1865 to 1868, when he became governor of the state. Hoffman was intimate with members of the Tweed Ring, and while he was mayor appointed Peter B. Sweeny city comptroller. This affiliation destroyed an otherwise promising political career.

"Ask them what rations they have." From their answer, Grant said, "The victory will fall to the first attacking party," and he immediately ordered an assault which decided the fate of the fort.

Mr. Young came in late in the evening.

Spent the morning at the Woman's School of Design. Mr. Bierstadt was kind enough to go with me there and look through the school. I must try to attend to my duties there a little more thoroughly, although Mrs. Field may be chairman.

Went through all the rain yesterday to the Union Home and School for soldiers' children[18] to see how the changes I had ordered in buying butler's meal wholesale worked. Found it would be much more economical and much better liked.

November 25, 1865

The charter election for mayor and alderman, etc., comes on next week. O'Gorman has got the nomination for corporation attorney, an office worth $4,500 a year. He does not deserve it, after the unpatriotic part he has taken in this war.[19] Judge John [T.] Hoffman had been nominated for mayor. The Judge was urged to accept the nomination for mayor, but declined it peremptorily, saying he was too poor a man, and too proud to place himself in a position where he would be controlled by such a set of scoundrel politicians as the Ring.

Went on Friday evening last to Mrs. Botta's, to a reception

---

[18] For many years following the war, Mrs. Daly served as president of the Union Home and School, founded on May 22, 1861. Judge Daly was on its board of directors, beginning in the summer of 1865. The purpose of the Home was "to furnish board and tuition for all motherless children of the officers and soldiers who have volunteered in the service of our country and in the defense of our Union under the flag of this city." Some five thousand children were accommodated by the Home during its life.

[19] Mrs. Daly is apparently referring to Richard O'Gorman's affiliation with the Copperheads during the war.

given to Senator and Mrs. [Lafayette S.] Foster [Connecticut]. She is a firm looking woman still, and was very polite to me. Mr. [George] Ripley and his new wife; Osgood Crunch, a good many names. I wore Grandfather Lydig's miniature. It was very much observed and thought a beautiful antique. They seemed surprised to hear whose likeness it was.

Major General Barlow dined with us the day before. What a thoroughly practical New England character! He seems to look upon his military career now as only a good advertisement for him as a lawyer. He paid a high compliment to Irish soldiers, whom he said he grew much attached to; they would follow any leader who was brave anywhere. I esteem him and respect his bravery, but I do not know why it is that I feel so little sympathy with him. I think he looks as though he had a very sensuous temperament and might become a very hard, money-making, selfish man as he grows older. Although very courageous, he is neither romantic nor has he any sympathy with either the poetical or the philosophical. He very frankly confessed that he had read very little except Shakespeare.

December 3, 1865

Mr. Harris came in last evening. I was astonished to hear him say that he should not live long and he would be glad to have the end come as soon as possible. He is not thirty-five, but has exhausted life. Can it be possible? He added he had twice attempted to take his own life but had not succeeded. I asked him how he lived. He said he took but one meal a day, a cup of coffee at nine o'clock and a biscuit, rising at daylight and getting as hungry as possible. I told him that if he would take his coffee and something substantial earlier, he would have more interest in life.

Hackett the actor came in about the Shakespeare Monument, and likewise Baron Osten-Sacken. The Judge went asleep upon the sofa.

December 5, 1865

Went last night to see *L'Africaine*, Meyerbeer's new opera; thought it beautiful music and a very fine spectacle, well-managed and a great credit to the management. But what a bedizened audience! Had some wild man of the woods come in who had never seen a white woman, he would have asked, "What strange animals they, what wonderful plumage!" [In] one box Mrs. McBicker. She was bedizened with gold, silver, and glass, white and gold dress and cloak, hair *à l'empire*. She had a bevy of girls with her who looked like ballet girls. You felt sure they had scanty drapery, though you knew from their place that they had on long clothes. And how they did seize on the men and how they laughed and talked and shook their heads at them! I thought they would eat the young fellows up among them. Then the droll hats with gold cords and birds on them and glass beads, the wooly-looking hair crimped to death. What a perfect Vanity Fair!

December 15, 1865

Edwin Booth and [Cephas G.] Thompson the sculptor came in, spent last evening with us. Harriet Whetten is staying here. She was enchanted with Booth, thought him so princely and grand in manner, so self-poised, so beautiful. They stayed until near one o'clock looking over the Judge's dramatic collection.

December 19, 1865

The Judge went to a supper given to Mayor [Mayor-elect] Hoffman at the Steuben House by the German Republicans. It was beautifully served, tastefully and profusely—the best wines, etc. The flags of the Steuben regiment were in the room and the Germans had not forgotten who had presented them. So they called upon the Judge first to speak and as he did not allude to them [the flags], they afterwards called him again, referring to him as the first American who recognized the foreign element in this war and felt its worth, who had presented that Steuben cross but who had been too modest to notice them [the flags] or to allude to what he could not have forgotten—the enthusiastic manner in which his gift had been received. Mayor Hoffman at once rose and, ignoring any reference to the Judge, proposed the memory of the brave men who had fallen in that regiment. But the Germans were not to be satisfied, and they called for Judge Daly until he had to answer the call.

December 24, 1865

Been all day at the Union Home and School, busy getting a dinner for the soldiers' children on Christmas. Invited Major General Barlow and Parke, Mr. Townsend Harris, Judge Brady, etc.

Christmas, 1865

Had a most satisfactory and delightful morning. Went to eight o'clock mass, saw the sun just rising above the buildings and the park as I crossed Waverly Place, the sky as bright and clear as spring. I thought of the words of the old carol, "Royal day that chasest gloom." I went to St. Joseph's, where the congregation was mostly poor people; I like to go to church with the poor, particularly on Christmas.

Then home to breakfast, then sent off my presents and prepared for going to the soldiers' children. General Parke and Mr. Harris came in good time and we met General [Prosper

M.] Wetmore[20] at the Home. The Judge addressed the children, giving an account of Christmas—a little sermon in fact. The children sang hymns, a hymn on the nativity, and some patriotic songs, hurrahs, and gave three cheers for General Parke. They had a capital dinner prepared for them and we all came home very much touched by what we had seen. Poor little fatherless children! It was very delightful to see them all so happy.

Went to Laight Street to dinner, hoping for a pleasant family reunion. Found Kate and the Judge not coming, Hannah sick, and Uncle Lydig installed, Father having asked him. It showed plainly that Father has more consideration for him than for us. We shall dine there no more on Christmas! I will be patriotic and Christian and dine another Christmas with the poor by preference. I think we would be greater favorites if we were less esteemed outside the family, so that all the wounds we receive, all the dishonor, is from our own familiar friends, the members of our own household. Whilst my husband is with me and loves me, I am independent of the whole world. Should I be so unfortunate as to outlive him, it will be of little consequence who else may be left, either of family or of friends.[21]

December 30, 1865

This week has been very busy in getting an appropriation passed for the Union Home and School, in which I find myself deeply interested. We at last succeeded. . . .

---

[20] Prosper M. Wetmore (1798–1876) was a founder of the Union Defense Committee in 1861 and its secretary until the end of the war. The designation "General" applies to his service in the Connecticut State Militia before he became a regent of the University of New York in 1833. He was secretary of the New York Chamber of Commerce in 1843 and vice president in 1849.

[21] Judge Daly outlived his wife by five years; she died in 1894. They left no heirs.

Mr. Harris paid us a pleasant evening visit. He is full of intellect and has a great memory, has read an incredible amount for so young a man. Baron Osten-Sacken came in this evening at ten o'clock.

INDEX

Abdul-Aziz, Sultan of Turkey, 49
Academy of Music, 116, 227
Academy of Mount St. Vincent, 164n.
Adams, Henry, U.S. Minister to Britain, 78
Adie, James, 252
Agassiz, Jean Louis Rudolphe, 108, 109, 235
Aiken, (Governor) William, 346
Albert, Prince, 29, 106n., 229
Albion (newspaper), 28n., 276
Alexander II, Czar of Russia, 52, 254–255
Alfred, Prince, 149
Allston, Washington, 236
American Geographical Society, 206n., 321n.
Amerique devant l'Europe, L', 89n.
Ames, Mrs., 191–192
Anchinoty, Union soldier, 197–198
Anderson, (Major, later General) Robert, 9–10, 69, 100
Andrew, (Governor) John A., 182n.
Anschütz, Carl, 207
Antietam, battle of, 174, 177, 183, 184, 190, 241n., 299n., 333
Applegate, Captain, 128
Appleton, William H., 315
Archibald, Edward M., British consul, 336
Are the Southern Privateersmen Pirates?, 89n., 144
Ashburne, Mr., 350, 354
Astor, John Jacob, 76n., 144n., 145
Astor, William Blackhouse, 76, 106, 215, 223, 224, 320
Athenaeum Club, 328
Atlanta campaign, 216n., 312

Badeau, (Captain, later General) Adam, xiii, 62–63, 121, 182, 200, 215, 241, 222, 255–256, 267; promotion, 285–286, 295, 299; convalescent, 327; opinion of Grant, 333; 368, 371, 376
Bailey, Mr., 34, 165
Bailey, (Captain) Theodorus, 131

Baker, (Senator, then General) Edward Dickinson ("Ned"), 19, 20, 26, 66n.–67n., 105n.
Baker, Lafayette Curry, 344–345
Ball's Bluff, battle of, 19, 66n.–67n., 105n., 180
Bancroft, George, xiii, 106, 116, 117, 134, 223n., 308, 309, 320, 322, 338
Bancroft, Mrs. George, 107; Poet's Tea Party, 309–310
Banks, (General) Nathaniel Prentiss, 113, 115, 137n., 140, 168, 240, 242; disgrace of, 295–296
Barbour, (Judge) John M., 69
Barlow, Arabella Griffith (Mrs. Francis C.) xiii–xiv, 80, 146–147, 169, 172–173, 320, 345
Barlow, (Colonel, then General) Francis C. (Frank), xiii–xiv, 46, 80, 146, 173, 190, 228, 299, 345, 379
Barney, Hiram, 89, 94, 104, 176–177, 211, 212, 328
Barnum's Museum, 220, 317n.
Bartlett, Sidney, 233, 234, 235–236
Battle (of, at, etc.) See *under* place name.
"Battle Hymn of the Republic, The," 276n., 320
Beauregard, (General) Pierre Gustave Toutant, 10, 27, 36–38, 139, 294
Bedford Springs, 365–366, 367
Beecher, Henry Ward, xiv, 14; "political sermon," 313; 350
Beecher, Lyman, 14
Bell, Mrs. J., 133–134
Bell, Judge, 218, 220
Belle Isle (prison), 364–365
Bellows, (Rev. Dr.) Henry Whitney, 59n., 223n., 309n.
Belmont, August, 20, 200, 201, 202, 218
Bendix, (Colonel, later General) John E., 17, 30, 31
Benjamin, (Senator) Judah Philip, 6
Benson, Egbert, 137, 340
Benton, (Senator) Thomas H., 70–72

Bernheimer, Simon, 268, 350, 361–362
Berrian, Goodwin, 199
Berrian, (Reverend) William, 199n., 282n.
Bertinatti, Chevalier, 257
Bierstadt, Albert, xiv, 100, 136, 202, 209; description of painting, 215; 217, 224, 231, 274, 279, 286, 292, 297, 324, 329, 361, 373, 374
Big Bethel, battle at, 24, 26
Birney, (Congressman) James G., 14
Black Brigades, 212, 219, 223n.
Black Horse cavalry, 45
Blair, Francis P. (Frank), Jr., 71–72
Blair, Francis P., Sr., 71, 335
Blair, (Postmaster General) Montgomery, 10, 71
Blenker, (Colonel, later General) Louis, 16, 20, 38, 40, 85, 161, 171
Blenker's First Rifles, 40, 86
Blunt, Orison, 267n.
Boileau, Baron Gauldieu, 288
Boileau, Madam (Baroness Gauldieu Boileau), 275, 276
Boker, George Henry, 308, 310
Boole, Francis, 267n.
Booth, Edwin Thomas, xiv–xv, 220, 260, 289, 291, 292, 316–317, 325, 345, 346, 347, 360, 365, 380
Booth, John Wilkes, 316n.; shooting of Lincoln, 353, 354; death of, 359
Booth, Junius Brutus, 316n.
Bosworth, (Judge) Joseph S., 261
Botta, (Professor) and Mrs. Vincenzo, 310, 378–379
Bouck, William C., 126
Brady, (Judge) James Topham, xv, 19, 20, 25, 31, 34, 81, 82–83, 114, 124, 137, 142, 143, 144–145, 202, 211, 214; wedding, 214; 223, 251, 306–307, 323, 324, 334, 336
Brady, Mrs. James Topham. See Lydig, Catherine.
Brady, John R., xv, 83n.
Bragg, (General) Braxton, 32, 169, 207, 241, 253n., 265, 266
Brandhead, Mr., 288
Breckenridge, (Vice President) John Cabell, 1, 162
Bright, John, 89, 264
Bristed, Charles Astor, 277
Broadhead, (State Senator) James O., 72
Broglie, Jacques Victor Albert, Duc de, 148

Bronx Park Zoological and Botanical Gardens, 34n.
Brooke, Sir James, 263
Brooks, James, 218n.
Brooks, (Representative) Preston, 193n.
Brown, Henry Kirke, 100
Brown, John, 320
Bruce, Sir Frederick, 353, 354, 363–364
Bryant, William Cullen, 307–309, 310, 320
Buchanan, Franklin, 116
Buchanan, (President) James, 1, 4, 7, 9–10, 81, 162, 163n.
Buckner, (General) Simon Bolivar, 105
Buell, (General) Don Carlos, 169, 207
Bull Run, both battles of, 45–46, 135n.
Bull Run, first battle of, 36–41, 45–46, 62, 137n., 139, 147–148, 149
Bull Run, second battle of, 90n., 111, 219n., 241n.
Burke, Edmund, 237
burning of New York City, attempt at, 317
Burnside, (General) Ambrose Everett, 90, 98, 104, 123, 164, 179; succeeds McClellan, 196, 197n.; 208, 209, 212, 219, 265; opinion of Philip Lydig, 274
Burnside, Mrs. Ambrose E., 204, 288
Busteed, (General) Richard, 169–170
Busteed, Mrs. Richard, 96
Butler, (Senator) Andrew P., 193n.
Butler, (General) Benjamin Franklin, 24, 26, 31, 49, 53, 218; in New Orleans, 224–226; 294, 295 310, 313–314, 315; at Fort Fisher, 330–331; 332, 333
Butler, Charles E., 323
Butterfield, (Colonel, later General) Daniel, 11, 46

Cahil, Miss ("Vivian"), 56, 62, 81, 93
Calhoun, (Senator) John Caldwell, 9
Cameron, Simon, Secretary of War, xvii, 44–45, 67, 99n.
Campbell, John A., 335
Canby, (General) Edward R. S., 296, 336
Cardozo, (Judge) Albert, 334, 342
Cardozo, Benjamin Nathan, 334n.
Carson, Caroline Petigru (Mrs. William A.), 95, 215, 224, 267

Catholic Publication Society, 83n.
Cavendish, Lord Spencer Compton, Marquis of Hartington, 201, 207, 216
Cavendish, William, 7th Duke of Devonshire, 201n.
Cedar Creek, battle of, 304
Central Park, 153n., 291, 292
Central Relief Association, 132
Century Club, 107, 130n.; Bryant festival, 307–309, 310, 320
Chancellorsville, battle of, 241n., 242–243, 299n.
Charleston, 337, 338; celebration of victory, 341, 342–343
Charleston Convention, 355
Chartres, duc de, 104n.
Chase, Salmon P., Secretary of Treasury, later Chief Justice, 85, 87, 147, 154n., 240, 286
Chattanooga, 253, 254, 258, 265, 266
Cheneworth, William, 365–366, 367
Chengwatana, 202n., 222
Chicamauga, 253n., 254n.
Choate, Joseph Hodges, 100, 224
Christian Inquirer, 309n.
Church, Frederick Edwin, 215, 286
Clay Compromise, 127n.
Clift, Mrs. Smith, 189, 268
Cobden, Richard, 264
Coffin, Mr. (Charles Carleton), 217
Cogswell, (Colonel) Milton, 30, 46, 66
Colden, Cadwallader David, 322
Cold Harbor, 296; battle of, 297–298
Colored Orphan Asylum (New York), 247
Committee for the Relief of Ireland, 137, 226, 237
Compromise of 1850, 311n.
Comstock, (General) Cyrus B., 375
Confiscation Acts, 72, 115
Congress, U.S.S., 116
Connolly, Archbishop Thomas Louis, 79, 83–84
Conolly, Lieutenant, 100–103, 316
Conyngham, (Captain) David P., 15n.
Cooper, Peter, 324
Cooper's Institute, 223, 307, 324
Cooper Union, 324n.
Copperhead(s), 15n., 62n., 182n., 194, 223, 238n., 267n., 301, 378n.
Coppinger, Captain, 319, 349
Corcoran, (Colonel, later General) Michael, xv–xvi, 11, 15, 18, 39, 41; prisoner, 45–46; 77, 79, 83, 96, 100, 101, 102, 138, 151, 153; freed, 166–167; 170, 174, 175, 180, 186–187, 188, 196, 219, 221, 222; shoots Col. Kimball, 230, 231, 238, 256; death, 270–271; 273
Corcoran, Mrs. Michael, 186
Corinth, evacuation of, 124, 139
Coxe, (Reverend, later Bishop) Arthur Cleveland, 277
Cranston, Henry, 370
Cropsey, Jasper F., 289
Cross Keys, battle at, 73
Crunch, Osgood, 379
Cullum, (Major, later Colonel) George Washington, 69, 70
Cumberland, U.S.S., 111, 116
currency. See money troubles.
Cushman, Miss Charlotte S., 260, 308n.
Cutting, Mrs. Francis B., 200
Cutting, Francis Brockholst, 200n., 218
Cutting, Robert, 372

Dahlgren, (Admiral) John Adolphus Bernard, 5, 24
Daly, (Judge) Charles Patrick, xvi, xxxii–xxxiv; opinion on Trent affair, 78; letter on privateering, 85, 89, 104–105, 113, 144; proposed changes of constitution, 110; will, 120; career as sailor, 124, 125–126; and Irish Relief, 137; 145; land speculation, 162, 202n.; formation of "Union League," 223; article on "Naturalization," 257; on committee to receive Russians, 260; Shakespeare tribute, 291, 292; support for McClellan, 302–303; salary increase, 328–329; Lincoln's confidence in, 350; refusal to meet Lee, 359
Daly, Sir Dominick, xvi, 12, 34, 97, 120, 255, 368
Daly, Elizabeth (Mrs. Michael), 165n.
Daly, John George, 97
Daly, Michael, 165 and n.
Dana, Charles Anderson, 115, 274, 308, 314
Darley, Felix O. C., 314
Davis, Charles Henry, 215, 216
Davis, George Thomas, xvi–xvii, 44–45, 89, 191, 193, 217, 233, 234, 276
Davis, James, 324
Davis, Jefferson, xvii, 138, 147, 171, 335, 349, 352, 360–361, 362–363

Day, James Gamble, 231, 232
de Broglie, Duc. See Broglie.
De Lancey family, xxxv, 34n.
Delmonico's Restaurant, 202
Delusy, Mrs. H. See Field, Mrs. Henry.
Democratic Club, 370
Democratic rally, Union Square, 302–303
Dempsey, Lieutenant, 91, 102, 138, 149–150
Dent, Frederick, 375
Detmold, Christian Edward, 259
Detmold, Mrs., 360
de Tocqueville. See Tocqueville.
Devlin, John A., 201, 202
Devlin, Mrs. John A., 202, 332
Devonshire, Duke of. See Cavendish, William.
Dickinson, Anna Elizabeth, 232–233, 349
Dickinson, John, 232n.
Dix, Charles Temple, 283
Dix, Miss Dorothea L., xliv; directress of nurses, 76, 128
Dix, (General) John Adams, xvii–xviii, 27–28, 30n., 31, 33, 81, 141, 195, 223n., 252, 283, 310, 320, 338, 342
Dix, Mrs. John Adams, 192
Dix, (Reverend) Morgan, 282–283
Donelson, Fort, 104, 105, 106, 377–378
Donovan, Lieutenant, 175–176
D'Oremieulx, Theophile Marie, 31
D'Oremieulx, Mrs. (née Laura Wolcott Gibbs), 31, 58, 241
Doubleday, (Captain) Abner, 69n.
Douglas, (Senator) Stephen Arnold, 4, 5, 142, 355
Doyce, Mr., 237
Draddy, Daniel, 293
Draft Riots (of 1863), 141n., 246–251, 261n., 274n., 277n.
Draper, Simeon, & Co., 30n.
Dred Scott Decision, 311
Duncan, Dr., 267
Dunsandel, Earl of, 97–98
du Pont, (Commodore) Samuel Francis, 121, 122, 249
Duranquet, (Father) Henry, 186
Dykes, Mr., 251, 314

Early, (General) Jubal Anderson, 243; "Early's Raids," 303–304
Edward VII, 149
Edwards, Miss Anne S., 290n.

Edward's Ferry, See Ball's Bluff.
Eleventh Army Corps, 146n.
Elgin, Lord, 206
Ellsworth, (Colonel) Elmer Ephraim, 17
Ely, (Congressman) Alfred, 103
Emancipation Proclamation, 177–178, 179, 181, 193n., 206, 244, 365
Emerson, Ralph Waldo, 308, 309
Emory, (Colonel, later General) William H., 80
Episcopal Church, 74
Ericsson, John, 111
États-Unis en 1861, Les, 89n.
Ethnological Society, 24, 206
Evarts, William Maxwell, 99, 116, 205, 309, 350
Everett, Edward, 263–264

Fair Oaks, battle of, 146, 172, 175n.
Farragut, (Admiral) David Glasgow, 124n., 131, 258; at Mobile, 304, 312, 325
Faulkner, Charles James, 103
Fay, Theodore Sedgwick, 313
Fenian Brotherhood, 231n.
Fenton, Reuben E., 302, 312
Field, Cyrus West, 107n.
Field, David Dudley, 107n., 342
Field, Mrs. Dudley (née Harriet Davidson), 293 and n.
Field, Henry Martyn, 107n., 314
Field, Laure Desportes (Mrs. Henry M.), 107
Fifth Avenue Hotel, 371, 375
Fifth Regiment, 75
Fifty-sixth New York Regiment, 73
Fillmore, (President) Millard, 127
Fire Zouaves, 40
First German Rifles, 16
Fish, Hamilton, 30n., 95n., 99
Fisher, Fort, 330–331, 333
Fisher's Hill, battle of, 304
Five Forks, 304
Floyd, John Buchanan, 2, 45, 54, 106
Folsom, George, 24
Foot, (Senator) Solomon, 188–189
Foote, (Commodore) Andrew Hull, 104, 105
Ford's Theatre, 220n., 353
Forrest, Edwin, 164n.
Fort. . . . See under second word.
Forty-second Infantry Regiment. See Tammany Regiment.
Foster, (General) John Gray, 69, 123

Foster, (Senator) Lafayette Sabine, 379
Foster, Martha Lyman (Mrs. Lafayette Sabine), 79
Francis, Sir Philip ("Junius"), 63n.
Frank Leslie's Illustrated Newspaper, 245n., 287
Franklin, Sir John, 228n., 321n.
Fredericksburg, 198n., 202, 206–207, 208–209, 241
Free-soil Democrats, 89n.
Frémont, Jessie Benton (Mrs. John C.), xviii, 72–73, 275–276, 292, 321, 338
Frémont, (General) John C., 47n., 56–57, 59; sponsored by Benton, 70–72; retirement, 73, 88n., 168, 276
Friendly Sons of St. Patrick, 223, 224n.
Frobisher, Sir Martin, 228, 229

Gaines's Mill, battle of, 175n.
Gamble, (Governor) Hamilton R., 72
Garibaldi Guard. *See* Thirty-ninth Infantry Regiment.
Garnet, (General) Richard B., 35
Garrison, William Lloyd, 13–14, 122n.
Gasparin, Count Agénor Étienne de, 89, 148
Gerard, James, 322
Gerhard, James Watson, 136
Gerolt, Carlotta von, 48, 64–65, 239
Gerolt, Dorothea von, 64, 65
Gerolt, Baron Friedrich von, xviii, 3, 20, 47–48, 50, 51, 55, 64, 112, 114, 119, 154–155, 159, 170, 184, 239, 257, 259, 275, 286, 287, 288, 314, 329, 338–339, 354, 361, 374
Gerolt, Madam von, 54–55, 60, 64–65, 170–171
Gescheidt, (Dr.) Louis Anthony, 16, 163, 232, 256
Gettysburg, battle of, 198n., 243–244, 299n.
Gibbs, (Captain, later Colonel) Alfred, 58, 222
Gibbs, Mrs. Alfred, 133
Gibbs, George (lawyer), 58n.
Gibbs, Laura Wolcott (Mrs. Colonel) 132–133, 222, 290n., 297
Gibbs, Oliver Wolcott, 31n., 58n.
Gibbs, Mrs. Tom, 209, 210
Gifford, Sanford Robinson, 100, 231, 286, 309

Gilbert, John Gibbs, 201
Gillmore, (General) Quincy Adams, 121n., 337
Gilmer, (General) Jeremy F., 347
Ginoux (artist), 100, 286
Godwin, Parke, 309, 310
Goldsborough, (Admiral) Louis Malesherbes, 104
Gould, Charles, 107, 223, 232, 325, 327
Gould, Miss, 107–108, 233
governors' convention, Altoona, 182
Gracie, Archibald, 33
Grant, Ulysses S., xix, 71, 104, 105, 239, 242, 260n.; drinking, 265; promotion, 294; message to Halleck, 296; 297–298; at Appomattox, 351; at opera, 371–372
Grant, Mrs. U. S. (Julia Dent), 371–372, 375
Grant reception, 368, 371, 373, 374–377
Gray, John Chipman ("Chip"), 3
Gray, Miss (of Baltimore), 286, 289
Great Bethel. *See* Big Bethel.
Great Eastern, 207
Greeley, Horace, 115n., 223, 311–312
Greenough, Mrs. William, 290n.
Grenough, Mrs., 337–338
Griffin, Christine Kean (Mrs. William Preston), 131
Grim, David, 138
Grinnell, Henry, 321
Grinnell, Joseph, 94n.
Grinnell, Moses Hicks, 94–95
Grinnell, Sylvia, 324
Gunther, (Mayor) Charles Godfrey, 267n.
Gurowski, Count Adam de, 226, 262

Habicht, Mrs. Claudius Edward, 259
Hackett, James Henry, 114, 288–289, 289–290, 291, 292, 314, 379
Hale, (Senator) John Parker, 4
Halifax, Archbishop of. *See* Connolly, Archbishop Thomas Louis.
Hall, Abraham Oakey, 323
Hall, Charles Francis, 228–229
Halleck, Fitz-Greene, 144
Halleck, (General) Henry Wager, 60, 119n., 124n., 184, 208, 243
Hamersley, Mrs. John W., 331
Hamilton, Colonel, 142
Hamilton, Miss Mary, 299, 375
Hamilton, (General) Schuyler, 119n.

Hamlin, (Vice President) Hannibal, 188

Hampton Roads, battle of, 111, 112, 116

Hancock, (General) Winfield Scott, 211, 332–333

Hardee, (General) William Joseph, 336–337

Harper's Ferry, evacuation of, 27; Jackson's victory, 174, 178

Harrington, George, 94

Harris, Captain, 173

Harris, (Senator) Ira, 85, 89, 210

Harris, Townsend, xix, 205–206, 216, 230, 232, 262–263, 284, 297, 317, 327, 330, 352, 359, 360, 365, 366, 373, 374, 379, 381, 383

Harrison's Landing, 168, 172, 175n., 197–198

Hartington, Marquis of. See Cavendish, Lord Spencer Compton.

Hasson, Father, 275

Hatteras, Fort, 47, 49, 53

Hawkins, (Colonel, later General) Rush Christopher, 19

Hawks, (Dr.) Francis Lister, 120

Hayes, Isaac Israel (explorer), 216

Hays, (General) Alexander, 297

Hayward (sailor), 116

Hecker, (Father) Isaac Thomas, 83–84

Hecksher, Pauline, engagement to Philip Lydig, 363; marriage, 367–368

Henry, Fort, 103, 104, 105

Hermann, "Professor" (magician), 61

Herndon, William H., 305n.

Herries, Mr., 371

Hewitt, Mrs. Abram Stevens, 95

Hicks, (Governor) Thomas H., 163

Hilegard, Colonel, 377–378

Hill, (General) Ambrose P., 175n.–176n., 243

Hill, (General) Daniel Harvey, 176n.

Hillard, George Stillman, 192, 234, 236, 237

Hilton, (Judge) Henry, 126, 137, 153, 201, 250, 257, 261, 283, 370

Hilton, Mrs., 152, 158

Histoire politique des Etats-Unis, 264n.

History of the Civil War in America, 104n.

Hoffman, (Mayor) John Thompson, 216n., 377n., 378, 380, 381

Hoffman, Murray, 223n.

Hoffman, Mrs. Ogden, 290n.

Holmes, Oliver Wendell, 308

Holt, Joseph, 58

Hone, Philip, 339

Hood, (General) John Bell, 312

Hooker, Dr., 236

Hooker, (General) Joseph, 46n., 183, 212n., 237–238, 241, 242, 244

Hosmer, Miss Harriet Goodhue, 308 and n., 309, 310

Howard, (General) Oliver Otis, 146, 243

Howe, Julia Ward (Mrs. Samuel), 14, 276–277, 308, 309

Hoyt, Mrs. Emy Otto, 301n.

Hughes, (Archbishop) John 79, 187, 188, 227n.; death, 274

Humboldt, Baron Alexander von, 152

Hunt, Richard Morris, 100n.

Hunter, (General) David, 121, 135

Hunter, R. M. T., 335

Huntington, Daniel, 281

Hutton, (Dr.) Mancius S., 245

Irish Ball, 229

"Irish Brigade." *See* Sixty-ninth New York Regiment. *Or see* Twenty-third Illinois Regiment.

Irish relief. *See* Committee for the Relief of Ireland.

Irving, Washington, 144, 281 and n.

Island No. 10, 114, 168

Jackson, (President) Andrew, 71, 188n.

Jackson, (Reverend) M., 189

Jackson, (General) Thomas Jonathan ("Stonewall"), 73, 137, 141, 155, 157–158, 164, 167–168, 169, 171, 174, 178, 208, 224; death, 243

Jarvis, Nathaniel, Jr., 215, 251, 336

Jerome, Mother, 164–165

Johnson, (President) Andrew, 91n., 99n., 193n., 301, 307; at Lincoln's inauguration, 343; becomes President, 353; amnesty, 362

Johnson, (General) Bushrod, 105

Johnson, Eastman, 216–217, 309

Johnson, (Senator) Reverdy, 8

Johnson, (Dr.) Samuel, anecdote, 373

Johnston, (General Albert Sidney, 50, 54, 106

Johnston (General), Joseph E., 36–37, 38, 146–147, 242, 266, 298, 335, 337, 351, 357

Johnston, Mrs. Joseph, 150n.
Joinville, Prince de, 104
Journal, Boston, 217n.
"Judge Daly Guards," 15n., 186
"Junius." *See* Francis, Sir Philip.

Kearny, (General) Philip, 147–148, 171
Keene, Laura, 220
Kennedy, (Senator) Anthony, 3, 289
Kennedy, Mrs. Anthony, 289
Kennesaw Mountain, battle of, 298
Kensett, John Frederick, 286, 324
Kent, (Chancellor) James, 300, 309, 314, 338, 339, 340
Kimball, (Colonel) Edgar Allen, 230, 231
Kindersley, Sir Richard, 113
King, Charles, 150n., 160, 297
King, Henrietta Liston Low (Mrs. Charles), 150, 347
"King Log" (Lincoln), xli, 158
Kingman, Mr., 188
Kirby-Smith, E., 37, 169
Kirke, 324
Kirker, Captain, 89, 138, 149–150, 167, 256
Kirkland, Caroline Matilda Stansbury (Mrs. William), 293 and n.
Knickerbocker Kitchen, 279–280, 285, 287
Knights of the Golden Circle, 317n.
Know-Nothing party, 128n.

Laboulaye, Édouard René Lefebvre de, 264
Lacy, Mrs., 174
Lafayette, Fort, 157
Laing, Mr., 17, 119, 143, 286
Lander, (General) Frederick W., 110
Lander, Mrs. Frederick W., 337
Lane, Miss Harriet, 79, 82
Lawrence, (Dr.) Francis E., 209
Leader, The, 141
Lee, Miss Mary, 69, 76, 79
Lee, (General) Robert E., xx, 32, 147, 168, 173–174, 180, 183, 184, 208, 240, 242–243, 244; in the Wilderness, 294; 296, 298, 348; surrender, 351
Lee, Mrs. Watkins, 133–134
Lefferts, (Colonel) Marshall, 11
Leonard, James, 251
Leslie, Frank, 245, 248
Leutze, Emanuel, 286

Lexington (Missouri), siege of, 86n., 88
Libby Prison, 285
Lieber, Francis, 81n.–82n., 338, 377
Lieber, Mrs. Francis, 290n.
Limburg, Mr., 338
Lincoln, (President) Abraham, 10, 23; proposed duel with Gen. Shields, 61–62, 67–68; conflict with Frémont, 72–73; on office-seekers, 73, 86; nomination for President, 87–88, 99n., 103, 135–136, 140–141, 154, 158, 168, 170, 171, 172, 177, 179, 181–182, 194, 196, 199, 208, 216; at Antietam, 218; assassination, 220n., 244; on Grant's drinking, 265; renomination, 301; 304–305; partners, 305n., 307, 311; reelection, 312; sayings, 313, 320; "malice toward none," 343; assassination, 352–353; Mrs. Daly's summing up, 354–355; mourning and funeral, 356–357, 358
Lincoln, Mary Todd (Mrs. Abraham), xx, 44–45, 53, 61, 62, 86, 87–88, 216, 245, 248; purchase of china, 305, 307, 329, 350
Lincoln War Democrats ("cowboys"), 315
Linton, Mary, 32–33, 39
Longstreet, (General) James, 168, 174, 219n., 244, 265
Lookout Mountain, battle of, 266
Lowell, James Russell, 14, 235, 308
Lowry, Major, 336
Loyal League Club, 314, 315, 328, 370
Luckerman, Lucius, 281, 317
luxuries. *See* Women's Patriotic Association.
Lydig, Catherine ("Kate") (Mrs. James T. Brady), xv, xx–xxi, 17, 25, 31, 56, 61, 81, 129, 130; engagement, 144–145, 154, 211, 214; wedding, 214, 275, 324, 382
Lydig, Catherine Mesier Suydam (Mrs. Philip Daly, the elder) ("Mother"), xx–xxi, 214, 217, 275, 288, 328
Lydig, David ("Grandpapa"), xxi–xxii, 18, 114, 223, 340, 379
Lydig, David (the younger), xxi, 66, 86, 164, 211; to college, 223; 240, 332
Lydig, Florence ("Fuggie"), 66, 118, 123, 211, 230, 231, 287
Lydig, Margaret ("Mag") (Mrs.

Karl Otto), xxii, 52–53, 65, 269–270, 275, 282, 297; return, 300
Lydig, Maria Mesier (Mrs. David Lydig, the elder), xxii, 52
Lydig, Philip (the elder) ("Father"), xxiii, 55, 85–86, 145, 161, 166, 185–186, 214, 217, 249, 269, 303, 330, 367, 368, 382
Lydig, Philip (the younger) ("Phil"), xxii–xxiii, 55, 66, 85–86, 90–91; leaves for army, 93, 94, 98, 100, 106, 109, 112, 119, 122–123, 128, 134–135; commission, 140, 145–146, 162, 164, 166, 170, 179, 189–190, 197, 202; return on leave, 209, 211–212; return to war, 222, 230, 238, 240, 265, 274, 284, 288, 290, 296; home on leave, 330–331; return to duty, 334, 348, 352; engagement to Pauline Hecksher, 363; marriage, 367–368
Lydig, Rosalie, 189, 285, 331, 368
Lydig family, xxxiv–xxxvi, 141
Lynch, James, 62, 69
Lyon, (General) Nathaniel, 47, 59, 70n., 71, 88
Lyon, Samuel E., 50
Lyons, (Colonel) George, 11
Lyons, Lord Richard Bickerton Pemell, 256

McCall, (General) George A., 176n.
McClellan, (General) George Brinton ("Little Mac"), xxiii–xxiv, 34, 35, 39, 50; rise to power, 67–68, 98, 100, 103, 104, 105, 111, 115, 124, 128, 135, 139, 140, 146–147, 152, 157, 160, 164; deposed, 168; reinstated, 169, 171–172, 173–174, 175n. 179, 181, 183, 184, 196; relieved of command, 197n., 198, 207–208, 212, 224, 227, 229, 241; nomination for President, 301, 302, 304; defeat, 313, 315, 329–330; post-election career, 330n., 365
McClellan, Mrs. G. B. (Mary Ellen Marcy), 127, 128, 199, 289, 374
McClernand, (General) John A., 242
McCloskey, (Archbishop) John, 376
McCunn, (Judge) John H., 261
McDonough, (Commodore) Thomas, 133
McDowell, (General) Irvin, 36–37, 39, 67, 135, 140, 147–148, 154n., 168, 171, 219n.
MacGowan, (Dr.) D. J., 206, 209
Mackay, Charles, 112, 118–119

Madrid Bend, 114n.
Mahan, Dennis Hart, 127
Malvern Hill, battle of, 175n.
Manassas, Pope's defeat at, 169, 173
Manning, (Governor) John Lawrence, 158
Mansfield, (General) Joseph King Fenno, 154
Manton, Mrs., 16, 17, 18
Marcy, Randolph Barnes, 304
Marcy, Mrs. Randolph Barnes (Mary A. Mann), 68, 127, 199, 304, 329
Marié, Pierre, 280
Marye's Heights, 208
Mason, (Senator) James Murray, 66, 77–79, 89n., 90, 192
Mason-Slidell incident. See Trent affair.
Massachusetts Fourth Regiment, 123
Mathews, (Reverend) James M., 339–341
Matsell, George Washington, 284
Maximilian, Archduke, 109, 256, 335
Meade, (General) George Gordon, 90n., 241, 243, 244, 245, 294
Meagher, (Colonel, later General) Thomas Francis, xvi, xxiv, 39, 40–41, 57, 63, 64, 68–69, 75, 79, 93, 96, 97, 98; at Bull Run, 101, 105, 136, 153, 190, 201, 211, 227; on Corcoran's death, 270, 271; for reelection of Lincoln, 311
Meagher, Mrs. Thomas F., 202, 229
Mechanicsville, battle of, 175n.
Medical College for Women, 338
Merrimac, 111, 112, 116, 127, 154
Mesier, Jane, xxi
Mesier family, xxxv, 138
Messer, Christina, 61
Metropolitan Fair. See Sanitary Commission Fair.
Miles, (Colonel) Dixon S., 178
Milne, Admiral Sir Alexander, 254
Minnesota, U.S.S., 111
Minturn, Robert Bowne, 130n., 223n.
Mississippi, C.S.S., 131
Mississippi River, Union control of, 242
Missouri Compromise, 311n.
Mitchell (commissioner), 217
money troubles, 180, 184, 185, 222, 239, 284, 306
Monitor, U.S.S., 11, 112
Monroe, Colonel, 137
Monroe, Fort, 24n., 47, 49, 138, 141, 154, 362

Montalembert, Charles Foster René de, 148
Monticello, U.S.S., 53
Morgan, (Governor) Edwin Denison, 23, 194, 374
Morris, (Lieutenant) George U., U.S.N., 116
Morris, Mrs. Harry, 252
Morris family, 34n.
Mosby, (Major) John Singleton, 319, 366, 367
Mount St. Vincent, College of, 164n.
Mozart Hall, 62, 261, 267
Mulligan, (Colonel) James A., 86–87; heroic dying statement, 86n., 88
Murfreesboro, battle of, 213, 241
Murphy, (Colonel) McLeod, 19, 25, 31
My Diary, North and South During the Civil War in America, 217n.
My Diary: Notes on the Civil War, 262n.

Napoleon, (Emperor) Louis, 89–90, 109, 149, 153, 155, 169, 182, 274n.
Nashville, C.S.S., 66
Nathan, Mrs. Benjamin, 290n.
National Academy of Design, 230–231, 361
National Cadets, 137
Naval Academy, U.S., 122n.
Negro brigades, 177. *See also* Black Brigades.
Nelson, (Judge) Samuel, 127
New Berne, battle of, 122n., 123
New Jersey Zinc Company, 259n.
New Madrid, 114n.
New Orleans, surrender of, 124, 131
Niblo's Theatre, 289, 292
Nicollet, Joseph N., 70
Ninth Army Corps, 240, 265, 349
Nolan, Lieutenant, later Captain, 200, 357
Norfolk (Va.), 127, 154, 160
Nutt, "Commodore," 220n.

O'Brian, Colonel, 249
O'Conor, Charles, 42, 163, 174, 327
O'Conor, Mrs., 82, 215, 331
O'Dalys, 368
O'Gorman, Richard, 15, 18, 19, 85, 180, 185, 227, 229, 237, 378
Olgerman (commissioner), 217
Olmstead, (General) C. H., 121n.
Olympic Theater, 220n.
O'Mahony, John, 231–232, 259

O'Meara, Colonel, 180
Opdyke, (Mayor) George, 26n., 167, 223
O'Reilly, (Father) Bernard, xxiv, 41, 45, 46, 63, 83, 97, 119, 148–149, 152–153, 175, 178–179, 180, 222, 254
Osgood, (Rev. Dr.) Samuel, 309
Osten-Sacken, Baron Carl Robert Romanovich von der, xxv, 190, 206, 231, 254, 257, 284, 297, 327, 330, 377, 379
Otis, Harrison Gray, 236n.
Otis, Mrs. Harrison Gray, 236
Otto, Margaret Lydig. *See* Lydig, Margaret.
Our American Cousin, 220n., 352
Owen, Johnny, 186–187

Paris, Comte de, 104
Park Barracks, 129, 130, 132, 134
Parke, (General) John Grubb, 90, 112, 123, 219, 284, 285, 375–376, 381, 382
Patterson, (General) Robert, 36–37; at Bull Run, 62
Paulist Fathers, 83n.
"Peace Democrat(s)." *See* Copperhead(s).
Peach Lake, 300
Pea Ridge, battle of, 70n.
Peck, (General) John James, 238
Peirce, (General) Ebenezer W., 30–31
Peltz, Edward, xxv, 23, 36, 99–100, 115, 202; biographical sketch, 203–204, 210, 226
Pendleton, George Hunt, 301, 307
Peninsula Campaign, 299n.
Perryville, 207
Peters, (Dr.) John Charles, 322
Peters, Mrs. John Charles (Georgiana Snelling), 322
Petersburg, battle of, 298, 304; siege, 347–348; surrender of, 349
Petersburg mine, 90n., 298
Petigru, James Louis, 95, 267n.
Petigru, Mrs., 347
Petrel (Union privateer), 77
Phelps, William Walter, 69, 70, 76
Philips, Adelaide, 337
Phillips, Wendell, 14, 122
Pierce (Seneca Chief), 278
Pierrepont, (Judge) Edwards, xxv–xxvi, 94, 99, 134–135, 140–141, 160, 172, 179, 181, 182, 205, 211, 251, 306, 310, 316, 334, 342, 344

Pierrepont, Maggie, 123, 231
Pillow, (General) Gideon Johnson, 106, 114n., 158
Pinckney, (Colonel) Joseph C., 11
Piper, Count, 257
Pleasant Hill, battle of, 295, 373n.
Polish Central Committee, 227
Polk, (General) Leonidas, 114n., 216
Pope, (General) John, 114n., 168, 169
Porter, (Admiral) David D., 242, 295, 330n.
Porter, Fitz-John, 169, 219; court martial, 219n.
Porter, (Colonel) Peter Buell, 320
Port Hudson, 113n., 240
Port Royal, battle of, 75
Portsmouth, capture of, 126
Portsmouth Hospital, 200, 229
Potter, (Bishop) Alonzo, 328n.
Potter, (Bishop) Horatio, 220, 286, 328n.
Potter, (General) Robert B., 327, 328
Potts, (Dr.) George, 91, 161
Powell (alias Payne), Lewis, 353
Powers, (Dr.) John, 165, 340
Praslin, Duchess de, 107
Price, (General) Sterling, 88n., 260n.
Prime, Temple, 100, 110, 119, 211, 287, 295, 297, 324, 331–332
Public Advertiser, 63n.
Pulaski, Fort, 121, 122

Raasloff, (Colonel) Valdemar Rudolph, xxvi, 50–51, 57, 74–75, 76, 181, 183, 184, 295, 297, 338, 354
Raasloff, Mrs. Anna, 275, 324
Randolph, Franklin F., 329
Rapidan, crossing of, 295
Raymond, Henry J., 311
Read, Miss, 128, 320, 337
Read, Thomas Buchanan, 309–310
Red Jacket, 278
Reid, William J., 221, 222, 230, 317, 327–328
Reilley, Capt., 239
Republic, Fort, battle of, 156–157
Reynolds, (General) John F., 176n.
Rhinelander, William Christopher, 16, 145
Rice, (General) James Clay, 299
Richmond, capture of, 348–350
Ricketts, (Captain, later General) James Brewerton, 95n., 97, 150
Ripley, George, 310, 379

Ritchie, Mrs. William F., 213
River Queen, conference aboard, 335
Roanoke Island, 90n., 103, 104
Roberts, Mrs. Marshall O., 290n.
Robertson, (Judge) William Henry, 323–324
Rockwell, (Judge) John Arnold, 8
Rodman, (Colonel, later General) Isaac Peace, 122–123
Rodman, (Reverend) W., 56, 165–166
Ronaldi, Mrs. (née Carter), 214, 280
Roosevelt, (Justice) James I., 79n.
Roosevelt, Mrs. James I., 79, 120, 200, 279–280, 287
Rosecrans, (General) William Starke, 213n., 241, 253, 254, 260, 266
Royal, Fort, 122n.
Royal, Port, 137n.
Ruggles, Mrs. Philo (Ellen Buckley), 331
Ruggles, Samuel B., 127, 331
Ruggles, Mrs. Samuel B. (Mary Rosalie Rathbone), 331
Russell, Helen, 201, 322
Russell, Judge, 233, 234
Russell, Sir William Howard, 21, 25, 40; report of battle of Bull Run, 63, 217; diary, 217n.
Russian fleet, visit of to New York, 254, 256, 258–259, 260; to San Francisco, 255

Sabine Crossroads, battle of, 113n., 295, 373n.
Salons de Paris, Les, 115, 118
San Jacinto, U.S.S., 78
Sanders, Colonel, 284–285
Sanitary Commission, U.S., 59, 130–131, 260 and n., 278, 299n., 309n., 315
Sanitary Commission Fair, 276, 278–279, 281–282, 285; opening, 286–287, 287–288, 289, 291, 293, 315, 374
Savage, John, 42, 74, 79, 125, 174, 175, 180, 222, 273
Savage, Mrs., 187, 188
Savage's Station, battle of, 175n.
Sayre, David Austin, 245
Schaack, Baron George W. von, 48–49
Schaffner, Adjutant, 26, 30
Schleiden, Rudolph Matthias, 20, 50, 60, 206, 223, 224, 256, 257

Schofield, (General) John McAllister, 337

School of Design for Women, at Cooper Union, 95, 107, 378

Schurtz, Carl, 146n.

Schuyler, George Lee, 95n.

Schuyler, Miss Louisa Lee, 299

Schuyler House, Albany, 174–175

Schwarzwaelder, (Colonel) C., 11

Scott, (General) Winfield, xxvi–xxvii, 2, 4, 8, 10, 22, 27, 32, 35, 36, 39, 40, 53; end of career, 67–68, 89–90, 93, 104, 110, 154n., 162–163, 196, 294, 358

Scrilles, Mrs., 138

Sedgwick, (General) John, 299

Sermon, Mr., 305

Seven Days, battles of the, 175n.

Seven Pines. See Fair Oaks.

Seventh New York Regiment, 15, 18, 30, 137

Seventy-first Regiment, 40

Seward, William Henry, xxvii, 4, 5–6, 23, 58, 89n., 90, 163, 164, 181, 192, 240, 264, 335, 353

Seymour, (Governor) Horatio, 182, 194, 195, 196, 198, 213, 261n., 302, 312

Shakespearean celebrations, 288–289, 291, 292

Shakespeare Monument Fund, 314, 316, 337, 372, 379

Sharpsburg, battle of. See Antietam.

Sheaff, (Cousin) Mary, xxvii, 54–55, 205

Shenandoah Valley, end of Confederate resistance in, 304, 337

Sheridan, (General) Philip H., 304, 337, 348, 349, 351, 363

Sherman, (General) William Tecumseh, 121, 122, 240, 242; advance into Georgia, 298; capture of Atlanta, 312; "March to the Sea," 318–319, 333, 334–335, 336, 337, 348; "softness" toward South, 357, 358, 363

Shields, (General) James, xxvii–xxviii, 35, 52; challenge to Lincoln, 61–62; marriage(?), 56, 59, 62, 81, 86; married, 90, 93–94; 96–97, 98, 105, 110, 113–114, 115, 117–118, 123, 140, 155–158, 159, 160, 164, 171, 172, 221; resigns, 230, 271, 368–369

Sickles, (Colonel, later General) Edgar, 22, 240, 244

Sigel, (Colonel, later General) Franz, 70, 184, 294

Sisters of Charity (of St. Vincent de Paul), 164n.

Sixty-first New York Regiment, 146

Sixty-ninth New York Regiment ("Irish Brigade"), 15–16, 18, 40, 41–42; war song, 42; at Bull Run, 45, 63, 64; speech for "Irish Brigade," 57; flags for 60, 63, 75, 79; departure, 138, 151, 187; confirmation ceremony, 187–188; new flags for, 201–202

Slemmer, (Lieutenant) Adam Jacoby, 26–27

Slidell, (Senator) John, 6, 7, 66, 77–79, 89n., 90, 163, 192

Smith, Mrs. Augustus F., 290n.

Smith, Caleb Blood, 196

Smith, Elizabeth Oakes (Mrs. Seba), 104

Smith, Goldwin, 320, 323, 328

Smith, (Lieutenant) Joseph B., U.S.N., 116

Smith, Seba, 104n.

Smith, Tangur, 324

Southern Literary Messenger, 3

South Mountain, battle of, 174, 179, 183

Spalding, 172

Spotsylvania Courthouse, battle of, 294, 296, 299

Stafford Heights, 208

Stahel, (Colonel, later General) Julius, 16, 20, 104

Stannard, Mr., 3

Stannard, Mrs. Robert, 95–96

Stanton, Edwin McMasters, Secretary of War, 99, 122, 128, 135, 141, 153–154, 160, 172, 184, 260n., 306, 307, 352

Star of the West, 10

Statue of Liberty, 105n.

Stebbins, Emma, 308

Stephens, Alexander Hamilton, 91, 335

Stephens, William Allan, 29n.

Steuben, Baron von, 17, 18

Steuben Regiment, 17, 26, 30, 49, 380

Stevens, John Austin, 281n., 345

Stevens, Mrs. John Austin, 320

Stewart, Alexander Turney, 223n., 224, 370, 375

Stewart, manager of Winter Garden, 346, 347

Stewart, A. T., 158, 332

Stiles, (Colonel) John W., 11
St. John's College, 227n.
St. Nicholas Society, 205
Stoddard, Richard Henry, 14n.
Stone, (General) Charles Pomeroy, 66n.–67n.; accused of treason, 105, 180; reinstated, 239
Stone, William Oliver (artist), 309
Stoneman, (General) George, 238
Stone's Brigade, 46n.
Stone's River. See Murfreesboro.
Stout, Mrs. George H., 197–198, 281–282
Stowe, Harriet Beecher, 14, 121
St. Patrick, Friendly Brothers (Sons) of. See under Friendly.
St. Patrick's Cathedral, 79n., 227n.
St. Patrick's Day dinner, 217, 223–224
Street, Alfred Billinger, 308, 310
Stringham, (Commodore) Silas, 53
Strong, Charles Edward, 281n.
Strong, Mrs. Charles Edward, 132
Strong, Ellen Caroline Ruggles (Mrs. George T.), 106, 131, 134, 321–322, 331–332
Strong, George Templeton, 322
Strong, Peter Remsen, 281; divorce, 345
Strong, Mrs. Peter R. (Mary Emmeline Stevens), 281
Struve, (Captain) Gustav, 21
Suffolk, Virginia, 221
Sumner, (Senator) Charles, 192n., 193, 276–277, 344, 353
Sumter, Fort, 9–12, 69, 337
Suratt, John H., 353
Suratt, Mrs. Mary E., 212n.
Sutherland, Duchess of, 84
Suydam, "Grandmother," 165, 291
Suydam, ("Uncle") Lydig, 269–270, 286
Suydam family, 323
Sweeny, Peter B., 261, 268, 377n.
Swinton, John, 77

Tammany Hall, 62n., 94, 157, 159, 196, 261 and n., 267–268, 303
Tammany Regiment (42nd Inf.), 46
Taney, (Judge) Roger Brooke, 311 and n.
Taylor, Bayard, 14, 310
Taylor, Moses, 223n.
Taylor, (General) Richard, 373
Taylor, (Reverend) Thomas House, 120, 220
Taylor, (President) Zachary, 127n.

Tenth Street Studios Building, 100, 215
Tenure of Office Act, 99n.
Terry, (General) Alfred Howe, 330n., 333
Thayer, Samuel Richard, 263–265
Thirty-ninth Infantry Regiment ("Garibaldi Guard"), 178
Thomas, (General) George H., 254n., 260n., 319
Thompson, Cephas G., 309, 380
Thompson, Jacob, 317n.
Thompson, John Reuben, 3
Thomson, James, 27–28
Thomson, (Senator) John Renshaw, 4, 5
Thumb, Tom, 220
Tiffany, Mr., 288
Tiffany & Co. (originally Tiffany & Young), 192n., 248
Tilden, Samuel J., 371
Tocqueville, Alexis Charles Henri Maurice Clérel de, 139, 143
Tompkins, (Colonel) George W., 11
Townsend, (Colonel, later General) Frederick, 26, 30
Townsend Regiment, 26, 30–31
Treanor, (Father) Thomas, 275
Trent affair, 66, 77–79, 90, 106n., 113, 192, 217, 350, 362
Tribune, New York, 14, 115, 274n., 310n., 311, 369
Trollope, Anthony, 82
Tucker, Gideon J., 69, 100
Tuckerman, Henry Theodore, 43–44, 82
Turner, Mr., 252
Tweed, William Marcy ("Boss"), 261n., 323n.
Tweed Ring, 261n., 268, 334n., 370, 378
Twelfth Army Corps, U.S.A., 154n.
Twelfth Regiment, 46
Twentieth New York Regiment, 212n., 278
Twenty-third Illinois Regiment ("Irish Brigade"), 86n.
Twiggs, (General) David Emanuel, 15n.
Tyler, (President) John, 162

Union Defense Committee, 30, 382n.
Union Fair, 87
Union Home and School, 378 and n., 381–382

Union League Club, 130n., 223n., 232n.

Vallandigham, Clement L., 90n., 238, 301
Van Buren, John, 196, 199, 205, 223, 224, 306–307, 323, 342
Van Buren, (President) Martin, 196n.
Vanity Fair, 29
Van Lew, Mrs., 360; extract from diary, 364–365
Van Tassel, Katrina, 281–282
Vernon, Mrs. (Jane Marchant Fisher), 201
Vicksburg, 213, 239, 241, 242, 244
Victoria, Queen, 106, 149, 229
Viele, (General) Egbert Ludovickus, 153–154, 288
Viele, Mrs., 277, 288
Virginia, C.S.S. *See* Merrimac.
Von Cuserov, 374
Vosburgh, (Colonel) A.S., 11

Wade-Davis Bill, 311–312
Wadsworth, (General) James Samuel, 194, 198; death, 198n.; daughter, 213, 297, 299, 320
Wales' Cut, 122
Wallack, James William, 201n.
Wallack's Theater, 201, 220
Wall Street, 180n., 349
Ward, Elijah, 210
Ward, Margaret, 145
Ward, Samuel, 145n.
Ward, (Dr.) Thomas, 128, 143, 317
Warren, Mrs. Judge, 234
Warren, Lavinia, 220
Warren, Minnie, 220n.
Washington, Martha Custis (Mrs. George) 140
Washington, siege of, 98
Washington Market, 60–61, 200
Weed, Thurlow, 23n., 89n., 311
Weitzel, (General) Godfrey, 348, 362
Welles, Gideon, 94
West Farms, 34n.
Western Sanitary Commission, 119
Weston, (Reverend) Sullivan Hardy, 13, 22, 23, 25, 34, 189, 270, 282
Wetmore, (General) Prosper M., 382
Wheatley, William, 292, 337
Whetten, (Miss) Harriet Douglas, xxviii, 29, 38, 56, 74; desire to nurse

wounded, 76–77, 84–85, 118, 120, 131; nursing wounded, 139, 140, 172–173; at Portsmouth Hospital, 200; on furlough, 229–230, 276, 380
Whili, Judge, 159
White, Grant, 291
"White House," New Kent, Va., 140
White Oak Swamp, battle of, 175n.
Whittier, James Greenleaf, 14
Widow's Society, 222
Wigfall, (Senator) Lewis Trezevant, 8
Wilcox, (General) Orlando B., 337
Wilderness, battle of the, 198n., 294, 296
Wilkes, (Captain) Charles, U.S.N., 78–79, 90, 192, 217
Wilkins, Gouverneur Morris, 55
Willis, Nathaniel Parker, xl, 3, 114, 205, 206, 309
Wilmington, Mrs., 341
Wilson, Dr. (Cayuga Sachem), 277–278
Wilson, (Colonel) William ("Billy"), 21, 22–23
Wilson's Creek, Battle of, 47n., 70n., 88n.
Winchester, battle of, 86n., 304
Winter Garden, 220, 346
Winters, Mrs. Richard Thomas, 128
Winthrop, Theodore, 26
Wolcott, Oliver, 57n.
Women's Patriotic Association for Diminishing the Use of Imported Luxuries, 290n., 299–300, 306
Wood, Benjamin, 195
Wood, (Mayor, later Congressman) Fernando, 26, 62n., 195, 198–199, 201, 261, 268, 370
Wood, Henry, 220
Wood, Matilda C. (Mrs. Henry), 222
Wool, (General) John Ellis, 141, 154 and n., 247
Woolsey, Miss ("Colonel"), 230
Workingwomen's Protective Union, 283–284, 317, 323
World, New York, 170, 315, 334
Wyckoff, 86

Yorktown (Va.), capture of, 124
Young, Alice and Anna, 295, 324
Young, William, 28–29, 51, 276

Zagoni, Colonel, 327